Griffin, John Chandler

Abraham Lincoln's
Execution

24.95

Abraham Lincoln's
EXECUTION

Abraham Lincoln's
EXECUTION

John Chandler Griffin

PELICAN PUBLISHING COMPANY
Gretna 2006

*The word "Pelican" and the depiction of a pelican are
trademarks of Pelican Publishing Company, Inc., and
are registered in the U.S. Patent and Trademark Office.*

Library of Congress Cataloging-in-Publication Data

Griffin, John Chandler, 1936-
 Abraham Lincoln's execution / John Chandler Griffin.
  p. cm.
 Includes bibliographical references.
 ISBN-13: 978-1-58980-395-4 (hardcover : alk. paper)
 1.   Lincoln, Abraham, 1809-1865—Assassination. 2.
Conspiracies—United States—History—19th century. 3.
United States—Politics and government—1861-1865. I.
Title.

 E457.5.G795 2006
 973.7092—dc22

                                        2006003630

Printed in the United States of America

Published by Pelican Publishing Company, Inc.
1000 Burmaster Street, Gretna, Louisiana 70053

To my daughter, Alexis Griffin Ballard, one of the most determined and courageous young women I've ever known. All my love to you and yours, and keep up the good work.

Contents

Acknowledgments

In addition to a great many others who must by necessity remain anonymous, I wish to thank the following persons for giving so unselfishly of their time and efforts on my behalf. Dr. Patrick Scott, Director of Special Collections at the Thomas Cooper Library, the University of South Carolina, made numerous issues of old magazines and journals available to me, materials which proved invaluable to this work. (Plus he permitted me to type a note on Joseph Heller's typewriter, the one he used when writing *Catch-22*!) And there is Nathaniel Orlowek of Silver Springs, Maryland, who spoke with me at great length concerning his work on the John St. Helen/David George theory, and the very real possibility that the body buried in Booth's tomb at Green Mount Cemetery in Baltimore is not that of John Wilkes Booth.

My thanks to Gaile Heath, a handwriting analyst with the South Carolina State Law Enforcement Division (SLED), for devoting so much of her free time to studying the handwriting of John Wilkes Booth, Lafayette Baker, and others. Her findings proved invaluable. And also my gratitude to Bethany Crooks, a photographic expert with SLED, for comparing photos of Booth with a likeness of John St. Helen. She was unable to reach any definitive conclusions because unfortunately the image of St. Helen is a painting and she can work only from photographs.

A special thanks to F. W. Wilson in Special Collections at Georgetown University for locating and sending me the photos of John St. Helen and David George. These were indeed a rare find and added much to my work.

So many of the finest photos of John Wilkes Booth and his family members are on file in the Harvard University Theater Collection. I wish to thank Virginia Dent, Curatorial Assistant at that institution, for all her help. This volume would not have been the same without those fine photos on file in the Harvard Theater Collection.

As for Lorraine Whiting of Geneva, Florida, my sincere gratitude. Lorraine is the great-grandniece of Lewis Powell and a deep storehouse of knowledge concerning Powell's childhood and adolescence in Fair Oaks, Florida. Lewis Powell was her great-grandfather's youngest brother, and Lorraine's knowledge of Powell is based on numerous family stories passed down from generation to generation. She was most gracious in sharing those stories with me. I am a long-time admirer of Lewis Powell, and I truly enjoyed my long conversations with Lorraine Whiting.

And there is Jim Kushlan, editor of the *Civil War Times Illustrated,* and his assistant, Brenda Wilt, who truly moved mountains in their efforts to track down the authors of several articles that appeared in their venerated journal many years ago. I spoke at some length with those authors and learned a great deal that I did not know.

Too, my gratitude to the widow of Robert Fowler, the original editor of the *Civil War Times,* for her kind permission to republish herein Ray Neff's "The Secret Papers of Lafayette Baker." Neff's discovery of those papers must rank as one of the most sensational finds of the twentieth century, and it sheds much light on who was truly behind the assassination of Abraham Lincoln.

I'd also like to thank Rae Emerson, an official with the Ford's Theatre National Historic Site of the National Park Service. She went to a great deal of trouble to send me photocopies of John Wilkes Booth's very controversial diary, the one Edwin Stanton was finally forced to turn over to authorities, the one from which someone had torn eighteen pages.

Closer to home, I wish to thank Blake Faulkenberry, our computer wizard at USC-Lancaster, for his help on the many occasions when I ran into glitches with my computer. As for our librarians, much gratitude to Shari Eliades, Linda Guess, and Lori Harris. No matter how obscure the material I needed, they always managed to find it somehow and get it to me straightaway. And always with nice smiles! Very good people to work with.

And what can I say about my Dean at this institution, John Catalano, to whom I owe much gratitude for his moral and financial help while I was putting this little volume together? John truly has his head on straight, and an impressive title has not turned it in the least. And the same is true of our Academic Dean, Ron Cox, to whom I owe a big debt of gratitude. Ron has a new book due out, *1963: The Year of Decision*, which I am truly looking forward to reading.

As for my wife, Betty, my daughter, Alexis, and my grand-daughers, Emmalee Grace Ballard and Serrah Roxanne Ballard, I suspect they have heard all they want to hear about John Wilkes Booth and Abraham Lincoln, at least for a while. I promise not to mention either again. Let's just cut on *Barney* and forget about things of lesser importance.

Introduction

Assassinate: *1: to murder by sudden or secret attack. 2: to injure or destroy unexpectedly and treacherously.*

Execute: *1: to do what is required by a decree. 2: to put to death in compliance with a legal sentence.*

By the summer of 1864 an overwhelming percentage of young Southerners between the ages of eighteen and thirty-eight had been either killed or maimed on far away battle-fields while a like percentage had died of various illnesses and diseases. The South of course simply had no way to replace those men. Whereas the South had earlier found itself outnumbered two to one, by 1864 its soldiers were inevitably outnumbered three or even four to one. And the Union by now refused to exchange prisoners of war. The Union, unfortunately, since they had an unlimited supply of soldiers, more than enough to supply their every need, refused to cooperate. But, hoped the Confederates, if they could get their hands on Lincoln, they could use him as leverage to force the Union to exchange prisoners, thereby giving them the manpower they so badly needed.

It might be pointed out that the South's desire to exchange prisoners of war was also motivated by humanitarian impulses. According to Federal War Department statistics, some twenty-four thousand Union soldiers died of wounds, starvation, and disease in Southern prisons during four long years of war, a very tragic rate. Even more tragic, however, was that some twenty-six thousand Confederate soldiers died in Union prisons during that same period. This despite the fact that the Union army had a wealth of food and medical supplies they easily could have made available to their Southern prisoners; but Union authorities very malevolently refused to do so.

Even apologists for Edwin Stanton admit it was purely from malice that the Union War Department intentionally withheld food and medical treatment from their Confederate prisoners, resulting in such an incredibly high number of fatalities. The Confederates on the other hand made available to their Union prisoners the same food and medical treatment that was available to their own soldiers. Unfortunately, there was very little food and medicine available, especially following the blockading of Southern seaports.

Confederate authorities were only too aware of the desperate situation faced by Union soldiers in their prison camps. Thus Southern representatives visited Secretary of War Edwin Stanton and offered to exchange prisoners of war, man for man. Stanton refused to even consider this proposal, reasoning that if the South was starved for manpower, well, let them starve. Two weeks later, these same Confederate representatives again met with Stanton. This time they proposed a total exchange of prisoners. If the North would agree to release all Southern prisoners, the Confederacy would release all Union prisoners. They offered this exchange despite the fact that the Confederacy held a great many more Union prisoners than the Union did Southern prisoners. Again Stanton refused to even consider the matter. As a result, a desperate South began exploring the idea of abducting Lincoln and using him as leverage to force the Union into a massive prisoner-of-war exchange.

As for Booth's plan to *assassinate* the president, it appears, based on the best available data, that prior to April 14 Booth had never entertained the least intention of harming the president. In fact, on March 20, just prior to his attempt to abduct the president on his way to Soldiers'

Home, Booth had several cases of delicate foodstuffs and toilet articles sent on to Maryland to ensure that Lincoln would suffer no privations during his sojourn to Richmond. And on several occasions Booth was heard to remark that he felt a great deal of admiration, and even some affection, for Abe Lincoln the man. It was Abe Lincoln the president whom Booth was sworn to abduct. During Lewis Powell's trial, when asked why he attempted to assassinate William Seward, he responded, "I am a Confederate soldier. I was simply doing my duty." That was also Booth's attitude.

Indeed, there is no evidence to suggest that Booth had ever considered bringing physical harm to Lincoln or anyone else prior to April 14. But on April 14 something happened, something of such extraordinary magnitude that Booth suddenly became convinced that Lincoln must be *executed,* and he must be executed immediately. What that something might have been is open to speculation, but it was of such a sensational nature that Booth, who was by no means a violent man, was persuaded that the president's death was now the only solution to an intolerable problem.

Today there is compelling circumstantial evidence to suggest that it was not Wilkes Booth who first thought of assassinating the president, rather Wilkes Booth was little more than a pawn, a tool, in the hands of certain high-ranking Federal officials who had been waiting and scheming for several weeks, or even months, to rid the Federal government of Abraham Lincoln and Secretary of State William Seward. In the end, they merely used Booth as a dupe to carry out their nefarious ends.

Who those people were and how they persuaded Booth to become a willing collaborator can only be conjectured. But the best evidence strongly suggests that the prime movers in this scheme were Secretary of War Edwin Stanton and Vice Pres. Andrew Johnson. Both men were incredibly ambitious and equally unscrupulous.

Edwin Stanton was known throughout Washington as a man of limitless ambitions, and his greatest ambition in 1865 was to see himself become president in 1868. With

Lincoln no longer in the picture and Congress in recess until December, the door to a military dictatorship in this great nation would stand wide open, with Stanton of course serving as the supreme dictator.

Though Stanton would totally dominate and manipulate Andrew Johnson throughout the early months of his presidency, Johnson was a man of unbridled ambitions. However, since he had made a drunken display of himself at Lincoln's second inauguration in March 1865, Lincoln had repeatedly snubbed him, and Johnson was keenly aware that his political career would soon be over if Abe Lincoln lived, that in fact Lincoln planned to drop him from the ticket as soon as possible. But should Lincoln suddenly die, Andrew Johnson would instantly realize his ultimate ambition: He would become president of the United States.

According to the "Secret Papers of Lafayette Baker" (see chapter II), Stanton, Johnson, and the Radicals in Congress hated Lincoln and were in a fever to rid the government of him. To achieve their ends, Stanton laid the plans, then appointed his chief of the National Detective Police, Lafayette Baker, and his assistant secretary of war, Maj. Thomas Eckert, to recruit the people needed to carry out those plans. And what was their motive in attempting such a daring maneuver? After all, assassinating the president of the United States is not child's play. Obviously they were motivated by greed and a lust for power, and certainly they had nothing to fear concerning punishment or retribution since they would be in charge of any subsequent investigation. Indeed, these two men were well aware that they could totally manipulate any investigative committee (and in fact they did just that), so that they themselves would run little risk of discovery.

But an even greater motive for Lincoln's execution concerned his recently announced program of amnesty for the defeated South. Indeed, after four long years of brutal warfare, Lincoln had in the spring of 1865 suddenly changed his attitude towards the seceded states. Now, under Lincoln's plan of amnesty, the South would not be occupied by a cruel

Federal army, its citizens robbed and pillaged at every turn. To the contrary, Lincoln was now preaching to one and all that the Confederate states should be welcomed back into the Union as though they had never been away. Citizens of the South, he said, would return to the Union with all the constitutional rights enjoyed by citizens of the loyal Northern states.

Such talk was casting a dark pall over the Radicals in Congress and their plans to occupy and loot the devastated Southland.

With Lincoln's new support of amnesty for the South, all those highly outspoken abolitionists who had eagerly supported Lincoln through four long years of warfare were also beginning to look askance at one another. Based on Lincoln's earlier words, as well as his Emancipation Proclamation, they had assumed that with war's end he would immediately make first-class citizens of millions of former slaves, granting them the same civil rights enjoyed by white citizens. But now Lincoln was backtracking there as well, shuffling his feet and looking uncomfortable when asked about the future fate of all those former slaves. Well, perhaps those former slaves would be given the vote, he hemmed and hawed, but only those who were "extremely intelligent and had served in the Union army."

In late 1864 he had confided in William Seward, "I cannot visualize millions of freed black slaves walking the streets of America." Indeed, Lincoln was now saying that all those former slaves would likely be much happier if the government undertook a massive resettlement program that would take them back to their native Africa. In fact, a dozen boatloads had already deposited several thousand former slaves in Liberia.

For those seeking a final straw, it should be pointed out that the one move that sealed Lincoln's fate was his secret meeting in early April 1865 with Judge John Campbell, a Virginian and a former member of the Supreme Court prior to the war. During that meeting, Lincoln assured Judge Campbell that he would allow the Virginia State Legislature to convene within the coming week at the State House in Richmond to discuss matters of importance to Virginia now that the war was coming to an end. Not only would he allow them to meet, said Lincoln, but he would order Gen. Godfrey Weitzel, commander of Union forces in Richmond, to furnish military escorts for the individual legislators as they came and went about state business.

According to Chief of Detectives Lafayette Baker, when Weitzel received his orders, he passed the message to Stanton, who flew into a rage and very brazenly countermanded the president's orders, instructing Weitzel to forbid the Virginia legislators to meet. Writes Baker, "Then for the first time I realized his mental disunity and his insane and fanatical hatred for the president. . . . He laughed in a most spine chilling manner and said, 'If he would to know who rescinded his order we will let Lucifer tell him.'" A day later, as Stanton predicted in his above statement, Lincoln was dead.

And what of Lincoln's secretary of state, the rabid Radical, William Seward? Oddly enough, his attitude now towards the Southern states was almost identical to that of the president. Seward had recently denounced any plans to make the South an occupied territory under military governors and martial law, advocating instead a rapid return of the Southern states to full participation in the political life of the nation. To the contrary, he had recently shouted to a stunned Congress that the Southern states should be welcomed back into the Union with all their constitutional rights totally restored.

Thus, in the eyes of Stanton and Johnson, Seward was just as much a traitor to the nation and the Republican Party as Abe Lincoln. Both men were extremely depressed at this recent turn of events and silently pondered the situation. Then, in a flash of inspiration, perhaps it suddenly occurred to Stanton and Johnson that it would be fortuitous if both traitors, Lincoln and Seward, should tragically perish on the same evening. And it could be claimed that their assassins were wild-eyed stooges of Jefferson Davis and the Confederate government.

What Lincoln was preaching now was downright treason, a betrayal of both his nation and his Republican Party. Of course if Lincoln should restore constitutional rights to citizens of the South, that would include their right to vote. And of course, every former Confederate would vote for the Democratic nominee in 1868. Indeed, that year would sound the death knell for the Republican Party and for all those loyal party workers who had labored so long to see that Republicans stayed in power for the next thirty years. Among those workers, unfortunately, were Edwin Stanton and Andrew Johnson. Johnson was a Democrat, but he was a Unionist and had served as military governor of Tennessee during the war. Certainly come 1868 Johnson would be gone along with all the rest.

Stanton and Johnson were Radicals—highly opinionated, self-righteous, power-mad Radicals, who did not suffer traitors gladly. And now Lincoln and Seward had become the worst of traitors.

If Lincoln and Seward should suddenly be removed from office, the Radicals, aided and abetted by Andrew Johnson, would be free to exact their own terribly vindictive Reconstruction policies towards the South. Under their domination, Southerners would enjoy no constitutional rights; to the contrary, they would be occupied by a hostile Federal army. White males who had supported the Confederacy (about 99 percent of the white male population) would be disenfranchised while all black males would be given the vote, especially if they wished to vote Republican—and of course they all would. Then they would see what would happen to the Democrats and Republicans in the election of 1868.

The Radicals would send their civilian representatives, those thieves and thugs known derisively throughout both the North and South as Carpetbaggers, whose job it would be to see that Radical procedures were being suitably implemented. Their first task was to ensure that certain servile blacks were elected to public office at all levels of government. Then, once they had their black representatives in place, it would be a simple matter to have them raise property taxes for white farmers in their particular locale, at least enough to make sure that few could pay. Then black officials could confiscate farm property and the Radicals would auction off that land to those Northern industrialists who were constantly searching for cheap natural resources and labor. What wonderful places to build their cotton mills! As for cheap labor, those displaced farmers who were daily watching their wives and children starving before their very eyes would beg for jobs—at any wages. All in all, agreed the Radicals, it was a wonderful and very profitable proposition, a wonderful payback to those Northern industrialists who had financed the Republican Party for the past four years.

And think of those tens of thousands of bales of cotton, white gold, sitting in warehouses and on wharves and hidden in swamps throughout the South. That cotton would be confiscated by the Federal government and auctioned off to the great entrepreneurs of New York, Boston, and Philadelphia who would then sell it to the cotton-starved nations of Europe.

But what about those poor Southern farmers who had lost all their cotton and land? Would they not wish to have their cases heard in court? Well, of course they could have their cases heard in court, military courts directly under the supervision of Edwin Stanton since no civil courts were allowed to function in the South. The outcome of such cases was a foregone conclusion.

And certainly with the Democratic Party essentially disenfranchised in the Southern states, the Republicans were assured power for years. Andrew Johnson, naive as he was, must have greeted Stanton's plans with glee. In 1868 he would simply move from the Democratic Party to the Republican Party. With the support of Edwin Stanton, he could remain president for the next two terms.

Stanton smiled benevolently. Of course Johnson could count on his support—at least for a year or two, until it became convenient to dump him. Then Stanton himself would become the nominee of the Republican Party. At last, he, Edwin Stanton, would become president of the United States. Indeed, given enough time, he would become what he had been during the war, the supreme dictator of the United States.

After pondering Stanton's solution to the problem, Johnson very possibly observed, "So you are proposing that we assassinate the president of the United States."

Not the most tolerant of men, Stanton shook his head in exasperation. "No, I am not proposing that we *assassinate* the president of the United States, Mr. Johnson. I am proposing that we *execute* a traitor. There is some difference, you know."

It was a wonderful idea, the perfect solution to a real dilemma. According to Lafayette Baker's secret papers, Stanton unabashedly brought in Radical congressmen, industrialists, bankers, and military leaders to discuss his Reconstruction plans for pillaging the South. Of course, he would then explain quietly and solemnly, Lincoln and Seward would have to be executed in order for any of those plans to be realized.

With big dollar signs floating before their eyes, those who listened to Stanton's whispered lectures reluctantly agreed. Abe Lincoln and William Seward would have to be executed. Besides, traitors generally are executed, aren't they? As reprehensible as such a move might be to them personally, it was certainly the best thing for the nation.

Once that decision had been made, says Lafayette Baker, Stanton assigned him and Maj. Thomas Eckert to arrange the details of the execution. It should happen as soon as possible, now that the war had ended, before Lincoln could do any more damage to the party, before he could further broadcast his policy of amnesty for the South. Likely, Friday night, April 14, would be an opportune time for the executions. That night the Lincolns, accompanied by Gen. Ulysses S. Grant, would be in attendance at Ford's Theatre. It would be a simple matter for an assassin or two to slip into the president's box and execute him. As for the fate of the assassins following the execution, it would be up to those worthies to plan their own escape, though they would certainly receive all the help the War Department could furnish. Indeed, the War Department wanted them to escape, or die, since dead men tell no tales.

Which would explain Boston Corbett's inexplicable murder of John Wilkes Booth on the morning of April 26. (Murder charges against Corbett were later dropped upon orders from Edwin Stanton.) It would also explain why the four conspirators who were known to have spoken with Booth on April 14 were later arrested and held totally incommunicado until all four were hanged on July 7, silencing their tongues forever.

And just how did John Wilkes Booth enter into this plotting and conniving? Back on February 20 a boarder at Mrs. Surratt's boardinghouse, Louis Weichmann, a clerk in the Commissary Office, reported to his commanding officer, a Captain Gleason, that he had observed many strange occurrences and many strange characters back at the boardinghouse, and he suspected that they might somehow be conspiring against the president. Weichmann then rattled off the names of the various strange characters he had observed, including that of John Wilkes Booth. Captain Gleason, afraid that Weichmann might be on to something, then reported the matter to Edwin Stanton's War Department.

Thus, as early as February 20, the War Department had the names of all those involved in the conspiracy to abduct the president. And once the decision was made to execute Lincoln, it would have been a simple matter for Major Eckert to contact John Wilkes Booth. No one knows what transpired between the two (or if such a meeting did in fact take place), but it is likely that Eckert could have persuaded Booth, who really did not require much persuading, that Abe Lincoln intended a vindictive Reconstruction policy that would totally destroy what remained of the South. But should Lincoln be eliminated, said Eckert, then Andrew Johnson, a Southern boy born and bred and a good Southern Democrat from Tennessee, would become president, and Johnson had privately sworn to welcome the South back into the Union with open arms. Under Johnson, there would be no reprisals. The Southern states would become full-fledged members of the Union, with all the rights enjoyed by other citizens.

And besides, it was well known that Johnson and Booth were old friends and had been for several years.

But in order for that to take place, Eckert cautioned, they would first have to execute Abe Lincoln, along with his major henchman, William Seward.

But what about Johnson's fate following the execution? Everyone knew that since his faux pas at Lincoln's second Inaugural (Johnson had become falling-down drunk), the president had snubbed him at every opportunity and was actively searching for an excuse to dump him. And now, following Lincoln's assassination, he should suddenly become president of the United States? Would that not strike people as suspicious? Would there not be certain individuals, people of great authority even, who might suspect that the ambitious Johnson had played some role in the assassination?

Yes, decidedly so, and this explains why Booth assigned poor George Atzerodt to assassinate the vice president. It is well known that Atzerodt was the most cowardly man east of the Mississippi River. Yet, on the evening of April 14, according to Atzerodt's later confession, Wilkes Booth assigned him of all people to murder Vice Pres. Andrew Johnson. Was Booth serious? What possibly could have motivated Booth to assign passive George Atzerodt to murder Andrew Johnson, the second-highest-ranking figure in American government? Certainly Booth was an unusually intelligent and perceptive young man, and he doubtlessly knew that Johnson would live forever if he waited for George Atzerodt to assassinate him. Obviously Booth never intended for Atzerodt to make a move against the vice president.

In the first place, Booth knew that if any attempt were made against the life of Andrew Johnson, then Abe Lincoln, the primary target, would definitely not appear at Ford's Theatre on the intended evening. He and his entire cabinet would be in hiding under heavy military guard. So why then would he even mention such a daring assignment to poor Atzerodt? The answer may be conjectured: If Johnson was involved in the conspiracy to execute Lincoln and Seward, then Booth created a very clever ploy to divert suspicion from the vice president. Certainly there would be those who might suspect that Andrew Johnson, the primary beneficiary of Lincoln's death, had played a role in the execution conspiracy (and in fact, his accusers were legion), but now Johnson would have a plausible cover story, an iron-clad alibi. Would he be foolish enough to plot his own assassination? Of course he had nothing to do with it!

Such reasoning also explains why Booth instructed David Herold to plant the revolver and knife in Atzerodt's room at the Kirkwood House late in the afternoon of April 14. Booth knew that once the news of the president's assassination had become public, the desk clerk at the Kirkwood would inform authorities that a highly suspicious character was registered there in a room directly above that of Vice President Johnson. Once those authorities searched Atzerodt's room they would find the incriminating evidence, and it would be only a matter of time before Atzerodt was arrested. And Booth, an astute judge of human character, was fully aware that once Atzerodt was arrested, he would immediately crumble before his interrogators and tell everything he knew concerning the conspiracy, including the fact that he had been assigned to assassinate Vice Pres. Andrew Johnson.

If Johnson did conspire with Stanton, Baker, Eckert, and others in planning and carrying out Lincoln's execution, then it would be well for him to be able to swear that he was totally innocent of any such plot. And now he could. Why, he himself had been a target of the assassins! It was only a matter of luck that he had escaped with his life! All in all, if this scenario is accurate, then it was a very clever ploy.

Too, it should be remembered that in 1865 the vice president was second in rank only to President Lincoln. If Booth truly wished to throw the government into disarray by eliminating the heads of state, as numerous historians have claimed, he would have targeted the vice president and not the secretary of state. And he would have assigned Lewis Powell to carry out the execution, not George Atzerodt. Had Lewis Powell been given the assignment, there would have been no failure. By Saturday morning, Andrew Johnson would have been just as dead as Abe Lincoln.

Therefore, it seems safe to conclude that those who planned the executions were not after the heads of state. They were after Lincoln and Seward, the two officials who advocated a conciliatory Reconstruction program for the South.

(It might be pointed out that had Seward succumbed to his wounds, he was slated to be succeeded as secretary of state by Sen. Ben Butler, the infamous Ben "The Beast" Butler, to whom "amnesty" meant hanging every Southerner in America, making him just the man the Radicals wanted to see in that office.)

Eckert might also have promised Booth help from the War Department in making his escape. For example, the army telegraph (Eckert was also head of the army's Telegraph Office), which had functioned without a hitch during four years of war, suddenly went silent at almost the exact moment that Lincoln was shot and did not begin functioning again for another four hours. Thus news of the execution and Booth's identity could not be telegraphed across the country for another four hours, certainly enough time for Booth, had he not broken his leg, to have made his escape through Maryland and to the coast of Virginia, where he hoped to catch a ship for Matamoros, Mexico.

Eckert also might have told him that sentries posted at the Navy Yard Bridge would receive instructions to allow him to pass. Nor would Union cavalry be dispatched to search the route Booth would surely travel (the same route taken by Confederate agents throughout the war) until he had long passed that area. Indeed, Union cavalry was alerted in such far off areas as Baltimore, New York, and Philadelphia, but *not* on the route that any sane Confederate agent would travel.

Doubtlessly Eckert would have advised Booth that he need not fear the presence of bodyguards at the theater. Stanton had already agreed to forbid Grant's presence, and as for Eckert (called the strongest man in Washington), certainly he would make up a plausible excuse not to attend. Probably he would be too busy with his telegraphic work.

And that is exactly what happened. Grant, a West Point graduate, was very much aware that an army officer does not snub a social invitation from his commander in chief. But inexplicably that is what Grant did, and for the flimsiest of excuses: at five that afternoon he sent Lincoln a note explaining that he and his wife had decided at the last minute to catch the afternoon train out of Washington for Brunswick, New Jersey, where they planned to visit their children. So sorry. Maybe next time. Please give his best to the hundreds of citizens gathered at Ford's Theatre that evening to shout their congratulations for his winning the war. Love, Sam.

As for Major Eckert, Lincoln himself, once he learned of Grant's sudden impulse to cater to his paternal instincts, went to Stanton and requested that the major be allowed to accompany him and Mrs. Lincoln to the theater. But Stanton responded that the major had too much work to do in the Telegraph Office that evening. Obviously disappointed, Lincoln then walked next door to Eckert's office and personally appealed to Eckert. But Eckert echoed Stanton's remarks. He shook his head and stated that he simply had too much work to do that evening to take off for the theater.

In fact, later testimony would prove that both Stanton and Eckert were lying. Eckert left the office at five that afternoon, went home, and did nothing for the rest of the evening—except to await the startling news from Ford's Theatre.

Certainly Booth was fully aware before he ever accepted his grim assignment that the president would be without bodyguards at the theater. Why else would he have armed himself with nothing more reliable than a small *single-shot* Derringer? He had in his possession several army Colt *six-shot* revolvers. Had he anticipated any resistance whatsoever, he would have carried one of those Colts. But he knew before he arrived at the theater that neither Grant, Eckert, nor any other bodyguards would be present. The question is, how could Booth possibly have known that the president would be alone and unprotected, unless he had been assured of that fact in advance.

The president would have *one* bodyguard, an officer from the Metropolitan Police Department, a drunken debauchee by the name of John Parker would be assigned to sit in a chair just outside the president's box. Officer Parker unfortunately had a lengthy record of reprimands for his drunken misadventures while on duty. Yet, Mrs. Lincoln herself, at Stanton's urging, had naively requested that Officer Parker serve her husband on this night of all nights. And sure enough at the moment that Booth entered the president's box, Parker was standing at the bar in the saloon next door becoming quite inebriated. Parker then vanished following the shooting and did not reappear until the next morning when he staggered into police headquarters with a disheveled woman in tow, a woman whom he happily claimed he had arrested for prostitution. He himself was immediately arrested and charged with dereliction of duty. (Charges against Parker were later dropped thanks to an order from Edwin Stanton.)

Eckert might well have concluded his persuasive talk with Booth by pointing out that everything was ready and in place. Booth had only to agree now to pull the trigger, and Lincoln's execution was an accomplished fact. Would Booth refuse and allow an evil tyrant to remain in office, or would he perform a deed that would win the lasting gratitude from citizens throughout the nation, especially those in his beloved South?

Sen. Ben Butler, during Johnson's impeachment trial of 1867, shouted from the floor of the senate:

> How clear himself? By disclosing his accomplices? Who were they? If we had only the advantage of all the testimony, Mr. Speaker, we might have been able to find out who, indeed, were these accomplices of Booth; to find out who it was that could profit by assassination who could not profit by capture and abduction, who it was expected would succeed to Lincoln if the knife made a vacancy.

Ben Butler did everything but name Pres. Andrew Johnson as the moving force behind Lincoln's execution, an opinion held by many. Unfortunately, at this late date, no one will ever know for certain just who Booth's "accomplices" were. We can only speculate based on circumstantial evidence.

What is known for certain is that Booth did execute the president on the night of April 14, and with Lincoln's death died his great and benevolent plans for a constitutional Reconstruction program for the South.

I

Abe Lincoln: His Sordid Political Career

Save The Union! (The Constitution Be Damned!)

Save the Union! That phrase was simply Abe Lincoln's way of saying, I shall deny the American citizens of some fifteen Southern states their constitutional right to secede from the Union. I shall deny them the freedom to pursue their own destiny, as guaranteed in the Constitution, even if I have to wage a terrible war and kill over three hundred thousand of their citizens to do it. I need those Southern states to carry out my own economic plans, and by God I shall have them, the Constitution be damned!

But despite his many sins as president, the image of Abraham Lincoln has grown to such heroic proportions since his death in 1865 that today it is difficult to find a truly objective portrait of the man. Yet one notes that in many of the biographies and histories of Lincoln, especially in those that most idealize him, historians do not attempt to simply record his behavior as much as they try to rationalize or excuse his behavior. This is especially true among the revisionist, or Marxist, historians. To them Lincoln has become so intertwined with the Civil Rights legislation of the 1960s, that to attack one is to attack the other, and to attack either has become an unforgivable sin. Indeed, say the revisionists, Lincoln fought a great Civil War for no other reason than to free his beloved black Americans. That war remains for our revisionists the number one most-heroic Civil Rights act of all time. To attack Lincoln, in their eyes, is to attack Civil Rights and to label oneself an inveterate racist.

The Great Emancipator, who denied civil liberties to citizens throughout the North. Was he so fixated on his own economic policies that he pushed the nation into a great Civil War just to attain those policies? Library of Congress

The revisionists, unfortunately, are wrong. Lincoln, like most politicians, had his blemishes. In fact, he had a great many blemishes, as any objective study will prove. In evaluating Abraham Lincoln, the first thing to remember is that throughout his political life he was first and foremost a Whig. Indeed, his hero and model during his formative years was Henry Clay, and like Clay he was totally devoted to an economic system that Clay had earlier labeled "the American System," sometimes referred to as mercantilism. From 1832, when Lincoln first ran for the state legislature in Illinois, until his death in 1865, he repeatedly declared his devotion to the American System, which meant that he advocated protectionist tariffs, taxpayer subsidies for railroads, and other corporations, as well as the nationalization of the money supply to help pay for those subsidies.

But the Whig's (and Lincoln's) big problem in realizing their economic dream prior to the War Between the States had been the Constitution, as one president after another vetoed internal improvement and national bank bills. Indeed, from Thomas Jefferson onward, it had been the Southern congressmen who led the opposition to the Whig's American System, prompting politicians like Clay and Lincoln to seethe with anger and frustration.

But then came the defeat of the South in 1865, and with that defeat came an immediate and fundamental change in American government. Prior to the war the government had been the highly decentralized, limited government established by our Founding Fathers, a nation of individual states that firmly believed in states' rights. But the end of the war sounded the death knell for states' rights and the birth of the highly centralized, all-powerful federal government we see today. As historian Richard Bensel points out in his work *Yankee Leviathan,* "Any study of the origins of the American state should begin no earlier than 1865."

Of course Lincoln and his Whigs did not think of themselves as dark subversives but as enlightened heirs to the Hamiltonian political tradition, which preached a strong centralized government, with Washington giving all the orders. It would be Washington that would plan the nation's economic development with corporate subsidies financed by protectionist tariffs and the printing of money.

This idea enjoyed little success during the first seventy years of America's existence, again thanks to the Constitution, but it was fully implemented during the first two years of Lincoln's administration. This was what he had always wanted, and he would brook no interference from anyone in seeing it become a political reality.

Indeed, as early as 1832, when Lincoln first ran for the Illinois state legislature, he stated in a speech:

> I presume you all know who I am. I am humble Abraham Lincoln. I have been solicited by many friends to become a candidate for the legislature. My politics are short and sweet, like the old woman's dance. I am in favor of a national bank, in favor of the internal improvements system and a high protective tariff.

This was also a statement of the Whig Party's political-economic agenda, dedicated as they were to protectionism, government control of the money supply through a nationalized banking system, and government subsidies for railroad, shipping, and canal-building businesses. One notes that Lincoln rarely spoke of slavery prior to 1854, but he did speak frequently with great conviction on the Whig economic agenda.

When the Whig Party dissolved in 1855, Lincoln switched to the Republican Party, though he repeatedly assured his Illinois constituents that there was little difference between the two. Having labored for the past twenty-five years to affect Clay's American System, the program that associated economic development with a strong centralized government, Lincoln was not about to surrender.

Perhaps the best description of Lincoln and his American System economic policies was written by Edgar Lee Masters, the Illinois poet, author, and law partner of Clarence Darrow, in his work *Lincoln the Man*.

> Henry Clay was the champion of that political system which doles favors to the strong in order to win and to keep their adherence to the government. His system offered shelter to devious schemes and

corrupt enterprises. . . . He was the beloved son of Alexander Hamilton with his corrupt funding schemes, his superstitions concerning the advantage of a public debt, and a people taxed to make profits for enterprises that cannot stand alone. His example and his doctrines led to the creation of a party that had no platform to announce, because its principles were plunder and nothing else.

For the American System to work we must have a strong centralized government. For that reason the American System had been a controversial issue from the time of the founding until 1861. At that point, with the coming of the War Between the States, a war that Lincoln badly needed and wanted, the debate over states' rights versus a strong centralized government came to a sudden halt: Lincoln and his cohorts won the debate by force of arms.

Another facet of the American System was the quest for empire. In this regard the Republican Party's treatment of Native Americans from 1865 until 1890 is a fine example. In order to take lands earlier granted to the Plains Indians, and thereby exploit the gold and oil being found in the Western territories, the Republicans, with almost no debate, simply dispatched the Federal army to the West, where they systematically exterminated any Native Americans (men, women, and children) who refused to be moved to those great wastelands so euphemistically known as reservations. Reading that black chapter in our history today, one is tempted to ask, was the Holocaust of Adolph Hitler during World War II any worse than what the Republicans perpetrated against Native Americans in the late nineteenth century?

Lincoln and the Negro

As the consummate politician, Lincoln had an innate ability to say one thing to one audience and the opposite to another. Indeed, economist Murray Rothbard, in his work *America's Two Just Wars, 1776 and 1861* writes, "Lincoln was unsurpassed as a politician, which means that he was

a master conniver, manipulator, and liar." The finest example of his duplicity possibly lies in his attitude towards racial
equality. Indeed, prior to 1863 Lincoln, "the Great
Emancipator," stated repeatedly that he was opposed to
racial equality. For example, in his debate with Stephen
Douglas in Ottawa, Illinois, in 1858, Lincoln stated,

> I have no purpose to introduce political and social equality between
> the white and black races. There is a physical difference between the
> two, which, in my judgment, will probably forever forbid their living
> together upon the footing of perfect equality; and inasmuch as it
> becomes a necessity that there must be a difference, I, as well as Judge
> Douglas, am in favor of the race to which I belong having the superior
> position. I have never said anything to the contrary.

In that same revealing debate with Stephen Douglas,
Lincoln stated that he

> was not and never had been in favor of making voters or jurors of
> Negroes, nor of qualifying them to hold office, nor to intermarry with
> white people. Anything that argues me into his [Douglas's] idea of
> perfect social and political equality with the Negro is but a specious
> and fantastic arrangement of word, by which a man can prove a horse
> chestnut to be a chestnut.

If Lincoln was not in favor of racial equality, as he repeatedly stated, then what was his solution to the problem of
slavery and slaves? According to Lincoln, Afro-Americans
should first be freed, then colonized. Which was another idea
he inherited from Henry Clay.

During the war he was asked what should be done with
the slaves if they were ever freed. He responded that he
would "send them to Liberia, to their own native land." To
that end, during his presidency, he developed plans to send
every black person back to Africa, Haiti, or Central America.

This colonization idea was the brainchild of Henry Clay,
who was the founding member and president of the
American Colonization Society. Upon Clay's death in 1852,
Lincoln presented a eulogy in which he pointed out that
Clay's colonization ideas did not die with him, but would

live on with Abe Lincoln. To that end, in an 1862 message to Congress concerning the problem presented by thousands of freed slaves now flooding into the North, Lincoln stated, "I cannot make it better known than it already is, that I strongly favor colonization."

But Lincoln's ideas concerning colonization cannot be dismissed as simple racism. To the contrary, he was truly troubled by the possibility that freed blacks would be competing with whites for the limited number of available jobs, especially in the Western territories. In his Cooper Union speech of February 20, 1860, he advocated "the peaceful deportation of blacks, so that their places be filled up by free white laborers." Some three years earlier, in 1857, with apparently this same goal in mind, he had urged his colleagues in the Illinois legislature to appropriate money to remove all free blacks from the state of Illinois. Where they were to go Lincoln did not say, but the important thing was to get them out of Illinois. According to Roy P. Basler in his *Abe Lincoln: His Speeches and Writings,* Lincoln in 1857 explained to his fellow Illinois state legislators that "eliminating every black person from American soil would be a glorious consummation."

In 1862, when slavery was finally abolished in Washington, D.C., Lincoln had Congress appropriate six hundred thousand dollars to fund his plan to export these freed blacks to the Danish West Indies, Dutch Guiana, British Guiana, British Honduras, Guadeloupe, Ecuador—anywhere but the United States. He asked Sen. Samuel Pomeroy to supervise his resettlement efforts, and the senator later suggested that these blacks be sent to a Central American location to be called "Lincolnia."

As for the institution of slavery, certainly Lincoln had no intention of making any moves to eradicate that dismal chapter from our history, or at least he had no intention of interfering with *Southern* slavery. In his First Inaugural Address he stated, "I have no purpose, directly or indirectly, to interfere with the institution of slavery in the States where it exists. *I believe I have no lawful right to do so, and I have no inclination to do so"* [emphasis added].

Indeed, none of the four candidates for president in 1860

advocated the abolition of Southern slavery. They were aware that to do so would first be to violate the Constitution and second to commit political suicide. True, there existed a small abolitionist movement in the North, but for the most part there was very little public support for interfering with Southern slavery. And indeed when politicians at that time spoke of banning slavery, they were speaking not of banning slavery in the Southern states but of prohibiting slavery in the new Western territories. Their opposition to extending slavery to the West was based not on moral grounds but on fears that black labor would compete with white labor for a limited number of jobs. Lincoln spoke on this point to the Illinois state legislature in 1854:

> Whether slavery shall go into Nebraska, or other new territories, is not a matter of exclusive concern to the people who may go there. The whole nation is interested that the best use shall be made of these territories. We want them for the homes of free white people. This they cannot be, to any considerable extent, if slavery shall be planted with them. Slave states are the places for poor white people to go and better their condition.

Lincoln, in his above statements, sets forward very accurately the position of the Republican Party in 1860. Indeed, *New York Tribune* editor Horace Greeley, a staunch Republican and rabid abolitionist, explained in an 1860 editorial that "all the unoccupied territory shall be preserved for the benefit of the white Caucasian race—a thing which cannot be except by the exclusion of slavery."

Paul M. Angle in his *Lincoln Reader* quotes Lyman Trumbull, a senator from Illinois and a Lincoln supporter, on this point:

> We, the Republican Party, are the white man's party. We are for the free white man, and for making white labor acceptable and honorable, which it can never be when Negro slave labor is brought into competition with it.
>
> When we say that all men are created equal, we do not mean that every man in organized society has the same rights. We don't tolerate that in Illinois.

It might also be pointed out that the Republicans of 1860 feared the political impact of extending slavery to the Western territories. The three-fifths clause in the Constitution allowed every five slaves to count as three white citizens when it came to determining the number of Congressional seats in each state. The Republicans pointed to Maine and South Carolina as examples of the unfairness of this law, saying that while Maine had 581,813 white citizens, South Carolina had only 274,567; yet both were accorded the same number of representatives in Congress because South Carolina also counted 384,984 slaves. Thus, to extend slavery to the new territories would be to worsen this Congressional imbalance in favor of the Democrats, which is another reason that Lincoln led Republican opposition. Yes, Lincoln and his Republican Party opposed the extension of slavery, but not on moral grounds. They were intent on protecting their own political hides.

Officially, at least according to the revisionists, the War Between the States was fought to eradicate slavery from our great nation. But the facts suggest that the revisionist are only partly correct. It is true that there existed a strong abolitionist movement in some parts of the North, but it was a very small movement. So small, in fact, that politicians like Lincoln would not risk their political futures by associating themselves with it. Note for example that no abolitionist was ever elected to any major political office in any Northern state. Indeed, the vast majority of white Northerners cared nothing for the welfare of the slaves and treated the freed blacks who lived among them with contempt and sometimes violence. As Eugene Berwanger wrote in *North of Slavery,*

> In virtually every phase of existence in the North, Negroes found themselves systematically separated from whites. They were either excluded from railway cars, omnibuses, stagecoaches, and steamboats or assigned to special "Jim Crow" sections; they sat, when permitted, in secluded and remote corners of theaters and lecture halls; they could not enter most hotels, restaurants, and resorts, except as servants; they prayed in "Negro pews" in the white churches, and if partaking

of the sacrament of the Lord's Supper, they waited until the whites had been served the bread and wine. Moreover, they were often educated in segregated schools, punished in segregated prisons, nursed in segregated hospitals, and buried in segregated cemeteries. Racial prejudice haunts its victim wherever he goes.

Too, Alexis de Tocqueville in *Democracy in America* wrote that "the prejudice of race appears to be stronger in the states that have abolished slavery than in those where it still exists; and nowhere is it so intolerant as in those states where servitude has never been known."

And there were those Black Codes that had existed in the North for some forty years before such cruel laws were enacted in the South during the Reconstruction period (1868-1877). *The Revised Code of Indiana of 1860,* for example, prohibited freed Negroes and mulattos from entering the state; all contracts with Negroes were null and void; any white person who encouraged blacks to enter the state was subject to a fine of up to five hundred dollars; Negroes and mulattos were not allowed to vote; no Negro or mulatto having even one-eighth part of Negro blood could legally marry a white person, an act punishable by ten years' imprisonment and a fine of up to five thousand dollars; any person counseling or encouraging interracial marriage was subject to a fine of up to one thousand dollars; Negroes and mulattos were forbidden from testifying in court against white people, from sending their children to the public schools, or from holding any political office. In other words, the freed slave in Indiana in 1860 had no rights. He could not operate a business, for example, for if he did and that business was robbed or plundered by a white man, there was nothing the black owner could do since he could not testify against a white in a court of law. And certainly, since he could not vote, he had no political representation. Yes, perhaps he was a freed slave, but such state laws that were prevalent throughout the North in 1860 made a mockery of his freedom.

In 1860 the only Northern states that allowed blacks to vote were Massachusetts, New Hampshire, Vermont, and Maine. And only Massachusetts allowed blacks to serve on juries. That same year, Illinois, Indiana, and Oregon amended their state constitutions to prohibit the emigration of freed blacks into those states. Illinois senator Lyman Trumbull explained, "There is a great aversion in the West—I know it to be so in my state—against having free Negroes come among us. Our people want nothing to do with the Negro."

In fact when Virginia statesman John Randolph had freed 518 slaves in 1847, the state of Ohio prohibited their resettlement there. An Ohio congressman threatened that if any black tried to cross the border into Ohio "the banks of the Ohio River will be lined with men with muskets on their shoulders to keep off the emancipated slaves."

With such laws and attitudes so prevalent throughout the North, it is not difficult to understand Lincoln's opposition to the spread of slavery into the new territories. From Lincoln's political standpoint, the best course, the safest course, was not to mention slavery at all. He would certainly win no friends in the North by doing so.

Of course such racism was not limited to the population at large but extended to even well-educated newspaper editors. On November 22, 1860, the *Philadelphia Daily News,* bemoaning the fact that freed slaves were flocking to Philadelphia, would state, "It is neither for the good of the colored race nor of our own that they should continue to dwell among us to any considerable extent. The two races can never exist in conjunction except as a superior and inferior. The African is naturally the inferior race." And on December 7, 1860, the *Daily Chicago Times,* also frightened at the prospect of freed slaves migrating to Illinois, commented: "Evil and nothing but evil, has ever followed in the track of this hideous monster, Abolition. Let the slave alone. Send him back to his master where he belongs." And speaking of the blessings of slavery, on March 11, 1861, the *New York Herald,* which had the largest circulation in the country at the time, would write, "The immense increase in the numbers of slaves within so short a time speaks for the good treatment and happy, contented lot of the slaves. They are comfortably fed, housed and clothed, and seldom or never overworked."

Stephen Douglas, the candidate of the northern Democrats for president in 1860. We can only wonder how the nation's history would differ today had he defeated Lincoln for the presidency that year. Library of Congress

As for Lincoln's plan to colonize the blacks of America, the *Concord (N.H.) Democrat Standard* lent their support when their editor wrote on September 8, 1860, "The proposition that the Negro is equal by nature, physically and mentally, to the white man, seems to be so absurd and preposterous, that we cannot conceive how it can be entertained by any intelligent and rational white man." Then two weeks later the *Boston Daily Courier,* fearing apparently that the mulatto had somehow been ignored in all the racial controversy raging about the country, added, "We believe the mulatto to be inferior in capacity, character, and organization to the full-blooded black, and still farther below the standard of the white race."

The foregoing discussion is intended to contradict the popular myth that morally outraged Northerners elected Lincoln to the presidency in 1860 as a result of their deep concern for the welfare of black slaves in the South. In fact, nothing could be further from the truth. Blacks in the North suffered terrible discrimination at the hands of their white neighbors and were deprived of the most basic human freedoms by the Black Codes in effect in most of the Northern states. Considering the racist attitudes so prevalent in the North, it is absurd to assume that any concern for black slaves would motivate hundreds of thousands of young Northerners to sacrifice their lives on foreign battlefields. To the contrary, they were fighting merely to preserve the Union.

Lincoln and Secession

From the very beginning our Founding Fathers believed that among our most fundamental rights was the right of any state to secede should that state feel that it was in its best interests to do so. In fact, the Declaration of Independence is little more than a justification for the secession of the American states from the British government. Our Founding Fathers, in other words, were themselves secessionists. With such precedence, Southern secessionists of 1861 quoted the

Declaration of Independence as a basis and justification for their belief in states' rights and as the most powerful defense against a strong centralized government.

Citizens sometimes forget that America has fought two wars of secession: 1776 and 1861. In 1776 the thirteen colonies seceded from the tyranny of the British government. In 1861 eleven Southern states seceded from what they considered the tyranny of Washington, D.C., using as their reasoning the words of Thomas Jefferson, the principal author of the Declaration of Independence, who stated that governments derive their just powers from the consent of the governed and that whenever a government becomes destructive of the rights of life, liberty, and property, citizens have a right to secede from that government and form a new one. In fact, in his First Inaugural Address in 1801, Jefferson declared, "If there be any among us who would wish to dissolve this Union or to change its republican form, let them stand undisturbed as monuments of the safety with which error of opinion may be tolerated where reason is left free to combat it."

Abraham Lincoln himself in an 1848 speech before the Illinois state legislature declared his own belief in the inalienable right of any state to secede from the Union:

> Any people anywhere, being inclined and having the power, have the right to rise up and shake off the existing government, and form a new one that suits them better. This is a most valuable, a most sacred right—a right which we hope and believe is to liberate the world. Nor is this right confined to cases in which the whole people of an existing government may choose to exercise it. Any portion of such people, that can, may revolutionize, and make their own of so much of the territory as they inhabit.

Alexis de Tocqueville in his *Democracy in America* also commented on the unique right of any state in this Union to secede should it be in that state's best interest to do so:

> The Union was formed by the voluntary agreement of the States; and in uniting together they have not forfeited their nationality, nor have they

been reduced to the condition of one and the same people. If one of the states chooses to withdraw from the compact, it would be difficult to disprove its right of doing so, and the Federal Government would have no means of maintaining its claims directly either by force or might.

Of course de Tocqueville had no way of knowing that in 1861 Abe Lincoln would dispatch his Federal army to invade and kill some three hundred thousand Southerners to prevent them from exercising their constitutional right to secede, a right that had traditionally been the very foundation of American government. Recall that at the beginning of the Revolution, each state declared its independence from Great Britain on its own, and following the war each state was individually recognized as sovereign by the defeated British government. These states then formed the Articles of Federation and Perpetual Union, which created a federal government to act as an agent for the thirteen states. But when the Constitution was adopted, the states dissolved the Perpetual Union, and the words "Perpetual Union" do not appear anywhere in the Constitution. From the very beginning each state was sovereign and each state remained so until 1861.

By 1861 the constitutional right of a state to secede was well known in the North as well as in the South. And the pervasive sentiment in the North was to allow the South to go in peace. Edward.Everett, who had campaigned as vice president with John Bell on the Constitutional Union Party ticket in 1860, voiced the common Northern attitude towards the South and secession: "To expect to hold fifteen States in the Union by force is preposterous. The idea of a civil war, accompanied as it would be, by a servile insurrection, is too monstrous to be entertained for a moment."

In Maryland in April of 1861, immediately following the firing on Fort Sumter, state leaders favored peaceful secession for the Confederate states, but President Lincoln, who had suspended the writ of habeas corpus, had all those leaders arrested and thrown in jail before they could assemble in the state legislature to even discuss secession. Lincoln ordered the Federal army to occupy the state and posted armed guards at the doors of the State House to prevent the state legislature from meeting to discuss secession. The governor of Delaware was warned that Delaware must support Abraham Lincoln and the Union or else the state would be bombarded by the Union gunboats sitting in the harbor.

Though Lincoln employed forceful means of preventing secession, newspaper editors throughout the North favored a peaceful exit for the Southern states. A sampling indicates the following attitudes:

On November 17, 1860, the *Providence Evening Press* editorialized, "Sovereignty necessarily includes what we call the right of secession. This right must be maintained lest we establish a colossal despotism against which the founding fathers uttered their solemn warnings."

On November 21, 1860, the *Cincinnati Daily Press* wrote, "We believe that the right of any member of this Confederacy to dissolve its political relations with the others and assume an independent position is absolute."

On December 17, 1860, the *New York Tribune* would write, "If tyranny and despotism justified the Revolution of 1776, then we do not see why it would not justify the secession of five million Southrons from the Federal Union in 1861."

On February 5, 1861, the *Tribune* would take an even stronger position:

> Lincoln's latest speech contained the arguments of the tyrant—force, compulsion, and power. Nine out of ten people in the North are opposed to forcing South Carolina to remain in the Union. The great principle embodied by Jefferson in the Declaration is that governments derive their just power from the consent of the governed. Therefore, if the Southern states want to secede, they have a clear right to do so.

Following the revolution our Founding Fathers, who had just fought a great war against a highly centralized government, had absolutely no intention of creating another such monster of their own. Even during the war the Continental Congress was nothing more than a standing committee of the various states that coordinated the war effort. And these colonial delegations even awaited instructions from home before approving the Declaration of Independence. All of which is to say that there can be no doubt that the individual states created the Constitution and delegated certain powers to the Federal government as their agent while reserving the right to secede from that compact should it be in their best interests to do so.

Prior to 1861 our Constitution always presented a great obstacle to those politicians who advocated a powerful centralized government (with themselves, of course, wielding the power). But in order to protect the individual states from such centralized power, that is exactly the way our Founding Fathers wanted it.

There was one way to circumvent the intentions of our Founding Fathers. Beginning with Daniel Webster, another of Lincoln's fellow Whigs, and continuing through the nineteenth and twentieth centuries, those politicians who advocated an all-powerful federal government simply rewrote American history to meet their own political ends. In 1833, Webster, angry at losing political battles with Andrew Jackson over the nationalized banking system, apparently decided that a rewriting of our history would greatly increase his chances of achieving his political agendas. Thus he began telling his great lie, that the federal government had somehow created the states.

Donald W. Livingston of Emory University states in his *Secession Tradition in America* that Webster's words constituted not only a lie but a "spectacular lie." It was this "spectacular lie" that Abraham Lincoln adopted as his justification and rationale for denying the right of secession to the Southern states in 1861.

Too, argued Lincoln, to allow the Southern states to secede would destroy the federal government. But the events of the next four years would prove how erroneous that statement was, as the federal government immediately fielded one of the largest, most well-equipped and powerful armies in the history of the world. Without doubt, despite Lincoln's dire warnings of catastrophe, the federal government grew and prospered more than ever following the departure of the Southern states.

The Gettysburg Address

Oddly enough in his Gettysburg Address, Lincoln argued that the war was being fought in defense of "government by consent," but in fact the opposite was true. Under Lincoln the Federal government fought to deny Southerners the right of government by consent. Indeed, in 1930, the great American satirist H. L. Menken, in an essay entitled simply "Gettysburg," took Lincoln to task for misleading a gullible public in his Gettysburg Address:

> It is poetry, not logic; beauty, not sense. Think of the argument in it. Put it into the cold words of everyday. The doctrine is simply this: that the Union soldiers who died at Gettysburg sacrificed their lives to the cause of self-determination—that government of the people, by the people, for the people, should not perish from the earth. It is difficult to imagine anything more untrue. The Union soldiers in the battle actually fought against self-determination; it was the Confederates who fought for the right of their people to govern themselves. The Confederates went into battle free; they came out with their freedom subject to the supervision of the rest of the country—and for nearly twenty years that veto was so efficient that they enjoyed scarcely more liberty, in the political sense, than so many convicts in the penitentiary.

Lincoln's War

By the spring of 1861 it had become obvious to almost everyone that Abe Lincoln wanted a war with the South. But it must not appear that the North was the aggressor. In order to quiet criticism in the North, he must find a way to compel the Confederates to fire the first shots. And that he very cleverly did, despite the fact that the last thing the Confederacy, one of the weakest nations on earth, wanted was a war with one of the world's most powerful nations. In hopes of avoiding a war, Pres. Jefferson Davis in March 1861 dispatched five peace commissioners to Washington to negotiate with Lincoln. They were to offer to pay the government for any Federal property located on Southern soil that the Confederacy might confiscate. They were also to offer to pay the government the Southern share of the national debt. Lincoln, rather than negotiating with them, refused to meet or acknowledge them. Napoleon III of France, who happened to be in New York at the time, offered to mediate the dispute, but he was also snubbed by Lincoln, who refused to meet with him as well.

Certainly newspapers throughout the North understood that Lincoln was itching for a war and that he was trying to maneuver the South into firing the first shots. On April 13, 1861, the day following the opening of hostilities at Fort Sumter, the *Providence Daily Post* stated, "For three weeks the administration newspapers have been assuring us that Fort Sumter would be abandoned, but Mr. Lincoln saw an opportunity to inaugurate civil war without appearing in the character of an aggressor, and so did just that." And on April 16, 1861, the *Buffalo Daily Courier* editorialized that "the affair at Fort Sumter has been planned as a means by which the war feeling at the North should be intensified." The following day the *New York Evening Day Book* wrote, "The event at Fort Sumter was a cunningly devised scheme contrived to arouse, and, if possible, exasperate the northern people against the South."

But one of the most damning and accurate portrayals of Lincoln's actions during this period appeared in the *Jersey City American Standard* on April 12, 1861. Writing of Lincoln's decision to send an unarmed ship to Charleston to supply the garrison at Fort Sumter, the *Standard* editorialized, "There is a madness and ruthlessness in Lincoln's behavior which is astounding. This unarmed vessel is a mere decoy to draw the first fire from the people of the South, which act by the pre-determination of the government is to be the pretext for letting loose the horrors of war."

And of course the *Standard* was absolutely correct. After all, what did the Confederacy have to gain by a war with the United States? Obviously, they had nothing to gain, and everything to lose. By April 1861 the Confederate states already had what they most desired—freedom. At that point, following their secession, they were free of an oppressive federal government, free to pursue their own destiny. Would they be foolish enough to risk their freedom, their very existence, by starting a war with the United States over Fort Sumter? Not unless they had been driven beyond endurance into firing the first shots. And that is what Lincoln engineered. He was aware that the Confederacy could no more tolerate a Federal fort sitting in Charleston Harbor than Boston could tolerate a British fort sitting in its harbor. Jefferson Davis already had informed Federal authorities that the Confederacy did not consider Fort Sumter to be a military threat, but it did consider it a threat to the Confederacy's bid for national sovereignty, especially at a time when the Confederacy was struggling for international recognition.

Lincoln was most aware of the Confederacy's touchy position in this matter, and he easily could have negotiated the peaceful surrender of the fort to the South (the Confederacy already had offered to purchase it). After all, what was the Federal government's purpose in constructing Fort Sumter in Charleston Harbor in the first place? The answer is obvious: to protect Charleston and its citizens from foreign invasion. But now, with South Carolina no longer a state of the Union, the protection of Charleston and its citizens was no longer the responsibility of the Federal government. Such protection was now the responsibility of South Carolina. Thus it would seem that the Federal government would be happy to relinquish that responsibility (and expense) to South Carolina. But such would not have served Lincoln's purposes. In order to achieve his secret agenda, he must have a great civil war, and thus he goaded the Confederacy into making the initial hostile move.

Lincoln's personal secretary, John Hay, also agreed that Lincoln very cleverly maneuvered the South into firing the first shots of the war. In Charles Ramsdell's *Lincoln and Fort Sumter,* Hay was quoted as having written, "Abstractly it was enough that the Government was in the right. But to make the issue sure, Lincoln determined that in addition the rebellion should be 'put in the wrong.'"

Of course Lincoln's hopes were realized. Not only determined to have a war, Lincoln seems to have been convinced that this war would last only a short time before the Confederates were forced to beg for peace. Indeed, in a speech before Congress on July 4, 1861, Lincoln very piously stated, "Having thus chosen our course without guile and with pure purpose, let us renew our trust in God, and go forward without fear and manly hearts."

However, Jefferson Davis and his cabinet were not fools. For the most part they were highly respected statesmen who had earlier held responsible positions in the national government, and they knew exactly what Lincoln planned. On April 9, 1861, Confederate secretary of state Robert Toombs warned his fellow cabinet members that to fire on Fort Sumter "is suicide, murder, and you will lose every friend in the North." But Davis and the others felt that their backs were to the wall. They had been maneuvered into giving the Federal government an ultimatum, and there was no way they now could retreat gracefully. To do so would be to lose face with England, France, and the other European countries where the Confederacy was seeking recognition.

But Toombs was quite right. Not only did the firing on Fort Sumter diminish support among much of the general population of the North, it also quieted many of the newspapers that had openly supported the right of the Southern states to secede. Once the war began, it was considered less than patriotic to offer any support for the South—and it could land editors in jail. Following the firing on Fort Sumter, the Lincoln administration imprisoned without trial thousands of war opponents and shut down or destroyed dozens of newspapers that opposed Lincoln or his war policies. Without question, it was Lincoln's suspension of civil liberties in the North that squelched public support for the constitutional rights of the South.

To say that he was leading a great crusade to abolish the abysmal institution of slavery would have proven a convincing justification for Lincoln's going to war with the South. But he never made such a case. Throughout the war and until the day he died, Lincoln insisted that the war was being fought to prevent Southerners from seceding from the Union. Preventing the spread of slavery, said Lincoln, was only a byproduct of the war's real purpose, "saving the Union." Following Fort Sumter, he immediately called up seventy-five thousand troops to put down a rebellion, not to free the slaves.

Confederate vice president Alexander Stephens, in his postwar book *A Constitutional View of the Late War Between the States,* explained that since the Northern abolitionist movement was so small in numbers and the federal government was powerless to put an end to slavery, it is likely that "not one in ten thousand" Northerners who voted for Lincoln did so because they thought he would end slavery. Nor was the war fought over slavery. Said Stephens:

> The contest, which ended in the War, was indeed a contest between opposing principles; but not such as bore upon the policy of African subordination. . . . They involved the very nature and organic Structure of the Government itself. The conflict, on this question of Slavery, in the Federal Councils, from the beginning, was not a contest between the advocates or opponents of the Peculiar Institution, but a contest, as stated before, between the supporters of a strictly Federative [decentralized] Government, on the one side, and a thoroughly National one, on the other.

From the South's point of view, in addition to states' rights and slavery, there also existed the issue of fiscal and trade policies, which the national government has been unfairly imposing on the South for many years. Indeed, the primary source of federal revenue at that time was derived from tariffs. Since the South had a very limited manufacturing base, it purchased most of its manufactured goods from the North so that in 1860 the South was paying 80 percent of all tariffs. But the vast majority of this money was being spent in the North, which led Southerners to feel that they were being plundered. And now Lincoln was promising his Northern constituents, to whom he owed his political existence, that he would impose even higher tariffs. To Southerners, whom Lincoln owed absolutely nothing, this meant the plunder would prove even greater.

The idea that they were being plundered from a fiscal standpoint was widespread throughout the South, and on January 18, 1860, the *Vicksburg Daily Whig* editorialized, "The North has been aggrandized, in a most astonishing degree, at the expense of the South, taxing us at every step, and depleting us as extensively as possible without actually destroying us." To continue in this vein, stated Southern statesmen, was intolerable. Something must be done.

And in March 1861 an editor in Montgomery wrote of the new Confederacy, "No more to pay duties to enrich Northern industrialists at Southern expense, and to pour money into Washington's treasury. This new nation will give the South a chance to profit from their own wealth and prevent the North from siphoning away an estimated $100,000,000 annually."

Citizens of the North did not deny that Southerners were being unfairly penalized for their lack of manufacturing, and on March 18, 1861, on the eve of war, the *Boston Transcript* wrote:

> It does not require extraordinary sagacity to perceive that trade is perhaps the controlling motive operating to prevent the return of the seceding States to the Union. Slavery is an issue, yes, but the mask has been thrown off, and it is apparent that the people of the principle seceding States are now for commercial independence.

The *Transcript* went on to warn that the Confederate constitution forbade protectionist tariffs, which meant the South would be devoted to free trade. If free trade were permitted to exist in the Southern states, then merchants in New Orleans, Charleston, and Savannah would soon take all the trade from Boston, New York, and other Northern ports. Such a thing would prove devastating to Northern merchants, and therefore secession must not be allowed.

It was a widespread belief throughout the country that this battle between the protectionist North and the free trade South was the real motive for Lincoln's pushing the South into the War Between the States. In hindsight, it appears that Lincoln and his Republican cronies were strongly motivated to impose a highly centralized mercantilist state on the people of the United States, a goal that seemed within their grasp in 1860—but only if they could subjugate the Southern politicians who stood in their way. To Southerners on the other hand the only escape from Lincoln and his oppressive political and economic policies was secession. In the end, they would pay an enormous price for their bid for social and economic freedom.

In the beginning, the South made their bid for freedom by forcing the evacuation of Fort Sumter following a day of heavy bombardment. They had fired on the United States flag, yes, but they had done the same earlier, back in January 1861, when they opened fire on *The Star of the West,* the Union ship that had attempted to resupply the fort, and absolutely nothing had come of that. The Federal government had not used that incident as a pretext for going to war. Thus the Confederate government felt confident that the forced evacuation of Fort Sumter would be viewed in the same manner.

Ah, but they reckoned without Abe Lincoln and his supporters in Washington. It must be remembered that Buchanan was president when *The Star of the West* had been fired on, but now Abe Lincoln was president, having been sworn in less than a month earlier. And Fort Sumter was just the excuse he was looking for. Nor could he have found a more ideal time to put his plan into action. For in April 1861, Congress was in recess, and Lincoln would be spared having to face a bevy of politicians who doubtlessly would have been aghast at the thought of unleashing a great war on the Southern states of America. However, with Congress in recess, he could play a lone hand.

It must be admitted that Lincoln was as clever as he was unscrupulous, and he had a most creative mind when it came to destroying an enemy. No one could deny that the Confederates had fired the first shots, and the Union had been attacked by the Southerners; thus Abe Lincoln had no choice but to defend the Union, as much as he dreaded the thought of shedding American blood.

Lincoln wasted no time. On the same day that Fort Sumter was fired upon, April 14, 1861, he drew up a proclamation of war. The next day he issued an executive proclamation ordering the Federal army and navy to cross the state lines of Maryland and Virginia and force the Confederacy to submit to Union authority. He also ordered the Northern states to furnish seventy-five thousand soldiers to enforce that proclamation.

The text of the Lincoln's proclamation follows:

By the President of the United States.
A PROCLAMATION

Whereas the laws of the United States have been for some time past and now are opposed and the execution thereof obstructed in the States of South Carolina, Georgia, Alabama, Florida, Mississippi, Louisiana, and Texas by combinations too powerful to be suppressed by the ordinary course of judicial proceedings or by the powers vested in the marshals by law: Now, therefore, I, Abraham Lincoln, President of the United States, in virtue of the power in me vested by the Constitution and the laws, have thought fit to call forth, and hereby do call forth, the militia of the several States of the Union to the aggregate number of 75,000, in order to suppress said combinations and to cause the laws to be duly executed.

The details for this object will be immediately communicated to the State authorities through the War Department.

I appeal to all loyal citizens to favor, facilitate, and aid this effort to maintain the honor, the integrity, and the existence of our Federation and the perpetuity of popular government and to redress wrongs already long enough endured.

I deem it proper to say that the first service assigned to the forces hereby called forth will probably be to repossess the forts, places, and property which have been seized from the Federal Government; and in every event the utmost care will be observed, consistently with the objects aforesaid, to avoid any devastation, any destruction of or interference with property, or any disturbance of peaceful citizens in any part of the country.

And I hereby command the persons composing the combinations aforesaid to disperse and retire peaceably to their respective abodes within twenty days from this date.

Deeming that the present condition of public affairs presents an extraordinary occasion, I do hereby, in virtue of the power in me vested by the Constitution, convene both Houses of Congress. Senators and Representatives are therefore summoned to assemble at their respective chambers at 12 o'clock noon on Thursday, the 4th of July next, then and there to consider and determine such measures as, in their wisdom, the public safety and interest may seem to demand.

In witness whereof I have hereunto set my hand and caused the seal of the United States to be affixed.

Done at the city of Washington, this 15th day of April, A.D. 1861, and the independence of the United States the eighty-fifth.

By the President: ABRAHAM LINCOLN.

It should be noted that in his proclamation Lincoln very cleverly avoided mentioning the Confederacy by name, referring to that free and independent foreign nation as "combinations too powerful to be suppressed by the ordinary course of judicial proceedings." He also avoided mentioning Fort Sumter. Instead, he wrote that a state of rebellion existed in seven American states and suggested that the states of the North were in danger of suffering great harm from those seven states. He also demanded seventy-five thousand soldiers "to conquer the persons composing the combinations."

According to the Constitution, only Congress has the authority to declare war, and the Constitution clearly forbade Lincoln from using military force against a state government. But in his proclamation Lincoln used highly esoteric legal language intended to circumvent both Congress and the Constitution. In fact, to ensure that his war was well underway and in no danger of being nullified by a pesky Congress, Lincoln closed his proclamation with a call for Congress to reconvene at noon on July 4, 1861, some three months down the road, at a time when his unconstitutional war would be too far advanced to be halted by Congress or anyone else.

It should also be noted that as justification for his proclamation Lincoln drew on "The 1792 Act for Calling forth the Militia" invoked by George Washington to suppress the so-called Whiskey Rebellion in Pennsylvania during that year.

This, despite the fact that the secession of seven Southern states in no way resembled the rebellion of several hundred Pennsylvania moonshiners who refused to pay tax on their homemade whiskey. Despite his best efforts, Lincoln could find no other legal justification for his unconstitutional move to invade the South.

In Montgomery, Jefferson Davis and his cabinet were stunned when they were informed of Lincoln's latest move. These men, former members of the United States government, certainly were very familiar with the Constitution, which states, "The House and Senate shall have power to provide for calling forth the militia to execute the laws of the Government, suppress insurrections, and repel invasions." Clearly, no such power was vested in the chief executive. Davis and his cabinet realized that with Congress in recess Lincoln had simply usurped their authority. He was determined to have a war whatever the cost.

Freedom to Abe Lincoln

It has already been demonstrated that in 1861 the vast majority of Americans agreed that the Constitution granted the right of secession to individual states. However, immediately upon taking office, Lincoln launched a series of unconstitutional acts that still stun historians. He launched an invasion of the South without consulting Congress, as required by the Constitution; declared martial law; blockaded the Southern ports; suspended the writ of habeas corpus for the duration of his administration; imprisoned without trial thousands of Northern citizens; arrested and imprisoned critical newspaper publishers and editors; censored all telegraph communication; nationalized the railroads; created several new states without the consent of the citizens of those states; ordered Federal troops to interfere with elections in the North by intimidating Democratic voters; and confiscated private property and firearms, a violation of the Second Amendment. His ideas at that time were considered quite radical, yet he had many of those radical ideas put into practice despite the fact that they had not been debated in Congress or by the courts. Indeed, Lincoln had no respect for constitutional liberty.

He generally excused his suspension of constitutional liberties by equating the Constitution with the Union. Thus, whatever action he felt necessary to "preserve the Union" he also considered constitutional. The fallacy in this reasoning is that the Constitution makes no mention of such a Union as Lincoln advocated. To the contrary, the Constitution very clearly grants each state the right to secede should that state desire to do so. With such actions, rather than the Great Emancipator, Lincoln very quickly became the Great Dictator.

It was Lincoln's suspension of the writ of habeas corpus that gave him a license to perform almost any act he chose, no matter how illegal. If anyone protested, he simply had that person arrested. One of the first victims of Lincoln's suspension of habeas corpus was Francis Key Howard of Baltimore (the grandson of Francis Scott Key), who was imprisoned at Fort McHenry after his newspaper criticized Lincoln's decision to invade the South without the consent of Congress as well as Lincoln's suppression of civil liberties in Maryland. Howard remained in that Federal prison without being charged and without trial for over two years. Following the war, he would write a book about his experiences titled *The American Bastille.*

How Lincoln justified such unconstitutional and dictatorial actions is difficult to understand. But it must be remembered that he was aided and abetted by such political thugs as Secretary of State William Seward and Secretary of War Edwin Stanton. Together these three radical and extremely clever politicians discovered unheard-of means of manipulating the Constitution. They discovered that the commander-in-chief clause of the Constitution, when combined with the duty of the president to "take care that the laws be faithfully executed," gave Lincoln a license to ignore laws. He could even ignore the Constitution itself in the name of "war powers."

The Suspension of Habeas Corpus

Initially, there was widespread sympathy in the North for the South and her efforts to secede peacefully from the Union. This was especially true among the abolitionists, for they wanted more than anything to disassociate themselves from the slave-owning states. Opposition to Lincoln's using military force was almost universal, and the Union army's terrible defeat at First Manassas merely intensified that opposition.

It was at that point that Lincoln decided he must silence his critics, otherwise he would be forced to make peace with the South or resign from office. He wanted to do neither. As a viable alternative, on April 27, 1861, just a few days following the opening of hostilities at Fort Sumter, he issued a declaration that he was suspending the writ of habeas corpus. This allowed him to order the military to arrest and jail anyone who voiced disagreement with his war policies—and in time, even his domestic policies.

The writ of habeas corpus is, of course, a most important part of the rule of law in a free country. It protects citizens from arbitrary arrest and imprisonment by the state for political reasons. Thanks to the writ of habeas corpus, American citizens accused of a crime have a constitutional right to a speedy public trial by an impartial jury, to be informed of the nature and cause of the accusation, to be confronted with witnesses against them, to bring witnesses in their favor, and to have the assistance of legal counsel. As of April 27, 1861, American citizens no longer enjoyed such legal protection. Nor would they as long as Lincoln lived.

In England the suspension of habeas corpus could be enacted only by an act of the legislature, and legal scholars always had assumed the same was true in this country as well, that the writ of habeas corpus could only be suspended by a majority ruling of Congress. According to James Randall in his *Constitutional Problems under Lincoln*, the chief justice of the Supreme Court, Roger B.

Taney, answered Lincoln's order suspending habeas corpus by issuing an opinion that the president of the United States lacked such legal authority. He pointed out that the provision regarding habeas corpus is located in a section of the Constitution that pertains to legislative, not executive, powers and explained that our Founding Fathers would never have given an American president "more regal and absolute power" over the personal liberties of the citizens than any king of England ever enjoyed.

Taney went on to state that even if Congress did support the suspension of habeas corpus, such support still would not justify holding a citizen in jail indefinitely without trial, as Lincoln was doing. Even treason, argued Taney, should be dealt with by the normal judicial process. If not, then "the people are no longer living under a government of laws; but every citizen holds life, liberty and property at the will and pleasure of the army officer in whose military district he may happen to be found." As a final parting shot, Taney admonished Lincoln to see that the laws were faithfully executed and that the civil processes of the United States were respected and enforced.

Taney's decision was delivered to Lincoln personally by courier. The courier later reported that Lincoln read the decision, then in a fit of rage tore the pages to pieces. Before the day was out, Lincoln would meet with William Seward and Edwin Stanton. Their advice? Ignore Taney's decision and continue his measures against his critics. Which is what Lincoln did.

At this time Secretary of State William Seward established a secret police that arrested thousands of citizens suspected of disloyalty, which meant that those citizens had somehow expressed disagreement with Lincoln's war policies. For the most part, those arrested were not told why they were being arrested, no one investigated the charges against them, and no trials were held. An Episcopal minister in Alexandria, Virginia, was arrested, for example, for failing to pray for the president of the United States during his church service as required by the Lincoln administration. And in New Orleans, Gen. Ben "the Beast" Butler hanged a citizen for removing an American flag in front of his business establishment.

In May 1861 a special election was held to fill ten empty seats in the Maryland House of Representatives. The ten men elected were some of Maryland's leading citizens, but because Seward suspected them of having secessionist sentiments, they were arrested and sent to Fort Lafayette, where they remained for the next two years though no charges were ever brought against them.

Despite Lincoln's interference with free elections throughout the North, on November 7, 1861, the Maryland legislature issued a proclamation declaring that

> the war now waged by the government of the United States upon the people of the Confederate States is unconstitutional in its origin, purposes and conduct; repugnant to civilization and sound policy; subversive of the free principles upon which the Federal Union was founded, and certain to result in the hopeless and bloody overthrow of our existing institutions.

Of course this proclamation fell on deaf ears. In fact, the Federal military used Maryland as a major launching pad for their excursions into the South for the rest of the war.

Lincoln and the Free Press

Once Lincoln sent Federal troops into Virginia in June 1861, he saw anyone who disagreed with his war policies as a possible traitor. These so-called traitors included dozens of newspaper editors and owners throughout the North. Lincoln's response was to have such miscreants imprisoned and their newspapers shut down.

His suppression of the press began with the big New York City newspapers, which dominated much of the nation's news. In particular, the *Journal of Commerce* and the *New York Daily News* were extremely critical of Lincoln's war policies, and their articles and editorials were reprinted in newspaper across the North. In May 1861 the *Journal of Commerce* printed a list of over one hundred Northern newspapers that had editorialized against going to war. Lincoln gleefully responded by ordering the postmaster general to forbid these newspapers the use of the mail for their deliveries. Within a week every one of those one hundred newspapers was out of business.

As for the *New York Daily News,* its editor was Ben Wood, the brother of New York City mayor Fernando Wood. In June 1861, Wood denounced Lincoln as "an unscrupulous Chief magistrate whose recent message to Congress was an ocean of falsehood and deceit." Lincoln responded by having Federal marshals confiscate the *Daily News* in cities throughout the North. At that point the *Daily News* went into bankruptcy.

In Washington, D.C., Federal soldiers were dispatched to destroy the offices and printing facilities of the *Democratic Standard* after it criticized military blunders during the Battle of First Manassas. A day later the same thing happened to the *Bangor Democrat,* only this time the soldiers also attempted to hang the editor.

As the war progressed, brave newspapers across the North renewed their efforts to persuade the Lincoln government to find a peaceful solution to the crisis. In response, Lincoln increased his repression of the free press, squelching any further mention of peaceful solutions.

Lincoln's Emancipation Proclamation

In January 1863 Lincoln's much-heralded Emancipation Proclamation was to be put into effect. According to revisionist historians, that edict proved Lincoln's humanitarian regard for the slaves of America. But that was decidedly not the case. In fact, Lincoln cared little if nothing for the slaves, and he was certainly not about to give them their freedom—at least not in those areas loyal to the Union.

As early in the war as the summer of 1861 Gen. John Frémont was in charge of Federal military operations in Missouri. In a move to deter Confederate guerilla operations in that state, Frémont issued a proclamation in August 1861 imposing martial law throughout the state and declaring that anyone who resisted the Federal army would have their property confiscated and their slaves freed. Those loyal to the Union, however, would be allowed to keep their slaves.

When Lincoln was informed of Frémont's proclamation, he furiously wired the general that he must immediately nullify that part of the proclamation dealing with the freeing of slaves. Several days later Lincoln informed Frémont that he was relieved of command. He was, to put it bluntly, fired.

When informed of Lincoln's actions, Sen. Ben Wade of Ohio wrote, "The president don't object to General Frémont's taking the life of the owners of slaves, when found in rebellion, but to confiscate their property and emancipate their slaves he thinks monstrous."

In a well-known letter to *New York Tribune* editor Horace Greeley in 1862, Lincoln wrote:

> My paramount object in this struggle is to save the Union, and is not either to save or to destroy slavery. If I could save the Union without freeing any slaves I would do it; and if I could save it by freeing some and leaving others alone I would also do that. What I do about slavery, and the colored race, I do because I believe it helps to save the Union.

This letter is primarily of interest because in it Lincoln contradicts the statements he made in his First Inaugural Address, where he explicitly pointed out that he lacked the constitutional authority to free any slaves. But by late 1862 Lincoln paid little attention to the Constitution and cared even less. Indeed, his Emancipation Proclamation, issued in January 1863, was in total conflict with the constitutional rights of citizens throughout the Confederacy, as Lincoln was certainly aware. It did not free a single slave in any of the states loyal to the Union. It applied only to slaves then being held in the Confederacy. And even at that, Lincoln exempted from emancipation those areas of the Confederacy then occupied by the Federal army: Missouri, Maryland, Kentucky, West Virginia, and large parts of Virginia and Louisiana.

In other words, the Emancipation Proclamation was nothing more than a political gimmick that freed few slaves, leading the *New York World* to editorialize on January 7, 1863:

> The President has purposely made the proclamation inoperative in all places where we have gained a military footing which makes the slaves accessible. He has proclaimed emancipation only where he had notoriously no power to execute it. The exemption of the accessible parts of Louisiana, Tennessee, and Virginia renders the proclamation not merely futile, but ridiculous.

Even Lincoln's most trusted collaborator, Secretary of State William Seward, as recorded in James Randall's *The Civil War and Reconstruction*, had the audacity to jeer, "We show our sympathy with slavery by emancipating slaves where we cannot reach them and holding them in bondage where we can set them free."

Basically, the proclamation says that no man can own slaves in America, unless he is loyal to the Federal government, in which case he is exempt from that mandate. Even Lincoln himself admitted on several occasions that his proclamation was not sanctioned by the Constitution. It was, he said, a "war measure." He was aware that most of the great nations of Europe had recently abolished slavery peacefully, and they would be unlikely to recognize or support the Confederacy if emancipation was one of Lincoln's objectives in the war. In January 1863 the Confederacy had recently enjoyed great successes on the battlefield, and Lincoln was desperate. At that point, had England or France offered economic assistance to the Confederacy or offered to negotiate a peace deal, Lincoln might have been pressured to end the war. Now, hopefully, his Emancipation Proclamation would keep England and France at bay—at least for a while.

At home, Northerners, many of whom prided themselves on their anti-black sentiments, were shocked and outraged by the Emancipation Proclamation. This was the first they had heard that they were dying by the tens of thousands on distant battlefields to free black slaves whom they despised. Their anger finally erupted in New

York, in July 1863. Terrible race riots erupted, with thousands of furious white ruffians running through the streets beating and killing any blacks unfortunate enough to cross their paths. The mob was also protesting the new conscription law, which declared that any man who could afford to pay three hundred dollars to the government would be exempted from the draft, which meant that only the poor would be doing the fighting.

Col. Arthur Freemantle, a British emissary to the Confederacy, was in the city awaiting passage back to England when the riots were in full force. In his later work *Three Months in the Southern States* he wrote of the riots:

> The reports of outrages, hangings, and murder, were now most alarming, the terror and anxiety were universal. All shops were shut: all carriages and omnibuses had ceased running. No colored man or woman was visible or safe in the streets, or even in his own dwelling. Telegraphs were cut, and railroad tracks torn up. The draft was suspended, and the mob evidently had the upper hand.
>
> The people who cannot pay $300 naturally hate being forced to fight in order to liberate the very race who they are most anxious should be slaves. It is in their direct interest not only that all slaves should remain slaves, but that the free Northern Negroes who compete with them for labor should be sent to the South also.

The mob burned down an orphanage for black children and began searching tenement houses by the waterfront for black men and boys, whom they beat unmercifully. They also turned their wrath on anyone associated with the Republican Party and began to burn down expensive Republican homes on Lexington Avenue. Then they remembered that one of the most prominent Republicans in the country, Horace Greeley, was in New York. Thus they made their way to Greeley's *New York Tribune* office and burned down the newspaper. They then lynched a black man named William Jones and burned his body. Other murders followed.

When informed of this great insurrection and fearing that his proclamation and new draft law would unleash a backlash throughout the North, Lincoln immediately dispatched five regiments of troops to New York, where they shot over a thousand citizens in order to quell the riot.

In Gary Gallagher's *The Confederate War,* Gallagher states that the Emancipation Proclamation caused over two hundred thousand Federal soldiers to desert the army and almost one hundred thousand Northern men to avoid conscription by fleeing to Canada or to the mountain areas of Pennsylvania. "They were willing to risk their lives for the Union, they said, but not for black freedom."

But Lincoln cared nothing for the emancipation of the slaves. To him emancipation was only a means of achieving his real goal: the consolidation of government power. State governments must become subordinate to the federal government, and all power must rest in the hands of the federal government. This was a theme Lincoln mouthed repeatedly, but he made it more palatable to Northern citizens by calling it "saving the Union." Of course the Union could only be saved by destroying that decentralized, voluntary union of states known as the Confederacy.

The War's Consequences

In his First Inaugural Address, Lincoln underscored the fact that it would be unconstitutional for the government ever to attempt to free the slaves in the South, and he originally had no intention of doing so. His invasion of the South in 1861 had nothing to do with abolishing slavery. To the contrary, Lincoln and other leaders of the Republican Party were in favor of Southern slavery, for they feared the possibility of a million freed slaves moving into the Northern states. Illinois, for example, Lincoln's home state, had recently amended its state constitution to prohibit the emigration of black people into the state, as had several other Northern states. And almost all the Northern states, with the exception of Massachusetts, had adopted Black Codes that discriminated terribly against freed blacks. There had been few blacks in the North prior to 1861, and Northern politicians and voters wanted it to remain that way.

Once the war began Lincoln and his Republicans were only opposed to the *extension* of slavery into the new territories. They felt that the territories must remain the domain of the white man. Also, Lincoln feared the three-fifths clause of the Constitution, which might have increased the number of Democrats in Congress had blacks been permitted to live and vote in the territories.

No, according to Lincoln, the war had nothing to do with freeing slaves. His purpose, he repeatedly stated, was to "save the Union." Which meant, accurately translated, that he wanted to destroy once and for all the belief in federalism and states' rights that had frustrated ambitious politicians like himself since the founding of the republic, politicians who wanted a highly centralized and enlarged federal government. As a Whig-Republican, it was Lincoln's ambition to dispense taxpayers' money to corporations and finance them with protectionist tariffs and a nationalized banking system (the American System).

Such a revolutionary idea had been strongly opposed since the founding of the republic by such Southern statesmen as Thomas Jefferson, James Madison, James Monroe, Andrew Jackson, and John C. Calhoun. But with his Republican Party in power, and the Southern states seceded from the Union, Lincoln and his Republicans were at last free to enact those economic policies they had been refused for so long. And this, most modern historians agree, was the real reason that Lincoln wanted to unleash his war against the South and why he repulsed all overtures from the South to peacefully end the dispute. He wanted a war. He *needed* a war.

At the beginning of 1861 he believed that such a war would last only a few months at most. Once the Confederacy had capitulated, he and his Republicans could easily accomplish their goal of a centralized federal government and do so without even addressing the issue of slavery. This turned out to be the greatest and most tragic political miscalculation in the history of this nation.

Lincoln preached Daniel Webster's theory that the Union had created the states, a theory with no factual basis. He then waged the most costly and bloodiest war in history to prove his theory. Approximately 620,000 young men lost their lives in that war, including one-fourth of all the white males in the South between eighteen and forty years of age. Viewed in terms of today's population, that number would translate into the deaths of over five million young men, nearly a hundred times the number of young Americans who were killed in Vietnam over a ten-year period.

Despite Webster and Lincoln's theory, our Founding Fathers determined that states' rights should be an integral part of the federal system they created. Later, this idea would be debated at great length by Alexander Hamilton and Thomas Jefferson, and for the first seventy years of the country's existence it was the Jeffersonians who easily had the upper hand. By 1865, the Hamiltonians, now calling themselves Republicans, had finally won this argument by emerging victorious in the terrible war they had imposed on the nation. Now they could impose their mercantilist American System on the entire country even if they had to destroy much of the nation in the process.

Thanks to Abe Lincoln and his great victory over the South, states' rights was essentially erased from the Constitution. Thanks to Lincoln's all-powerful federal government, the people would no longer be sovereign. The federal government became the citizens' master, rather than servant. Indeed, thanks to Lincoln's war, the federal government had the authority to draft young men into military service and the right to impose federal income taxes on its citizens—revolutionary and oppressive measures at best.

But the very word "Union" suggests a voluntary confederacy of states, which is what our citizens had until the empowerment of Abe Lincoln. He forced the states to remain in the Union, violating the very tenets of choice and freedom upon which the Union was based. It's admirable to desire to preserve your family, but what kind of a family would you have if you had to destroy eleven cousins in order to force them to remain in the family?

The Execution of Abraham Lincoln

Despite Lincoln's many sins, he is still remembered in the South for the very humane Reconstruction program that he planned for the Confederate states once the war ended. By April 1865, Lincoln was publicly advocating a complete return to constitutional government for the defeated Southern states. They would be welcomed back into the Union, said Lincoln, with all the constitutional rights guaranteed citizens of every other state. There would be no military occupation. There would be no carpetbag government. Southerners would immediately become American citizens again.

Edwin Stanton and the Radical Republicans in Congress were aghast. In promising a Reconstruction policy of reconciliation for the South, Lincoln took a political direction that was opposite that planned by the Radicals in Congress. The Radicals wished to punish the Southern states for having the audacity to secede from the Union. Even more, they viewed Reconstruction as a license to continue their robbing and pillaging of the South. They were extremely self-righteous, highly opinionated men who truly despised anyone who disagreed with their opinions. Lincoln, in their eyes, had not merely disagreed with them, he had absolutely betrayed them. After four long years of preaching punishment for the South, Lincoln was now changing his stance, doubtlessly for political reasons. They now saw Lincoln as a traitor, and these Radicals were men who did not suffer traitors gladly, especially when the issue involved taking control of the prostrate Southland, a vast empire consisting of millions of acres of rich cotton land and millions of dollars in commerce and trade. Indeed, the Southland had become a deal the Radicals and their Northern capitalist supporters eyed greedily.

As for the bankers, businessmen, and industrialists of the North, the newly risen capitalist class, they were truly impatient to reap the wealth awaiting them. But first, the South must be occupied by the Union army, placed under the new regime of the North. Under the new political system, the lands of formerly wealthy plantation owners could be confiscated and auctioned off at a great profit to Northern capitalists to build their mills and factories. Their cotton would be purchased by Northern entrepreneurs, then sold at incredible profits to the European nations in great need of the white gold, thereby enriching all involved. As for cheap labor, those Southerners who had lost their farms and were watching their families starve would take jobs at whatever wages their carpetbag bosses wanted to pay. But such financial windfalls could only come about if Abe Lincoln and his ideas of clemency for the South could be superseded. Perhaps our capitalists should talk with Edwin Stanton.

And in the Union army, there were numerous glum generals who saw their chances to rule over these occupied Southern territories, a quarter of the country, quickly fading away. And what would they do when peace and self-rule returned to the nation? There was nothing they could do. America would disarm and demobilize while its generals were relegated to lesser tasks, waiting to retire—probably as colonels. But, if Lincoln, that great Rebel-lover, should be removed somehow, things would be different. Then the Federal military would remain the most important element of American society.

And as soon as the South was occupied, which would require only a small part of that massive Federal army, those generals could set their sights on conquering the Western territories and gaining access to that area's oil and gold deposits. Soon those territories would become states, Republican states, and America would become a vast Republican empire stretching from sea to shining sea. The generals pondered the problem. Their horizons were certainly limitless, but only if Abe Lincoln should somehow pass suddenly from the scene. Perhaps they should speak with their secretary of war, Edwin Stanton.

As for the Radicals, doubtlessly it also occurred to them to secretly sit down with Secretary Stanton, a wise and experienced politician and a member of Lincoln's cabinet, to discuss just what could be done to terminate Lincoln's presidency. After all, he had just been elected to his second term less than six months before, which meant that he had another three and a half years before the next election. Far too long. By then the Civil War would be a distant memory, and the Radicals' opportunity to benefit from Reconstruction would be just a distant memory.

Stanton, as it turned out, was far more outraged by Lincoln's conciliatory policies towards the South than anyone else. In fact, according to Lafayette Baker's secret papers (see chapter II), Stanton was already taking steps to solve the problem. Indeed, not only must Lincoln be eliminated, but his chief ally, William Seward, must also go.

Yes, Booth pulled the trigger. But standing close behind Booth were Col. Lafayette Baker, Maj. Thomas Eckert, Edwin Stanton, and Vice Pres. Andrew Johnson.

Indeed, in his landmark work, *Why Was Lincoln Murdered* (1937), Otto Eisenschiml writes:

> Congressman Julian, a leader of the Radical Republicans, boldly stated that the accession of Andrew Johnson to the presidency would prove a blessing to the country. In this sentiment he was not alone. On April 15, only a few hours after Lincoln's death, a caucus of Republican leaders was held, at which the tragedy was described as a gift from Heaven, and it was decided to get rid of Lincolnism. Ben Butler was chosen Secretary of State. Unfortunately for that plan, William Seward's injuries were not fatal, and his position did not become vacant. Blunt Senator Wade told the new President: "Johnson, we have faith in you. By the gods, there will be no trouble now in running the government!" Johnson had been ranting for weeks past that secession was treason, that treason must be made odious, and that all Confederates should be hanged.

Congressional Republicans, led by the Radicals in their midst, feared that citizens of the Southern states, if allowed their constitutional rights, would vote a solid Democratic ticket in 1868. Combine these Southern Democrats with those Democrats in the Northern and Border states, and in

1868 the Republican Party would likely be overwhelmed at the polls, and the tremendous power and prestige they had enjoyed during the war years would be erased. And if there is anything a congressman cannot bear to contemplate, it is the thought that he might be defeated in an upcoming election, that he might lose his power and prestige. If it took the death of Abe Lincoln to avoid such a disaster, then so be it.

Besides, in the end Lincoln had proven a traitor to his party; therefore he totally deserved whatever might happen. After all, traitors generally are executed, aren't they? Once Andrew Johnson, that old Rebel-hater, was seated in the president's office, things would return to normal. The South could once again be slated for punishment and pillage, and the Republicans could maintain their power and prestige for decades to come.

Unfortunately for the Republicans, once Johnson ascended to the office of the presidency, he seemed to forget his stringent Reconstruction policies for the South. With his eyes cocked on the election of 1868, Johnson began advocating a return of all constitutional rights to the seceded states. At the same time, he began courting Southern statesmen, powerful politicians who could easily arrange for Johnson to receive the Democratic nomination for president in 1868, and would do so if he would veto all Reconstruction programs for the South. A smiling Andrew Johnson said that he was more than eager to do so. As always, he only wanted to do the right thing.

So what could the Republican congressmen do? They had just executed one traitor. To shoot another at this point might appear suspicious. Thus in 1867 they began impeachment proceedings against Johnson, accusing him of every sin imaginable, including the assassination of President Lincoln. Luckily for Johnson, he avoided conviction by one vote. Still, following his impeachment hearing, Johnson became a nonentity in Washington, and in 1868 Congress passed, over Johnson's veto, a Reconstruction bill for the South that ushered in one of the most wretched decades in the history of this great nation, a disgraceful era that is still remembered with great bitterness by Americans across the South.

II

The Secret Papers
of Lafayette Baker

In 1960 a New Jersey chemist, Ray A. Neff, whose lifelong hobby had been studying the Civil War, discovered coded messages in the secret papers left behind by Lafayette Baker, Edwin Stanton's master spy, upon his death in 1868. Neff finally succeeded in having these messages decoded by professional cryptographers, and in the end he learned to his amazement that Baker had named Edwin Stanton himself (aided and abetted by Vice Pres. Andrew Johnson) as the primary conspirator behind the murder of Abraham Lincoln. Neff also uncovered evidence that Baker might very well have been poisoned to keep him quiet about Stanton's involvement.

If Lafayette Baker is to be believed, this work represents the "smoking gun" for which historians have so long searched, and these pages prove that the devious Edwin Stanton, assisted by Andrew Johnson and various members of Congress, was the prime mover behind Lincoln's assassination. The motive for such a drastic act was to put an end to Lincoln's lenient Reconstruction policies for the South.

Lafayette Baker's words are presented here just as they appeared in the August 1961 issue of *The Civil War Times*.

"The Secret Papers of Lafayette Baker"[1]

By Robert H. Fowler, Editor, Civil War Times

Did Edwin M. Stanton engineer the murder of Abraham

Lincoln as part of a vast, well-financed plot to seize control of
the Federal Government at the end of the Civil War and prevent an easy peace for the conquered South?

Was the chief of Stanton's powerful, secret National
Detective Police force, Brigadier General Lafayette C. Baker,
poisoned in 1868 to insure his silence about the plot?

Ray A. Neff, shown holding his secret-laden copy of Colburn's
United Service Magazine *for the last half of 1864.* Courtesy
Civil War Times Illustrated

These possibilities are raised by a series of discoveries claimed by a Gibbsboro, N. J. research chemist and longtime student of the Civil War, Ray A. Neff. Unless what Neff has uncovered is merely an intricate hoax by Lafayette C. Baker, the suspicion that has lingered through the years concerning Stanton's role in the assassination of Lincoln may well be based on brutal fact.

Neff, a 37-year-old native of Virginia, has discovered two ciphered messages left by Baker in a bound volume of *Colburn's United Service Magazine, Series II, 1864,* in which the one-time secret police chief presumably:

—Told how Stanton plotted the murder of Lincoln and headed a conspiracy involving "at least eleven members of Congress . . . no less than twelve Army officers, three Naval officers and at least 24 civilians, of which one was a governor of a loyal state. . ."

—Indicated he had entered the names of the supposed conspirators in another bound volume of the same military journal—a book, incidentally, which Neff and *Civil War Times* have tried to locate for more than a year without success.

—Spoke of "constantly being followed" and expressed fear for his life.

After spending many weeks digging in the files of the Philadelphia City Hall in an effort to authenticate these amazing charges, Neff finally found the transcript of a hearing conducted by the Philadelphia Register of Wills in 1872 concerning a long-suppressed codicil to Baker's will. This remarkable document contained testimony:

—describing two attempts on Baker's life by shooting and one by cutting.

—Establishing the strong suspicion that his death, July 3, 1868, was due to arsenic poisoning, a suspicion that is strengthened by a last-minute diagnosis of his illness as "meningitis" so that his body was sealed immediately in a coffin.

—Indicating that Baker possessed a large sum of money (at least $275,000) when he died and that the money was secretly removed immediately after his death by the wife of a cousin.

But perhaps the most surprising part of the testimony that Neff found was that given by a former national detective who told of visiting Baker just before his death and finding him writing in cipher in an "English military journal!" This same witness said that at Baker's insistence, he had taken another volume of the same journal and had found cipher written in it.

In a painstaking search of records which had not been examined for years, Neff also located an inventory of Lafayette Baker's personal property which listed bound volumes of *Colburn's U.S. Service Magazine* complete from 1860 through 1865 except for the first half of 1864—the very volume in which Baker's ciphered message said the names of the conspirators were listed.

There can be little doubt that the volumes of magazines in Neff's possession was left by Lafayette Baker and that the cipher in them was written by him. Two handwriting experts have authenticated Baker's signature in the book. What Baker said about Stanton and the conspiracy against Lincoln can hardly be regarded as final proof of the Secretary of War's long suspected guilt, however. It can only be treated as new and possibly perjured evidence.

From what is known about Baker, he was capable of leaving the coded message simply to embarrass Stanton. Truthfulness was not his outstanding virtue. He was a scoundrel.

Even so, *Civil War Times* felt that Neff's findings did deserve a careful hearing when he first brought them to our attention in July 1960. This magazine agreed to assist him in searching for the missing volume of the military journal while he ran down his remaining leads. Repeated advertisements in *Civil War Times* and attempts elsewhere have not brought forth a single copy of the military journal, with or without Baker's cipher.

And Neff's attempts to locate Baker's grave to have his remains tested for traces of arsenic have been fruitless. That part of the cemetery where the detective chief was buried was taken over as a public playground in 1924 and the bodies therein were removed to another Philadelphia graveyard,

Neff learned. The records of which bodies went into which plots in this removal cannot be found.

Likewise Neff has been unable to find several boxes of Baker's impounded personal papers and books which may be stored somewhere in the vast Philadelphia City Hall. After he had gone as far as his single-minded efforts could take him, *Civil War Times* decided to print the evidence turned up through his arduous and dedicated research.

First, however, this magazine enlisted the help of the Pennsylvania Historical and Museum Commission in authenticating the will and codicil left by Baker. Neff turned over the copy of the military journal to be examined as closely as we wished.

The professional cryptographer who helped Neff decode the relatively simple cipher left by Baker died last year. Therefore *Civil War Times* submitted the code to two U.S. Government historians for checking. One handwriting expert had already verified Baker's signature in the volume but we had Captain Stanley S. Smith of Harrisburg, Pa., a veteran handwriting expert, double check it with Baker's signatures on his will and the codicil. As specified in his accompanying statement, Captain Smith testifies to the authenticity of the signature in the volume. This book apparently did belong to Baker. The messages, whether true or false, do appear to have been written by him. The story can now be told.

This story, for Ray A. Neff, began four yeas ago when he innocently bought a bound volume of *Colburn's United Service Magazine* at Leary's Bookstore in Philadelphia. He paid 50 cents for the volume which contains issues of the journal for the last half of 1864.

"Some months later" he recalls, "I noticed that there were numbers and letters written in pencil in the inner margins next to the binding. They appear as cipher but are not grouped as cipher usually is."

Neff enlisted the aid of Leonard Fousche of Collingswood, N.J., a professional cryptographer. (Fousche died in 1960.) With the help of his wife and Fousche, Neff deciphered the two messages, the text of which are printed several pages over.

*Lafayette Baker, Stanton's chief of the National Detective Police.
In 1960 Ray Neff discovered Baker's secret coded messages
naming Stanton as the mastermind behind the assassination of
President Lincoln. In 1867 Baker was fired after President
Johnson learned that he had placed spies in Johnson's office.*
National Archives

The first message is in what Neff calls "substitution cipher" of a "sliding variety." Each letter in the message is represented by another letter with frequent changes or "slides" back and forth through the alphabet to make solution more difficult. Each word is separated from the next by a number. Punctuation, absent in cipher, was inserted by Neff.

The first part of this cipher, found on Page 181 of the volume, is dated 2-5-68 and runs: "I am constantly being followed. They are professionals. I cannot fool them."

Then on Page 183 there begins this allegorical message in the same cipher:

> In new Rome there walked three men, a Judas, a Brutas and a spy. Each planned that he should be king when Abraham should die. One trusted not the other but they went on for that day, waiting for that final moment when with pistol in his hand, one of the sons of Brutus could sneak behind that cursed man and put a bullet in his brain and lay his clumsy corpse away. As the fallen man lay dying, Judas came and paid respects to one he hated, and when at last he saw him die, he said, "Now the ages have him and the nation now have I." But alas as fate would have it Judas slowly fell from grace, and with him went Brutus down to their proper place. But lest one is left to wonder what happened to the spy, I can safely tell you this, it was I.
>
> Lafayette Baker 2-5-68

Anyone with a smattering of knowledge about Lincoln's assassination would assume that "Judas" referred to Edwin M. Stanton to whom is attributed, wrongly or rightly, the quotation about Lincoln, "Now he belongs to the ages." John Wilkes Booth, Lincoln's killer would be "one of the sons of Brutus."

Of course some bright schoolboy could have written the foregoing. The other cipher Neff found in the military journals employed an even simpler system of cryptology. Dots were placed under letters on the printed page to form words. But the message called for intimate knowledge of the period on the author's part. The full text is printed on Page 10.

This message said that the author, presumably Baker, learned of the plot against Lincoln on April 10, 1865. When he approached "E. S." (Edwin Stanton) about it, the Secretary of War first acted surprised but then said Baker was a party to it.

On the next day, the message said, Stanton showed Baker a forged document making it appear that he (Baker) "had been in charge of a plot to kidnap the president . . ." There are two interpretations of the rest of this sentence. One would indicate that Vice President Andrew Johnson was also to have been kidnapped; the other, that he was the instigator of the conspiracy.

The message also says that when Stanton learned that Lincoln wanted to permit the Confederate legislature of Virginia to assemble to withdraw the state's troops from the war "He fermented immediately into an insane tirade" and sent a telegram rescinding the President's order.

Finally the cipher yielded this amazing message:

> There were at least eleven members of Congress involved in the plot, no less than twelve Army officers, three Naval officers and at least 24 civilians, of which one was a governor of a loyal state. Five were bankers of great repute, three were nationally known newspaper men and eleven were industrialists of great repute and wealth. There were probably more that I know nothing of. The names of these known conspirators is presented without comment or notation in Vol. one of this series. Eighty-five thousand dollars was contributed by the named persons to pay for the deed. Only eight persons knew the details of the plot and the identity of the others. . . . I fear for my life. LCB.

Naturally these disclosures excited Neff whose Civil War studies go back to his days at Bridgewater College but "I was quite cautious about disclosing the message since cipher is without character and very difficult, if not impossible, to authenticate." He began "a detailed study" to see if the volume held more secrets.

Neff, a professional chemist, found several discolored places which he subjected to "ultrashort wavelength ultraviolet radiations." One of these spots emitted a purple glow but prolonged exposure to the lamp produced no results. Neff then spread a tannic acid solution over the spot and up came the signature: "L. C. Baker."

At the time, Neff was working in the office of the medical examiner of the City of Philadelphia under a Walter G. Karr graduate fellowship. He had the signature examined by a city handwriting expert. The signature was declared genuine.

In Neff's view "this signature was made with an invisible ink having a ferrocyanide base." As he points out, "Ink of this type was widely used by secret agents on both sides during the Civil War and would become visible after exposure to the sunlight for about an hour." He thinks that the ink lost some of its properties over the years so that it would not respond to the "UV lamp." He says that "Ferric ion plus tannic acid yields ferric tannate, a blue ink" and that the "the ferric ion would remain intact for a couple of centuries after the writing no longer would respond to sunlight or ultraviolet rays."

Despite his discovery, Neff kept the story to himself. He started digging into the life of L. C. Baker. Plenty of surface information was available in standard reference works and in Baker's own *History of the Secret Service,* which he wrote with the help of a New York journalist just after the War. Neff went far beyond these published sources. He knew that Baker had moved to Philadelphia after his dismissal in February, 1866 following Andrew Johnson's discovery that the National Detective Police had the White House under surveillance. He knew that Baker had died on July 3, 1868 in Philadelphia. So Neff began an exhaustive examination of the records in the City Hall there.

On file in the Register of Wills office he found the will of Lafayette C. Baker, dated April 30, 1866. Baker left specific amounts to his three brothers and three sisters and willed the residue of his estate to his wife, Jane Curry Baker.

Newspaper accounts of Baker's death said he died of typhoid but Neff found a different story on the death certificate. Signed by Dr. William S. Rickards, it listed "meningitis" as the cause of death. This discrepancy was to take on greater significance as Neff's investigation wore on.

Luther Byron Baker, a cousin and fellow spy, on July 29, 1868 declined to serve as executor as named in the will. The full duties devolved upon co-executor Joseph E. Stidfole who on August 24 reported to the Register of Wills that he had been unable to find any personal property belonging to Baker. This report, too, did not appear significant until later.

Neff then began checking out the legal records of the four witnesses to Baker's 1866 will. Only one provided results, but what results! Mary Baker, a cousin of Lafayette, lived next door to the former master spy at the time of his death. She died in 1870 of tuberculosis. She left a will signed June 11, 1867. Among her records at City Hall was an unprobated codicil to the will of L. C. Baker dated "June 31," 1868—three days before his death, assuming that "June 30" rather than "31" was the date. The codicil provided for "all books, diaries and personal papers not of a financial nature to be given to "my longtime friend Laura Duvall of Washington, D.C." And across the bottom of the codicil was written the notation: "Rejected by Orphans Court, MBF January 6, 1879."

"When I saw that, I knew that somewhere in the City Hall there had to be a record of the hearing into that codicil," Neff relates. He began another search. He learned the book number of the transcript of the hearing but looked through piles of old documents for day after day without finding the transcript itself. This was the most discouraging part of the investigation for Neff. There was the nagging thought that even if he found the transcript it might contain only routine material. For a long time, it appeared that he was chasing after a needle of information hopelessly concealed in a haystack of dusty and long-neglected official records.

"Then one day I moved a pile of old books aside and found the ledger with the number the clerk had told me to look for," Neff recalls.

The ledger contained a handwritten transcript "in the matter of the probate of a paper propounded as a Codicil to the Last Will and Testament of LAFAYETTE C. BAKER, deceased."

The information in the transcript of the two-day hearing

(held Oct. 14 and 15, 1872) went far beyond anything Neff had expected to find. The full text printed on pp. 16-23, of this issue of the *Civil War Times*, makes fascinating reading. To relate its entire story here would obscure Neff's main points, (1) that the messages in the English military journal were written by Baker and (2) there was justification for the suspicion that he was poisoned to keep him silent either about the conspiracy against Lincoln or some other matter.

Mary Baker, a poor woman when her illustrious next door neighbor and cousin of her husband died in 1868, left an estate of approximately $275,000 when she herself died four years later. Her daughter Elizabeth, executrix of her estate, found the unrecorded codicil and six boxes of Lafayette Baker's books and papers among her mother's effects. On the advice of her lawyer, she submitted the codicil to the Register of Wills. The remaining personal possessions of Lafayette Baker were then inventoried and impounded and the hearing ordered.

Exactly why it had been reported to the Register of Wills in 1868 that Baker had left no personal possessions came out very quickly at the hearing. Elizabeth Baker testified that on the night of "Uncle Lafe's" death (he was actually her cousin), her mother, Mary, had two colored men bring several "heavy wooden boxes" from the L. C. Baker home and store them in the attic of her own home next door. Although Elizabeth refused to admit that her mother had deliberately suppressed the codicil dealing with these boxes, that was obviously what had happened. Mary Baker had signed the codicil as a witness.

Now the heirs of Lafayette C. Baker did not call the hearing just to gain possession of a few boxes of books and papers. They were certain that Baker had left a large amount of cash among his personal possessions, cash which they felt belonged to them under his will of 1866.

The lawyer for Baker's heirs tried to prove that Lafayette Baker was insane during the last few months of his life and that his talk of attempts on his life and of having large sums of money was simply evidence of mental unbalance. These allegations were strongly contested by witnesses for the legatee of the codicil, Laura Duvall. To wit:

Dr. William M. Rickards, personal physician of Lafayette Baker, told of taking six stitches in a knife wound inflicted on Baker the night of Dec. 23, 1867. The attack occurred on the front porch of Baker's home. Dr. Rickards told of removing from Baker's face splinters caused by a bullet striking the door of the master spy's carriage "about December 28" of the previous year. And he told of Baker coming to his office on January 5, 1868 for "nerve medicine" because of these attacks. What's more, the doctor testified, he had observed two men shadowing Baker after the former National Police director had left his office. And the same day, two men pounced on Baker, beat him and tried to force him into a carriage. The attack was halted by a policeman, Dr. Rickards said. For a time thereafter, a police guard was assigned to Baker, he said.

The physician detailed Baker's final illness thusly: On Jan. 12, 1868, soon after eating with his wife at the home of friends in the Germantown section of Philadelphia, Baker became violently ill with "ptomaine poisoning." On Feb. 14, he developed a high fever which was diagnosed as "typhoid." On July 1, Baker showed symptoms of having meningitis and died at 12:10 A.M. July 3. Two hours later a magistrate signed an order to have the coffin sealed because of the contagious nature of the disease. This was done at 2:30 A.M., after which the house was fumigated. (By this time the boxes of personal possessions had been taken next door to Mary Baker's house.)

Dr. Rickards, a highly respected citizen of Philadelphia and an ardent abolitionist, represented himself as a close personal friend of Baker's as well as his personal physician. He said he regarded Baker as a brilliant man who was "perfectly sane."

Evidently the family of Lafayette Baker suspected he had died of arsenic poisoning for at the hearing their lawyer, Walter Marshall, bore down heavily on this possibility.

Dr. Rickards said, "I know he was not poisoned because no one had the opportunity."

But he replied "yes" to the question: "In other words, the symptoms shown by General Baker show more similarity to arsenic poisoning than they do to typhoid fever?" And he admitted that at one point during his treatment of Baker he himself had suspected that the master detective was being poisoned "by accidental means." He had Baker's medicine checked carefully but it proved non-toxic.

His suspicions were aroused, he said, when "General Baker was having very severe headaches and I applied leeches behind his ears." Dr. Rickards said: "The leeches stuck at first and then dropped off. When reapplied they would again drop off. I returned them to the apothecary and got others. These did the same. I watched these second leeches and observed that they soon died."

What would this indicate?

"It could indicate some sort of poison. After consulting an associate I concluded that it was due to the toxin of typhoid."

Dr. Rickards, speaking as both a friend of the Baker family and as a physician, said he didn't think this could have been caused by arsenic. But he replied "yes" to the question: "Speaking solely as a physician, could it have been arsenic?"

(Ray Neff who is now doing graduate work in toxicology at Jefferson Medical College, points out that snails and leeches are "particularly susceptible to arsenic poisoning." On the other hand, he says, "the toxins of typhoid would be proteinaceous and would be likely to be slow acting." Neff also points out that arsenic poisoning often is misdiagnosed because its symptoms resemble those of several other ailments.)

Dr. Rickards spoke of Baker as "a very kind and generous man," adding that "Much of the false things which had been written about him gave him worry. It made no difference whether it was good or bad, if it was untruthful it worried him. He was very apprehensive about what history would say about him. He wanted it to be good but he also wanted it to be accurate. He often told me of his concern about this."

The physician also testified that Baker "said he had no ideas as to who was behind the attempts on his life or why they were trying to kill him." He insisted that Baker was sane until his death and that the possibility he had committed suicide was "unthinkable."

Kathleen Hawks, who worked in the Baker home from Feb. 1, 1868 to June 1, 1868, testified that in her opinion Baker "was as sane as you or I." As for his fears of being killed, she said, these were well-founded.

"The General was standing by the window and someone shot at him," she said. "The bullet narrowly missed him and struck the wall near my head. I screamed and ran out of the room."

Miss Hawks said that Baker was not hurt "but he looked frightened and said they would get him yet. I asked him who and he said, 'My old friends. . .'"

Did he say why? "He said he had papers which would send them to prison."

The witness also told of "Mr. Cobb" whose visits upset Baker. "One time he said to me that Mr. Cobb would like to see him dead. Another time he said that Mr. Cobb wanted some papers which he had." She also told of overhearing Cobb say on one occasion: "Our patience is running short, Baker, you haven't much time."

As for Baker's having a large amount of money, Miss Hawks said she knew this was true. When she asked for her back wages of "about eight dollars," Baker had given her a key and sent her to the attic for a tin box which he opened. "The box was plumb full of new money, mostly in fifty and hundred dollar bills." He paid her $20.00 because she "had been a good nurse."

Mrs. Bridgit McBane, the nurse who replaced her, said she thought Baker "was daft." In her words, "He was always talking about how somebody was trying to do him in and as how he had papers to prove it and as how he had a lot of money hidden and they was after it."

She had never seen the money, she said, adding "I'm still owed for me last two weeks work there." But she did tell of seeing Baker sign the codicil in question. And she testified that Mrs. Baker rarely slept in the house, preferring to stay at the homes of relatives because "she said she was afraid."

The testimony that cinched the importance of Neff's find was that offered by William Carter, then a "drummer for American Household Supply Company" but who had "worked under" Baker during the War. He told of visiting Baker on June 30, 1868, three days before his death and of finding him "in fair spirits." Carter said Baker seemed "mentally sharp" but added that "He did say some things which made me wonder though."

> When I came into the room he had a stack of books by his bed and he had one open and was making marks in it. I asked him what he was doing and he said, "I'm writing my memoirs." I asked him to repeat that to make sure I had heard him right and he said it over again. Then I said, "But General, them books is already wrote," and he said, "Right, they are going to have to get up early to get ahead of old Lafe Baker." And then he laughed. I picked up one of the books and looked at it and I saw that he was writing cipher in it. But it was a different cipher than I'd ever seen before. I learned to read and write cipher when I was in the National Detective Police during the war and I never seen anything like he was writing that day. I asked him what it was and he just laughed.

Asked whether Baker had seemed "strange or insane," he replied:

> No, he didn't seem insane but he didn't seem hisself. It could have been the medicine but he seemed sort of funny. He kept laughing and kind of cackling. All the time that I was there he kept writing in the book. Once, I picked up one of the books and looked at the title in it. It was an English military journal and it had a story in it that I was interested in. When I said that I was interested in it he gave me the book and told me to take it home with me.

Carter said he had found cipher in the book but could not read it. Yes, he still had the book.

Neff believes that the book in Carter's possession in 1872 was *Colburn's United Service Magazine* for the first half of 1864 and that it contained the names of the "known conspirators" to whom Lafayette Baker referred in the coded message in Series II of the same year. As pointed out before,

Baker's set of the magazine as listed in the inventory ordered by the Register of Wills, was completed in 1872 except for this one bound volume. Neff thinks that the copy of the issues for the last half of 1864, which he bought for 50 cents, must have been pilfered from the impounded belongings sometime after the hearing.

Of course the persons at the hearing had little interest in ciphered messages of military journals. It was the large sum of cash Lafayette Baker had left in which they were interested. Attorney Walter Marshall, representing the heirs of Baker's main will, finally observed that "the late Lafayette C. Baker, was, prior to June 31, 1868, mentally deranged and incompetent." Marshall didn't say so, but the fact the codicil is dated "June 31," a non-existent date, might be considered evidence of mental confusion on Baker's part.

His clients couldn't have cared less who got the personal papers "not of a financial nature" which Baker left in the codicil to one Laura Duvall. Proving the sanity of the late detective chief no longer seemed important, perhaps. But Marshall asked the Register of Wills to "note the testimony concerning the possession by the late L. C. Baker of a large sum of money as late as June 1, 1868 and further that the late Mary Baker had access to the L. C. Baker household at the time of and immediately following the death of the late L. C. Baker, that it has been testified that she was alone in the household with his corpse before the undertakers arrived and further, that there is no apparent source of the large estate left by the late Mary Baker.

One person at the hearing said little until the proceedings were ended. He was John F. Smallwood, a representative of the United States War Department who moved "that certain papers which are in the inventory of contents of the six boxes found with the effects of the late Mary Baker be released to the War Department."

Said Smallwood: "These documents were pilfered from War Department files many years ago and they are important. I am here prepared to take charge of them for the Government."

The register told Smallwood he would have to select the

papers and turn them over to the clerk to be read into the record before they could be released, war department or no war department.

"It is the desire of the Government to have these documents kept secret," Smallwood declared and upon refusal of the register to give up the papers without recording them, withdrew his petition.

Laura Duvall, who would have received the personal property under Baker's codicil, was not present for the hearing. She was represented by John R. Rodgers. Elizabeth Baker identified her as a woman who paid frequent visits to Lafayette in his final sickness and who had been "very kind" to him. General Baker's wife was jealous of Miss Duvall, according to Elizabeth Baker. Other than that Miss Duvall had brought Baker flowers, had once appeared as a witness for him in a government case and had got a job through his influence. Miss Baker knew nothing more about her.

Laura Duvall is mentioned in Baker's *History of the Secret Service* as a witness against a Treasury Department official, Spencer H. Clark, with whom she admitted intimacies. She appears to have been one of the demi-prostitutes who worked in government offices in Washington during the War. If our analysis of her character is incorrect, we apologize to the memory of Miss Duvall. Whether Baker's bequest to her was merely a casual gesture in his dying days or a token of deeper affection cannot be said 93 years later on the basis of the skimpy records.

At any rate she never got the papers Baker wanted her to have. She was killed in Philadelphia during the summer of 1876 by a runaway team. On January 6, 1879 the codicil was rejected by the Orphans Court. In July of that same year the estate of Mary Baker was finally settled with an award of $80,000 going to the heirs of Lafayette. By that time the estate had grown to $458,299 of which the various lawyers got $38,272.

Exactly what happened to the impounded personal possessions of Lafayette C. Baker is a question that haunts Ray A. Neff. He thinks that what has not been pilfered may be lying somewhere in one of the dozens of storerooms of the City of Philadelphia.

The inventory lists 10 volumes of Baker's journals for the years 1858-1868 plus five volumes containing binders of correspondence and 22 volumes of photographs. These papers, if located, might prove of immense historical importance, Neff believes.

As for what he has uncovered so far, Neff makes no extravagant claims. He is quick to admit that Baker may indeed have been lying or was "mentally incompetent when he wrote the letters and numerals in the book now in my possession." But he also points out how what Baker wrote fits in with known details of the assassination of Lincoln.

For instance, the ciphered message tells of Baker's learning "on the tenth of April Sixty-five" that some kind of plot had been laid against Lincoln. He says "Eckert had made all the contacts, the deed to be done on the fourteenth."

Lincoln had wanted Eckert as a bodyguard at the Ford Theater the night of April 14, 1865. First Stanton refused to assign Eckert, saying that the major had work to do. Then Lincoln spoke directly to Eckert who declined on the pretext of work. Yet it has been established that this strong man in fact did not work that night and was at home when notified Lincoln had been shot. A further indication this was the same Major Thomas Eckert can be found in Baker's cryptic quotation of Stanton's "Be off *Tom*, and see to the arrangements."

Baker wrote:

> [On the thirteenth Stanton] discovered that the president had ordered that the legislature of Virginia be allowed to assemble to withdraw the states troops from action against the U.S. Stanton fermented immediately into an insane tirade. . . . However, during that insane moment he sent a telegram to Gen. Weitzel countermanding the presidents order of the twelfth. Then he laughed in a most spine chilling manner and said, "If he would to know who recinded his order we will let Lucifer tell him."

Baker's memory failed him by a few days here. On April 6, while the beaten Confederate Army of Northern Virginia

Maj. Thomas Eckert, chief of Stanton's Telegraph Office who refused to accompany the Lincolns to the theater on the night of the assassination. Baker's secret messages name Eckert as having arranged the details of the murder and having worked with the conspirators. The day following the assassination, he was promoted to brigadier general. National Archives

was retreating toward Appomattox, Lincoln sent the following telegram to Maj. Gen. Godfrey Weitzel, whose 25th Corps occupied Richmond:

> It has been intimated to me that the gentlemen who have acted as the legislature of Virginia, in support of the rebellion, may now desire to assemble at Richmond, and take measures to withdraw the Virginia troops and other support from resistance to the General government. If they attempt it, give them permission and protection, until if at all, they attempt some action hostile to the United States, in which case you will notify them and give them reasonable time to leave; and at the end of which time, arrest any who may remain. Allow Judge Campbell to see this, but do not make it public.

Judge John A. Campbell was a Virginian who had been on the U.S. Supreme Court before the War and had served as assistant secretary of war for the Confederacy. It appears that Campbell spoke and wrote more freely about Lincoln's telegram than the President intended.

Stanton's anger toward Lincoln in this case is indisputable. He and others in the government took Lincoln's telegram as open recognition of the Confederate legislature and regarded this as a further sign he would be too easy on the South.

The Official Records carries a message from Stanton to Weitzel dated 8 P.M. April 9 in which the Secretary of War upbraids the officer for permitting the Episcopal churches of captured Richmond to hold services without prayers for the President of the United States, and adds:

> You are, moreover, directed to hold no further conference with Mr. Campbell on any subject without specific authority, to be given by the President or this Department; but if he desires to make any communications to you it must be in writing, and transmitted by you to this Department for instructions.

There is also a record of a telegram from Lincoln to General Weitzel dated April 12, 1865, 6 P.M., in which the President refers to the assumption "that I have called the insurgent legislature of Virginia together, as the rightful legislature of the State, to settle all differences with the United States." Wrote Lincoln: "I have done no such thing. I spoke of them not as a legislature but as the gentlemen who have acted as the legislatures of Virginia in support of the Rebellion . . ."

Lincoln countermanded his own instructions of April 6, ending his telegram: "Do not now allow them to assemble, but if any have come allow them safe return to their homes."

It is conceivable that Stanton did send another message "recinding" the President's misunderstod instructions in secret. But it could not have been on the 13th because (1) Lincoln had already sent his telegram the day before and (2) whether Baker remembered it or not, he went to New York on the 13th and was there when Lincoln was shot.

A comparison between the style of the substitution cipher beginning: "In New Rome . . ." and Baker's own *History of the Secret Service* shows interesting similarities. Obviously Baker was obsessed with Roman history. His book contains frequent references to Julius Caesar and his cryptic message is one long Roman allegory. The inventory of his personal possessions, too, lists three books on Roman history (and one titled *How to Be a Detective*).

His book in one passage implies that Stanton had prior knowledge of the plot against Lincoln. He tells how, on learning of the assassination, he rushed back to Washington and:

> As I entered the Secretary's office, and he recognized me, he turned away to hide his tears. He remarked—"Well, Baker, they have now performed what they have long threatened to do; they have killed the President."

And his book contains this scantily veiled threat in the form of an unsigned letter praising "Gen. L. C. Baker, Chief Detective of the War Department during the late rebellion":

> And now about certain facts Baker may state with respect to men high in official relation with the Government or otherwise! The half he will not tell. I know of many things he will not state which I would. I have no mercy on men who will corrupt and contaminate all with

whom they come in official contact; and men who, in time of peace, after treason has been put down, again secretly plot the overthrow of a Government at once the best and noblest that the sun of the Eternal ever shone upon.

I hope to see truth come, let it cut where it may, as I believe the country to be still in danger; and unless some master hand will seize the knife and lay open the festering wound, the disease of the Republic will never heal!

And the so-called letter is unsigned. Surely someone was threatening someone. It may well have been Baker's oblique way of trying to throw a scare into Stanton.

During an inquiry by the House Judiciary Committee into Lincoln's death in 1867, Baker gave testimony implying that Stanton had destroyed several pages from the diary found on John Wilkes Booth's body. The House report on the hearing practically called Baker a liar.

Neff points out that at the time Baker's book was released— in the summer of 1867—a power struggle was in progress between Stanton, who was still Secretary of War, and President Johnson over the latter's relatively lenient Reconstruction policy. The contest ran through sordid impeachment proceedings which began March 5, 1868 and ended on May 16, 1868 with the Radicals failing by one vote to gain the two-thirds majority in the Senate necessary for conviction. The first of the series of attacks on Baker occurred in December, 1867. One year after the release of his book, he was dead either of typhoid, meningitis or arsenic poisoning.

Baker obviously left far more money than an honest, hardworking detective could have amassed by honest, hard work. He apparently had good reason to think someone was trying to kill him and from what is known of his high-handed police methods during the War, if nothing else, many had good reason to wish him dead. And unless someone has gone to fantastic ends to perpetrate a hoax, he was the author of the cipher charging Stanton with heading up the conspiracy against Lincoln.

The only question remaining then is: Did Lafayette Baker tell the truth or was he merely trying to settle an old score with Stanton?

Despite his long months of personal sacrifice and incredibly persistent research, Ray A. Neff does not feel qualified to answer the question.

He'd like to locate the spot where Baker's bones are buried. If he were poisoned and if any fragments of hair or skeleton remain, traces of the arsenic could be detected.

And he would like to find the rest of Baker's personal papers.

Finally, he would like to get his hands on that bound volume of *Colburn's United Service Military Journal* for the first half of 1864.

Until he can run down these last important pieces of evidence, Neff will remain an unfulfilled man. Until he does, he will not accept the word of Lafayette Baker. For as he explains it: "One can readily imagine the pleasure Baker would have gotten from the knowledge that one day he would again be in the national spotlight, although dead more than ninety years, pointing the accusing finger at his 'old friends'."

Texts of Ciphered Messages

The following page numbers refer to the pages of Colburn's United Service Magazine *on which Baker's messages were written.*

[p. 181] I am constantly being followed. They are professionals. I cannot fool them. 2-5-68.

[p. 183] In new Rome, there walked three men, a Judas, a Brutus and a spy. [pp. 185-211] Each planned that he should be king when Abraham should die. One trusted not the other but they went on for that day, waiting for that final moment when with pistol in his hand, one of the sons of Brutus could sneak behind that cursed man and put a bullet in his brain and lay his clumsy corpse away. As the fallen man lay dying, Judas came and paid respects to one he hated, and when at last he saw him die, he said, "Now the ages have him and the nation now have I." But alas as fate would have it Judas slowly fell from grace, and with him went Brutus down to their proper place. But lest one is left to wonder what has happened to the spy, I can safely tell you this, it was I.

[p. 106] It was on the tenth of April, sixty-five when I first knew that the plan was in action.

[p. 107] Eckert had made all the contacts, the deed to be done on the fourteenth. I did not know the identity of the assassin but I knew most all else when I approached Stanton about it.

[p. 108] He at once acted surprised and disbelieving. Later he said, "You are a party to it too. Let us wait and see [p. 109] what comes of it and then we will know better how to act in the matter. I soon discovered what he meant that I was a party to it [p. 110] when the following day I was shown a document that I knew to be a forgery but a clever one, which made it appear that [pp. 111, 112] I had been in charge of a plot to kidnap the president, the vice-president being the instigator. Then I became a party to that deed even though I did not care to.

[p. 113] Discovered that the president had ordered that the legislature of Virginia be allowed to assemble to withdraw their states troops from action against the U.S. Stanton fermented immediately into an insane tirade. Then for [p. 114] the first time I realized his mental disunity and his insane and fanatical hatred for the president. There are few in the War Department that respect the president or his [p. 115] strategy but there are not many who would countermand an order that the president had given. However during that insane moment he sent a telegram [p. 116] to Gen. Weitzel countermanding the president's order of the twelfth. Then he laughed in a most spine chilling manner and said, "If he would to know who recinded his order [p. 117] we will let Lucifer tell him. Be off Tom, and see to the arrangements. There can be no mistakes." This is the first that I knew that he was the one responsible [p. 118] for the assassination plot. Always before I thought that either he did not trust me, for he really trusted no one, or he was protecting someone [p. 119] until it was to his benefit to expose them. But now I know the truth and it frightens me no end. I fear that somehow [p. 120] I may become the sacrificial goat. There were at least eleven members of Congress involved in the plot, no less than twelve Army officers, three Naval officers and at least

the whole, of the Austrian force engaged, had had ~~
of actual warfare, whereas the Danish army was compo
young, middle-aged, and almost old, who had neve
fired in anger. That the Danes would have fought b
doubts, but in war mere bravery is not sufficient to s
As it was, the troops suffered severely before the retrea
upon. The cold was intense; heavy falls of snow and
followed by a partial thaw, which filled the air witl
vapour that soaked in their clothes and chilled ther
depressed their spirits to an extent which experien
enable a man to realise. Add to this that they wr
quately sheltered at night from the inclemency of the
it will be evident to the most unexperienced person, t
more hours would have rendered a considerable porti
unable to fight from mere sickness. That Gener;
wisely in abandoning the Dannewerk will eventua
even in Copenhagen, where the excitement was very
its first becoming known. His determination wa
nearly every officer under his command competer
opinion, though there were some whose bravery w
their judgment, who gave way to expressions of in
they heard of what had been decided upon. It
Bishop Monrad that neither the Government nor
previously sanctioned the retreat; but it is impos
cile this statement with the reports current in Sc
King, when he visited the Dannewerk on the p
agreed with Meza that the works were untenabl
small against an enemy so numerous. That the Ki
the retreat is possible: but that General Meza t
Majesty his opinion on the subject is altogether

A page from Colburn's United Service Magazine *with Baker's signature in the left margin. A handwriting expert has verified that this is the signature of Lafayette Baker.* Courtesy *Civil War Times Illustrated*

24 civilians, of which one was a governor of a loyal state. Five were bankers of great repute, three were nationally known newspaper men and eleven were industrialists of great repute and wealth. There were probably more that I know nothing of.

The names of these [p. 126] known conspirators is presented without comment or notation, in Vol. one [p. 127] of this series. Eighty-five thousand dollars was contributed by the named persons to pay for the deed. Only eight persons knew the details of the plot and the identity of the others.

[p. 245] I fear for my life. LCB.

Baker's Secret Papers: A Brief Discussion

The most intriguing part of Baker's coded messages is his naming of the three persons responsible for the execution of Pres. Abraham Lincoln. Baker speaks allegorically of course but it seems safe to assume that those three persons were men of power and great ambition who violently disagreed with Lincoln's policies. The question is, just who were the three men to whom Baker refers? There is no doubt that Baker himself is one of those men. When he writes that "Each planned that he should be king," Baker indicates that the other two were men who dreamed of becoming the nation's leader once the president had been executed.

Just how Baker, "the spy," became aware that the other two wanted Lincoln dead is uncertain. It seems highly doubtful that he met with these two at the same time to discuss how Lincoln's death should be accomplished. To the contrary, it seems more likely that he met with them individually, privately, and then walked away with the idea that both individuals, both "Judas" and "Brutus," wanted to see the president executed.

And why would these two men risk their careers (and very lives) to meet with Baker? Obviously someone had to supervise the details of the execution, and Baker would be the logical choice since he was an agent well known throughout the government as a man without moral scruples, a man who would work tirelessly to see an idea become reality. He was also Edwin Stanton's most trusted ally. Baker leaves little doubt that Judas is none other than Edwin Stanton as he links him to the famous incident by Lincoln's deathbed when Stanton is alleged to have commented, "Now he belongs to the ages." Indeed, if the secret papers had been discovered and deciphered immediately following Baker's death in July 1868, as he had planned, Edwin Stanton and Andrew Johnson would have found themselves in a very uncomfortable position (perhaps at the end of a rope).

For reasons known only to himself, Baker leaves it to the reader to guess the identity of Brutus. But it is obvious that Brutus was a man of high rank in the Federal government and a man well acquainted with Lafayette Baker. According to Baker this unknown individual would have had essentially the same relationship with Lincoln as Brutus had with Caesar. He would have been an intimate of the president, and he must have held an office from which he could move directly into the president's shoes once the execution took place. In other words, he was either a high-ranking member of Lincoln's cabinet or the vice president himself. Otherwise, the order of succession would have placed the office of president beyond his reach. But most importantly, he must have been a Rebel-hater, a man whose Reconstruction policies for the South were the opposite of Abe Lincoln's. Otherwise, Lincoln's execution would have been unnecessary. Certainly with this man as president, there would be no amnesty for the South. The other assassin must have been well acquainted with Lafayette Baker as well; he must have been a close associate of Lincoln, a man of at least cabinet rank; a man whose love of power was well known; and a well-known Rebel-hater who would approve the most stringent Reconstruction policies that Congress could formulate.

It is a fact that in 1865 Lincoln's cabinet was dominated by two members, Edwin Stanton and William Seward. But Stanton has already been identified as Judas. As for William Seward, his Reconstruction policies were in almost total agreement with those of Abe Lincoln, which would seem to eliminate him as Brutus. It also must be remembered that Seward himself was marked for assassination on the evening of April 14.

Therefore, simply by process of elimination, we are led to the conclusion that Brutus could have been none other than Vice Pres. Andrew Johnson. If Baker's secret papers had been discovered and deciphered following his death in July 1868, as he had planned, Andrew Johnson would have had a very bad time of it. In fact, during his impeachment trial of 1867, he avoided conviction by only one vote. However, should Baker's confession have come to the attention of Congress during that trial, Johnson might very well have been dragged out and hanged (alongside Edwin Stanton) from the highest apple tree.

Thus it is evident that Lafayette Baker was the Spy; Edwin Stanton was Judas; and Andrew Johnson was Brutus. Of course it has been strongly rumored for a century and a half now that Andrew Johnson was involved in the plot against Lincoln, and Baker's words would seem to verify that rumor. Too, according to Baker, it was "the son of Brutus" who murdered Abe Lincoln. And who was the "son of Brutus"? The answer is obvious: John Wilkes Booth, the son of the great actor Junius Brutus Booth. In other words, John Wilkes Booth was literally the "son of Brutus." Baker did everything but draw a picture of the assassin and those who prompted him.

For those searching for a motive in this matter, it is well known that in 1865 both Stanton and Johnson felt that Lincoln's very humane Reconstruction policies for the South would mark the end of hostilities and by extension their political careers. But should Lincoln and his lenient Reconstruction policies be suddenly eliminated, then Johnson, aided and abetted by Edwin Stanton and the Radicals in Congress, could institute a harsh Reconstruction program for the South that would last for years. Truly, Reconstruction was the answer to all their prayers. Now, with Lincoln's death, they could further their own personal ambitions and keep the Radical Republicans in perpetual power. And that is exactly what happened. Following Lincoln's execution, Congress did indeed pass Reconstruction policies that kept the Radical Republicans in power for years, though both Stanton and Johnson had fallen from grace before that wretched period came to pass.

Booth's role in this chicanery is open to question. But it is known that he and Andrew Johnson had been close friends in Nashville in 1863, when Booth was on stage there and Johnson was serving as military governor of Tennessee.

Johnson's private secretary, William Browning, testified during the impeachment trial of 1867 that Booth and Johnson were very close friends. They had kept two sisters as mistresses, and they were frequently seen together in various Nashville hotels and nightspots.

It seems very possible that they continued their relationship in Washington after Johnson was chosen as vice president in 1864. (It is a historical fact that Booth visited Johnson at his hotel room on the afternoon of his inauguration as vice president on March 4, 1865.) Following Louis Weichmann's report of the conspiracy to the War Department in February 1865, Johnson must have been aware that his old friend Wilkes Booth was leading a movement to abduct the President—or perhaps he was made aware of it prior to that time by Booth himself. Thus, after Lincoln suddenly expressed his determination to treat the South as a long-lost brother rather than as a defeated criminal, it seems likely that Johnson and Stanton put their heads together to determine what could be done to eliminate such a treasonous attitude.

Who was the first to mention execution? Johnson? Stanton? No one knows. But according to Lafayette Baker, it was Stanton who arranged for his assistant secretary of war, Maj. Thomas Eckert, to make the contacts and handle the details of that execution. And it is a fact that Baker was in New York during the days immediately preceding April 14. Therefore, it stands to reason that Maj. Thomas Eckert, who was certainly aware of the abduction conspiracy already in progress, would have immediately made contact with Booth.

If so, this would explain Booth's easy escape from Washington on the night of the assassination, as well as his unimpeded escape through Maryland and into Virginia. It could very well explain why it was essential that Booth not be brought back alive. He knew too much. It could also explain Booth's enigmatic statement in his diary: "I have a greater desire and almost a mind to return to Washington and in a measure clear my name, which I feel I can do." Possibly he meant that he could return and report that when he pulled the trigger he was simply a Federal agent acting under orders from two of the highest-ranking members of the United States government.

This situation could also explain Edwin Stanton's reluctance to arrest or extradite John Surratt once he fled Washington. Stanton clearly knew that Surratt was in hiding in Canada. Later, he was informed almost daily of Surratt's movements in England and Rome, yet he refused to take any steps to have him returned to the United States. In August 1865 Stanton announced that the twenty-five-thousand-dollar reward for Surratt's arrest had been terminated, which quieted the numerous informants who were frantic to claim the reward money.

At his first trial the jury was unable to reach a verdict, and so Surratt was again brought to trial. Only this time, instead of charging him with murder, the government reduced the charge to treason. In court, Surratt's attorney calmly stood up and informed the court that the statute of limitations had expired for the charge of treason. At that point a smiling judge agreed that the attorney was correct and declared Surratt a free man. Surely the judge, prosecutor, and everyone else associated with the case against Surratt was aware that the statute of limitations had expired on charges of treason. So the question is why? Why would government officials drop the murder charges and simply charge him with treason, a charge that was no longer valid since the statute of limitations had long expired on such a charge? Again, as with Booth, perhaps a deal had been struck, a deal to keep Surratt quiet. In later years, when queried about his acquittal, Surratt would only say, "I traded my freedom for my silence."

Government complicity in Lincoln's execution could also explain why the four conspirators who were known to have spoken with Wilkes Booth on April 14 were all held incommunicado following their arrests, and why all four of them were hanged on July 7. Even Mary Surratt, who was obviously innocent of any role in the conspiracy, was hanged. Her greatest crime was that she had spoken with Booth on April 14. Thus, if she did know any secrets, she took them to the grave.

III

The Case against
Stanton and Johnson

For almost a century and a half persistent rumors have floated across this great nation concerning Edwin Stanton and Andrew Johnson and the role they possibly played in the execution of Abraham Lincoln. Indeed, it is almost impossible to read any study of the assassination without finding at least some hint that the secretary of war and the vice president were far more involved in that terrible event than some would like to admit. Still, the reader should be warned, the case against Stanton and Johnson, as damning as it appears on the surface, is almost totally circumstantial. After more than 140 years, there still exists no physical evidence of wrongdoing in this case, and it is unlikely that such physical evidence will emerge over the next 140 years. Yet it must be remembered that a great many criminals have been convicted and sent to the gallows based solely on circumstantial evidence.

Obviously, if Stanton was involved in the conspiracy, then his disreputable hireling, the director of the National Detective Police, Lafayette Baker, was also involved. And he was involved—up to his ears, in fact. According to Baker's own words, it was he, aided and abetted by Edwin Stanton and Stanton's assistant secretary of war, Maj. Thomas Eckert, who planned the entire execution.

In 1937 a German-born chemist named Otto Eisenschiml, whose lifetime hobby had been investigating the Lincoln assassination, published a work entitled *Why Was Lincoln Murdered*, a work that is meticulously researched, finely reasoned, and extremely well written. In this work Eisenschiml presents a case against Edwin Stanton that is most difficult to refute. Even the Stantonphiles in our midst have remained silent before Eisenschiml's onslaught. Unfortunately for Eisenschiml, he did not have access to the secret papers of Lafayette Baker, which lay hidden until 1960. That material could have provided the semi-physical evidence for which he had so long searched.

Edwin Stanton: A Machiavelli without Peer

Looking at the individual members of Lincoln's cabinet, the one man who had the most to gain from his death (aside from Andrew Johnson) was his secretary of war, Edwin Stanton. Generally described as brusque, insolent, and cruel, he was loathed and feared not only by those who worked under him, but by other members of Lincoln's cabinet as well. On numerous occasions Lincoln was pressured by other members of his cabinet to terminate Stanton, but for reasons that remain a mystery, he always refused. Of course it could be that Lincoln himself felt a bit intimidated by Stanton. After all, as director of the National Detective Police (a forerunner of the FBI), Stanton made it a point to know and remember where everyone of importance, including Lincoln, had buried their political bodies.

Eventually, Stanton's treatment of Pres. Andrew Johnson was so disgraceful that it became a matter of gossip throughout Washington. The question became, why does Johnson tolerate such treatment? He is the president, why does he not terminate Stanton? It was truly a puzzling question, and many reached the conclusion that Johnson himself was involved in Lincoln's assassination and Stanton could prove it and was holding that information over the president's head.

Stanton was first appointed to office on December 20, 1860, when President Buchanan named him attorney general upon the strong recommendation of Secretary of State Jeremiah S. Black. Still, Buchanan had some misgivings, and in 1862 he would write to his niece, "He was always on

Edwin Stanton, who began his career as a staunch anti-abolitionist Democrat under President Buchanan, went on to become a Radical Republican under President Lincoln. Outraged at Lincoln's conciliatory Reconstruction program for the South, Stanton, aided and abetted by Andrew Johnson, in early 1865 reached the fatal decision that Lincoln must be executed. Library of Congress

my side, and flattered me *ad nauseam.*" Indeed, Buchanan was suspicious of Stanton from the beginning, and for good reason.

Jeremiah Black, who had recommended Stanton to Buchanan in the first place, said of him at the time of his appointment, "His condemnation of the abolitionists was unsparing for their hypocrisy, their corruption, their enmity to the Constitution, and their lawless disregard for the rights of States and individuals. Thus he won the confidence of the Democrats."

Later, during the impeachment trial of Pres. Andrew Johnson, Jeremiah Black would testify:

> Secretary Stanton, this indomitable foe of all Secessionists, who never spoke or wrote of those at war against the government but as rebels and traitors, was, while a member of Buchanan's Cabinet, distinctly of the opinion that the government had no right to make war on a state for the purpose of coercing it to remain in the Union. Stanton endorsed this point of view with extravagant and undeserved laudation.

But time would prove that Stanton's disdain for the Republicans and their abolitionist masters was only a pose, a disguise he was forced to assume in order to win a place in Buchanan's cabinet. From the very moment he became attorney general, he also became a self-appointed spy for Buchanan's Republican enemies in Congress. Certainly he was aware that a Republican administration would be coming into power within the next few weeks, and he deemed it wise to curry favor with the Republicans while at the same time pretending undying loyalty to Buchanan and his Democratic allies. While serving Buchanan and the Democrats during the day, he was holding secret meetings behind closed doors at night with some of the most deeply avowed abolitionists in the country. From the very beginning, according to the diaries of various Republican congressmen, Stanton kept them informed of "the fearful condition of affairs" in the president's office. Indeed, Stanton on one occasion sat down with several Republican Congressmen and verbally outlined for them a basis for articles of impeachment of

President Buchanan should such a course of action become necessary before Abe Lincoln could be sworn in.

Stanton was nothing if not resourceful. He was one of the most ambitious and unscrupulous politicians ever to hold public office, and he was extremely clever when it came to playing both sides of Congress. He would smile in Buchanan's face by day, then plot and scheme with the Republicans by night, paving his way for an important cabinet position once Lincoln assumed office.

However, following Lincoln's swearing in, Stanton was dismayed to learn that his name was not among those War Democrats chosen to serve in Lincoln's cabinet. Stanton seethed with silent rage and plotted how he could wreak revenge. Over the next few weeks it was Stanton himself who coined the term "black" Republicans, and he blamed "the imbecility of this Administration" for the Union disaster at Bull Run. He referred to Lincoln as "the original gorilla," and he told Gen. George B. McClellan that with Lincoln in the White House, Paul du Chaillu had made a mistake "in going all the way to Africa to look for an ape."

Stanton was venomous in his hatred of Lincoln. But then Lincoln's secretary of war, Simon Cameron, ran afoul of Lincoln and his administration by publicly advocating the arming of slaves in the Southern states. Deeply embarrassed, Lincoln demanded that Cameron withdraw his proposal, but an obstinate Cameron refused to do so. As a result Lincoln fired him in December 1861. At that point, such influential Republicans as William Seward, Charles Sumner, and Salmon P. Chase, recalling Stanton's clandestine services over the past few months, pleaded with Lincoln to name him the new secretary of war. Despite his great reluctance, Lincoln agreed to their proposal and submitted Stanton's name to Congress on January 13, 1862.

Lincoln, of course, was not aware that it was Edwin Stanton himself who had secretly advised Cameron concerning the arming of slaves. It was none other than Edwin Stanton who had actually written Cameron's slave proposal and then offered him legal advice as the controversy between Cameron and Lincoln intensified. But this is merely another example of Stanton's talent for creating and then exploiting controversial situations. Frank A. Flowers, in his biography of Stanton, would write a glowing tribute to this master of intrigue:

> Interesting indeed is the fact that Lincoln was unaware that the iron-willed giant he was putting in was more stubbornly in favor of arming the slaves than the man he was putting out. Lincoln was also unaware that the recommendation which, with his own hand, he had expunged from Cameron's report and which was the means of forcing its supposed author out, was conceived and written by the very man now going in, and so it may be said that Stanton wrote his own appointment.

Once Stanton, this Machiavelli of the Potomac, became firmly entrenched as Lincoln's secretary of war, he began to hatch long-range plans to further his personal ambitions. Incredibly enough, and as difficult to believe as it might seem, there is much evidence that he intentionally prolonged the war in hopes of assisting the abolitionists in their scheme to finally disenfranchise the Democratic South. By prolonging the war, he would create the world's mightiest army, one that could become a terrible weapon in the hands of a president who had been a former military idol. Of course it was his fondest dream that he, Edwin Stanton, would become that man in 1868.

One of Stanton's first moves as secretary of war was to assume total control of the press. David Bates, in his *Lincoln in the Telegraph Office,* writes that "from January, 1862, when Stanton entered the cabinet, until the war ended, the telegraphic reins of the Government were held by a firm and skillful hand. Stanton centered the telegraph in the War Department, where the publication of military news could be supervised, and, if necessary, delayed."

On February 25, 1862, Stanton appointed himself the military supervisor of telegrams. "What his blue pencil erased," said Bates, "had to be left out, and reporters frequently spent hours in procuring some choice bit of news which was never transmitted over the wires."

Within a few months Stanton assumed control of all telegraph lines in the country, and on March 2, 1862, he moved
all telegraphic machinery into a room next to his office at the
War Department and appointed Maj. Thomas Eckert as the
officer in charge. Not even President Lincoln was exempt
from being forced to send and receive messages through
Stanton's common channel in the Telegraph Office. In fact, it
has often been said that Lincoln spent more time in the
Telegraph Office than he did in his own office.

This arrangement, combined with his censorship of the
press, gave Stanton powers never dreamed of by any other
politician, powers he inevitably used to his own political
advantage. Stanton soon realized that by controlling the press,
he could also control opinions and mold attitudes throughout the country. His next move was to use this new power to
help himself and his allies while destroying his enemies.

As the war progressed, an ever alert Edwin Stanton began to
view Gen. George McClellan as a possible competitor for the
1868 presidential nomination. He released news to the press
that General McClellan had informed the War Department
that the Army of Northern Virginia was on its knees and the
surrender of Richmond was expected at any moment. This
news was flashed to newspapers across the country and met
by Northern citizens with great joy. Days later, however, when
Richmond failed to surrender, Northern joy turned to dismay.
Was McClellan insane? Just who was this McClellan, this
apparently mad individual leading the Army of the Potomac?
Thus, in just one very clever Machiavellian move, Stanton successfully eliminated McClellan as a competitor for the 1868
Republican nomination.

In fact, there were numerous occasions when Stanton
engaged in subterfuge when the truth would have served
just as well, apparently delighting in his ability to manipulate facts and people. For example, in September 1862, Gen.
Benjamin Butler, commander of Union forces in Louisiana,
wrote his old friend Sen. Henry Wilson, asking him to use his
influence with Stanton to have reinforcements sent to him at
once. Two days later Wilson responded to Butler that he had

spoken with Stanton and the secretary "agreed with me and expressed his confidence in you, and his approval of your vigor and ability." Unfortunately, neither Wilson nor Butler was aware that Stanton, by secret order, three weeks earlier had appointed Gen. Nathaniel Banks to replace the unsuspecting Butler as commander of Union forces in Louisiana. In describing Stanton's behavior in this bizarre episode, Butler would later write, "Can lying, injustice, deceit, and tergiversation farther go?"

Stanton even effectively manipulated the president. It was well known that the sanguine Abe Lincoln tried whenever possible to avoid confrontations with others, a trait that the perceptive Stanton detected immediately and interpreted as a weakness of character. As the months progressed, the domineering Stanton began gradually to bend Abe Lincoln to his own will. By the summer of 1863 those close to Lincoln noticed that Stanton was beginning to order the president about like a mere clerk. In Edward Rice's *Reminiscences of Abraham Lincoln*, he writes that when news of General Hooker's resignation reached Stanton, "he sent for the President to come to the War Office at once. It was in the evening, but the President immediately appeared." Who else in Washington would have had the audacity to send for the president to come to his office to read a telegram, rather than delivering the telegram to him? Only Edwin Stanton.

Stanton Suffers Misgivings Concerning Lincoln

Following Lincoln's reelection in 1864, Stanton and the Radicals must have suffered some misgivings concerning his incumbency. Was he, with his liberal attitude towards reconstructing the South, really the man they wanted to serve another four years as president? True, he had signed the Emancipation Proclamation, but he did so with the utmost reluctance and certainly had never demonstrated the least enthusiasm for enforcing the proclamation.

By 1864 Lincoln, at least in public, was insisting that the

abolition of slavery was a condition to ending the war. But by April 1865 it was well known throughout Congress that Lincoln wanted peace so badly that he was weakening on the slavery issue and planned to make the reestablishment of the Union the only real condition for a cessation of hostilities.

Sen. Orville Browning would write in his diary for November 24, 1864:

> I said to General Singleton I thought the President would make the abolition of slavery a condition precedent to any settlement. He replied that he knew he would not—that he had a long interview with him before the election—that the President showed him all the correspondence between himself and Greeley and said it put him in a false position—that he did not mean to make the abolition of slavery a condition, and that after the election he would be willing to grant peace with an amnesty, and restoration of the union, leaving slavery to abide the decisions of the judicial tribunals.

Browning supposed that Singleton must have been terribly mistaken concerning Lincoln's attitude towards the abolition of slavery, and thus, on December 24, he himself paid a visit to the president to learn firsthand just how Lincoln felt on that point. He would later write:

> In the evening went to the President and had an interview. During the evening the President showed me all the correspondence between him & Greeley in regard to the negotiations at Niagara in July last with Clay and Tucker, and assured me that he had been misrepresented, and misunderstood and that he had never entertained the purpose of making the abolition of slavery a condition precedent to the termination of the war.

Stanton and the Radicals in Congress considered Lincoln's attitude treasonous to the party. He had been reelected in 1864 with the understanding that with the end of the war, slavery would be abolished throughout the nation. Now that war's end was at hand, he was beginning to drastically change his position, saying that the abolition of slavery was not a matter for the federal government to decide. Such would never do, not if the Republicans wished to maintain power in America.

But by March 1865 Lincoln gave the Radicals in Congress a new worry to occupy their time. Earlier, the Wade-Davis Manifesto had made it clear that Congress would impose their own Reconstruction program upon the South with no interference from the president. Thanks to Wade-Davis, the Radicals could proceed with abolition despite what Lincoln might think about it. But Lincoln, still eager to abide by his resolution of 1861, was determined to restore all political and civil rights to the Confederate states immediately upon their return to the Union. Therefore, in order to circumvent Wade-Davis, he very cleverly arranged for his generals in the field (Grant and Sherman) to conclude armistices that amounted to a peace without penalties. By the time Congress learned of the generals' treaties with Lee and Johnston, they already would be accomplished facts, and Congress would be powerless to change them. Indeed, in April 1865 Congress would go into recess and would not meet again until December. By then the war would be long over, and the time to change any treaties long past.

To that end, on March 27, 1865, Lincoln met with Generals Grant and Sherman and Admiral Porter aboard the *River Queen* at City Point on the James River. There he gave them secret orders for what one historian called "one of the most cunning examples of the 'double cross' that the whole range of American politics, before or after him, could show." These orders were for Grant and Sherman simply to grant to Lee and Johnston a truce based on the situation as it had existed before the beginning of the war. And in his memoirs, General Grant writes that President Lincoln took him aside during the conference at City Point and quietly said to him, "Give Lee anything he wants if he will only stop fighting." Thus when Sherman signed the treaty with Joe Johnston on April 17, he was only following orders given him by Lincoln on March 27. The treaty stated that the president of the United States was to recognize the state governments on the condition that the officers and legislators would take the oath prescribed by the Constitution. Federal courts would be reestablished, and the people of the Confederacy guaranteed their political rights, as well as their rights of person and of property. A general amnesty was to be announced and the war declared over.

Of course, when this treaty was reported to Washington on April 21, a week following Lincoln's execution, Stanton persuaded Andrew Johnson to call an emergency cabinet meeting. Initially, Stanton stood alone in his denunciation of Sherman's treaty with Johnston, but finally, through threats and intimidation, he persuaded other cabinet members and President Johnson to join him in having the armistice disapproved. Then, without the knowledge of Johnson, he released to the Associated Press a diatribe that branded Sherman a traitor to the nation: "Sherman gave terms that had been deliberately, repeatedly, and solemnly rejected by President Lincoln, and better terms than the rebels had ever asked in their most prosperous condition."

Unfortunately for Stanton, Admiral Porter had taken notes during the conference aboard the *River Queen,* and in an 1868 article in the *New York Gazette,* long after his words could have helped General Sherman, he would write:

> The terms of the treaty were exactly in accordance with Mr. Lincoln's wishes. Sherman could not have done anything which would have pleased the President better. Mr. Lincoln did in fact arrange the liberal terms offered General Joe Johnston, and whatever may have been General Sherman's private views, I feel sure that he yielded to the wishes of the President in every respect. It was Mr. Lincoln's policy that was carried out. I was with Mr. Lincoln all the time he was at City Point, and until he left for Washington. He was more than delighted with the surrender of Lee, and with the terms Grant gave the Rebel general, and would have given Joseph Johnston twice as much had the latter asked for it.

For two years General Sherman adamantly refused to comment on the Sherman-Stanton controversy. But then, following Admiral Porter's article, Sherman finally gave his side of the story in a letter to Admiral Porter, dated October 19, 1868:

You will remember that last spring when I wrote you about the interview of Mr. Lincoln, yourself, Grant and me, at City Point, you wrote me a letter, and gave me at length the subjects therein discussed, principally that *Mr. Lincoln plainly foreshadowed the course to be pursued when the Rebel Armies were defeated. Tell me the substance of your memory of what Mr. Lincoln did say, likely to influence me in offering to Joe Johnston the favorable terms I did.* Being an interested party, I would prefer the testimony to come from you.

Even more ominous for Lincoln's future was the speech he delivered to hundreds of adoring fans from his White House window on the evening of April 11, publicly promising a Reconstruction policy of amnesty for the South. Holding a candle in one hand, his speech in the other, he emphasized to hundreds of war-weary citizens that his Reconstruction policy assured the restoration of self-government to the Southern states. He wanted no military dictatorship imposed on the South and its citizens, he said. Instead, all local and state governments should be placed in the hands of the Southern people, with local and state governments duly elected by the people.

But the one move that likely sealed Lincoln's fate occurred on the day prior to Richmond's evacuation. At that point Lincoln met secretly with Judge John Campbell of Virginia, who had served on the Supreme Court prior to the war, to discuss Lincoln's postwar policies for Virginia and the other Southern states. During that meeting Lincoln informed Judge Campbell that "the gentlemen who have acted as the legislature in support of the Rebellion" should be permitted to convene in Richmond to discuss matters pertinent to Virginia. Lincoln then dispatched his personal messenger to Gen. Godfrey Weitzel, Union commander in Richmond, to provide those Virginia legislators whatever protection they might need. Weitzel was cautioned to treat this entire matter with the utmost secrecy.

Lincoln met with Campbell in private and had hoped to have the Virginia legislature in session before the Radicals could even learn the event was in progress. But General

Weitzel immediately informed Stanton of Lincoln's plan.

According to Lafayette Baker, when Edwin Stanton received Weitzel's message, he furiously cursed the president's name and accused him of treason against his party. Stanton, against the wishes of Lincoln, then instructed General Weitzel not to allow the Virginia legislature to meet under any circumstances. Once those gentlemen arrived in Richmond, he said, Weitzel should arrange for their safe passage home, but they were not to be allowed to meet. Again, he made this insubordinate move with neither the knowledge or permission of President Lincoln. According to Lafayette Baker's recollection of this event. On the thirteenth Stanton

> discovered that the president had ordered that the legislature of Virginia be allowed to assemble to withdraw their states troops from action against the U.S. Stanton fermented immediately into an insane tirade. Then for the first time I realized his mental disunity and his insane and fanatical hatred for the president. There are few in the War Department that respect the president or his strategy but there are not many who would countermand an order that the president had given. However during that insane moment he sent a telegram to Gen. Weitzel countermanding the president's order of the twelfth. Then he laughed in a most spine chilling manner and said, "If he would know who recinded his order we will let Lucifer tell him."

A day later, on April 14, Lincoln was executed.

To prevent the president of the United States from pursuing his own political goals, death was obviously the answer. As Frank Flower, Stanton's biographer, says,

> Lincoln and Sherman labored under the same disability. The latter had suffered severely in history on account of his attempt to fix the political status of the rebellious sections. Yet Sherman was only a soldier, whose terms could be reversed and annulled, while Lincoln was president of the United States with supreme discretion in military affairs. Therefore, when, by the secret letter to General Weitzel, he undertook to hand over to the Virginia legislature that which the Confederate armies had been unable to secure, he entered the vortex leading to destruction.

Stanton's Lust for Power

By January 1865 things were going very well for Edwin Stanton. The war had been prolonged, his army was now the greatest the world had ever seen, slaves in the seceded states had been freed, and the South would soon lay helpless beneath his feet. Within months, as soon as Lee admitted defeat, it would become necessary to construct a new nation upon the ruins of the old, and it would be up to the ruling Republican Party to assume that responsibility. And who would be the leader of the Republican Party? If things went as scheduled, the leader by 1868 (or perhaps even before) would be Edwin Stanton.

He was aware that throughout history military heroes had found great favor with the public following a military victory, such as the one now at hand. But certainly Gen. George McClellan had fallen from grace and could not be considered a serious contender for the Republican nomination. Who could take his place? At the moment, Stanton could think of no other great heroes to capture the public's imagination.

There was Gen. Ulysses S. Grant, but who could view such a dull man as a great hero? Sen. Richard Dana of Massachusetts, who just happened to meet Grant in the lobby of the Willard Hotel, described him as "a short, round-shouldered man, in a very tarnished uniform. He had no gait, no station, no manner, and rather a scrubby look." In the hands of the aggressive Stanton, Grant would crumble. In fact, Stanton had already gone out of his way on several occasions to humble Grant in front of others, ordering him about as though he were an office clerk, leading Adam Badeau, an assistant in the Telegraph Office, to later write that Stanton would roughly send for Grant as he would for a lowly lieutenant.

Of course there was Gen. William T. Sherman, the leader of the infamous March to the Sea, but Stanton soon disposed of Sherman as well. When Sherman proposed Lincoln's peace terms to Gen. Joseph Johnston in North Carolina, Stanton, without President Johnson's consent or knowledge, sent to the press nine reasons why he had rejected Sherman's peace agreement. Stanton's reasons for his rejection made it appear that Sherman was guilty of treason, and editorials across the North accused him of such. Stanton even made it sound as though Sherman had been bribed to make such liberal peace terms and to allow Jefferson Davis to escape to Mexico or Europe:

> The orders of General Sherman to General Stoneman to withdraw from Salisbury and join him will probably open the way for Davis to escape to Mexico or Europe with his plunder, which is reported to be very large, including not only the plunder of Richmond banks, but previous accumulations.

Sherman, who had little use for politicians of any stripe, was of course outraged when informed of Stanton's treachery, but he was powerless to retaliate. In his memoirs, however, he charged Stanton with "deadly malignity" and expressed the wish to "see deeper into the diabolical plot." But Sherman was just another potential rival for the presidency whom Stanton cleverly disposed of with a single stroke of his poisoned pen.

Indeed, as the war came to a close, Stanton felt that at last he stood at the zenith of his political career. Salmon P. Chase, the secretary of the Treasury, had just been named to the Supreme Court, and Generals Grant, McClellan, and Sherman had been disposed of, which meant that Stanton stood second only to the president in power and public esteem. According to a lifelong friend Donn Piatt, "Stanton was drunk with the lust for power and fairly rioted in its enjoyment."

Still, Stanton was troubled. He wondered if the public blamed him for President Lincoln's suspending the writ of habeas corpus and for initiating a conscription program. Indeed, between 1861 and 1865, some 38,000 Northern citizens had been thrown in jail for political reasons and were kept there without charges and without recourse to trial. As for total arrests, it is estimated that some 260,000 citizens were arrested and jailed during the war years under what Stanton referred to as his "arbitrary authority." Though he had *suggested* to Lincoln that he should suspend the writ of habeas corpus, its implementation was the president's doing. How could citizens hold him responsible for the president's actions?

As for the Conscription Act, Stanton had made sure that the majority of those young men drafted for service were recent immigrants to this country, mainly young men from Ireland and Germany. He had given orders to his conscription officers that young men from influential American families should not be bothered. But in case they were, they could easily pay someone else three hundred dollars to take their place. True, it was he who had persuaded Lincoln that such stern measures were necessary if they were to successfully prosecute the war, but Lincoln had agreed with him. Lincoln was the president and was thus ultimately responsible.

During the waning days of the war, Stanton was very much aware that he had enemies in both Congress and Lincoln's cabinet, men who were clamoring for Lincoln to discharge Stanton now that the war was ending. For Stanton, who craved power, that would have been an unbearable fate. He pondered that troubling situation and finally arrived at a solution. Just days prior to Lee's surrender, with the war obviously over, he decided to force the issue. He sat down and wrote his resignation, which he then carried to President Lincoln.

He knew that Lincoln, after four long years of war, would not have the heart to accept his resignation at this moment of great triumph. And sure enough, he was correct. Lincoln refused to accept his letter of resignation despite the fact that he obviously wished to be rid of him, allowing Stanton to stay on as one of the most powerful men in America. Again, he had outsmarted all his enemies—as well as Abe Lincoln.

Then came the blow that no one, least of all Edwin Stanton, had expected. Lincoln suddenly announced that he would not follow the Radical Republicans' punitive ideas for bringing the South back into the Union, but would welcome them back with full rights. To Stanton and the others, congressmen as well as members of Lincoln's cabinet, this

meant that the Southern states, full of Democratic supporters, would soon be readmitted to the Union. Their first move,
of course, would be to vote the Republicans out of office.
The sunshine of yesterday turned suddenly to gloom.

In promising a Reconstruction policy of reconciliation for
the South, Lincoln assumed a direction that was directly
opposed to that desired by the Radicals in Congress. The
Radicals wished to punish the Southern states for having the
audacity to secede. Even more, they wished to rob and pillage the South. At that very moment there were thousands of
bales of cotton, acres of land, and innumerable resources
waiting to be confiscated. Such men as Thaddeus Stevens,
Ben Wade, Ben Butler, Wendell Phillips, and other Radicals
of their ilk were delirious with greed, and the South was lying
there, virtually helpless, just waiting to be plucked. And it
would be plucked, if they could just find some way to remove
the obstinate Lincoln from office. The bankers, businessmen,
and industrialists of the North were even more impatient to
get their hands on the resources of the South. And they
could do so, if the Radicals kept their promises.

Stanton, as it turned out, was far more outraged by
Lincoln's conciliatory policies towards the South than anyone else. In fact, according to Lafayette Baker's secret
papers, Stanton was already way ahead of his Radical colleagues. He assured them that Lincoln would cease being a
problem in the very near future.

Indeed, upon his arrest David Herold testified that Booth
had told him there were at least thirty-five influential citizens
involved in the conspiracy to assassinate the president. For
a century it was assumed that either Booth was guilty of a
gross exaggeration or that he was referring to peripheral
Southern collaborators. But in his secret papers, discovered in 1960, Lafayette Baker verifies Booth's statement and
says that in fact it was primarily Northern Republicans who
collaborated in the conspiracy. Though no records exist
proving a relationship between Stanton and John Wilkes
Booth, Lafayette Baker wrote that Stanton appointed Maj.
Thomas Eckert to arrange the details of Lincoln's execution,

and since it was Wilkes Booth who carried out the execution, it follows that he must have been in contact with either Baker or Eckert. And it is known that both Baker and Booth were in New York in the days just prior to the assassination. Did they meet there? Perhaps, though there certainly exists no record of such a meeting.

It seems improbable that Booth played a lone hand in the execution of the president. In the first place, how likely was it that a telegraph system that had worked fine throughout the war years suddenly would shut down at the moment Booth fired the fatal shot? Why would Stanton wait until 2:30 A.M., some four hours following Lincoln's wounding, to mention the name John Wilkes Booth to the press, too late for it to make the morning newspapers? And how was Booth able to pass over the Navy Yard Bridge at that time of night when others were being turned back? It is apparent that had Booth not broken his leg, he could easily have made it to the coast of Virginia, where he would have caught a ship to Mexico and freedom.

Perhaps it is newsworthy to note that on April 17, the Monday following the assassination, thanks to Edwin Stanton, Colonel Lafayette Baker became General Lafayette Baker, and Major Thomas Eckert became General Thomas Eckert.

At 7 A.M., the morning following Lincoln's wounding, Stanton was standing by, of course, in the back bedroom of the Petersen's rooming house when the attending physicians announced that President Lincoln finally was dead. At that point, reports Frank Flower, Stanton did a strange thing:

> He slowly and with apparent deliberation, straightened out his right arm, placed his hat for an instant on his head, and then just as deliberately returned it to its original position. To some of those present it must have appeared as if Stanton were crowning himself King of America.

Stanton immediately returned to the War Department the morning following Lincoln's death. Despite going without sleep the previous night, his steps were jaunty. At last, his future was assured. On the morning of April 15, Stanton already viewed himself as *de facto* president of the nation.

Since Congress was not in session, the defeated South was now lying completely at the mercy of the president. Secretary William Seward was confined to bed in critical condition while General Grant was wholly intimidated by Edwin Stanton. Andrew Johnson, a harsh master, would punish and pillage the South for years to come, and of course Johnson would look to Stanton for advice and guidance, at least until 1868, when Stanton himself could become president of the United States.

Of course there is much circumstantial evidence (and logic) that suggests it was Andrew Johnson who instigated the assassination. During his impeachment trial of 1867, his personal secretary, William Browning, would testify that Johnson and Booth had been the best of friends for several years in Nashville. Perhaps this relationship would explain Booth's known attempts to see Johnson on the day of the assassination. He called for him twice at the desk of the Kirkwood House and was told that Johnson was out. But there is every reason to believe that Booth might have ignored the desk clerk and gone directly to Johnson's room. Perhaps he did see Johnson, who could have persuaded him that Lincoln must be terminated immediately; otherwise his beloved Southland would be ravaged by Lincoln's vindictive Reconstruction plans.

Had Booth been motivated by a desire to throw the Federal government into total confusion by eliminating the heads of state, then he would have executed the president and vice president, not the president and secretary of state, since Seward was not in line to succeed Lincoln as president. His execution, therefore, made no sense, because it would *not* have thrown the Federal government into a state of confusion. Once Lincoln was executed, Andrew Johnson succeeded him as president and the government functioned with no break in continuity, experiencing no confusion whatsoever. Seward's death, therefore, was in fact unnecessary and superfluous.

The question must also be asked, if Booth hoped to throw the Federal government into confusion by eliminating the heads of state, why did he choose to execute Seward rather than Edwin Stanton, the scourge of the South for the past four years and the man who was actually running the government? Certainly Stanton would have made a much more appealing (and reasonable) target than the innocuous William Seward.

There can be only one answer to these questions: Booth was an intelligent man, and had he been aware of the true state of affairs, he would have protected Lincoln and Seward with his very life. But Booth was lied to and misled. He was told that it was Lincoln and Seward who planned a vindictive Reconstruction program for the South. Only the old Southern Democrat, Andrew Johnson, could save the South from further destruction. But that could happen only if Lincoln and Seward were eliminated.

The Stanton-Johnson Enigma

Strangely enough, almost immediately following Lincoln's execution, Andrew Johnson began to follow Lincoln's lead in his attitude towards the defeated South. Seemingly with each day Stanton's dream of a continued dictatorship began to fade. In fact, the hitherto compliant Johnson was beginning to grow far more assertive than Lincoln had ever been. Despite his earlier boasts of punishing the South, he was now making every effort to restore the South to its proper place in the Union, and since Congress was adjourned, he was making rapid progress in that direction. Stanton and his Radical allies were furious, but there was nothing they could do. Until Congress should again convene, nothing could be done to stop the new president. While Stanton and the Radicals fumed, Johnson went blithely on his way, welcoming visiting Southern politicians to his office on a daily basis, smiling, shaking hands, slapping backs, and making friends for himself throughout the South.

When the thirty-ninth session of Congress finally did open in December 1865, Rep. Thaddeus Stevens, the most radical

Andrew Johnson, an old friend of John Wilkes Booth, appeared visibly inebriated at his inauguration as vice president in March 1864, much to the lasting consternation of Abraham Lincoln. Aware that Lincoln would remove him from office at his first opportunity, Johnson collaborated with Stanton in plotting the president's own removal from office.
Library of Congress

of the Radicals, organized a steering committee of fifteen members whose sole purpose was to prevent representatives from the Southern states from occupying their seats in Congress. It was a revolutionary move and totally unconstitutional, but it was also very effective. Against this solid wall of Radical opposition, all of Johnson's appeals and arguments went for naught. The Southern states would pay dearly in blood and money for their transgressions. The Constitution be damned!

As the conflict between Johnson and Congress worsened, Stanton resorted to a most daring—and unscrupulous—ploy to keep himself and his Radical friends apprised of the president's every move. He ordered his chief of detectives, Lafayette Baker, to collect a half-dozen spies from among his detective force and place them in Johnson's office. They would masquerade as secretaries of one sort or another and keep Stanton informed of Johnson's every move and every word. Stanton then would carry this information to his Radical allies in Congress.

Gideon Welles, secretary of the navy, would later write in his diary:

> Stanton contrived to have the President surrounded most of the time by his detectives, or men connected with the military service who are creatures of the War Department. Of course, much that was said to the President in friendly confidence was directly communicated to Stanton. In this way a constant espionage was maintained on all that transpired at the White House. Stanton, in all that time had his confidants among the Radicals—enemies of the President—in Congress—a circle to whom he betrayed the measures and purposes of the President and with whom he concocted schemes to defeat the measures and policy of the Administration.

Johnson was certainly aware of Stanton's machinations, and one cannot help but question why he refused to fire him from his cabinet. Even Johnson's friends counseled him to rid himself of Stanton as quickly as possible. Yet Johnson remained passively unconcerned. This state of affairs eventually led to rumors that either Johnson or Stanton, or perhaps both, were somehow linked to Lincoln's assassination. To insure the continued silence of the other, they would remain together. George Milton in his *Age of Hate* writes:

> The country could not understand why Johnson did not discharge the faithless Secretary. Radicals were as amazed as Conservatives. Senator Doolittle of Wisconsin wrote the venerable Francis Preston Blair of a rumor so damnable that Blair sat down immediately to present it to the President, to force the latter to act.
>
> "For six long months," Doolittle had written, "I have been urging the President to call on Grant temporarily to do the duties of the War Department."
>
> But Stanton remains, and so the report has spread all over the State that there is something sinister. It started through the *Milwaukee Sentinel* printing the letter of a correspondent from Washington, which says that Stanton is not removed because it is rumored and believed that Stanton has testimony to show that Mr. Johnson was privy to Lincoln's assassination.

But through it all the president just smiled and shook his head—and Stanton stayed on. Even the ugly rumors could not force Johnson to act.

While the storm raged around the ambitious Stanton, he continued to build up his military machine. On February 13, 1867, the Reconstruction Bill passed the House. According to this bill, Stanton proposed that the Southern states be dissolved and then divided into military districts, a plan which President Lincoln had rejected out of hand some five years earlier. Each state would be under the control of a military governor with unlimited power. These military governors would be appointed not by the president, but by the general of the army, Ulysses S. Grant. Grant of course was directly under the control of Edwin Stanton. Essentially, then, Edwin Stanton would become the supreme dictator of the Southern states of America, thanks to this Reconstruction Bill of 1867, and the citizens of the South would become a people without constitutional rights. Once that had been accomplished, they could also be robbed of their money and property. Northern bankers and industrialists held the purse strings of the

Republican Party at that time, and this Reconstruction Bill would be their payoff for years of support. Needless to say, Johnson immediately vetoed this Reconstruction Bill, pointing out that it gave the military governors of the various states as much power as absolute despots, their mere whim enough to replace the law. Stanton's disappointment and anger knew no bounds.

At the same time the Reconstruction Bill was under consideration, the Tenure-of-Office Bill was very slyly concocted by Edwin Stanton and presented to his Radical friends for passage. Thanks to this outrageous bit of legislation, Johnson was deprived of his right to remove appointed officials without the express consent of the Senate. In other words, Stanton could now spy on Johnson and conspire against him all he wished, and there was absolutely nothing Johnson could do about it. Over the president's veto, the Tenure-of-Office Act passed Congress on March 2, 1867. On that same day, with Stanton now firmly protected from Johnson's wrath, and again over the President's veto, Congress passed their infamous Reconstruction Act, which substituted elected civil governments in the South with federal military governments.

Thanks to the Tenure-of-Office Act, Johnson's hands were finally tied. He could not force Stanton out without incurring the danger of impeachment. But Johnson's impeachment was exactly what Stanton was hoping for, and he seemed to delight in insulting and betraying Johnson at every turn. Should Johnson be impeached, there was no vice president in line for succession, so the duties of the executive would devolve upon Ben Wade, president of the Senate, a timid man who would depend heavily on Stanton for advice and direction. Stanton, who already had the South under his thumb, could, by extending the suspension of the writ of habeas corpus, also control the North. His dreams seemed at last within reach.

On August 12, 1867, throwing caution to the wind, a furious Andrew Johnson sat down at his desk and wrote the following gem of a letter to Stanton:

Sir: Public considerations of a high character constrain me to say that your resignation as Secretary of War will be accepted.
Andrew Johnson
President of the United States

Stanton received this brief bombshell, read it, then angrily tore it to shreds. A moment later he had a secretary inform the president that he had not the least intention of resigning, nor, thanks to the Tenure-of-Office Act, could Johnson force him. Still, Johnson did not totally surrender, and on February 21, 1868, he informed Congress that he had removed Edwin Stanton from office. Three days later Congress impeached him for "high crimes and misdemeanors." Stanton, meanwhile, refused to vacate his office. Things were going just as Stanton had planned, and now, if Johnson should be found guilty, the secretary of war would become the most powerful man in America. And the election of 1868 was less than a year away.

Johnson's impeachment trial began on March 23. At its conclusion, when the final vote was taken, the result was thirty-five to nineteen. Johnson had escaped conviction by a single vote. It was said that when Stanton was given this devastating news, he collapsed in a dead faint on his office floor. After all he had been through, after all his great battles, after years of lies and betrayals (and perhaps an assassination or two), his great dream of becoming president of the United States had come to nothing. Now it would be Gen. Ulysses S. Grant who would become president in 1868. (Following Grant's election, Andrew Johnson would return home to Tennessee, and in 1872 he would be elected to the U. S. Senate from that state.)

As for Stanton, his great hope now was to resume his old position as secretary of war in Grant's cabinet; therefore he actively campaigned for Grant during the campaign of 1868. When that appointment was not forthcoming, he began to publicly slander Grant, just as he had done with Lincoln and Johnson. Oddly enough, Grant signed an order naming Stanton to a seat on the Supreme Court. Fortunately for the nation, Grant never issued that order, and Stanton died before he could assume a seat.

More Incriminating Evidence

Again, if Edwin Stanton (aided and abetted by Andrew Johnson) did play a role in the execution of President Lincoln, the case against him is totally circumstantial. Still, his possible role in that memorable event is certainly worthy of discussion.

In the first place, it was to Stanton's advantage to dispose of Abraham Lincoln. With Lincoln out of the way, so Stanton must have reasoned, he could maintain his position in the cabinet, where he would have even more power over a new and supposedly weak Andrew Johnson. Using his present position as a launching pad, he considered his chances of becoming president himself in 1868 to be excellent. And of course after Lincoln's elimination, Andrew Johnson, with his anti-Confederate sympathies, would become president, thereby insuring military occupation and harsh treatment of the South for years to come. And certainly a grinning Johnson would grant the Republicans and their carpetbagger minions a license to pillage the South at every turn. Thus · the Radical Republicans, and by extension Edwin Stanton, would continue their political domination of the nation throughout the nineteenth century.

It might also be pointed out that Stanton refused to protect the president's life on the evening of April 14, even though an unusually nervous Abe Lincoln repeatedly requested a bodyguard.

As for General Grant's refusal to accompany the Lincolns to the theater, it should be noted that Grant was a West Point graduate and well versed in military etiquette. And West Point graduates do not snub official invitations from their commander in chief. After visiting with Stanton late that afternoon, however, Grant did just that. Of course this was not just any visit to the theater. Grant was credited with winning this most terrible of all wars some five days earlier, and tonight he would put in a personal appearance at the theater, where adoring citizens could catch a glimpse of him. All the newspapers in Washington had headlined this

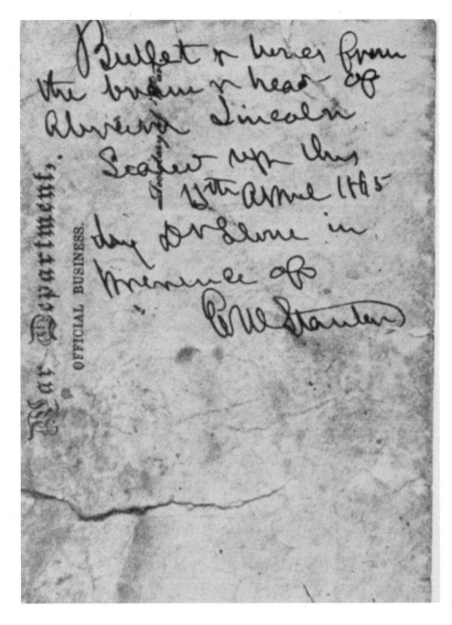

The envelope in which Secretary of War Edwin Stanton kept the "bullet and bones from the brain and head of Abraham Lincoln." U.S. War Department Archives

event. Grant would appear at Ford's Theatre that very evening as a special guest of the president of the United States. The entire city was agog at the prospect of seeing both men together.

In his biography, published in 1883, Grant briefly glosses over this astonishing chapter from his life, the day he refused an invitation from the president of the United States, a blatant snub that may have allowed the execution of the president. According to his biography, at approximately 5 P.M., Grant blandly sent a message to Lincoln informing him that his wife, Julia Dent Grant, wished to visit their children as soon as possible, and they would be catching a late afternoon train bound for New Jersey; therefore, he would be forced to refuse the president's invitation. And this came about immediately following Grant's 4 P.M. meeting with Edwin Stanton, which should arouse the suspicions of even the most passive critic.

With both Eckert and Grant out of the picture, Lincoln was essentially alone in his box, a ready target for anyone wishing to assassinate him. Not only that, but Grant was out of town, a passenger on a train far out of the city at the time of the murder. He certainly could never be accused of being an accessory to the crime.

Other trails leading from Lincoln's assassination all seem to connect at Stanton. It was due to Stanton's efforts that all charges of negligence against Washington policeman John F. Parker were finally dropped and the report suppressed. It was Stanton who directed the pursuit of Booth, and directed it in such a way that Booth would doubtlessly have escaped had it not been for his broken leg. For reasons that have never been adequately explained, Stanton's military telegraph suddenly ceased functioning immediately following the assassination and was out of order for the next four critical hours. Indeed, Booth's name was not telegraphed to newspapers across the country for almost five hours following the assassination, providing Booth time to make his escape.

A week later, it was Stanton who recalled cavalry leader

Maj. James R. O'Beirne when that officer reported from Virginia that he was on the track of Booth and expected his capture within hours. Once he had recalled the very frustrated O'Beirne, Stanton assigned his own trusted lieutenant, Luther Baker, the first cousin of Lafayette Baker, to go after the assassin. And of course Booth was not brought back alive. Somehow, inexplicably, he was shot dead in Garrett's barn by Sgt. Boston Corbett. It was Stanton who ordered that all charges against Corbett be dropped.

All suspects known to have collaborated with Booth were immediately silenced upon their arrests. Not only were they thrown into solitary cells, they were also forced to wear tight-fitting, thickly padded hoods that prevented them from hearing or speaking with any other persons. Those who escaped hanging were banished to a desolate fortress in the Dry Tortugas. The four persons who were known to have spoken with Booth on the day of Lincoln's execution were all hanged.

The arrest and extradition of John Surratt were delayed for months after the government became aware of his whereabouts. In fact, there is some evidence that efforts were made to prevent his return to this country altogether for there was fear that Surratt might reveal details of the conspiracy that could prove highly incriminating to government officials, especially Edwin Stanton.

During President Johnson's impeachment trial of 1867, William Browning, his private secretary, testified that Booth and Andrew Johnson were friends, implying that it was Johnson who had introduced Booth to Stanton. This would explain the strange hold that Stanton seemed to have over Johnson, who kept Stanton in office for unknown reasons long after Stanton's treachery had become a matter of public knowledge.

In 1867, after two years of blatant treachery, Andrew Johnson finally fired Edwin Stanton. Two years later, in 1869, after confessing that "That Surratt woman haunts me," Stanton passed on to the other world. Officially he died of natural causes, but Ben P. Poore in his *Reminiscences* says, "There are many in Washington who believe that Mr. Stanton committed suicide by cutting his throat with a razor. Caleb Cushing was positive that he did." Certainly that act could be attributed to the guilt of a man who engineered so many of those events that comprised the most accursed period in American history.

IV

The Conspirators
and Their Conspiracies

Oddly enough, of the seven young men actively involved in the conspiracy against Abraham Lincoln, all seven of them— John Wilkes Booth, John Surratt, Lewis Powell, David Herold, Michael O'Laughlin, Samuel Arnold, and George Atzerodt— grew up in a home where he was his family's youngest child. Booth had three older brothers and four older sisters; Surratt had one older brother and one older sister; Powell had two older brothers and six older sisters; Herold had seven older sisters; O'Laughlin had at least one older brother; Arnold and Atzerodt had at least two older brothers.

One noted historian very aptly described Booth and his collaborators in the plot against Lincoln as "a conspiracy of foolish and misguided boys." And such was indeed the case. In the autumn of 1864, when Booth apparently first began a serious effort to organize a group of conspirators, he was only twenty-six years old; Samuel Arnold, the senior member of the group, was only thirty; Michael O'Laughlin was twenty-four; John Surratt and David Herold were twenty; and the fearless Lewis Thornton Powell was a lad of only nineteen.

With the exception of Powell, the son of a Baptist minister, the conspirators were all of the Catholic faith (Booth apparently converted to Catholicism late in his career), which led to widespread rumors that the Vatican was somehow behind the plot to execute the president. But it must be remembered that all the conspirators (again with the exception of Lewis Powell) were all from Maryland, traditionally a Catholic colony.

John Wilkes Booth, one of the most successful actors in America, by 1864 was making nearly twenty thousand dollars a year, a princely sum at that time. Certainly his conspiracy against Abraham Lincoln was motivated not by hopes of personal gain but by his misguided love for the South. Library of Congress

It has been denied that the Confederate government played any role in the plot to abduct the president, but recently discovered documents indicate that the Southern government was deeply involved. In fact, the Booth conspiracy, it is now known, was not the first such conspiracy approved and financed by the Confederacy. Booth, Surratt, and Powell were all three active agents of the Confederate Secret Service, and all three were working on behalf of that clandestine agency when they plotted to abduct the president. As for Booth's later decision to execute the president, it seems highly doubtful that Confederate authorities would ever have sanctioned such an extreme move.

Booth's father, Junius Brutus Booth, despite severe problems with alcohol, eccentric behavior, and occasional fits of madness, was considered the leading Shakespearean actor (and one of the wealthiest) on the American stage. He was born in the parish of St. Pancras, London, on May 1, 1796. He first married a Belgian girl named Christine Adelaide Delannoy, but after six years of marriage he blithely deserted her (and their two-year-old son, Richard) without a backward glance. Soon he met another beautiful girl, Mary Ann Holmes, and despite the fact that he never bothered to divorce Adelaide, he became the common law husband of Mary Ann.

Together, in April 1821, possibly in hopes of escaping his complicated marital problems, Junius and Mary Ann migrated to America, landing at Norfolk, Virginia, on June 30. He immediately traveled to Richmond, where he introduced himself to Charles Gilfert, the manager of the Richmond Theater. Gilfert had heard of Booth and hired him immediately to play Richard III in the play of that same name. The play folded, but Booth's performance was considered so sensational that from then on he secured all the engagements he could fill.

In the summer of 1822, while the yellow fever raged in Richmond and Baltimore, Booth purchased a farm in Hartford County, Maryland, about twenty miles from Baltimore. Here his children—Junius Brutus, Edwin Forrest, Joseph, John Wilkes, Asia, and three other daughters—were

Booth's father, Junius Brutus Booth, who prior to his death in 1858, had become America's leading stage actor. Harvard Theater Collection

born. It was to here, to his peaceful farm, that Junius Booth fled when free from his theater engagements.

A divorce was finally granted to Junius and Adelaide on April 18, 1851. Adelaide charged him with adultery, a charge he could hardly deny since Mary Ann had now given birth to eight children. Finally, Junius and Mary Ann were legally married in Baltimore on May 10, 1852, on Booth's thirteenth birthday.

Junius Booth's final appearance on stage occurred in New Orleans on November 19, 1852, as Sir Richard Mortimer in *The Iron Chest.* Following this run in New Orleans, he booked passage on a steamship and became ill during the trip upriver,

Booth's mother, Mary Ann Holmes, lived with Junius Booth for thirty years and bore him eight children prior to their marriage on May 10, 1851 (Booth's thirteenth birthday). The Kimmel Collection, Library of Congress

dying suddenly on November 30, 1852. In 1858 his remains were reburied at the Green Mount Cemetery in Baltimore.

Of all his sons, Edwin Forrest Booth, more than any of the others, showed genius for the stage and was considered at least the equal of his celebrated father. The eldest son, Junius Brutus Booth, Jr., played for years on the stage but never with any great success. He devoted the final years of his life to managing a hotel in Massachusetts, where he died in 1898. Joseph A. Booth never felt any attraction for the stage but became a highly respected New York physician.

He died in 1902, and like the rest of the family is buried in Green Mount Cemetery.

Daughter Asia Booth, a beautiful girl, married John S. Clark, a serious professional man with no ambition for the stage. Asia had refused to marry him until he tried his hand at play acting. To win her hand, he went on stage and eventually became one of America's most celebrated comedians. Following the execution of Abe Lincoln, Asia and John Clark fled to England to escape the notoriety. Asia would die there in 1888.

John Wilkes Booth (he was known to his family and acquaintances as Wilkes Booth) was born on the Booth farm near Bel Air, Maryland, on May 10, 1838. His proud father named him John Wilkes in honor of his great-great-grandfather, the well-known British agitator and statesman of the same name. His early school years were spent at St. Timothy's Hall, an Episcopal military academy in Catonsville, Maryland. There, he was a schoolmate of both Samuel Arnold and Michael O'Laughlin, apparently the first two men he would enlist in his conspiracy to abduct the president.

Booth left school following his father's death in 1852 and spent several years working on the family farm. At that time he was considered an excellent athlete and could ride and shoot as well as any young man in the county. Those who knew him would later describe him as a cheerful and cordial young man with a rich sense of humor, a young man who seemed to thoroughly enjoy life. He was always friendly and outgoing and seemed totally oblivious to class distinctions, enjoying the company of the poorer members of the community as well as that of the well-to-do. In 1855, at the age of seventeen, he secured employment at the Arch Street Theater in Philadelphia (thanks to the influence of Edmund Booth and John Clark), at a salary of fifteen dollars a week. Fortunately, he had found his calling at a very young age, though it would be several years before he truly hit his stride as an actor.

Indeed, when appearing in a play in Baltimore at that time, Booth, playing the part of Arcanio Petruccio, was on stage with Eliza Wrenn when she asked him, "Who art thou?" But the nervous youngster could not recall his unusual

Booth's sister Asia Booth in 1859 married John Clark, who would himself become a celebrated actor. She would later write a most informative biography of Wilkes Booth, The Unlocked Door. The Kimmel Collection, Library of Congress

name. Aware that he was facing disaster, the distraught Booth stuttered about the stage for a moment, then paused, flashed Eliza a big grin, and blurted out, "Ah heck! I can't remember. Who am I anyway?" A forgiving audience roared with laugher, and Booth continued on with the play.

At the age of twenty-one in 1859, he stood five foot seven, had jet black hair, ivory skin, and was trim and well muscled.

It was later claimed that his eyes were black, but in her book, *The Unlocked Door,* Asia writes that his eyes were of the deepest blue. At the time, he was often called the handsomest man in America. He was courteous and cordial to all. Men sought his company and members of the opposite sex found him irresistible.

As fate would have it, on November 19, 1859, he was appearing on stage in Richmond when John Brown, who had attempted to incite slave insurrections across the South, was captured at Harpers Ferry. Fascinated by all the excitement, Booth borrowed a uniform from a member of Company F, Richmond Volunteers, talked his way aboard the troop train bound for Charles Town and was assigned guard duty once he arrived there. He would later witness the execution of John Brown.

Almost a year later he would agree to star with Matthew Canning's company on a tour of the South. The company opened on October 1, 1860, in Columbus, Georgia, with Booth playing Romeo and Mary Mitchell as Juliet. Then on October 12 there occurred an event that could have had far-reaching consequences for Booth and those investigating the execution of President Lincoln. Booth and Canning were practicing with a revolver at Cook's Hotel when Canning attempted to cock the revolver. The hammer slipped and the revolver fired, the ball striking Booth in the left thigh. It was a serious wound, and Booth was immobilized for weeks. On December 16, in a letter now on file at the Peale Museum in Baltimore, Asia Booth would write to a friend, "Wilkes Booth is at home. He is looking well, but his wound is not entirely healed yet. He still carries the ball in him." The importance of this wound to historians should not be overlooked. If Booth's body is ever exhumed, the presence (or absence) of that ball in the casket should settle once and for all the identity of the body in the grave at Green Mount Cemetery.

Despite this setback, Booth soon became a favorite of playgoers in Richmond and appeared in play after play. At that point, there he was, a young man of twenty-two, the darling of respectable young ladies throughout the land (and a few not so respectable young ladies, as time would prove). Minus family restraints and totally on his own, it is said that he enjoyed a wild life.

Even with Booth's successes as an actor, his life and interests began to follow a new and radically different direction following the outbreak of war between the North and South in 1861. He became a dedicated Southern partisan, and soon he would be a working member of the Confederate Secret Service. By the summer of 1864 he would be concentrating his energies in a bizarre plot to abduct the president and bring him South, where he could be exchanged for Southern prisoners of war.

September 1864: Booth Recruits Arnold and O'Laughlin

As far as can be determined, Wilkes Booth began taking practical steps to put his scheme to abduct the president into effect in September 1864, when he made his first effort to recruit other Southern sympathizers. Obviously at that point he already had devised a general plan, an outline of sorts, for the abduction and realized that it was something he could not do alone. In order to abduct the president while he rode alone in his buggy to the Soldiers' Home would require the help of at least several other persons. If he could abduct Lincoln from Ford's Theatre, a scheme Booth greatly preferred, he would still need the help of several others, a supporting cast if you will.

To that end, in September 1864 he contacted two of his oldest acquaintances, Baltimore natives Samuel Arnold and Michael O'Laughlin, and summoned them to his room at Barnum's Hotel. Considering their shaky backgrounds, Arnold and O'Laughlin would hardly make ideal recruits, but at this point they were better than nothing. Both were confirmed triflers and loafers, but they were loyal to the South and Booth knew he could depend on them.

Booth had attended St. Timothy's Hall Academy in Baltimore, as had O'Laughlin and Arnold, who was five years

At the age of thirty, Samuel Bland Arnold, an old friend of Wilkes Booth, was the senior member of the abduction team. One of the most reluctant members, Arnold withdrew from the conspiracy following the failed abduction on March 17, but nevertheless the Military Commission sentenced him to life in the Dry Tortugas. Pres. Andrew Johnson granted him a full pardon in 1869. Library of Congress

O'Laughlin's senior, and Booth was aware that both had served briefly in the Confederate army and still harbored Southern sympathies. Arnold, the son of a prominent Baltimore baker, had returned home in late 1862, discharged for medical reasons, taken the oath of allegiance, and still unemployed was living at home with his parents. O'Laughlin's situation was similar to Arnold's. He too had served in the Confederate army, been discharged in 1862, and was now living quite unemployed at home with his parents. In fact, the O'Laughlins were renting their home from Booth's mother, Mary Ann Booth.

According to Arnold's later testimony, he entered Booth's room at Barnum's Hotel and the two men warmly embraced. They seated themselves on the couch by a big open window and while enjoying brandy and cigars spent the next hour delightedly reminiscing about old times and old schoolmates. Their conversation was interrupted by a knock at the door: Michael O'Laughlin. Since O'Laughlin and Arnold did not know each other, Booth made the introductions and pointed O'Laughlin to a chair facing the couch. Then he poured his new guest a snifter of brandy and handed him a big cigar. Soon O'Laughlin too was happily involved in their discussion of old times and old friends.

An hour later Booth began steering the conversation to the Confederacy and the numerous evils they had suffered at the hands of the Federal government. Arnold and O'Laughlin heartily agreed with everything he said, then poured themselves another drink. Then he spoke of the thousands of Southern boys enduring terrible hardships in Northern prison camps. He explained that though the Union had exchanged prisoners early in the war, they now refused to do so. The North, unlike the South, had no lack of manpower, so they could allow their own troops to freeze and starve in Southern prisons rather than exchange them for Southern prisoners. The South, hardly able to feed and offer medical treatment to her own soldiers, was only too aware that she certainly could not feed and care for the thousands of Union prisoners then in her prison camps.

Michael O'Laughlin, another of Booth's reluctant patriots, was only twenty-four at the time of the assassination. Though he withdrew from the affair following the failed abduction of the president on March 17, the Military Commission found him guilty of conspiracy and sentenced him to life in the Dry Tortugas. He died there during the yellow fever epidemic of 1867. Library of Congress

And thus Southern officials repeatedly pleaded with Secretary of War Edwin Stanton to resume an exchange of prisoners, but to no avail.

Then Booth broached the real reason for meeting with his old friends. Clearing his throat and sitting forward on the edge of his seat, he explained to his awestruck companions the ease with which President Lincoln could be abducted and taken to Richmond, and how he could be used as a hostage to force the release of Confederate prisoners in

Union hands. Flabbergasted, Arnold and O'Laughlin looked at one another, then at Booth. Had he lost his mind? Booth smiled and brushed aside their objections. His plan was well thought out and really quite simple, he said. He pointed out that the president disliked military escorts and was in the habit of driving his carriage out to the Soldiers' Home in Washington totally alone. It would be no problem to stop the carriage in an isolated area, turn it about, and drive across the Navy Yard Bridge into Maryland, then across the Potomac into Virginia, and finally to Richmond. They would have speedy horses planted along the way to aid in their escape, and once they reached southern Maryland there would be Confederate cavalry (Mosby's Rangers) stationed there to discourage Union pursuit. All he needed to carry out his plans, said Booth, were a few fearless friends.

While Arnold and O'Laughlin sat stunned at this bizarre turn of events, Booth talked on, painting in glowing strokes their chances of success and the great honors that would come their way once their feat was accomplished. They would be toasted and feted throughout the South. Plus, said Booth, they would be paid a great deal of money for their services. At that these two young men, whose lives were studies in boredom, who had not a dollar between them, looked at one another and shrugged. Yes, they said reluctantly, they would go along with the plan, at least for a while. After all, it was not like they would be called on to do it today, and if they changed their minds, they could always back out. Besides, between now and the time for the abduction, they certainly could use some cash. They raised their right hands and swore an oath that they would never reveal Booth's plan to anyone. Then, with shaking hands, they poured themselves another snifter of brandy.

Almost immediately after this meeting Arnold took a job thrashing wheat on a farm just outside Baltimore with a friend named Littleton Newman. This job was hardly a boon to his financial situation, but it made his mother happy. A few days later he received a letter from Booth stating that he was laid up with erysipelas but he would meet again with

Arnold and O'Laughlin as soon as he was better. More importantly, from Arnold's standpoint, Booth enclosed a note for fifty dollars, a down payment of sorts, which Arnold was to share with O'Laughlin.

As soon as Booth was recovered he visited his mother in New York for a few days then took the train to the oil regions of Pennsylvania, where he purchased stock in a drilling company. Finally he made his way to Montreal for a meeting with Jacob Thompson and other members of the Confederate Secret Service. Upon his return, he visited briefly with Arnold and O'Laughlin in Baltimore. His purpose, apparently, was to give them more money, at least enough to further encourage and cement their relationship.

In October 1864, Booth again made the long trip to Montreal, where he was seen in the company of agents Jacob Thompson and George Sanders, leaders of what was appropriately known as the "Confederacy's Canada Cabinet." (Following the assassination of Lincoln on April 14, Jacob Thompson fled to France where he remained for several years, pursued by both Federal and Confederate agents alike since he had absconded with over three hundred thousand dollars in Confederate gold, money that was never recovered.) On the twenty-seventh of October, Booth deposited $455 of his own money with the Ontario Bank of Montreal, the same bank where Jacob Thompson kept funds entrusted to him by the Confederate government. At the time of his deposit, Booth also withdrew $300 in American gold, which he possibly used to help finance his campaign to abduct the president.

During this trip to Montreal, Booth was also frequently seen in the company of Confederate secret agent Patrick Charles Martin, a citizen of lower Maryland, who was involved in trading Canadian and American currency and other intriguing enterprises for the Confederate government. It was Patrick Martin who would write Booth a letter of introduction to his old friend Dr. William Queen of Bryantown in Charles County, Maryland. According to the later testimony of Dr. Queen, Booth visited him in early November and inquired about the price of land and horses in the

Bryantown area. He boasted that money really was no object. On November 5, Booth joined Dr. Queen and his family for Sunday services at St. Mary's Catholic Church in Bryantown, and it was there that Booth met Dr. Samuel Mudd for the first time. It was a meeting that would have far-reaching and tragic consequences for the good doctor. They were introduced by John C. Thompson, Dr. Queen's son-in-law, and soon Booth had convinced Dr. Mudd that he was very serious about investing in property in that region.

Booth Meets Dr. Samuel Mudd

Dr. Mudd was a highly respected citizen of southern Maryland whose life was totally dedicated to caring for his family and his fellow man. But as sometimes happens Dr. Mudd very innocently got caught up in circumstances far beyond his control. Dr. Mudd treated Booth as cordially as he would any other gentleman met at church. It is truly unfortunate that Mudd could not see into the future at that point, that he could not see that this first meeting with Booth would eventually lead him, as though driven by fate, to a Federal prison in the Dry Tortugas, where he was to serve a life sentence for aiding Booth in his escape.

He was born on December 20, 1833, on a large plantation in Charles County, Maryland, to Henry Lowe Mudd and Sarah Ann Reeves. He was educated at home until he was fourteen. At that point he entered St. John's College in Frederick, Maryland. Then he transferred to Georgetown College, where he remained for another two years. Finally, in pursuit of a medical degree, he entered the University of Maryland. He graduated in 1856 at the age of twenty-three. Upon graduation he returned home and began practicing medicine and helping with his father's farm. A year later, in 1857, he married Sarah Frances Dyer, his childhood sweetheart. Their first child, Andrew, was born in 1858. About a year later Dr. Mudd purchased a farm of his own about five miles from Bryantown and thirty miles

Dr. Samuel Mudd, whose guilt or innocence in the conspiracy has created much debate. His only proven connection with the crime was that of setting Wilkes Booth's broken leg on the night of the assassination. National Park Service, Ford's Theatre, Washington, D.C.

south of Washington. He and Sarah would have a daughter and two more sons by 1864.

With the outbreak of war in 1861, feelings in favor of the Confederacy ran high in southern Maryland, and Dr. Mudd, like most citizens of that area, if not a registered member of the Confederate Secret Service, became at the very least a working member of the Confederate underground. As such, he would relay messages and dispatches between Richmond and Washington, report Federal troop movements, and assist

Confederate agents and soldiers as they passed back and forth between the lines. These Southern agents created an underground railroad of sorts, with each agent knowing all the other agents in the region. Doubtlessly this is how Dr. Mudd became acquainted with John Surratt, one of Judah Benjamin's youngest and most daring Secret Service agents.

In retrospect, it appears that Booth had no intentions of buying land in Bryantown but was simply trying to familiarize himself with Confederate sympathizers in that area, knowledge that would prove invaluable once he had abducted President Lincoln. Subsequently, Dr. Mudd, who had apparently become aware of Booth's real purpose in surveying the land and citizens of Bryantown, introduced him to Thomas Harbin, a signal officer and spy for the Confederacy in lower Maryland. (The Confederate Secret Service was a part of the Confederate Signal Corps.) Booth then informed Harbin of his plans to capture the president. Indeed, said Booth, he had come down to Charles County to invite cooperation and secure partners for his conspiracy. Harbin expressed a great deal of interest in Booth's story and requested that Booth keep him informed of future developments.

Booth spent the night with Dr. Mudd, through whom he met a local farmer named George Gardiner, and it was from Gardiner that he purchased the bay horse, blind in one eye, that Lewis Powell would ride the night he attacked Secretary William Seward.

Booth arrived back in Washington on November 9 and took room 20 at the National Hotel. He departed the city two days later, returning on the fourteenth, then left again on the sixteenth. During those days of his absence, he was visiting with his new acquaintances in Bryantown. In the month of December, Booth appeared in Washington on three different occasions. According to Louis Weichmann, a War Department clerk and a boarder at Mrs. Surratt's boardinghouse, it was on December 23 that Dr. Mudd introduced Booth to John Surratt, the young man who would quickly become his most trusted lieutenant.[1]

Surratt, Weichmann, and Sainte Marie

According to Louis Weichmann's story, he and John Surratt first met in September 1859, when both were preparing for the Catholic priesthood at St. Charles College in Howard County, Maryland. Surratt was a hard-working and practical lad of only fifteen when Weichmann first introduced himself. Weichmann, as Surratt was soon to learn, was a very intelligent boy, though at times he could be annoyingly priggish, self-righteous, and terribly inquisitive. Still, Surratt and Weichmann spent much of their spare time together. As for Surratt, Weichmann describes him at he appeared in 1859 as "tall, erect, slender, and boyish, with a very prominent forehead and receding eyes. His nose was sharp, thin, and aquiline; his face bore an unusually keen and shrewd expression." He immediately aroused hostility in some of the older students, says Weichmann, "by wearing a white necktie." Over the next three years, until July 1862, Surratt and Weichmann would become extremely well acquainted with one another. But then, with the war raging throughout the South, both were forced to withdraw from college.

Surratt returned home to Surrattsville in Prince Georges County, Maryland, some twelve miles from Washington, to replace his recently deceased father as the village postmaster. From a military standpoint, Surratt's home was strategically located, situated as it was on the main road from Washington to Bryantown and the Potomac River and then on to Richmond. By 1862 this road was already heavily traveled by those running the blockade, spies, escaped prisoners of war, and Northerners who wished to join the Confederate army. Surratt's older brother, Isaac, was now in Texas in the service of the South, and soon John Surratt himself would volunteer his services, not as a soldier, but as a dispatch runner for the Confederate Secret Service.

Louis Weichmann, meanwhile, had taken a job as principal of a Catholic school in Washington, D.C., and very shortly thereafter he would renew his friendship with John Surratt. On April 2, 1863, Surratt and Weichmann decided

John Harrison Surratt was only twenty years old when he joined the conspiracy to abduct Abraham Lincoln. Among the conspirators, he was second in command only to John Wilkes Booth, but he later escaped conviction because his whereabouts on the night of the president's assassination could never be proven. Library of Congress

Louis Weichmann lived at the Surratt boardinghouse from the very beginning of the conspiracy and was a witness to much that transpired between Surratt and his fellow conspirators between November 1864 and April 1865. It was largely a result of his testimony before the Military Commission that Mary Surratt was sent to the gallows. Library of Congress

to pay a sentimental visit to St. Charles College to renew old friendships. Though neither knew it at the time, this trip, as innocuous as it appeared, would have far-reaching consequences for John Surratt. Once arrived there, they immediately met with a Father Dennis, who asked Weichmann if he would mind stopping in Little Texas, Maryland, on his way home and deliver a letter to a former student whom he had earlier taught at a college in Montreal. The young man's name was Henri Beaumont de Sainte Marie. He was a native of Montreal, but in 1863 he had decided to go South and join the Confederate army, booking passage aboard a blockade runner in New York with intentions of going to Wilmington, North Carolina. Unfortunately, off the coast of Maryland his ship was captured by a Federal warship and its crew interned at Ft. McHenry. However, thanks to the intervention of the British consul, Sainte Marie, a British subject, was released. He found a room in a Baltimore rooming house and employment on a farm near the city, where it was his duty to feed the cows and pigs. But news of this highly cultured and talented young man soon made the rounds, and he was hired to teach in the Catholic school in Little Texas. Soon Father Dennis became aware of his presence and thus asked that Weichmann deliver him the letter.

Weichman did as requested, delivering Father's Dennis's letter to Sainte Marie on April 3. He also introduced John Surratt to Sainte Marie. They spoke cordially, shook hands, and Surratt then bid both men goodbye since he had to return home immediately. It is unlikely that he spent more than five minutes in Sainte Marie's presence; yet that brief meeting would have nearly fatal consequences for John Surratt in years to come. When viewed in retrospect, it seems that the dark hand of fate was at work in this chance meeting between John Surratt and Henri Sainte Marie.

Sainte Marie, this adventurous young spirit, would suffer more than his share of misfortunes over the next four years. Indeed, just weeks after meeting with Surratt and Weichmann he would enlist in the Third Delaware Regiment, a Federal military unit, with intentions of again making his way southward. Once his unit was sent to the front, Sainte Marie deserted at the first opportunity. He hailed a group of Confederate soldiers and told them his story, but these battle weary Southerners listened to his tale with great skepticism. As a result, he was arrested and sent to Castle Thunder in Richmond as a spy. But as luck would have it, he soon learned of a plot by a group of Northern forgers in the prison and revealed that plot to

Confederate authorities. As a reward for his services, he was released and sent to Nassau in the Bahamas, where he took passage on a ship bound for England. From there he eventually managed to return to Montreal, where he was living at the time of the assassination.

The Charming Mary Jenkins Surratt

Meanwhile, the recently widowed Mary Surratt, in hopes of increasing her meager income, had leased her property in Surrattsville to a local resident, John M. Lloyd, for five hundred dollars a year and opened a boardinghouse at 541 H Street in Washington. On November 1, 1864, Louis Weichmann, who had met Mrs. Surratt on several previous occasions, took a room there. At that time there was also in residence a Miss Honora Fitzpatrick, a friend of Anna Surratt and a young lady of excellent reputation. There were also a Mr. John T. Holohan, a Washington tombstone cutter, and his wife and two children, as well as Apollonia Dean, a child of nine, who was boarded out by her mother.

The dwelling itself was a brick structure, three stories in height with an attic. There was a basement on a level with the pavement containing two large rooms, one used as a dining room and the other as a kitchen. On the second story were front and back parlors, the back parlor being used as a bedroom by Mrs. Surratt. A long flight of wooden steps ran from the pavement to the second story. The third floor contained three rooms, the two front ones occupied by Mr. Holohan and his family, the back one by Weichmann and John Surratt. In addition to the downstairs rooms, the attic contained two large rooms and a small one. One of these was occupied by Anna Surratt and Honora Fitzpatrick while the other one was vacant. The small room was occupied by the servant.

Mary Surratt, the mother of John Surratt and the first woman ever to be executed in America, was born in May 1823 in Waterloo, Maryland. In 1840, at the age of seventeen, she married John H. Surratt, a man eleven years her

The very handsome Mary Surratt at the age of forty-one in 1865. She became the first woman to be executed in America. It was in her boardinghouse that the real conspirators fre-quently met, but Mary Surratt was a sociable woman and naively welcomed her son's friends into her home. Courtesy the Surratt House Museum

senior. Over the next three years, living in a house her husband had inherited in Washington, she gave birth to three children: Isaac, Anna, and John, Jr. In 1851 the family decided to move to Maryland, where John built a combination house/tavern. Two years later John opened a post office at this location, and in 1853 the area became known officially as Surrattsville. That same year the prosperous John Surratt purchased a large house in Washington, which would eventually become Mrs. Surratt's boardinghouse.

For whatever reasons, Isaac, Mary's oldest son, moved to Texas in 1861, just prior to the outbreak of war, and later joined the Confederate army. A year later, following his escape from a Union prisoner-of-war camp, he fled to Matamoros, Mexico, and was living there at the time of the execution in 1865. (There is some evidence that Booth planned to escape to Matamoros following the execution.)

Sadly for the Surratts, John, Sr., died in August 1862 at the age of fifty. At that point, Mrs. Surratt, hoping to increase her meager income, opened her boardinghouse in Washington. As for her tavern, she leased that property to a local farmer named John M. Lloyd, a drunken lout infamous throughout the region for his frequent bouts with alcohol. It would be his highly suspect testimony that would later send Mary Surratt to the gallows.

By December 1864, John Surratt had been in the employ of the Confederate Secret Service for some time and was frequently absent from home. Louis Weichmann states that Mrs. Surratt's main reason for moving to Washington was to rescue her son from the dangers of working with the South. In Washington, he would be removed from the negative influences of their Maryland neighbors, many of whom were Southern sympathizers and underground agents. Plus, Washington was a thriving city with many opportunities for profitable employment. Thus Surratt's mother hoped her youngest child would no longer be tempted by the excitement and money of working for the Confederacy. To that end, on December 30 Surratt secured employment with the Adams Express Company. But it was a job that would not last long. It is obvious that he took the job only to make his mother happy.

According to Weichmann, the first meeting between John Surratt and Wilkes Booth occurred on December 23, 1864, though he was obviously mistaken about this date. It was about six o'clock in the evening, says Weichmann, just after dinner, and he and Surratt were standing in front of the boardinghouse engaged in pleasant conversation when they decided to take a stroll down Pennsylvania Avenue. They had just reached the Odd Fellows Hall when someone called Surratt by name. They turned around and there stood two men. One was an old friend of Surratt's from Charles County, Maryland, Dr. Samuel Mudd. The other man Weichmann did not recognize.

Surratt and Dr. Mudd warmly shook hands and Surratt then introduced Weichmann to Mudd. It was evident to Weichmann that Dr. Mudd, who stood just over six feet tall, was an educated man of refinement and culture, a true Southern gentleman. The man with him was much smaller in stature but obviously a man of the world and a gentleman. Dr. Mudd introduced his companion as "Mr. Boone," but this man was, in truth, John Wilkes Booth.

Booth then invited his three companions to join him for refreshments in his room, room 84, at the National Hotel. Once arrived there, they seated themselves comfortably about the room and were served milk punches and cigars. Following refreshments, Dr. Mudd stepped out into the hallway and called Booth out after him. They spoke quietly for some five minutes, then Dr. Mudd looked in and called Surratt out to join them. There followed more quiet conversation between the three men. A few minutes later Dr. Mudd returned to Weichmann and begged his forgiveness for leaving him alone, but he was trying to conduct some private business with "Boone," he said. He then revealed that Boone wanted to purchase some of his farm land in southern Maryland but they had not been able to agree on a price. Booth approached Weichmann, making the same apology and providing the same explanation.

Mary Surratt's boardinghouse at 541 H Street in Washington. Her husband originally had purchased this property in 1854, and Mary turned it into a boardinghouse in November 1864. A month later John Surratt met Wilkes Booth, and from then on Mrs. Surratt's boardinghouse became a headquarters for Booth and the other conspirators. Courtesy the Surratt House Museum

Then, according to Weichmann, who had obviously become a sore thumb at this meeting, Surratt, Booth, and Dr. Mudd grouped themselves around a small table in the middle of the room while he was left alone on a couch by a far window. They spoke very quietly and very intently, again excluding Weichmann from their conversation.

After about twenty minutes of such conversation, Dr. Mudd arose and invited everyone to accompany him to his room at the Pennsylvania House on C Street. Once they arrived, Dr. Mudd and Weichmann enjoyed a friendly chat on the settee by the window while Booth and Surratt engaged in an animated discussion over by the roaring fire in the hearth. Booth drew letters and photographs from his pockets and showed them to Surratt, who reacted by throwing his head back and laughing loudly. Weichmann was annoyed that he was excluded from their apparent merriment.

Around ten-thirty, Surratt and Weichmann took their leave of Booth and Dr. Mudd. On their way back to the boardinghouse, Surratt revealed to Weichmann that their new friend was the famous actor John Wilkes Booth and Booth was hoping to purchase a great deal of land from Dr. Mudd. He said that Booth wanted him to act as his agent in the transaction. A week later, when Weichmann told Mrs. Surratt that John planned to act as an agent for Booth in the purchase of Dr. Mudd's land, she angrily shook her head and retorted, "Oh, Dr. Mudd and the people of Charles County are getting tired of Booth and are pushing him off on John."

Still, from this point on, John Surratt would become Booth's chief ally and confidante. Indeed, in March 1865, when Arnold and O'Laughlin had taken upon Booth's orders rooms in Washington, Arnold would frequently complain that Booth would cancel meetings with the other conspirators because he was off with John Surratt. However, in an interview with John Surratt conducted by Hanson Hiss and published in the *Washington Post* on April 3, 1898, Surratt makes the following revealing, and somewhat contradictory, comments:

Ah! Wilkes Booth. I loathe him. In the first place, Wilkes Booth was never introduced to me by Dr. Mudd on the street or anywhere else. Booth came to me with a letter of introduction from a valued friend and trusted friend. In the second place, Weichmann was nowhere near when Booth presented his letter. I looked upon Booth as a hotheaded, visionary man, and the moment he broached his wild scheme to me of abducting Lincoln I simply laughed at him.

"It is utterly impracticable," I said to him.

"It is on that very account that I have come to you for your assistance, cooperation and advice," said Booth.

"And it's on that very account that I tell you that the idea is not feasible," I replied. "In the second place, you do not realize the danger."

"I don't consider that for a moment," said Booth.

"Nor I," I replied, "but it must be considered. After leaving Washington, provided we are able to leave with President Lincoln—which I doubt—we will have to drive over one hundred miles before we can cross the Potomac. After having crossed that in safety we will have to drive from one end of Midland Virginia to the other. Don't you know that that section is simply swarming with Yankees? I do, because I have just come through there. Granted that we do get through all right, we reach the Rappahannock, and cross it, we will be reasonably safe. But we stand about one chance in five hundred of surmounting all those obstacles. Inside of an hour, or, at most, two hours, from the time we get possession of Mr. Lincoln's person, the entire country will be in a furor. The President of the United States cannot be spirited away like an ordinary citizen."

Booth said he was willing to take any chance. I believe he was a monomaniac on the subject. He had brooded over the South's wrongs so much that his mind was unsettled on the subject. . . . No man in his right mind would have shot Lincoln. The South lost its best friend when it lost Lincoln.

No Turning Back

By November 1864 Booth's destiny was set. Following Lincoln's election to a second term as president, Booth gave up all hope that a peace agreement might be worked out between the North and the South. Such being the case, he became totally determined to capture the president at whatever the cost and hopefully strike a successful blow for the

Confederacy. But fearing that he might lose his life in the attempt or that people might misunderstand his noble motives, he wrote the following surprisingly erudite letter, placed it in a sealed envelope, and gave it to his brother-in-law John S. Clarke (the husband of Asia Booth), then living in Philadelphia, with directions that it should not be opened unless he (Booth) so directed.

To Whom It May Concern,

Right or wrong, God judge me, not man. For be my motive good or bad, of one thing I am sure, the lasting condemnation of the North.

I love peace more than life. Have loved the Union beyond expression. For four years I have waited, hoped and prayed for the dark clouds to break, and for the restoration of our former sunshine. To wait longer would be a crime. All hope for peace is dead. My prayers have proved as idle as my hopes. God's will be done. I go to see and share the bitter end.

I have ever held the South were right. The very nomination of Abraham Lincoln, four years ago, spoke plainly of war—war upon Southern rights and institutions. His election proved it. Await an overt act. Yes, til you are bound and plundered. What folly! The South was wise. Who thinks of argument or patience when the finger of his enemy presses on the trigger? In a foreign war, I too, could say, country right or wrong. But in a struggle such as ours where the brother tries to pierce the brother's heart, for God's sake, choose the right. When a country like this spurns justice from her side, she forfeits the allegiance of every honest free man, and should leave him untrammelled by any fealty [what]soever, to act as his own conscience may approve.

People of the North, to hate tyranny, to love liberty and justice, to strike at wrong and oppression, was the teaching of our fathers. The study of our early history will not let me forget it and may it never.

This country was formed for the white man and not for the black. And looking upon African slavery from the same stand-point as held by the noble framers of our Constitution, I, for one, have ever considered it one of the greatest blessings for themselves and for us that God ever bestowed upon a favored nation. Witness heretofore our wealth and power; witness their elevation and enlightenment above their race elsewhere. I have lived among it most of my life, and have seen less harsh treatment from master to man than I have beheld in the North from father to son. Yet heaven knows that no one would be more willing to do more for the negro race than I, could I but see a way to still better their condition.

But Lincoln's policy is only preparing the way to their total annihilation. The South are not nor have been fighting for the continuance of slavery. The first battle of Bull Run did away with that idea. The causes since for war have been as noble, and greater far than those that urged our fathers on. Even though we should allow that they were wrong at the beginning of this contest, cruelty and injustice have made the wrong become the right, and they now stand before the wonder and admiration of the world, as a noble band of patriotic heroes. Hereafter reading of their deeds, Thermopylae will be forgotten.

When I aided in the capture and execution of John Brown who was a murderer on our western border, who was fairly tried and convicted before an impartial judge and jury, of treason, and who by the way, has since been made a god, I was proud of my little share in the transaction, for I deemed it my duty, and that I was helping our common country to perform an act of justice. But what was a crime in poor John Brown is now considered by themselves as the greatest and only virtue of the Republican party. Strange transmigration. Vice is to become a virtue, simply because more indulge in it.

I thought then, as now, that the Abolitionists were the only traitors in the land, and that the entire party deserved the same fate as poor old Brown, not because they wish to abolish slavery, but on account of the means they have endeavored to use to effect that abolition. If Brown were living, I doubt whether he himself would set slavery against the Union. Most, or many in the North do, and openly curse the Union, if the South are to return and attain a single right guaranteed to them by every tie which we once revered as sacred. The South can make no choice. It is either extermination or slavery for themselves worse than death to draw from. I know my choice.

I have also studied hard to discover upon what grounds the right of a state to secede has been denied, when our name, United States and Declaration of Independence, both provide for secession. But this is no time for words. I write in haste. I know how foolish I shall be deemed for undertaking such a step as this, where on one side I have many friends and every thing to make me happy, where my profession alone has gained me an income of more than twenty thousand dollars a year, and where my great personal ambition in my profession has such a great field of labor. On the other hand the South have never bestowed upon me one kind word, a place where I have no friends except beneath the sod; a place where I must either become a private soldier or a begger [*sic*].

To give up all the former for the latter, besides my mother and sisters whom I love so dearly, although they differ so widely in opinion, seems insane; but God is my judge. I love justice more than a country that disowns it; more than fame and wealth; heaven pardon me, if wrong, more than a happy home. I have never been upon the battle field, but, O my countrymen, could all but see the reality of effects of this horrid war, as I have seen them in every state save Virginia, I know you would think like me, and would pray the Almighty to create in the Northern mind a sense of right and justice even should it possess no seasoning of mercy, and then he would dry up this sea of blood between us, which is daily growing wider. Alas, poor country, is she to meet her threatened doom? Four years ago I would have given a thousand lives to see her as I have always known her, powerful and unbroken. And even now I would hold my life as naught, to see her what she was. O, my friends, if the fearful scenes of the past four years had never been enacted or if what had been done were but a frightful dream from which we could now awake with over-flowing hearts, we could bless our God and pray for his continued favor. How I have loved the old flag can never be known.

A few years since the world could boast of none so pure and spotless. But of late I have been seeing and hearing of the bloody deeds of which she has been made the emblem, and would shudder to think how changed she has grown. Oh, how I have longed to see her break from the midst of blood and death that circles round her folds, spoiling her beauty and tarnishing her honor! But no; day by day she has been dragged deeper into cruelty and oppression, till now in my eyes her once bright red stripes look bloody gashes on the face of heaven.

I look now upon my early admiration of her glories as a dream. My love as things stand today is for the South alone. Nor do I deem it a dishonor in attempting to make for her a prisoner of this man to whom she owes so much misery. If success attends me, I go penniless to her side. They say she has found that last ditch which the North has so long derided and been endeavoring to force her in, forgetting they are our brothers, and it is impolitic to goad an enemy to madness. Should I reach her in safety and find it true, I will proudly beg permission to triumph or die in that same ditch by her side.

A Confederate doing duty on his own responsibility, John Wilkes Booth

Together on stage for the only time, the three Booth brothers—John Wilkes, Edwin, and Junius Booth, Jr.—performed Julius Caesar *in New York's Winter Garden on November 25, 1864. By this time Booth was deeply involved in the conspiracy to abduct the president.* Harvard Theater Collection, Harvard University

Clearly, in November 1864 Booth intended not to kill Lincoln but "to make for her a prisoner of this man to whom she owes so much misery." His plan from the very beginning had been to abduct Lincoln and take him South to be used as leverage to persuade the North to exchange prisoners of war. Indeed, Booth's decision to execute Lincoln appears to have taken place late on the afternoon of April 14. And what might have motivated him at that point? Perhaps the impetus for such an insane act was provided by a high-ranking government official, perhaps either Edwin Stanton or Andrew Johnson. At this point no one can know for certain.

(On the day following the assassination, John Clarke read Booth's foregoing letter and turned it over to authorities. He was arrested immediately.)

Enter David Edgar Herold

David Herold, according to his attorney at trial, was somewhat retarded, having the mind of a ten-year-old child. But such an assessment must have been simply a defensive ploy designed to mitigate his actions on the night of April 14. In fact, in 1860 Herold earned a certificate in pharmacy from Georgetown College, which would suggest that he was of at least average intelligence.

Born on June 16, 1842, he was the youngest of Adam and Mary Herold's ten children. Only twenty-two years old on the evening of April 14, Herold was another of Booth's "foolish and misguided boys." His family was well off financially and lived in a fine home at 636 Eighth Street, near the Washington Navy Yard. Herold's father, Adam Herold, was the chief clerk in the navy store at the Navy Yard for over twenty years. Herold's two older brothers died early and his father soon thereafter, leaving young "Davy" to be raised by an elderly mother and seven older sisters. Such being the case, he was spoiled and overindulged at every turn. He found refuge from the doting females in his life by escaping to the solitude of southern Maryland, where he could hunt and fish to his

David Edgar Herold, another of Booth's "misguided boys," was only twenty-two at the time of Lincoln's execution. Despite his attorney's claim that he had the mind of a ten-year-old child, he in fact held a certificate in pharmacy from Georgetown College. It was he who lost his nerve and abandoned Lewis Powell at Seward's residence on the evening of April 14, 1865. For his role in the conspiracy, he was hanged on July 7, 1865. Library of Congress

heart's content without fear of being reminded to do the "correct" thing. Herold was described as a "chatty" young man who talked endlessly of hunting and fishing, dogs and guns, a scatter-brained boy, but totally harmless. Having spent much of his youth hunting and fishing in southern Maryland, Herold knew the roads, streams, and rivers of that area as well as anyone, better than most. Thus he was of immense value to Booth in his conspiracy to abduct the president.

Oddly enough, in 1863, while employed at Thompson's Pharmacy in Washington, Herold once delivered a bottle of castor oil to President Lincoln at the White House. He would later recall how he had doubled over with laughter when the president looked at the price tag on the bottle, shook his head, and joked, "Can you charge this to the Federal Government?"

It is quite likely that Herold met John Surratt when both boys were enrolled at the Charlotte Hall Academy in Washington during the 1850s. And of course it was through Surratt that he was introduced to Wilkes Booth in December 1864. It has been recorded that Herold was in awe of Booth, one of the most well-known actors on the American stage at that time, and immediately became doggedly loyal to him. In time he would essentially sacrifice his own life to protect him.

Booth's Attempts to Recruit Others

As far as can be determined, by December 1864 Booth had successfully recruited Samuel Arnold, Michael O'Laughlin, and John Surratt, and through Suratt, George Atzerodt and David Herold (and perhaps Dr. Mudd). Still, since Lewis Thornton Powell had not yet arrived on the scene, he needed at least one or two more conspirators if he were to abduct the president as planned. To that end, he approached another old friend and fellow actor, Samuel Knapp Chester. According to Chester's later testimony before the Military Commission, Booth paid him a visit at his home at 45 Grove Street in New York City in late November.

Chester began their conversation by asking him why he was not acting at that time, and Booth replied that he did not plan to act again in the North, that he had in fact sent his wardrobe to a Patrick Charles Martin in Montreal (a Confederate Secret Service agent). He then informed Chester that he was involved in land speculation in lower Maryland and invited Chester to become a partner. But Chester sadly shook his head and replied that he lacked the funds to become involved in such a project.

At that point, recalled Chester, Booth suggested they go for a walk. They put on their hats and wool scarves to guard against the chill night air and departed Chester's home. After a frigid stroll of several blocks, they darted into a warm saloon, the House Of Lords, on Houston Street. They took a table, enjoyed a light dinner, and had a few drinks. They then braved the weather for two more blocks, down to the Revere House, another saloon, where they had more drinks. An hour or so later, they decided to take a sightseeing stroll up Broadway. It was during this walk that Booth said through chattering teeth that he wanted to tell Chester more about his land speculation. They ducked into another saloon.

It was then, said Chester, after seating themselves at a table by a roaring fire, that Booth revealed to him that he was involved "in a large conspiracy to capture the heads of the Government, including the President, and to take them to Richmond." In truth, said Booth, that was the land speculation he had mentioned earlier. Shocked beyond words, Chester told Booth that he could not possibly become part of such a conspiracy. Not only must he consider his own welfare, but that of his family as well. Booth shushed away his fears and pulling his wallet from a rear pocket, he told Chester that he would give him three thousand dollars immediately, which he could leave with his family if he would agree to become a part of the plot. Chester's role would be very simple, Booth said. The abduction was to take place at Ford's Theatre in Washington, and Chester had only to open the back door of the theater at a signal from Booth. Chester was acquainted with the theater, so his role would be both simple and natural, and he would run no risk to himself. He had only to open the back door. Plus he would be paid a great deal of money.

Chester, still frightened, silently shook his head. Booth, with obvious annoyance, then said, "You will at least not betray me. You dare not." He then informed Chester that he was a member of a large party of agents, and should Chester betray him, he would be hunted down and killed. Booth went on to tell Chester that there were a hundred other agents involved in the conspiracy and that Confederate forces would be waiting to assist in their escape once they crossed the Potomac into Virginia. Still, Chester shook his head. He could not become involved.

Some six weeks later, in early January, according to Chester, he received a letter from Booth containing a note for fifty dollars and saying that Chester must come to Washington immediately to further discuss the conspiracy. Again Chester refused.

In February, Booth again visited Chester in New York, and again they visited a bar where they had a few drinks. This time Booth informed him that he had attempted to recruit another old friend and actor, John Matthews, for the conspiracy, but Matthews was too terrified even to discuss the matter. Booth continued, saying Matthews was a coward and not fit to live. At that point Booth again urged Chester to become a part of the plot, telling him that should he do so, he would "never want for money as long as I lived." Indeed, said Booth, he intended to visit Richmond again in the near future and there he would secure the funding required for his project.

It should be noted that Chester's testimony mentions for the first time Booth's alternate scheme for abducting the president. Heretofore, Booth always spoke of waylaying Lincoln's carriage as he traveled to the Soldiers' Home. But for the first time he reveals his secret plan, his favorite plan, to abduct the president at Ford's Theatre. It must be remembered that Booth was an actor and harbored a deep affection for the dramatic.

Lewis Thornton Powell

From all that can be learned of Powell's background, he had grown up in a strict Christian home and later became one of the most outstanding young men ever to serve in the Confederate army, truly a hero among heroes. Most historians agree that he was by far the most fascinating character involved in the Lincoln conspiracy.

Born on April 22, 1844, to George Cader and Patience Caroline Powell, Lewis Thornton Powell was the youngest child in a family of ten children, with two older brothers and seven older sisters. When young Lewis was three, his father was ordained a Baptist minister, and the family moved from Randolph County, Alabama, to Stewart County, Georgia. Three years later, the family again moved, this time to Live Oak Station, Florida. He and his siblings were all educated at home by their father, a highly literate man, and their mother, who was also well educated for that era.

Having been raised in a religious home, young Lewis was described as a quiet, sensitive, and thoughtfully reserved boy who enjoyed reading and study. But his favorite pastimes, not surprisingly, were whittling and fishing. He was also an animal lover and made it his business to nurse back to health the sick and stray animals he found about the farm. As a result of his habit of caring for sick creatures, his sisters soon dubbed him "Doc," a nickname that stuck for the rest of his life among his family and friends. One of his sisters would later recall that he had been "a sweet, lovable, kind young boy" who was "pious and tender-hearted" and devoted to Sunday school, prayer meetings, and other religious activities. His father remembered that even as a young teenager, "Doc would hold prayer meetings and could speak with ease and force." He was very popular with everyone in the neighborhood, especially the ladies, both young and old, it was said.

Then, on May 30, 1861, at just sixteen years of age, the precocious Lewis Powell came home and casually announced to his dismayed parents that he had volunteered for the Confederate army and must soon report for duty. After a

Lewis Thornton Powell at the age of two in 1846, and his mother, Patience Caroline Powell. She was a well-educated woman for that era and worked endlessly with Lewis, the youngest of her ten children. Indeed, by the time he was twelve he was delivering sermons to his father's congregations. During the war he would become famous as "Lewis the Terrible," a man for whom death held no fear. Library of Congress

great deal of wailing and gnashing of teeth, his parents calmed down and bid him a tearful farewell. Initially, Powell was assigned to Captain Stuart's company of the Jasper Blues, which in time would become the Second Florida Infantry Regiment. Soon his regiment would be shipped off

Young Lewis Thornton "Doc" Powell as a handsome boy of twelve. He had delivered a sermon to his father's congregation just the day before, and his proud parents took him to town, bought him a gold watch, and had this photo taken. Library of Congress

to Virginia, attached to A. P. Hill's Corps, and would fight with distinction throughout the Peninsula Campaigns and then at Chancellorsville and Antietam.

In January 1863, Powell received the devastating news that his brother Oliver had been killed at Murfreesboro and his brother George badly wounded.

The following July, he marched with General Lee's dusty Confederate veterans into Gettysburg, Pennsylvania, and there, on July 2, he was wounded and taken prisoner. He was taken to Pennsylvania College, turned into a makeshift hospital, where he was soon up and around and helping look after the other wounded. There he met Miss Margaret Branson, a very attractive lady of thirty from Baltimore and an ardent secessionist, who had come to care for the Southern wounded. To her surprise, she found that all the patients by now, both Southern and Union, were referring to the assertive Powell as "Dr. Powell." Margaret informed Powell that her father operated a boardinghouse at 16 North Eutaw Street in Baltimore and that he was an agent for the Confederacy.

As luck would have it, on September 1, Powell was transferred to the Wests Building Hospital in Baltimore for further treatment, and of course Margaret Branson accompanied him there. A few days later she somehow slipped a Union uniform into the hospital. Within the hour she and Powell walked out the front door and made straightway for her father's boardinghouse. There she introduced him to her younger sister, Mary Branson, a beautiful young woman of twenty-eight. For the next two weeks, Mary, Margaret, and Powell happily whiled away their days sitting in the parlor, playing whist, drinking hot punch, and singing around the piano. (With seven older sisters, Powell doubtlessly delighted in the company of these young women.) But in early October, Powell, hearing the call of duty, bid the Branson sisters a tearful goodbye and began making his way southward towards Virginia.

Days later, now in northern Virginia, Powell was seen one warm afternoon casually strolling across the front yard of a large homestead known as Granville Tract. It was owned by

John Scott Payne, the uncle of Lewis Edmunds Payne, whose name Powell would adopt once he returned to Baltimore.

Lewis Payne, the son of a prominent Warrenton physician, would later become United States attorney for the state of Wyoming, but in 1863 he was a wide-eyed lad of only eleven. In the June 3, 1882, edition of the *Philadelphia Weekly Times*, Payne would recall his first sight of Powell: "He was wearing a ragged Confederate uniform. He was tall and well built, being particularly broad and robust about the chest and shoulders. He had one of those peculiar dark southern complexions, blue eyes, and dark hair." Lewis Payne then sat gazing silently at Powell, wondering what a boy of his age was doing in the Confederate army.

Following conversation and a wonderful dinner, Powell and the elder Payne's talk turned to the heroic ventures of Col. John Singleton Mosby and his Partisan Rangers (Company B, Forty-third Battalion, Virginia Cavalry), who were headquartered in Warrenton. John Scott Payne then told Powell that should he wish to join up with Mosby, he could take a room in the home of the Paynes.

To that end, the following day Powell did meet with Mosby, who personally selected members of his unit and did so with extreme care. He was impressed with Powell's physique, keen intellect, and fearless nature and immediately accepted him as one of his Partisan Rangers. It might be pointed out that Lewis Powell was a cousin to one of the oldest and most prominent families in Virginia. He was also a first cousin of Gen. John Brown Gordon, one of General Lee's most trusted lieutenants. Obviously his family connections might have helped him gain a place with Mosby. Powell's name appears on the role of Mosby's Rangers for the first time on October 1, 1863. He was nineteen years old.

The fearless Powell fit right in with this celebrated band of soldiers, and soon he became famous with both Union and Confederate troops as "Lewis the Terrible" Powell, a name he came by honestly. Mosby himself would later recall that his most outstanding Rangers were Syd Ferguson, Sam Alexander, Cab Maddox, Walter Gosden (the father of Freeman

Lewis Thornton Powell, a former member of Mosby's Partisan Rangers and an active member of the Confederate Secret Service, is pictured here in handcuffs and leg irons, still dressed in the navy uniform he was issued the night he was arrested. His father was a Baptist minister, and Powell himself neither drank, smoked, nor used profanity. When he was hanged on July 7, 1865, he had just turned twenty-one.
Library of Congress

Gosden, who would later gain fame as "Amos" on the nationally popular *Amos and Andy Show*), and Lewis Powell.

There was also a warmer, more human side to Powell's personality. John Scott Payne would later write that Lewis Powell was "a chivalrous, generous, gallant fellow, and particularly fond of children. Rarely would he visit Warrenton that he did not bring them some little thing. Often he would be seen in the streets of Warrenton with one of the Payne youngsters perched on the saddle in front of him on his horse."

John Scott Payne had a niece, Miss Betty Meredith, and soon she and Powell were in love. But in the final month of 1864, when his time with Mosby had come to an end and he was being dispatched to Baltimore to aid in the abduction of the president, he was forced to bid her goodbye. He left with her a photograph of himself and his personal diary. What happened to that priceless photograph no one today remembers, but Lewis Edmunds Payne did save the diary. He quoted one passage: "In battle, in the fullness of pride and strength, little recks [reckons] the soldier whether the hissing bullet sings his sudden requiem or the cords of life are severed by the sharp steel." Despite the Military Commission's later efforts to portray Powell as an ill-bred, semiliterate monster, he was no backwoods ignoramus, as proven by the above lines.

In December 1864, Colonel Mosby sent five of his Rangers, including Powell, to Richmond under mysterious circumstances. The Secret Service had carefully selected these men to assist Wilkes Booth in the abduction of the president. In later years Lewis Edmunds Payne would recall:

> After leaving Richmond, Powell would return to Warrenton a changed man. He seemed to be more grave and thoughtful than ever. He often spoke of his visit to Richmond and his intention soon to go to Baltimore to meet friends he had met in Richmond. He soon began to sell off his horses and dispose of his effects, saying he would be gone for several months on his Maryland expedition.

Once Powell began working for the Secret Service, it made perfect sense for him to assume the alias "Lewis Payne" since the Paynes were a well-known family throughout northern Virginia. After living with them for months, he could answer any questions about them if he were to be captured. Plus there exists the possibility that Powell also wished to protect his own family should he ever be executed for his efforts on behalf of the Secret Service. Powell did a masterful job of hiding his true identity. Throughout his trial he was known as Payne, and he finally went to the gallows on July 7 not as Lewis Powell but as Lewis Payne.

Upon his departure to begin work for the Secret Service, he sold his horse and caught a train for a Federal encampment in Alexandria, where he took an oath of allegiance to the United States government and requested that he receive protection as a civilian refugee. Now he was free to travel throughout the North without fear of capture.

Sleet was falling in Baltimore on that raw day in January 1865 when a frozen Powell eagerly knocked on the door of the Branson's boardinghouse. Reunited, he and Mary Branson embraced warmly, and he told her he would like to take a room there for several weeks. At his request, the Branson sisters introduced him to others as "Mr. Payne from Frederick County, Maryland."

The Branson sisters introduced him to a friend of their father, a Mr. David Preston Parr, owner of an exclusive china shop at 1211 Baltimore Street and a devoted Confederate secret agent. It was through Parr that he met John Surratt, who brought him money from Booth. Soon Powell would meet Booth himself.

At this point, Booth was beginning to feel much better about his recruitment efforts. By now he had recruited John Surratt and David Herold, men who were thoroughly familiar with the geography of lower Maryland and with every road leading from Washington to the Potomac River. And there was George Atzerodt, an expert boatman, who was thoroughly familiar with the Potomac and Rappahannock Rivers and had much experience in ferrying parties across the river from Port Tobacco to the Virginia shore. As for Arnold and O'Laughlin, both were former

The Reverend George Cader Powell, the father of Lewis Powell, was a gentleman farmer and educator, who was also related to one of Virginia's most prominent families. In 1871, the Reverend Powell, accompanied by his son George, would journey to Washington to claim his son's remains and have them interred in a grave next to that of his mother in Live Oak, Florida. Library of Congress

Confederate soldiers accustomed to handling firearms and were well-built, muscular men. With Lewis Powell, Booth was at last ready to make a move.

Booth visited Baltimore on January 10 and called for O'Laughlin and Arnold to again meet with him in his hotel room. This time he showed them a large trunk. Curious as to its contents, Arnold lifted the lid and beheld a number of deadly weapons. At Booth's bidding, he lifted out two Spencer repeating rifles, six Colt .44 revolvers, six bowie knives, canteens, handcuffs, and other items. A smiling Booth then informed him that these were the weapons they might need in their flight from Washington with the president.

Booth also informed his old friends that he had just purchased a horse, a set of harnesses, and a buggy, which he would leave with them to drive to Washington. In fact, they were to leave immediately. Both men then protested that they could not leave without informing their parents that they would be out of town for a few days. Booth paused thoughtfully for a moment then agreed reluctantly that they should indeed inform their parents of their whereabouts.

Because of the trunk's great weight, they shipped it by train to Washington while Arnold and O'Laughlin departed in the buggy. As luck would have it, both the trunk and the conspirators arrived in Washington at about the same time that evening. They picked up the trunk then drove immediately to Ford's Theatre, where they met Booth. He led them to a nearby restaurant, and there, over a bottle of brandy, he explained his alternate plan to abduct the president at Ford's Theatre should his plan to abduct Lincoln on his way to the Soldiers' Home fail. Thoroughly enjoying their new prosperity, Arnold and O'Laughlin were skeptical of such a radical idea, but they kept their reservations to themselves— at least for the moment. After all, this was Booth's show; they were merely supporting actors.

Following more drinks and a dinner of roasted oysters, Booth drove them back to Ford's Theatre. To demonstrate the feasibility of capturing the president at the theater, he showed them the president's box and all the rear exits.

By the time Booth had completed his demonstration, Arnold and O'Laughlin had to admit that this alternate plan really was not that bizarre. He also told them that he had just purchased two fast horses,which they would use in their escape.

Both Arnold and O'Laughin felt a mixture of excitement and anxiety. They wished Booth could be more definite concerning a time and date for this adventure, but in Arnold's later confession he would bitterly complain that Booth seemed to have little time for his old friends from Baltimore. Rather, he spent most of his time with a man unknown to them at that time, John Surratt. After two days of high living in Washington, Arnold and O'Laughlin returned home to await further orders from Booth.

John Surratt, meanwhile, doubtlessly at his mother's request, secured employment on December 30 as a clerk at Adams Express Company in Washington. But on January 13 he applied for a leave of absence, stating that his mother was going down to Prince Georges County and he felt obligated to accompany her as her protector. His employer replied that such a request could not be granted. Subsequently, Surratt left his office and never returned, not even to pick up the pay due him for two weeks of service.

Later testimony revealed that the cause of this flurry of activity on the part of Booth and his conspirators was an article that appeared in a Washington newspapers announcing that President Lincoln would attend a performance of *Jack Cade* at Ford's Theatre on Wednesday evening, January 18. This explains why John Surratt was forced to go to his superior, Mr. Dunn, at the Adams Express Company on January 13 and request a leave of absence: he would soon be busy abducting the president of the United States. When Mr. Dunn said no, Surratt had no choice but to quit. He then galloped down to Port Tobacco to meet with George Atzerodt.

In later years it would come to light that Atzerodt did manage to purchase the sort of flatboat needed for the abduction from Richard Mitchell Smoot, a Port Tobacco planter and an active agent of the Confederate Secret Service.

According to the testimony of one Eddie Martin at Surratt's trial in 1867, in mid-January he had already been in Port Tobacco for several days waiting for Atzerodt to ferry him across the river but Atzerodt kept delaying his departure. Finally on January 18 an angry Martin confronted Atzerodt and accused him of lying to him. Atzerodt shrugged apologetically and confessed that he had been hired by ten or twelve others to take them across the river that very evening. They had already bought a boat, said Atzerodt, and had relays of horses stationed between Washington and Port Tobacco and had already paid him to take them across. Eddie Martin, therefore, would just have to wait another day.

President Lincoln's appearance at Ford's Theatre on the evening of January 18 was a situation ready-made for Booth's abduction plans. Immediately he put his conspirators on notice and began issuing very definite orders. David Herold was dispatched to Prince Georges County to rent a team of horses. He was to wait with these steeds on the southern bank of the Anacostia River at a point near the Navy Yard Bridge. John Surratt was sent to Port Tobacco to have Atzerodt secure a flatboat that could hold a carriage and fifteen men. Booth also wired Arnold and O'Laughlin to return to Washington immediately. Their services would be essential.

January 18 was the date that would win the war for the Confederacy. Richmond was standing by, awaiting the miracle. Soon, Booth and his band would be hailed as heroes throughout the South. Confederate agents had been alerted throughout southern Maryland, as far away as Piscataway, Pope's Creek, Allen's Fresh, and Mathias Point. It was said that Mosby's Rangers would be standing by to distract any pursuing Union cavalry foolish enough to venture into Mosby's Confederacy.

But then came the inevitable hitch. Arnold and O'Laughlin, still celebrating with money Booth had recently sent them, failed to report for duty. Booth was livid with rage. Now, short two men, he stood totally alone on this night of all nights. However, he was determined to push on.

He sent a message for Surratt to race back to Washington as quickly as possible.

Late that afternoon Surratt reported to Booth's room at the National Hotel. Booth's plan, by necessity, was very simple. He had already arranged with a stagehand at Ford's Theatre (possibly Edman Spangler) to turn off the theater lights at a given cue. Then he and Surratt would hustle the president, who would be alone in his box, over the railing and down to the stage and out a rear exit. A buggy with side curtains would be stationed in the alley behind the theater.

By eight o'clock that evening, January 18, all was in readiness. Booth and Surratt, acting alone now, with no help from anyone else, would execute the most daring plan in the history of the Western world. Their excitement as seven o'clock approached was at a fever pitch. They could not fail. They must not fail. The future of the Confederacy depended on their success, and their names would go down in history.

But by the time they approached the theater that evening, the temperature had dropped below freezing. Sleet and a freezing rain had begun to fall, and a thick fog covered most of the city. His teeth fairly chattered as Booth asked the ticket manager at Ford's for two tickets. As the ticket manager passed Booth his tickets, he casually remarked that he had just received word that the president had canceled his plans to attend the theater that evening because of the inclement weather. Without a word, Booth turned and looked at Surratt. Surratt shrugged his shoulders and rolled his eyes. The two saviors of the South did an about-face and silently sloshed their way back through the sleet and frozen rain to the National Hotel. Fame and fortune would just have to wait another day.

With such an outcome how would Booth answer the questions of all those rabid partisans waiting in southern Maryland? And certainly agents in Richmond, Washington, New York, and Montreal would also be aware of his failure. Rather than a hero, he could quickly become a target for ridicule, the butt of jokes.

Lewis Thornton Powell in 1860, just a few months before he joined the Confederate army. At this time he was a gangly lad of sixteen, who stood 6 feet and weighed in at 140 pounds. By 1865 he stood 6 foot 2 inches and his weight was up to 220 pounds. In late 1864, because of his intelligence and fearless nature, the Confederate Secret Service selected him to assist Booth in the abduction of President Lincoln. Library of Congress

The following morning he was off to Baltimore to confront Arnold and O'Laughlin. Both loudly swore that they certainly were not guilty of negligence. Indeed, they said, raising their right hands, they had never even received Booth's telegram ordering their appearance in Washington. Had they only known, they would certainly have been there. Besides, Lincoln had failed to attend the play, so what difference did it make? They would get him next time. They also wondered if Booth could perhaps give them a small advance on their salary. Placated, smiling now that the fearless boys of his merry band were once again together, Booth slapped both men on the back and drew some American bills from his pocket. Arnold and O'Laughlin, pictures of humble gratitude, accepted the cash without comment.

On January 21, Surratt, accompanied by a babbling Louis Weichmann, took the train to Baltimore. Upon their arrival, they took a room in the Maltby House, where Surratt revealed to Weichmann that he was carrying three hundred dollars in gold from the Confederate government, and he must immediately see an unidentified gentleman on private business. The inquisitive Weichmann, typically enough, was terribly annoyed that Surratt refused to reveal to him the name of the gentleman or the nature of their business. Weichmann pouted for the rest of the evening.

By this time, late January, Lewis Thornton Powell, now using the alias Lewis Payne, had taken a room at the boardinghouse of his old friend and ally, the very handsome Miss Margaret Branson, on Eutaw Street. When he was not enjoying the company of the beautiful Branson sisters, Powell was frequently meeting with David Preston Parr, owner of Parr's China Hall at 1211 Baltimore Street. On the surface this gentleman, with his very expensive goods and his large upper-class clientele, was the ultimate in good breeding and respectability, a most patriotic Unionist who never failed to raise the Stars and Stripes by his front door each morning. But today it is known that his china shop was merely a front for his real occupation, serving as a spy for the Confederate States of America, his shop nothing more that a clandestine meeting place for other Southern agents in the area.

When he left Weichmann, Surratt made straight for Parr's China Hall, and there for the first time, on January 22, 1865, he met Lewis Thornton Powell. He gave Powell the money Booth had sent and made arrangements for Powell to meet with Booth the following week.

Powell was just what Booth's team needed. Physically powerful, unusually intelligent, and totally fearless, Powell was truly the missing element that Booth had searched for. Over the past three years he had fought on numerous battlefields throughout northern Virginia, was wounded, and captured at Gettysburg. Then, having escaped from a Federal hospital, he had been hand chosen to serve with Mosby's Rangers, a great distinction in itself. Truly, death held no fear for the stoic Powell.

Booth and Powell met for the first time in late January at Barnum's Hotel in Baltimore, where a very pleased Booth treated his star recruit to a sumptuous meal. While Powell wolfed down an entire fried chicken, Booth explained the conspiracy and Powell's role in it in some detail. As he spoke, Booth apprehensively observed Powell's every facial expression. He then very pointedly asked Powell's reaction to the plan. Powell looked up from his plate, gave Booth an approving little smile, and said he would not miss it for the world. It was just the sort of adventure he had joined the army for. Ecstatic at this response, Booth took Powell on a shopping extravaganza, buying him several new suits of clothes and giving him more cash.

From that point on, aware that Booth was now his commanding officer, Powell always referred to him as "Cap'n." Second only to John Surratt, Lewis Powell immediately became Booth's most trusted lieutenant, and Booth would make arrangements for him to stay at the Herndon House when he visited Washington, passing himself off as the Reverend Lewis Payne.

George Atzerodt, A Man in the Wrong Place at the Wrong Time

Several days following his return to Washington from Baltimore, Louis Weichmann came home to Mrs. Surratt's boardinghouse late one afternoon to find a stranger in the sitting room. Surratt immediately introduced the stranger to Weichmann as George Atzerodt. Mrs. Surratt, her daughter Anna, and her niece Miss Fitzpatrick were all there, listening to the humorous ramblings of their German guest. The ladies could not (or pretended they could not) pronounce Atzerodt's name, and, aware that he came from Port Tobacco, began to jokingly refer to him as Port Tobacco. The name stuck, and soon his fellow conspirators were calling him Port Tobacco as well.

In retrospect, it is possible that George Atzerodt remains one of the most innocent citizens ever to be executed in this nation. His role in the conspiracy simply was to row Booth and the others across the Potomac River should they ever abduct the president. This he promised to do not for patriotic reasons but for the few dollars that Booth tossed him on occasion to maintain his loyalty.

He had been born on June 12, 1835, in Dorna, Prussia. In 1844, at the age of eight, he came to America with his parents and settled in Germantown, Maryland. He never became an American citizen. In 1857 Atzerodt's father died, and he moved to Port Tobacco with his older brother, John, where they opened a carriage repair shop. The shop seemed to prosper, but for reasons known only to himself, John decided to move to Baltimore, leaving George alone in Port Tobacco.

Once the war broke out, Atzerodt, who felt allegiance to neither the North nor the South, began making extra money by rowing escaped Confederate soldiers, Secret Service agents, and blockade runners back and forth across the Potomac. One such Secret Service agent was Thomas H. Harbin, a resident of Surrattsville, who in January 1865 introduced Atzerodt to John Surratt. Surratt was deeply impressed with Atzerodt's knowledge of the back roads and escape routes out of Maryland, as well as his proven ability to ferry heavy loads across the river, and thus signed him on as a fellow conspirator. Shortly thereafter Surratt invited Atzerodt to Washington to meet John Wilkes Booth. Surratt also invited him (rather foolishly as it turned out) to spend several nights in an attic room at his mother's boardinghouse.

George Atzerodt, a German citizen, felt no special allegiance to either the North or the South, but became semi-involved in the conspiracy simply for the little money he could make. He was executed on July 7 and buried in St. Paul's Cemetery in Baltimore under the alias Gottlieb Taubert. Library of Congress

Azterodt was a man of swarthy complexion with eyes of a greenish hue. His figure was low and squat and his head badly shaped. Those unfortunate features, combined with his strong German accent, made him a man not easily forgotten. Despite his lack of education and refinement, he was described as a man full of fun, country humor, and quaint stories and not an unpleasant companion.

Mary Surratt, unfortunately, was not in the least amused by George Atzerodt. She was put off by his scruffy appearance and his inability to speak English, but, as she heatedly explained to her son, John, the major point of contention was Atzerodt's weakness for alcohol. She had smelled whiskey on his breath, she said, and had found several bottles of whiskey in his room. "Tell him he must go," Mrs. Surratt ordered. That was the end of George Atzerodt's relationship with Mary Surratt. He subsequently took a room at the Kimmel house, which was more in keeping with his station in life.

On January 25 Booth brought the one-eyed mare he had purchased from George Gardiner in Bryantown to the stable of William E. Cleaver on Sixth Street near Maryland Avenue. Then, on February 9, he brought another horse, a light bay, to the same stable. From that point on, Booth and Surratt were frequent visitors to the stable, Booth paying for the horses' keep there. Booth visited the stable on January 28 in the company of Samuel Arnold and told the stable keeper that he had sold the horse to Arnold and that Arnold would be paying for his keep in the future. Arnold then paid for the horses until February 8, and at that time they were moved to Howard's Livery Stable on G Street, almost in the rear of Mrs. Surratt's boardinghouse, where they remained until March 31.

February 1865

It was in early February that John Surratt paid a visit to E. I. Smoot of Charles County, Maryland, just a few miles from Surrattsville. The two had known each other for years and were old friends despite Smoot's Union sympathies. Smoot would later testify at Surratt's trial that on this occasion Surratt spent the night in his home, and Smoot began to joke with his visitor about his clandestine trips to Richmond. In response, Surratt laughed good-naturedly, drew his finger across his neck, and said, "If the Yankees knew what I have done or what I am doing, they would stretch this old neck of mine." Truer words were never spoken.

Upon his return to Washington, Surratt immediately took the train for New York to pay a visit with Wilkes Booth, who had departed Washington on January 28. Once arrived at the magnificent home of the Booth family, Surratt was welcomed by Wilkes with open arms then introduced to his mother, Mary Ann Booth, and to his brother Edwin. The Booths were the very pictures of hospitality. They treated Surratt to a fine dinner and insisted that he spend the night in their plush guest room. It was an experience that the young and impressionable Surratt would recall with pride for the rest of his days.

Around this time, according to Louis Weichmann, Surratt was continually on the go and away from home, much to his mother's distress. Oddly enough, he seemed to always have more money than he could spend, so he kept making excuses when his mother would hopefully suggest that he search for employment. Much of the time he walked around with knitted brow, as though preoccupied with weighty matters, matters that he refused to discuss with Weichmann, much to his old chum's annoyance.

On the afternoon of February 10, Arnold and O'Laughlin arrived in Washington and secured lodging at the house of Mrs. Mary T. Van Tine at 420 D Street. Booth called on them frequently when not in the company of John Surratt. If they were not in, Booth would leave a note asking that they meet him at the stable behind the theater. Once, Mrs. Van Tine would later recall, they met with Booth and then the three of them were out all night. On another occasion, said Mrs. Van Tine, she went in to clean their room and found a big bowie knife and several revolvers left on their bed. When queried about their business, they cleverly replied that they were in the "oil business."

It was in the latter part of February that Lewis Powell first put in an appearance at Mrs. Surratt's boardinghouse. According to Weichmann, it was rather late in the evening, just after dinner, with himself, Mrs. Surratt, Anna, and Honora Fitzpatrick all gathered in the parlor for an evening of piano playing and song when there came a knock at the front door. Weichmann answered the knock and there stood the young giant, Lewis Powell. He was wearing a dark felt hat and a seedy black overcoat. It was brutally cold outside, and his hands were buried deep in his overcoat pockets. He asked if this were the home of John Surratt and if he were at home. Weichmann, unnerved by the unusual appearance of the visitor, stuttered that this was indeed the home of John Surratt, but he was not in. Powell then asked if he might speak with Mr. Surratt's mother. My name, said Powell, is Mr. Wood.

At that point Weichmann ushered Powell into the parlor and introduced him to the ladies as Mr. Wood. Powell politely removed his hat and spoke very cordially to the ladies. He was a very handsome young man of twenty at this time, and Anna and Honora Fitzpatrick seemed to be in absolute awe of him. He gave them a friendly nod, smiled, then approached Mrs. Surratt, seated on the couch across the room, and spoke to her so quietly that Weichmann could not make out his words, though he strained to hear. A few moments later Mrs. Surratt called to Weichmann and informed him that Mr. Wood would like supper, but since her dining room had been closed for the day, she would be most appreciative if Weichmann would prepare Wood a plate and take it to him in his own bedroom.

Weichmann immediately did as requested, he says, taking Wood enough food for two men. Then he propped up on his bed and stared unabashedly while Wood sat in a hard chair at a small table eating voraciously. Weichmann would later observe, "He had the eye of an eagle and was very self-possessed." To Weichmann's endless questions, Powell mumbled only that he was from Baltimore and worked as a clerk in a china shop. He said nothing else but continued to devour his food as though he had not eaten all day. When he had finished, he washed his face and hands in a large porcelain bowl, thanked Weichmann for his troubles, then walked downstairs and asked Mrs. Surratt if he could retire for the night. She directed him to a bedroom in the attic, and Mr. Wood bade her and the two awed young ladies good night. When Weichmann awakened the next morning, Powell had already departed the house. He would not reappear for several weeks.

In his magazine article "Conspiracy Against Lincoln," in the February 1911 issue of *Magazine of History*, Capt. D. H. Gleason, an officer in the Commissary of Prisoners and Louis Weichmann's immediate superior, wrote that on February 20, 1865, Weichmann reported to him in a state of extreme excitement. It seems that over the past two months he had observed a series of strange happenings and even stranger individuals at the boardinghouse of Mrs. Mary Surratt. He did not know what these fellows were up to, he told Gleason, but it was obvious something was afoot. Besides, he added as a happy afterthought, they were all Confederate sympathizers—of that he was sure. Reported Weichmann, it could be that they were planning to kidnap or even assassinate the president. Gleason, aware of Weichmann's annoyingly inquisitive nature and his nose for sensational news, listened patiently to his story then urged him to report any further suspicious activities. Gleason was dubious of Weichmann's story, but as a precaution, he reported the matter to the War Department, along with the names of those allegedly involved in this possible conspiracy. It can be assumed, therefore, that as early as February 20 both Edwin Stanton and Lafayette Baker were aware of a possible plot against the president, as well as the names of those involved in that plot. This information could prove of vital importance to them later.

Indeed, on April 17, once Weichmann had been arrested and charged with aiding Booth in the assassination plot, it was this brief report to Captain Gleason, combined with his other damning testimony, that would save him from the gallows.

As verification that Stanton and Baker were already aware of the identities of those in conspiracy against the president, note that both Samuel Arnold and Michael O'Laughlin were arrested on April 17. (Arnold was then working at Fortress Monroe, Virginia). The question is, just how could Lafayette Baker's National Detectives move so quickly? How did they know who to look for and where to look for them? Weeks later Baker would offer a lame explanation, stating to the press that when his agents examined the contents of Booth's trunk at the National Hotel on the morning following the assassination, they found a letter from Samuel Arnold to Booth in which Arnold mentioned the names of the various conspirators. But this letter, as all historians know, was signed simply "Sam" and has always been referred to as the "Sam letter." Since there are a great many Sams in Maryland, Virginia, and Washington, Baker must have had better, more definite, leads to follow. The answer to this puzzle seems obvious: Baker's information was based on Louis Weichmann's report of February 20 to Captain Gleason, which listed the names of all the conspirators. Apparently Baker's men had been keeping watch on these individuals since February 20.

On February 22 John Surratt appeared outside his mother's boardinghouse driving a carriage in which sat an unusually handsome young lady. Mrs. Surratt called Weichmann from his seat in the sitting room to bring in the lady's small trunk, which he eagerly did. Weichmann noted that she was a rather small but sprightly lady in her late twenties, wearing a dark veil that covered her face down to her chin. She was Sarah Antoinette Slater, a North Carolinian, who became infamous with the Federal government during the war for her work delivering secret dispatches between Richmond and Montreal for the Confederate Secret Service. And she and Surratt were the best of friends.

That evening the mysterious Mrs. Slater had a long conversation with an oddly familiar "Mr. Spencer" on the sidewalk outside the boardinghouse. Soon the two of them came inside and Weichmann remembered then that Mr. Spencer had boarded with Mrs. Surratt for two days earlier in the month.

Apparently he had timed his arrival to coincide with that of Mrs. Slater. The entire situation struck Weichmann as highly suspicious. Thus he immediately made it his business to learn all he could about this Mr. Spencer. His real name, as it turned out, was Augustus Howell, and he was already well known to the Federal government for his clandestine operations on behalf of the Confederate Secret Service. Like so many Confederate agents, he was a native of Prince Georges County, Maryland, and had known the Surratts for many years.

The following morning he would escort Sarah Slater on to Richmond. A month later, on March 24, Howell would be arrested by Federal authorities and jailed as a spy at the Old Capitol Prison. This turned out to be the most fortunate misfortune of his life, as he was still there on the evening of April 14. He was eventually released for lack of evidence. Doubtlessly Weichmann reported the suspicious meeting between Mrs. Slater and Howell to Captain Gleason, who then passed the information on to the War Department.

March, a Critical Month in the Conspiracy

It was now March 3, 1865, and the North was all abuzz concerning Lincoln's inauguration, slated for the very next afternoon. For days now dozens of bands had been on hand playing lively patriotic music, and thousands of soldiers and officers dressed in colorful uniforms had been parading through the streets. Politicians of every rank and description had been standing up and making speeches wherever they could find an audience. Everyone, it seemed, wanted to be a part of what promised to be a memorable experience in the history of the United States: Lincoln's being sworn in for his second term in office on March 4, 1865.

The morning of the fourth dawned cold and wet with a heavy rain falling throughout the city. The rain stopped around eleven o'clock that morning, but the streets and roads were still a muddy mess, making it difficult for the inaugural procession to make it to the Capitol.

It was that morning that a most unfortunate and unforgettable incident occurred in the capital. While Lincoln was in the president's room signing the final bills of that session of Congress, the new vice president, Andrew Johnson, was across the hall in the vice president's room. He was welcomed by Hannibal Hamlin, the retiring vice president. Ben P. Poore, a journalist from New York, would report:

> The usual courtesies being exchanged, Mr. Johnson asked Mr. Hamlin if he had any liquor in his room, stating that he was sick and nervous. He was told that there was none, but it could be sent for. Brandy being indicated, a bottle was brought from the Senate restaurant by one of the pages.

Poore says that the liquor arrived, and Johnson quickly downed three tumblers of straight brandy. These had an immediate effect. When escorted to the Senate Chamber to take the oath of office, Johnson "was staggering." Then, to the surprise of everyone, Johnson

> insisted on making a maudlin, drunken speech. Republican senators were horror-stricken, and Colonel Forney vainly endeavored to make him conclude the harangue; but he would not be stopped; the brandy had made him crazily drunk, and the mortifying scene was prolonged until he was told that it was necessary to go with the President to the eastern front of the Capitol.

Johnson's performance that morning was so wretched he could never live it down. Even cordial Abe Lincoln snubbed him whenever possible.

Among the spectators present for the inauguration that day were Wilkes Booth and several of his conspirators. Thanks to his fiancée, Lucy Hale, the daughter of Sen. John P. Hale of New Hampshire, Booth had received a special pass that allowed him to take a place on the grandstand, where all the dignitaries sat, just to Lincoln's rear. Several of his conspirators, meanwhile, were standing just below the grandstand. Despite some historians' claims that Booth planned to assassinate Lincoln on this occasion, there is no indication that such was the case. Booth's own words to fellow actor Samuel Knapp Chester on April 7 would seem to refute such a surmise. He told Chester, "What an elegant chance I had to kill the President on inauguration day if I had wished." Obviously he did not wish—not at that point.

On March 12 Booth's plans almost came crashing down when Powell, now returned to Baltimore, was arrested by city detectives and charged with being a spy. Fortunately, he was released two days later for a lack of evidence, though he was required to sign another oath of allegiance. Then, as a happy afterthought, the provost marshal took a pencil and wrote on the oath that Powell (Lewis Payne) was hereby required to move to Philadelphia for the duration of the war. A relieved Powell then returned to the Branson boarding-house, borrowed a pencil from Mary Branson, and simply erased the note stating that he was required to move to Philadelphia. He then visited Parr's China Shop to see if he had received any messages since his arrest. Sure enough, there was a telegram awaiting him from John Surratt:

Preston Parr
210 W. Baltimore St., Baltimore, Md., March 13, 1865, 11:40 A.M.

Immediately telegraph if my friend is disengaged and can see me this evening in Washington.

(Signed) Harrison Surratt
541 H Street, Washington

Parr then asked Powell if he had a reply. Powell nodded and said, "Yes, will you telegraph him for me and say, 'She will be over this afternoon?'"

Thus Parr dispatched the following telegram to John Surratt:

Harrison Surratt
541 H Street, Washington, D. C., March 13, 1865

She will be over in the six P.M. train.

President Lincoln's Second Inaugural Address on March 4, 1865. In this photo Lincoln is seated just to the left of the little white lectern waiting to take his oath of office. Booth is standing behind the railing at top, just in front of the marble statue. His fellow conspirators are standing below the president. Lewis Powell is wearing the Western hat. National Archives

In this remarkable close-up of Lincoln's second inauguration, Booth can plainly be seen in his high silk top hat on the balcony above the stand from which Lincoln is speaking. The heavyset man with a beard standing in front of Booth and to his right is John T. Ford, owner of Ford's Theatre. National Archives

Powell returned to the Bransons, packed up his carpetbag, bid the Branson girls a tearful goodbye, and departed Baltimore for Washington.

Also on March 13, Booth himself sent a telegram to Michael O'Laughlin in Baltimore: "Don't fear to neglect your business; you had better come at once." Then he contacted the other members of his band and gave them instructions to meet with him in Washington on the following day. They were given no reason for the urgency, though they would soon find out. On March 14 Atzerodt drifted in from Port Tobacco. Arnold and O'Laughlin came from Baltimore.

March 14 also marked the reappearance of Lewis Thornton Powell at Mrs. Surratt's boardinghouse. As luck would have it, Louis Weichmann was again present when Powell rang Mrs. Surratt's doorbell. The scenario proceeded very much as it had on Powell's first visit. Weichmann answered the bell and Powell introduced himself, somewhat carelessly, under his latest alias, Lewis Payne. Oddly enough, Weichmann says that he did not recognize Powell on this occasion. Perhaps Weichmann's confusion was the result of Powell's attire. He had appeared rather scruffy on his first visit, but today he was wearing a new gray suit of a soft wool material, a starched white shirt, and a black tie. His black slippers were neatly shined, and his hair had been carefully combed. Dressed as he was now, Weichmann would later write, Powell was one of the most handsome and well-spoken men he had ever met. Apparently Powell had grown prosperous since his earlier visit, thanks to Wilkes Booth.

Powell asked if Mr. Surratt were at home. He was not, he was told. He then asked if he could see Mr. Surratt's mother, and Weichmann ushered him into the parlor. At that point, Weichmann introduced him to Mrs. Surratt, her daughter, Anna, and her niece, Honora Fitzpatrick. Powell was most courteous to the ladies, smiling, bowing slightly, and bidding all a good evening in a soft, pleasant voice. At Mrs. Surratt's invitation he seated himself in a comfortable chair facing the ladies and began making pleasant conversation. Having apparently forgotten his earlier visit, he informed them that

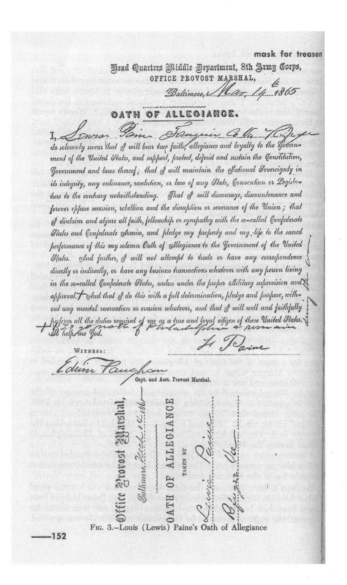

Fig. 3.—Louis (Lewis) Paine's Oath of Allegiance

Powell's oath of allegiance, which he signed in Baltimore on March 14, 1865, using the alias Lewis Payne. He was carrying this oath when arrested at Mrs. Surratt's boardinghouse on April 17. Erasures can still be seen where he deleted the order to "go north to Philadelphia and remain during the war." National Archives

his name was Lewis Payne and that he was a Baptist minister from Baltimore. Following his remarks, a frowning Honora Fitzpatrick commented that she thought his name was Mr. Wood. Powell looked confused for a brief moment, but then quickly recovering himself, he smiled and said that one of his best friends back in Baltimore was named Mr. Wood and that apparently his hostesses had misunderstood his remarks concerning his relationship with his best friend during his first visit. Of course! They all laughed politely at their mistake.

Having averted that disaster, Powell arose and lifted the piano lid for Anna Surratt and requested that she play *Rock of Ages.* Then he, Mrs. Surratt, and Honora stood around the piano and sang while Anna played. After singing several more songs, the ladies invited "Lewis the Terrible," the man for whom death held no fear, to sit down for a game of euchre. It must be remembered that Powell had six older sisters and was certainly no stranger to young ladies. He played with mock seriousness, and every time he trumped Anna's play, he would flash her a smile and a quick wink. She would flush deeply and drop her eyes.

Mrs. John Holohan, another boarder, entered the parlor, took a seat, and began closely observing the card game. An hour later, following Powell's departure, she observed, "Queer preacher. I don't think he'll convert many souls." This comment earned her frowns from both Anna Surratt and Honora Fitzpatrick.

The following afternoon, March 14, Weichmann and John Surratt were in their bedroom, Weichmann writing at a small table, Surratt lying on the bed, when the door suddenly opened and there, filling the doorway, stood Lewis Powell. Surprised, both men looked up. Powell nodded to Weichmann and asked in a soft voice if the gentleman on the bed was John Surratt.

"Yes, sir, it is," replied Weichmann.

"I would like to speak privately with Mr. Surratt if I may," Powell said.

Weichmann left the room, thoroughly convinced that

Powell and Surratt already knew each other, that Powell's question was intended merely to deceive him. Why they would play such a game he did not know, but he was convinced that it was a ruse of some sort.

The next afternoon, March 15, Weichmann returned from work and walked up to Powell's room in the back attic. Without bothering to knock, he threw open the door. There, seated on the bed, were Surratt and Powell surrounded by two revolvers, two bowie knives, and eight pairs of spurs. Weichmann's bursting into the room terribly alarmed both men, and they immediately threw out their hands as if attempting to conceal those articles. When they saw who it was, they visibly relaxed, and Surratt jokingly chastised him by asking if he had never heard of knocking before entering. Feeling spurned, the priggish Weichmann turned without a word and walked briskly downstairs to make a full report of what he had seen to Mrs. Surratt. Mrs. Surratt made light of his report and reminded him that her son was in the habit of riding in the country and that he needed those weapons as security. Besides, she added in a scolding voice, Mr. Weichmann would do well to mind his own business. He thus returned to his own room, his face burning with anger and embarrassment.

In order to introduce Powell to Ford's Theatre, Booth arranged a theater party, purchasing a ticket for the private box seat on the evening of March 15. This he passed to John Surratt with instructions to take Powell to the theater and make it appear as innocent as possible. They certainly did not wish to arouse further suspicions at this point.

After dinner that evening, back in his bedroom at his mother's boardinghouse, Surratt showed Louis Weichmann the ten-dollar ticket for a private box at the theater that Booth had given him. Weichmann playfully grabbed the ticket from his hand, and the two of them began wrestling boyishly about their room for possession of the ticket. Finally, Surratt threw Weichmann to the floor, jerked the ticket from his hand, and said that he and Payne planned to go to Ford's Theatre that evening to see *Jane Shore* and they would take Honora Fitzpatrick and little Apollonia Dean with them.

As the four theatergoers were about to depart that evening, Surratt asked Weichmann if Mr. Payne could borrow his blue military cloak. The evening was quite breezy and Payne wished to wear it to the theater. Weichmann, ever eager to please, darted upstairs to get his Union army cloak for Powell.

After a delightful trip to the theater in a covered carriage, the four of them entered their box and settled back to enjoy a wonderful comedy. Honora Fitzpatrick pleasantly surprised her companions when she opened and passed around a tin of fudge that Mrs. Suratt had baked specially for this occasion. The two girls would later describe attending the play this evening with John Surratt and Lewis Powell as one of the happiest evenings of their lives.

It was in the third act that Wilkes Booth suddenly put in an appearance. Silently, he motioned for Surratt and Powell to join him in the narrow hallway outside the box. There, he explained his plan for abducting the president at Ford's Theatre to Powell and the role he would play in that abduction. Powell nodded and said quietly that the he would not fail. Booth gave him a firm handshake and a hearty slap on the back. Powell and Surratt then hurried back to their seats to catch the very humorous ending of *Jane Shore*. Powell asked Miss Fitzpatrick if there were any fudge left. There was not.

It might be pointed out that Surratt, Powell, and the girls occupied the president's box at Ford's Theatre that evening—apparently for good reason. Two years later, during Surratt's trial of 1867, the prosecution called Miss Honora Fitzpatrick to the stand. Her questioning went as follows:

> *Q.* Do you recollect in the month of March going to Ford's Theatre, and if so state in whose company you went.
>
> *A.* I went with Mr. Surratt, Mr. Wood and Miss Dean.
>
> *Q.* State in what box of the theater you were seated, whether you occupied a box or a seat in the orchestra.
>
> *A.* We occupied a box, Sir.
>
> *Q.* When you say Mr. Surratt you mean John H. Surratt, the prisoner?
>
> *A.* Yes, Sir.

Q. And when you say Mr. Wood you mean Lewis Payne?

A. Yes, Sir.

Q. While your party was in the box did you see John Wilkes Booth? If so, state what he did.

A. Mr. Booth came there and spoke with Mr. Surratt. They both stepped outside the box and stood there at the door.

Q. You mean spoke to the prisoner?

A. Yes, Sir.

Q. State if any one else joined them while standing there.

A. Mr. Wood.

Q. Lewis Payne you mean.

A. Yes, Sir.

Q. How long were these three men talking together?

A. They remained there a few minutes.

Q. Could you hear what they said?

A. No, Sir; I was not paying attention; they were conversing together.

Q. State, if you please, where that box was—in what part of the theater.

A. I think it was an upper box. I do not remember what side of the theater it was on.

Q. In what part of the play was this conversation, in the middle or near the end?

A. It was near the last part.

Q. After they separated which way did they go, and which way did your party go?

A. We returned to Mrs. Surratt's house.

Further testimony at the trial would prove that Surratt and his guests occupied Box 10, the President's box, at Ford's Theatre that evening. Booth obviously wished to make them familiar with the president's box and with the theater in general in case his dream of abducting the president before a large audience should come to pass.

Following the play Surratt and Powell spoke briefly with a beaming Mrs. Surratt in the parlor. Surratt explained to his mother that he and Mr. Payne were leaving to attend a private party but that they would return shortly. Mrs. Surratt looked at the big clock on the wall and commented that it was very late to be going to a party, but Surratt assured her that he and Payne would only be gone for a short time. Then he slipped a deck of cards in his coat pocket, nodded to Powell, and the two young men quickly ducked out the front door, leaving Mrs. Surratt to worry that her son might have fallen in with the wrong crowd. Yet Mr. Payne was a Baptist minister. Likely she was worrying for nothing.

The Attempt to Abduct the President

As for the whereabouts of Surratt and Powell following the play, Samuel Arnold's later testimony would prove conclusively that they, along with all the other conspirators, met at Gautier's Saloon, a fashionable restaurant and bar located at the corner of Thirteenth Street and Pennsylvania Avenue, for a general meeting called by Booth. They entered the restaurant by the front entrance then walked down a dimly lit hallway to the rear of the establishment, where Booth had engaged a large private room. Once inside, they found a long buffet table located to the side of the door heaped with food, cheeses, slices of cold meat, and oysters. Numerous liquors and brandy stood on another table.

For the first time, Booth and his conspirators were all present for the meeting. After shaking hands with Booth, introductions were made all around since several of the conspirators had never met before. Lewis Powell was introduced to everyone simply as "Mosby," a testament to his service with that Southern hero. Atzerodt was "Port Tobacco."

After several friendly drinks, the men settled back to enjoy a hearty dinner. Then came more drinks and much laughter. Everyone was in a cordial mood. Finally, Booth, who enjoyed a good party as much as anyone, reluctantly called the meeting to order. Michael O'Laughlin, who enjoyed a good party more than most, had to be told to sit down and get quiet. It was then that Booth finally unveiled his great plan to abduct the president at Ford's Theatre. Many years later, recalling this particular meeting, Samuel Arnold would write: "It was a wonderful idea, said Booth, for now we could affect our plan, and do it before an audience of hundreds. There would be no applause, he warned, but still, it would be as though we were actors in the greatest drama ever produced."

The conspirators sat in stunned silence as Booth's great plan unfolded. Once he had finished speaking, some very subdued discussion followed. The conspirators looked skeptically at one another. Then man after man, with the exception of John Surratt and the stoic Powell, voiced reservations about such a bizarre idea. Things were not going well for Booth. Samuel Arnold, who had been a reluctant participant in the conspiracy from the very beginning, stated that he had some reservations about the theater idea. He was not sure that he wanted any part of it. At that point, he and Booth began to quarrel, and a furious Arnold suddenly announced to all that he was tired of waiting, and if the abduction did not take place within the next week he would withdraw from any further participation.

Booth became enraged at that ultimatum and stormed that Arnold should be shot for expressing such sentiments. Arnold jumped to his feet and replied that Booth had better shoot quickly or he might very well walk away with an extra hole in his own head. At that, now pale with anger, Booth stood silently for a moment, then he banged his fist down on the table and said, "Well, gentlemen, if worse comes to worse, I shall know what to do."

Alarmed at Booth's implied threat on Lincoln's life, four of the conspirators—Surratt, Arnold, O'Laughlin, and Herold—jumped to their own feet, and Arnold heatedly stated, "If I understand you to intimate anything more than the capture of Mr. Lincoln, I for one will bid you goodbye." As though on signal, the four men began putting on their coats and hats; they intended to depart the room immediately. Only Powell remained seated, intently eyeing Booth as though waiting for a signal to strangle these four malefactors.

At that point, sensing his grand conspiracy was about to fall apart, Booth raised both hands as a sign of surrender. Then he laughed and apologized, saying that he had imbibed just a bit too much champagne. No, he said, if things went as planned, they would certainly abduct the president not at the theater but on his way to the Soldiers' Home. In fact, he had heard from a reliable source just that very afternoon that President Lincoln would be attending a play, *Still Waters Run Deep,* at Campbell's Hospital two days hence, on March 17. The hospital itself was located on a very isolated road, with heavy woods on both sides, and the president would be alone in his carriage. It would be a simple matter to waylay him as he drove to the hospital then spirit him out of Washington. Once they crossed the Potomac, promised Booth, they would find friendly forces that would assist them in their escape to Richmond.

Arnold broke in at that point and asked what the reaction would be in Richmond when they came marching into Jefferson Davis's office with the president of the United States in tow.

"Maybe they'll give us all medals," smiled Booth.

"Or maybe they'll have us all shot," cracked Arnold.

Arnold's comments here simply underscore the fact that of all the conspirators, only Booth, Surratt, and Powell were aware of Richmond's complicity in the plot to abduct the president. As for the others, they all assumed they were working for John Wilkes Booth, that it was Booth and only Booth who was behind this conspiracy.

Following a good laugh all around at Arnold's little joke, Booth admonished his merry men to be prepared to move at a moment's notice on Friday afternoon, March 17, two days hence. These comments pacified Arnold and the others, and they all came forward and shook hands with Booth and embraced him while vowing that they would be ready when called.

It was just after sunup when Surratt, just a bit tipsy, and Powell arrived back at the boardinghouse. Very quietly, they tiptoed up the stairs, slowly opened the front door, and silently entered the parlor. It was then that they were discovered. Before their startled eyes sat a very angry Mrs. Surratt, who had gone sleepless most of the night, awaiting her son's return. She made no effort to conceal her anger but sternly reprimanded John and the deeply remorseful Lewis Powell for their lack of consideration. And was that alcohol she smelled on John's breath? She ordered them both to bed, promising to discuss the matter further when they awakened. Powell, who easily recalled the pain of being reprimanded by his own mother, mounted the stairs to his attic bedroom with leaden feet.

On March 16, the day prior to their planned abduction of Lincoln, Wilkes Booth very calmly played the role of Pescara, the infamous Duke of Alva, in *The Apostate* at Ford's Theatre for the benefit of his old friend and fellow actor John McCullough. (Booth, who obviously had the ability to compartmentalize all the facets of his life, was nothing if not versatile!) But this would prove to be his final performance. His next appearance on stage would be on the evening of April 14, the night he assassinated the president.

Booth gave Surratt two passes to the play, and Surratt invited the delighted Louis Weichmann to accompany him. Apparently Booth had been most generous with his passes, for once Surratt and Weichmann arrived at the theater they met on the sidewalk fronting the theater George Atzerodt, whose coat pockets were stuffed with cookies which he intended to munch during the performance. Inside the theater, they met David Herold and Mrs. Surratt's boarder Mr. John Holohan. Herold, who was from a very well-respected Washington family consisting of a mother and seven older sisters, had just had a fresh shave and haircut and was dressed to the nines in a dark suit and tie. Everyone, it seemed, was looking forward to seeing their old chum on stage.

Following Booth's very successful performance, Weichmann, Surratt, and Mr. Holohan left the theater together, trailed by Herold and Atzerodt. They were walking up Tenth Street when Surratt suddenly turned and noticed that his two friends were not following. He asked Weichmann if he would retrace their path, find Atzerodt and Herold, and invite them to join their party at Kloman's Saloon on Seventh Street for an oyster supper. Weichmann thus went in search of the two, finally glancing in the window of the saloon

John Surratt received the so-called Watson letter in March 1865. One handwriting expert has stated that Lafayette Baker was doubtlessly the author of this letter (see his two known signatures for comparison). If so, this would prove that Baker was a party to the conspiracy. It should also be noted that Watson was the alias Surratt used when serving with the Papal Zouaves in Italy following Lincoln's execution.

adjoining Ford's Theatre. There he spied Herold and Atzerodt involved in deep conversation with Wilkes Booth. As Weichmann approached the party, Booth came forward, shook his hand, and invited him to join them in a drink. Delighted at Booth's show of friendship, Weichmann sat down and drank a glass of ale. He then profusely thanked Booth for the free passes to the theater and expressed his admiration for his fine acting ability. While he and Booth engaged in conversation, Herold and Atzerodt rose from the table and bid everyone good night.

As for Booth's performance that evening, Weichmann would later write, "Never in my life did I witness a man play with so much intensity and passion as did Booth on that occasion. I cannot use language forcible enough to describe Booth's actions on that night."

Now Booth's energies were all concentrated on abducting Lincoln as he rode out to the Soldiers' Home to see *Still Waters Run Deep* on Friday afternoon. Booth had suffered a deep sense of humiliation back on January 18, when Lincoln failed to appear at Ford's Theatre because of bad weather, and felt that he had let everyone down. Indeed, Confederate agents in Richmond, Montreal, and throughout the South were beginning to look askance at Booth. His great scheme had begun in August 1864; it was now mid-March 1865, and Booth still had nothing to show for all his talk of abducting the president. The Confederate army was on the point of starvation, and still Booth did nothing but talk. Obviously he was the wrong man for the job. Booth was keenly aware of all the criticism. Well, this time he would not fail. Immediately, he locked himself in his room at the National Hotel and began working out the details of his plan.

The following Friday, March 17, Louis Weichmann returned home from the Prisoner of War Commissary to find the house empty of both Surratt and Powell. He asked the handyman, a mulatto named Dan, where they might be, and Dan replied that at about two o'clock that afternoon they had ridden away on horseback with Booth, Port Tobacco, (George Atzerodt), Herold, O'Laughlin, and Arnold. Weichmann then met Mrs. Surratt in the hallway. She was weeping bitterly. "Go down, Mr. Weichmann," she said, "and make the best of dinner that you can. John is gone away, John is gone away." It was obvious that her mother's instinct told her that her son had departed on some dangerous adventure and was unlikely to return in the foreseeable future.

Booth, meanwhile, was totally convinced that he and his band would succeed in abducting the president that afternoon. In further preparation of that great event and wishing to show Mr. Lincoln every courtesy, he had arranged for a large trunk to be delivered to a collaborator in lower Maryland to await his arrival with the president. Inside that trunk, it was later discovered, was a ham, cans of potted meats, sardines, crackers, several bottles of wine, flasks of brandy, and various toilet articles. In no way should Mr. Lincoln claim that he had been shown a lack of courtesy on his trip to Richmond. Booth on a number of occasions had expressed a great deal of admiration and even some affection for Lincoln. He harbored no hard feelings whatsoever for the man Abe Lincoln. It was the president whom he despised.

Booth had called for his comrades to meet at Mrs. Surratt's boardinghouse at 2 P.M. on Friday, October 17, a cold, windy day in Washington. Once assembled, Booth counted heads: all present and accounted for. At a signal from their leader, now terribly excited that their daring plan was at last coming to fruition, they looked at one another, swallowed hard, then galloped away to a heavily wooded area near Campbell's Hospital. There, obscured from sight by the heavy foliage growing alongside the road, they waited. Booth had armed them with Spencer repeating rifles and Colt revolvers. After months of talking, their deed was at hand. It was a frightening reality: To abduct the president of the United States was a serious offense. They fingered the cold, black steel of their rifles and wondered if they would live to see another sunrise or if they might be thrown into prison then hanged by the neck until dead. After waiting for what seemed an eternity, they spied the approach of a carriage. Booth silently raised his right hand, and the men looked at one another, their hearts pounding, their adrenaline pumping, their hands shaking, and drew their revolvers. Just as they were about to dash out to stop the carriage and grab the reins from Lincoln's hands, they realized it was not the president's carriage. They would later learn that the president had decided at the last minute to meet with a regiment of Indiana soldiers and had asked Chief Justice Salmon P. Chase to attend the play in his place.

Despite themselves, the men all felt a great sense of relief when they realized that Lincoln was nowhere to be seen. Perhaps they would live to see another sunrise after all. But almost immediately their relief turned to terror when they heard Davy Herold casually mention to Booth that he had heard from a reliable source that Lafayette Baker's National Detective Police had gotten wind of their conspiracy and their arrest could be imminent. At that point, hardly waiting to bid their leader goodbye, the conspirators scattered to the winds. Arnold and O'Laughlin, swearing they were finished with Booth, returned immediately to Baltimore. John Surratt, during his trial of 1867, swore that he too disavowed any further relationship with Booth following this failed abduction on March 17. Davy Herold and George Atzerodt, who seemed oblivious to the fact that abducting the president might be a violation of the law, and Lewis Powell, who considered himself a Confederate soldier merely following orders, remained loyal to Booth and his abduction efforts.

Meanwhile, back at Mrs. Surratt's boardinghouse, Weichmann recalled that during dinner that evening, with John Surratt's whereabouts still unaccounted for, Anna Surratt grew very angry when asked about her brother, and bringing the handle of her knife down hard on the table, she exclaimed, "Mr. Weichmann, do you know that if anything were to happen to my brother John through his acquaintance with Booth, I would kill him."

An hour or so later, about six o'clock, Weichmann returned to his bedroom and had just begun reading a novel when the door suddenly burst open and there stood a greatly excited John Surratt. His pants were tucked into his riding boots and he was wearing spurs. To Weichmann's surprise he then reached beneath his coat and pulled a Colt revolver from his waistband. He closed the door behind him, slammed his hat to the floor, and exclaimed to the startled Weichmann, "My prospects are gone. My hopes are blasted. I want something to do. Weichmann, can you get me a clerkship at the Prisoner Commissary?" Before Weichmann could answer, the door again flew open and this time Lewis Powell strode angrily into the room. His face was flushed, and he seemed oddly excited, which was uncharacteristic for the usually stoic Powell. He said nothing but flung himself on the bed, tightly closing his eyes as though to shut out the world. Weichmann could see that he was carrying a .44 Colt revolver in the big black holster on his hip.

The three men sat silently for a few moments, then again the door opened. This time it was Wilkes Booth. He was wearing a black suit and carrying a riding crop in his hand. As though oblivious to the others, he silently strode into the room and began walking in circles, totally distracted, his head bowed in deep thought. Then he stopped in mid-circle, looked pointedly at his two comrades, and made a slight motion with his head. At that Surratt and Powell arose and silently followed him upstairs to the attic room occupied by Powell. There they remained for the next thirty minutes, then the three came downstairs and left the house without saying a word to anyone.

Four days later, on March 21, Booth and Lewis Powell caught the six o'clock train to New York with intentions of remaining there until things cooled down, taking rooms at the fashionable Revere House Hotel. There is some evidence that Booth and Powell then traveled to Canada, where Booth introduced Powell to Jacob Thompson and Clement Clay, heads of the Confederate Secret Service. Indeed, one notorious agent in that area, Richard Montgomery, would later write:

> I saw him [Lewis Powell] again and had some words with him at the Queen's Hotel in Toronto. I had an interview with Mr. Thompson and on leaving the room, I met this man Payne, in the passageway, talking to

Mr. Clement C. Clay. While Mr. Clay was away, I spoke to this man Payne, and asked him who he was. I commenced talking about some of the topics usually spoken of in conversation amongst these men. He rather hesitated about telling me who he was. He said, "O, I am a Canadian." By which I understood that I was not to question him further. In about half an hour afterward, I asked Mr. Clay who this man Payne was, and he said, "What did he say?" I told him that he said he was a Canadian. Mr. Clay laughed and said, "That is so; he is a Canadian," and he added, "We trust him."

Booth's failure to capture the president on March 17 discouraged him only slightly. Let the other faint hearts fly away if they so desired, but as for him, he was now more determined than ever to strike a blow against Lincoln for both his beloved Southland and the nation as a whole. But his detractors were unimpressed by his latest failure. After all, Booth's conspiracy had been in effect since August, and now it was the middle of March, and Booth had little to show for seven months' effort. If the Confederacy wanted to get their hands on Lincoln, they had better forget Wilkes Booth and send John Singleton Mosby after him.

Apparently Samuel Arnold shared these sentiments, for following the failed abduction of March 17 he would have nothing further to do with Booth and his grandiose plans. He took a job in Fortress Monroe on April 1 and was in that village when Lincoln was assassinated on April 14. Still, he was arrested and thrown into prison along with all the others. Weichmann later testified that it was also on March 17, nearly a month prior to the assassination, that he last saw John Surratt have any personal contact with Wilkes Booth.

As for the firearms that Booth had distributed to his conspirators on the afternoon of March 17, he collected them once the abduction failed and instructed the ever-loyal David Herold to keep them at his home until further notice. To that end, some three days following the failed abduction, upon orders from Booth, Herold rented a horse and wagon and delivered those weapons to a hotel in Teebee, Maryland, a village some five miles below Surrattsville. The hotel was owned by John C. Thompson, and Herold informed him that he planned a big hunting trip on the Patuxent River. Thompson then called for his employee, William A. Norton, to take the trunk into the barroom. It was late afternoon by this time and Herold took dinner at the hotel. While eating, he asked both Thompson and Norton if they had seen his friend John Surratt, whom he was supposed to meet. They had not.

The following morning, having spent the night at the hotel, Herold loaded his trunk back on the wagon and set out on the road to Surrattsville. He had driven only a short distance when he met John Surratt and George Atzerodt on horseback. They greeted one another briefly, then all began the trip to John Lloyd's tavern.

John Lloyd would later testify that some six weeks prior to the assassination these three young conspirators had arrived at his tavern and treated themselves to several drinks. Then Surratt called him into the front parlor, and there, spread on a couch, were two Spencer carbines, several large Colt revolvers, ammunition, a length of rope some twenty feet in length, and a monkey wrench. Surratt asked him to take care of these items and hide the carbines and revolvers. But Lloyd, who had frequently been in trouble with the law because of his drunken misadventures, told Surratt that he wanted nothing to do with firearms, and besides he had no idea where to hide them. Surratt brushed aside his objections and led him to an unfurnished room over the storeroom in the back part of the building. There he hid the firearms underneath the ceiling joists. He merely wanted to leave these items for several days, he said, and then he would be back to pick them up. It was later determined that Booth and his conspirators planned to use the length of rope to stretch across the road to trip the horses of any cavalry that might be in pursuit following the abduction. As for the monkey wrench, that would be used to remove the wheels from the president's carriage so that it could be placed bodily upon the flatboat used to ferry them across the Potomac. Apparently Booth was leaving nothing to chance.

On the afternoon of March 21, following his return to

Washington from Lloyd's tavern, Surratt and Weichmann decided to take a stroll to the post office on Seventh Street. There Surratt approached the window and asked for any mail addressed to "James Sturdy." The clerk handed him a letter, which he read with some excitement. Weichmann, ever curious, asked him when he had become James Sturdy. Obviously annoyed at Weichmann's questions, Surratt made no response, but he did briefly flash the letter before his eyes. Weichmann did not have time to read it, but he did note the signature. It was signed "Wood," the alias Powell had used at Mrs. Surratt's boardinghouse. Weichmann decided that this was just more of Surratt's childish play-acting and put the matter out of his mind.

However, that same day, Weichmann's interest was again piqued when he received a telegram from Wilkes Booth in New York: "Tell John to telegraph number and street at once." Weichmann turned over the telegram to Surratt, telling him that he supposed it was intended for him. Weichmann then asked what the sender meant by street and number. Surratt replied, "Don't be so damned inquisitive."

The explanation for Surratt's sudden reliance on aliases when communicating with his fellow conspirators is fairly simple. By now he was convinced that Stanton's National Detective Police, headed by Lafayette Baker, had gotten wind of the conspiracy and were hot on his trail. It was a fear shared by his fellow conspirators, and they very well might have been correct. On the other hand, there is evidence that Lafayette Baker himself was involved in the conspiracy. If so, that would explain why Baker never took steps to arrest Booth and the others when he knew who they were and what they were planning.

At this time Surratt frequently had his mail addressed not to himself but to a Miss Annie Ward, a teacher in a Catholic school on Tenth Street in Washington. Late in the afternoon of March 23, a Thursday, Weichmann accompanied Surratt on a visit to Miss Ward at her school. They spoke briefly and in low tones, says Weichmann, so that he was unable to overhear their conversation. Then it was on to the Herndon House on Ninth Street, where Surratt talked with Mrs. Murray, the owner of the hotel. Weichmann overheard him say to Mrs. Murray, "Perhaps Miss Annie Ward spoke to you about a room. Did she not speak to you about engaging a room for a delicate gentleman who was to have his meals sent up to him?" He then went on to say that he wanted the room for the following Monday, March 27. Mrs. Murray assured him that Miss Ward had indeed reserved a room and that it would be ready the following Monday.

It might be pointed out that Lewis Powell registered at the Herndon House under the alias "Mr. Kincheloe," Captain Kincheloe being an old friend of his while serving with

This telegram, in which Booth asks Louis Weichmann to have John Surratt wire him Lewis Powell's new address, suggests that Booth and the government's star witness might have been much closer than either the government or Weichmann wanted to admit. (Booth mistakenly wrote the incorrect date on this telegram, March 23, 1864, months before the conspiracy even began. Obviously he intended to write in March 21, 1865.) U.S. War Department Archives

Mosby's Rangers. Like most secret agents, Powell always chose the names of old friends to use as aliases since they were easy to remember. It would be most embarrassing, and perhaps even fatal, for a secret agent to forget his name.

Despite the nosey Weichmann's repeated inquiries, Surratt refused to reveal the name of the "delicate gentleman" taking the room at Herndon's, much to Weichmann's annoyance. But Weichmann, resourceful fellow that he was, especially when his curiosity was aroused, happened to encounter George Atzerodt on the street the following Monday. He stopped Atzerodt and casually asked, "Is Lewis Payne now staying at the Herndon House?" Atzerodt replied that indeed he was.

And Atzerodt was quite right. Both Booth and Powell departed New York and arrived back in Washington on March 27 after an absence of ten days. Having conferred at great length with agents of the Confederate Secret Service in Canada, Booth returned more convinced than ever that steps must be immediately taken if they were to be taken at all. Lee's Army of Northern Virginia were on their last legs; therefore, if he was going to save the Confederacy, he must hurry.

The following day, March 28, his curiosity still not quite content, the resourceful Weichmann made it a point to speak with the "young colored waiter" at the Herndon House responsible for taking meals to the room of the "delicate gentleman" registered there. Weichmann asked him if "Mr. Kinchelow" was a "delicate eater." The waiter replied with a broad grin that he was not. "Why, if I served a young pig to him he would have eaten it, bones and all." Jubilant at his successful detective work, Weichmann returned to the boardinghouse and informed Mrs. Surratt that Lewis Payne was back in town. But instead of praising him for his clever deductions, Mrs. Surratt angrily told him to please mind his own business. Stung, Weichmann repaired silently to his room. However, he was quite satisfied that Surratt and the others had not been able to put one over on him. Plus, he knew, Powell's arrival also explained Booth's telegram to Surratt asking for "the street and number."

Two days earlier, at eight o'clock on the morning of March 25, a Saturday, Weichmann noticed Mrs. Surratt and her son sitting in a white carriage parked in front of the boarding-house. With them was the mysterious Sarah Antoinette Slater. Later testimony would indicate that she had departed Montreal several days earlier and was now on her way to Richmond bearing secret documents. Within the hour, accompanied by John Surratt, she would again be on the road to the Confederacy, this time in a carriage pulled by a fine team of white horses that Surratt had rented from Howard's Stable. Surratt would not be seen again in Washington for a period of nine days, or until the evening of April 3.

On the morning of March 26, a Sunday, Weichmann was just leaving the boardinghouse for church when he was stopped by Mrs. Surratt. She asked him if he would be kind enough to stop by the National Hotel and ask Wilkes Booth if he would call on her that afternoon. He of course agreed. Minutes later, as he was walking down Sixth Street, he encountered George Atzerodt, who was also on his way to see Booth. Once arrived in the lobby of the National Hotel they saw Booth and fellow actor John McCullough talking in the lobby. Weichmann shook hands with McCullough then delivered his message from Mary Surratt. Consequently, says Weichmann, Booth did visit with Mrs. Surratt that afternoon, and they sat on the kitchen stairs and conversed in soft tones for some thirty minutes. Weichmann, reading a book in the parlor during their conversation, was curious as to why Mary Surratt would wish to meet alone with Booth and why they would be speaking so intimately. Without raising his eyes from the book he was ostensibly reading, he strained to overhear their conversation. But he could not—to his great disappointment.

Weichmann would later testify that on the afternoon of March 28, just after he had satisfied himself that Powell was indeed back in their midst, he accompanied Mrs. Surratt, Anna, Honora, and Olivia Jenkins, Mrs. Surratt's niece, to St. Patrick's Church on Tenth Street. Following services, they walked to the Herndon House, and there Mrs. Surratt told the others to wait outside while she went inside to visit Powell. During Weichmann's testimony at the trial of Mary Surratt, it was this damning story that contradicted Mrs. Surratt's contention that she did not know Lewis Powell. It should also be noted that Anna Surratt, Honora Holohan, and Mrs. Murray all strongly denied that this visit with Powell ever took place. Indeed, Powell himself broke his stony silence before the Military Commission long enough to swear that he had never been visited by Mrs. Surratt at the Herndon House or anywhere else. Still, it was this story that tightened the noose around Mary Surratt's neck. As for Weichmann, he would spend the rest of his life vowing that he had told the truth, that the others had all lied.

Booth arrived in New York on March 21 for a visit with his mother. On his way back to Washington, he stopped briefly in Baltimore in an unsuccessful effort to contact Samuel Arnold. He arrived back at the National Hotel in Washington on Monday, March 27. Two days later, on March 29, he received the following letter from Samuel Arnold. This letter has become known as the famous "Sam letter":

Hookstown, Balto. Co.
March 27, 1865.

Dear John:
Was business so important that you could not remain in Baltimore till I saw you? I came as soon as I could, but found that you had gone to Washington. I called also to see Mike, but learned from his mother that he had gone with you and had not returned. I concluded therefore he had gone with you. How inconsiderate you have been! When I left you, you stated that we would not meet in a month or so and therefore I made application for employment, an answer to which I shall receive during the week. I told my parents that I had ceased with you. Can I then, under existing circumstances, act as you request? You know full well that the government suspicions something is going on, therefore the undertaking is becoming more complicated. Why not, for the present desist, for various reasons, which if you look into, you can see without my making any mention thereof? You nor anyone can censure me for my present course. You have been its cause, for how can I now come after telling them that I had left you? Suspicion

rests upon me now from my whole family, and even parties in the country. I will be compelled to leave home anyhow, and how soon I care not. None, no, not one, were more in favor of the enterprise than myself, and today would have been there had you not done as you have. By this, I mean the manner of proceeding. I am, as you well know, in need. I am, you may say, in rags, whereas, today, I ought to be well clothed. I do not feel right stalking about without means and more from appearance a begger [*sic*]. I feel my dependence, but even all this would have been forgotten, for I was one with you. Time more propitious will arrive yet. Do not act rashly or in haste.

I would prefer you first query, "Go and see how it will be taken in Richmond," and ere long I shall be better prepared to again be with you. I dislike writing. Would sooner verbally make known my views. Yet your not waiting causes me thus to proceed. Do not in anger peruse this. Weigh all I have said, and, as a rational man and friend you cannot censure or upbraid my conduct. I sincerely trust this nor aught [*sic*] else that shall or may occur will ever be an obstacle to obliterate our former friendship and attachment. Write me at Baltimore as I expect to be in about Wednesday or Thursday, or, if you can possibly come on I will Tuesday meet you at Baltimore at B.

Ever I subscribe myself, your friend,
Sam

Arnold's reference to Richmond reinforces the conclusion that Booth never informed his fellow conspirators that he had the blessings of Judah Benjamin and other Confederate authorities. From their standpoint, this conspiracy was Booth's idea, and they were working for him alone.

On March 27, the same day that Arnold wrote the foregoing letter, Booth would send the following telegram to Michael O'Laughlin:

M. O'Laughlin, Esq.,
No. 57 North Exeter Street, Baltimore, Md.

Get word to Sam. Come on with or without him Wednesday morning. We sell that day sure. Don't fail.
J. Wilkes Booth

Booth's plans for Wednesday, March 28, remain a mystery,

but ultimately they are irrelevant, for most of his conspirators seemed to be concerned with other matters at the time. O'Laughlin did not even respond to this telegram. As for the reluctant Arnold, he had just taken a job at Fortress Monroe and was apparently finished with the plotting. Davy Herold, at his mother's urging, had just taken a clerkship at the Base Hospital, Army of the James, and was finished with Booth, at least for the moment. And John Surratt was in Richmond conferring with Confederate authorities. It appears that only George Atzerodt and Lewis Powell were available to meet with Booth on March 28.

April 1-13, 1865

With Lincoln now out of the capital, discussing strategy with Generals Grant and Sherman at City Point, Virginia, Booth took a moment to check his bank account. He was nearly broke. Therefore, he sold his horses and caught the next train for New York, where he borrowed money from his mother—and squeezed fifty dollars out of Samuel Chester.

On that same day, Saturday morning, April 1, Mary Surratt's brother, Zadoc Jenkins, picked her up in a buggy rented from Howard's Stable and together they drove to Surrattsville, returning in the early evening. It seems that John Lloyd owed her money on the property he had leased from her months before, and Mrs. Surratt was in a dither to collect that badly needed cash.

The next morning, Sunday, April 2, Mary Surratt again approached Weichmann with a request that he see Wilkes Booth at the National Hotel and tell him to please visit her that afternoon. If Booth should be out, she cautioned, Weichmann should find Atzerodt and have him find Booth and send him to her. Weichmann did as she requested, but Booth was indeed out of town. He then walked down to the Pennsylvania House and found Atzerodt standing outside holding two horses by their bridles, one a fairly small one and the other a large bay horse, blind in one eye. (This was the horse purchased from

Mr. Gardner and ridden by Lewis Powell on the night he attacked Secretary William Seward.) Weichmann asked about Wilkes Booth and Atzerodt replied that Booth was in New York and would not return until the following Saturday, April 8.

Weichmann reported Atzerodt's information to Mrs. Surratt, and she, terribly disappointed at this news, then asked that he return to Atzerodt and request the loan of a horse so that her brother, Zadoc Jenkins, could return home without having to walk. The horses belonged to her son, she said, so Atzerodt could hardly refuse. Weichmann, accompanied by Jenkins, did as she requested. They met Atzerodt and there ensued a lengthy debate concerning the ownership of the horses. Atzerodt denied that they were the property of John Surratt, claiming that the one-eyed mare actually belonged to "Lewis Payne." Before he loaned Mr. Jenkins the horse, said Atzerodt, he would have to see Mr. Payne. (Booth and the conspirators never owned more than two horses, which they kept at Howard's Stables.) Despite Weichmann's arguments to the contrary, Atzerodt was adamant: The one-eyed mare belonged to Mr. Payne. To solve the dispute, Weichmann, Jenkins, and Atzerodt walked to the Herndon House to see Lewis Powell. While Weichmann and Jenkins waited outside, Atzerodt went up to Powell's room to learn what Powell's response would be. Minutes later he returned and said that Mr. Payne, fearing that Booth might disapprove, would not consent to the loan of either horse.

So Mary Surratt, in the space of two hours, was given the disappointing news that Booth would be out of town for the next week, and her brother would be forced to walk back to Surrattsville. In a fit of pique she blamed Atzerodt for the whole fiasco and complained that she had once loaned him five dollars out of her own pocket, a loan which he had never repaid, and now he should treat her like this.

However, Mrs. Surratt's disappointment paled in comparison to the news of the next day. Monday, April 3, 1865, will forever be remembered as a black day for the Confederacy. For it was on this day that the Confederate government was finally forced to evacuate Richmond.

On April 3 Booth was in Newport, Rhode Island, visiting with a female friend. Then it was on to Boston, where he visited with his brother Edwin.

Weichmann also remembered April 3, for it was on that evening that he next saw John Surratt, who had been in Richmond since March 25. Supposedly he had traveled to Richmond with Mrs. Slater on that date to seek employment. Weichmann, as usual, was sitting in the parlor when Surratt entered the front door. He was very neatly dressed in a new spring suit, light tan in color. Following preliminary greetings, Weichmann asked him if he had heard the news of Richmond's evacuation. Surratt denied that such was the case. "I just yesterday visited with Jefferson Davis and Judah Benjamin," he said, "and they assured me that Richmond would not be evacuated." It may be safely assumed that Davis and Benjamin did not meet with just anyone, which suggests that Surratt was an agent of some importance to the Confederacy. Whether they discussed the abduction of President Lincoln is not known. Nor is it known why he would share this news with Louis Weichmann, a loyal employee of the Federal army.

Surratt, followed by Weichmann, then walked upstairs and exchanged four hundred dollars in gold for American greenbacks with Mr. Holohan. Weichmann was surprised to see Surratt with so much money since he had no visible means of income. That evening Surratt, now wearing a new gray suit with a maroon shawl thrown over his shoulders, invited Weichmann to a saloon on Pennsylvania Avenue, where they enjoyed a fine dinner of roasted oysters. Following dinner they walked back together as far as the Metropolitan Hotel. There they paused and Surratt shook hands with Weichmann and bid him goodbye. He was aware that he was being closely watched by agents from Lafayette Baker's National Detective Police, he explained, and had been for some time, and thus he was afraid to spend the night at home, preferring instead to take a room at the Metropolitan. He was leaving for Montreal the next morning, he told Weichmann, but would soon write, a situation that doubtlessly explains what Surratt was doing with four hundred dollars in gold coins.

Certainly Surratt's fear of returning home that evening cannot be attributed to simple paranoia. In fact, since Weichmann had begun making his reports to Captain Gleason back in February, Lafayette Baker's police had doubtlessly kept close tabs on the denizens of Mrs. Surratt's boardinghouse. Why he had not arrested them earlier is puzzling, but Baker was famous as one of the most clever and conniving creatures ever to hold a military commission. It could well be that he anticipated a good use for these conspirators sometime in the near future. Perhaps he foresaw how these conspirators could very well become collaborators.

In point of fact, two years would elapse before Weichmann and Surratt would see each other again—in 1867 at the trial of John Surratt for the murder of Pres. Abraham Lincoln. That meeting would hardly be cordial. At the trial Surratt swore that Weichmann had been a part of the conspiracy and blamed his lies for sending Mary Surratt to the gallows. Surratt would also testify at his trial that during his final visit to Richmond, Judah Benjamin had given him dispatches hidden in a book entitled *The Life of John Brown,* which were to be delivered to Montreal. As for his bidding Weichmann goodbye at the Metropolitan Hotel that evening, he stated that he had been told that a detective had recently been to the boardinghouse looking for him and he was afraid that he might be arrested should he return home. He also pointed out that he encountered George Atzerodt later that evening and Atzerodt had asked the whereabouts of Wilkes Booth. Despite his earlier comments to Weichmann, Surratt told Atzerodt that Richmond had fallen, the war was essentially over, and he should forget about Wilkes Booth, return home, and find work.

As for Booth, after a violent argument over the war with his brother in Boston, he returned to Washington on Saturday, April 8, taking room 228 at the National Hotel. Two days later, on Monday, April 10, Booth paid a late-afternoon visit to Mary Surratt at her boardinghouse. If he had hoped to speak privately with her, he was disappointed. In addition to Booth and Mrs. Surratt, there soon gathered in her parlor her daughter and the rest of her boarders. With everyone seated, looking to Booth for all the latest war and theater gossip, Louis Weichmann rather boorishly remarked to everyone that Lee's army was finished and the Confederacy at an end. Booth, unflustered, responded by calmly pulling a battle map from his pocket and pointing out several routes that Joe Johnston's army might take across North Carolina to the Blue Ridge Mountains, where they could hold out indefinitely. Later, perhaps, they could even link up with Gen. Kirby Smith's Army of the Trans-Mississippi, then headquartered in Galveston, Texas. If that should happen, the Federal army would pay hell trying to root the Confederate army out of the Lone Star State. (In fact, Johnston finally surrendered his army to Gen. William T. Sherman on April 26, 1865, truly marking the end of the War of the Rebellion.) To Booth's way of thinking, the war did not end with Lee's surrender on April 9. As long as Joe Johnston was still fighting in North Carolina, there remained hope. And that hope could be strongly reinforced should Abe Lincoln be abducted.

Later, Weichmann asked Booth if he planned to take to the stage again in the near future. Booth, in a private jest, replied that the only play that interested him now was *Venice Preserved*. At the time no one present got the joke. The main plot of this drama concerns a hero saving Venice by assassinating the officers of the Venetian cabinet. To that end, four days later Booth would fire a shot into the back of President Lincoln's head, a shot which did anything but save the South and the nation.

Also present that afternoon was Annie Ward, the young lady school teacher who had secured the room for Lewis Powell at the Herndon House. She had with her a letter from John Surratt in New York, which she left with Anna Surratt. Following the departure of Booth and Miss Ward, Anna proudly showed the letter to Weichmann. It was a very well-written letter, but the text consisted of nothing but idle chitchat, certainly nothing to arouse his suspicions.

So, as of Monday, April 10, it is obvious that among his conspirators Booth had only George Atzerodt, David Herold, and Lewis Powell upon whom he could count in Washington. Surratt was in New York while Arnold and O'Laughlin were working in Baltimore. This placement of conspirators underscores the fact that Booth's decision to execute Lincoln on April 14 came about not as a matter of careful planning, but simply as a matter of impulse, an impulse possibly prompted by high-ranking government officials.

Of course, in addition to those who were actually indicted and brought to trial, there were many others involved in the conspiracy, their identities for the most part still unknown. The following letter, addressed to Booth, was delivered to the National Hotel just a day or two prior to the assassination, but the clerk there placed it in the wrong box, so Booth never received it. During the trial of the conspirators, this letter was brought to light and leaves no doubt that there were many others involved in the conspiracy.

> Friend Wilkes: I received yours of March 12th and replied as soon as practicable. I saw French, Brady and others about the oil speculation. The subscription to the stock amounts to eight thousand dollars, and I add one thousand myself which is about all I can stand. Now, when you sink your well, go deep enough, don't fail; everything depends upon you and your helpers. If you cannot get through on your trip after you strike oil, strike through Thornton Gap and across by Capon, Romney and down the Branch. I can keep you safe from all hardships for a year. I am clear from all surveillance now that infernal Purdy is beat.
>
> I send this by Tom, and if he don't get drunk you will get it the 9th. At all events, it cannot be understood if lost.
>
> No more, only Jake will be at Green's with the funds.
>
> Lon

In view of subsequent events, the contents of this letter strike one as extremely suspicious and are fairly easy to interpret. The conspirators used Booth's interest in the oil business as an analogy for the plot to kidnap the president; thus "when you sink your well, go deep enough" suggests that Booth should not take half measures, but make sure Lincoln was well in hand. Most of the letter informs Booth that once he moved against the president and flight became necessary, a plan of escape already had been established. Should that route not prove feasible, he should head for Thornton Gap, across by Capon and Romney, and down the Branch for the shelter his collaborators could offer him. The writer's "I am clear from all surveillance now" indicates that he is no longer being watched as he once was and that it will be safe for Booth to hide out with him "for a year." As for the total of eight thousand dollars the writer mentions, that is apparently money that will enable Booth and his conspirators to finance their final escape. What their final escape, or destination, might have been remains another mystery, though it should be remembered that John Surratt's older brother was then living in Matamoros, Mexico, which would been an ideal hiding place for the conspirators.

That this letter was not a fabrication was proven by the testimony of Robert Purdy (referred to in the letter as "that infernal Purdy") during the trial of the conspirators. Purdy testified that he was a detective for Stanton's National Detective Police in the spring of 1865 and that there were Confederate agents stationed in the areas mentioned in the letter. One was a noted Confederate agent living in Thornton Gap whom Purdy had earlier had under surveillance; another a freed black servant named Tom living in the area of the South Branch Bridge; and a man known to all as Lon lived at South Gap Bridge. There was also a little-known route through the Gap, as described in the letter.

Just how extensive the conspiracy might have been and who were really involved remains a mystery to this day. But as time goes by and more and more evidence comes to light, it becomes increasingly apparent that the desire to somehow eliminate Lincoln was extremely widespread. According to "The Secret Papers of Lafayette Baker," Edwin Stanton and Andrew Johnson were the masterminds behind the assassination, and, according to Baker, there were numerous other politicians, military men, and industrialists who had prior knowledge that Lincoln was marked for death.

On the morning of Tuesday, April 11, Mary Surratt asked Weichmann if he would drive her to Surrattsville to see John K. Nothey and John Lloyd in order to collect money they owed her. Weichmann agreed, and she then asked him if would go to Room 228 at the National Hotel and ask Wilkes Booth for his horse and carriage. Weichmann says that upon his arrival at Booth's room, he found Booth lying on his bed reading a book. He delivered Mrs. Surratt's message, but frowning as though troubled, Booth informed Weichmann that he had sold his horse and carriage and therefore could not loan them to Mary Surratt. But then, flashing Weichmann a quick smile, he pulled a ten-dollar bill from his pocket and told Weichmann to go to Howard's Stable and rent a horse and carriage. (The fact that he had sold his horses and carriage suggests that Booth already had abandoned any plans to abduct the president, either at the Soldiers' Home or at the theater.)

Weichmann did as Booth suggested, and he and Mrs. Surratt departed Washington about nine that morning. Before reaching Surrattsville, they met Mrs. Surratt's tenant, John Lloyd, and his sister, Mrs. Emma Offutt, in an approaching buggy. Weichmann stopped the carriage and Mrs. Surratt motioned for Lloyd to approach her. She leaned out the carriage and spoke to Lloyd in quiet tones. Later, at the trial of the conspirators, Lloyd testified that Mrs. Surratt mentioned nothing about the money he owed her, that her purpose in visiting him was to have the guns ready for Booth and his fellow conspirators.

> On the Tuesday before the assassination of the President I was coming to Washington and I met Mrs. Surratt on the road at Uniontown. When she first broached the subject about the articles at my place I did not know what she had reference to. Then she came out plainer and asked me about the "shooting irons." I had myself forgotten about their being there. I told her that they were hid far away back and that I was afraid the house might be searched. She told me to get them out ready: that they would be wanted soon. I do not recollect the first question she put to me. Her language was indistinct, as if she wanted to draw my attention to something so that no one else

would understand. Finally she came out bolder with it and said they would be wanted soon. I told her I had an idea of having them buried; that I was very uneasy about having them there.

As incriminating as this testimony might appear, Lloyd's companion on that morning, Mrs. Offutt, testified that Lloyd was so drunk when he met Mrs. Surratt that he could hardly stay in the saddle. Lloyd's wife testified that when he arrived home that morning he was too drunk to lie down, for when in a reclining position he became extremely nauseous and vomited all over the bedroom. Still, despite his drunken condition on the morning of April 11, his testimony was just what the Military Commission wanted to hear. It proved beyond a shadow of a doubt that Mary Surratt was involved in the conspiracy to assassinate the president, and she must be hanged.

Never mind that it had not occurred to Booth on Tuesday, April 11, to execute Lincoln or anyone else. Why would he have wanted the "shooting irons" made ready? The question might also be reasonably asked, why would Booth wish to alert John Lloyd, a totally untrustworthy drunk, that he was on the verge of taking some drastic action—unless he wanted the news spread all over southern Maryland.

At noon Weichmann and Mrs. Surratt arrived in Surrattsville to see Mr. Nothey about the money he owed her. Mr. Nothey was not in, so Mrs. Surratt sent a messenger to tell him to meet with her at two that afternoon. She and Weichmann then drove over to one Bennett Gwynn's place, where they enjoyed a nice lunch. Following lunch, Weichmann, Mrs. Surratt, and Mr. Gwynn returned to Surrattsville. There she met with Mr. Nothey, collected her money, and she and Weichmann returned to Washington.

It must be observed that if Mrs. Mary Surratt, whom everyone described as one of the kindest, most gentle, and Christian ladies on record, was on a mission to assist in the murder of the president of the United States, she certainly kept a tight rein on her emotions. If she could order up the "shooting irons" from Lloyd then calmly sit down to a nice lunch, she certainly had everyone fooled.

That evening, the Federal government and Washington celebrated General Lee's surrender. Throughout the day there had been fireworks, brass bands, bonfires, and parades, and as night fell, thousands of jubilant citizens continued to dance through the streets. Among those celebrants were two well-dressed gentlemen wearing somber frowns of defiance and determination: Booth and Powell. They followed the riotous crowd all the way to the White House and then stood silent and watchful on the lawn beneath the president's windows. The crowd began to chant, "Speech! Speech!"

Soon a French window opened and the tall, stooped figure of Abe Lincoln could be seen looking down at the crowd. An aide handed him a candle. A roar went up from the crowd. When the noise finally subsided, Lincoln began to read from a prepared statement. If the crowd had been expecting to hear a pledge to hang Jeff Davis, they were disappointed:

> Fellow citizens, we meet this evening not in sorrow, but in gladness of heart. The evacuation of Petersburg and Richmond, and the surrender of the principal insurgent army, give hope of a righteous and speedy peace, whose joyous expression cannot be restrained.
>
> Let us all join in doing the acts necessary to restore the proper practical relations between these States and the Union.

The president went on to explain his Reconstruction program for the South. He promised the restoration of self-government in the states of the Confederacy once the war ended. He wanted no military dictatorship imposed on the South and its citizens, but local governments should be placed in the hands of the Southern people, local governments duly elected by the citizens of those localities. Yes, said Lincoln, once the war ended, the people of the South would have restored to them all the constitutional rights they had enjoyed prior to the war. They would, in other words, be welcomed back into the Union just as though they had never been away.

Then, as a concession to his Radical supporters, he

broached a subject that he would rather have avoided: voting rights for freed slaves. Not all former slaves would be given the right to vote, he said, but only those who were "very intelligent" and those who had "served in the Union army." How Lincoln planned to measure the intelligence of former slaves is a question that cannot be answered here. Again, Lincoln truly had no intentions of extending the vote to black Americans though he would occasionally make such statements as a conciliatory gesture for the Radicals in Congress. In fact, he was already making preparations to have these former slaves resettled in Liberia.

Booth nudged Powell and shook his head. Things were starting to go exactly as he had feared. Not only had Lincoln given blacks their freedom, now he wanted to give them the right to vote. Next, they would be holding public office and control of the nation.

Two days later, on the evening of Thursday, April 13, Booth quietly sat down at the desk in his hotel room, took out pen and paper, and then, as any other young man might do, he calmly and quietly wrote a brief letter to his mother. By no means is it a "last goodbye" letter such as a young man bent on committing a terrible crime the following evening might write. To the contrary, it is one of those letters of obligation that young men frequently write to their mothers out of guilt for not having written sooner:

> Indeed, I have nothing to write about. Everything is dull, that is, has been until last night. Everything was bright and splendid. More so, in my eyes if it had been a display in a nobler cause. But so goes the world. Might makes right. I only drop you these lines to let you know that I am well and to say I have not heard from you. Excuse brevity, am in haste.
> I am your affectionate son, ever,
> Wilkes

Taken in toto, this certainly does not sound like the ranting letter of a wild-eyed fiend written on the eve of his bloodiest triumph. There is not the least hint of excitement or tension in this letter. In fact, Booth's dominant mood seems to have been one of utter boredom. He even mentions that the Union victory celebration of the previous evening was "bright and splendid," which seems an odd thing for a Southern sympathizer to say and suggests that perhaps he did not take Lee's surrender quite as seriously as one might expect. Indeed, it is only in passing that he alludes to his disappointment, but then he shrugs it off very philosophically with "But so goes the world."

Thus it should be obvious to any objective observer that on the evening of April 13 it still had not occurred to Wilkes Booth to execute Lincoln. So the question begs to be asked: What did happen during those intervening twenty-four hours to convince him that Lincoln must die?

V

Booth's Movements on That Fateful Day

It was not until late Friday morning, April 14, 1865, that John T. Ford, the owner of Ford's Theatre, was notified that President and Mrs. Lincoln, accompanied by Gen. Ulysses S. Grant, would be attending the play at Ford's Theatre that evening. (Mrs. Grant, who had run afoul of Mrs. Lincoln's temper in the past, did not receive an invitation and probably would not have accepted if she had.) Prior to Friday afternoon, it had been rumored all week that the Lincolns would accept an invitation from Leornard Grover to attend the play *Aladdin* at Grover's Theatre (later known as the National Theatre) on that evening, a rumor which for obvious reasons Leonard Grover did nothing to dispel. This rumor was so widespread, according to Grover's later testimony, that even his old friend Wilkes Booth came to him on Thursday afternoon and purchased a ticket for Friday night's performance, a ticket that would have placed him in the box adjoining the Lincolns had they chosen to attend. But as fate would have it, President Lincoln, who always enjoyed a good laugh, decided at the last minute to attend a comedy at Ford's Theatre. How events might have turned out differently had the Lincolns attended the play at Grover's instead of Ford's makes for interesting speculation. John Ford was delighted when notified that two of the nation's most prominent citizens would be in attendance at his theater that night. He immediately sat down and drafted a press release for Washington's afternoon newspapers. They would hit the streets at about 2 P.M.

231

Mary Todd Lincoln of Kentucky and Julia Dent Grant of Missouri both came from families with Southern sympathies. Mary Todd Lincoln's brother, a Confederate general, was killed in battle, while Julia Dent Grant was the first cousin of Gen. James Longstreet. Library of Congress

At noon that day Booth visited Ford's Theatre and learned for the first time that the President and Mrs. Lincoln had decided to attend the play there that evening. Some five hours would elapse before Booth learned, at 5 P.M., that the president would attend the theater that evening totally unattended by body guards or General Grant. Thus Booth's movements prior to five o'clock must be viewed as really irrelevant to this sad drama, for he was unaware until that time that it would be possible to execute the president.

Had Booth seen and spoken with every person across Washington, D.C. who later recalled having seen and spoken with him on April 14, he would have been far too exhausted to have executed the president that evening. But according to the most reliable testimony, his movements were as follows.

Where Booth spent the night of April 13 remains a mystery since three of his coconspirators (Herold, Powell, and Atzerodt) visited his room (No. 228) at the National Hotel at 7 A.M. on the morning of April 14 only to find him absent and his bed not slept in. They were stumped as to his whereabouts, as historians have been since, but it is well known that Booth was quite a ladies' man and generally was seeing several females at the same time, some reputable, some not. Therefore, it seems entirely reasonable that once he had completed writing the letter to his mother on Thursday evening, he might have spent the night in the company of a female friend.

He was seen, finally, in the dinning room of the National Hotel at nine o'clock having breakfast with his fiancée, Lucy Hale, daughter of Sen. John P. Hale of New Hampshire. They were laughing quietly and talking of nothing in particular. After breakfast he escorted her back to her family's apartment and very casually promised to call on her later that evening.

By ten o'clock that morning Booth was observed as he leisurely strolled into the Booker and Stewart Barber Shop on E Street near Grover's Theatre. There, Charles Wood trimmed his hair and gave him a fresh shave. Finding Booth in a good, talkative mood, Wood used this opportunity to catch up on the latest theater gossip. Wood would later testify, as did so many others, that if Booth planned to murder someone later that evening, he certainly gave no indication of it that morning.

Then it was on to Grover's Theatre, where Booth sat down and spoke at some length with Leonard Grover. Grover would remember that the main point of Booth's visit seemed to be to confirm whether the Lincolns would be in attendance at the play that evening. Grover could only tell him that he still was unsure since he had received no confirmation at that point. Their conversation was soon interrupted by the excited appearance of Mrs. C. D. Hess, the wife of Grover's partner, who was on her way to visit the White House. Booth greeted her with a smile, rose, and shook her hand. In later years Mrs. Hess would boast that on April 14 she had shaken hands with both John Wilkes

Booth and Abraham Lincoln, certainly a unique experience.

Still in the dark as to the Lincolns' intentions for that evening, Booth next appeared at the Kirkwood House, where Andrew Johnson rented a suite of rooms. He told the desk clerk that he wanted to see the vice president, but the clerk shook his head and told him that Johnson was out.

At this point, one cannot escape the nagging question: Why would John Wilkes Booth wish to visit with Vice President Johnson on the very day that Lincoln would die? Ostensibly, and according to Johnson's later testimony, Booth's motive probably was to request a military pass from Johnson that would allow him to ride into Maryland that night without fear of being stopped by army pickets guarding the roads in and out of Washington. This explanation, based totally on conjecture, simply does not hold up, as Booth's visit to Johnson occurred prior to noon that day, prior to the time when Booth became aware that he would attempt to execute Lincoln that evening. Certainly, at that point, it had not dawned on him that he might need a military pass to flee Washington that evening. Too, if Booth truly planned to execute the president that evening in front of a thousand people, he must have known that no military pass in existence could prevent his capture should he be stopped by U.S. soldiers at the Navy Yard Bridge. No, his only hope for survival would have to come from elsewhere. Fortunately for Booth, it did—when Edwin Stanton's telegraph system went dead at the very moment that Booth pulled the trigger.

As incredible as it might seem, that very afternoon Booth again tried to see the vice president, a fact that presents the historian with an enigma. Was Booth setting Johnson up to be assassinated later by George Atzerodt or, to the contrary, was Johnson more involved in the conspiracy than he ever would admit? Mrs. Mary Lincoln (among many others) went to her grave believing that Johnson was behind her husband's assassination. Two years later, during Johnson's impeachment trial, charges were hurled at him from the floor of the Senate that it was he, the vice president, who had been behind the plot to assassinate Lincoln. Missouri's senator,

Benjamin Loan, roared, "An assassin's bullet wielded and directed by a Rebel hand made Andrew Johnson President. The price that he was to pay for his promotion was treachery to the Republicans and fidelity to the party of treason and rebellion!" And Ohio senator J. M. Ashley denounced

> the man who came into the Presidency through the door of assassination. And I would call attention to the dark suspicion which crept over the minds of men as to Johnson's complicity in the assassination plot. The country demands that the incubus which has blotted our country's history with the foulest blot should be removed.

It must be remembered that Loan and Ashley were not merely private citizens voicing unfounded suspicions. Both were high-ranking members of the federal government, and both were privy to confidential information and Congressional gossip not available to the public at large. They, and numerous other government officials, believed until their dying days that Andrew Johnson was the driving force behind the scheme to murder Abe Lincoln.

Their beliefs would later find some support from a strange quarter. Some twenty-five years following the execution of President Lincoln, a man by the name of John St. Helen would confess on his deathbed in Enid, Oklahoma, that he was in fact John Wilkes Booth. The story that St. Helen related concerning the execution is most convincing (see chapter IX). He swore that late in the afternoon of April 14, 1865, he and his fellow collaborator, David Herold, visited with Andrew Johnson in his room at the Kirkwood House. Johnson, he says, was fully aware of their conspiracy to abduct the president, and they had visited with him on numerous occasions over the past few months to discuss the progress of their conspiracy. This time they did not bother the desk clerk but went directly to Johnson's room.

Booth was concerned with the military ramifications of General Lee's surrender to General Grant, and so was Andrew Johnson. In fact, Johnson convinced him that abduction was now out of the question. He said that the only solution now, the only way to save the South, was assassination, and it must be done this very night, at the theater. Shocked, Booth raised several objections. First, there would be no way he could approach the president at the theater if were accompanied by General Grant. Secondly, there would be no way he could escape Washington following the assassination.

Johnson brushed aside his fears, saying that if Booth would agree to pull the trigger, he would make sure that General Grant would not be in attendance and that Booth would have plenty of time to escape before the call went out for his arrest. Not only that, said Johnson, but if Booth ever were prosecuted for the assassination, he would use his powers as president to see that he received a presidential pardon. At that point Johnson excused himself and left his room. Upon his return an hour later he informed Booth that all arrangements had been made. General Grant had suddenly been called out of town, and Maj. Thomas Eckert had promised that the military telegraph would be shut down. With all arrangements made, Booth had little choice but to follow through with the plan to save the South by executing President Lincoln.

Though this tale seems bizarre upon its first reading, there is much to suggest that John St. Helen was in fact John Wilkes Booth. If so, this account of the events leading up to the assassination could explain why Booth suddenly moved from an aborted plan of abduction to execution for Abraham Lincoln.

Returning to the generally accepted timeline of Booth's movements that day, following Booth's attempt to see the vice president, he returned to his room at the National Hotel. He had walked only two blocks when he met the editor of the *Daily Constitutional Union,* Thomas R. Florence. The next day Florence would write that he had talked with Booth only hours before Lincoln's assassination. Booth told him that he might soon be going to Canada, where several theater owners were offering him engagements. He also complained that he had recently lost six thousand dollars in oil as a result of the recent floods at Oil City, Pennsylvania.

Finally arrived at the National Hotel, Booth found a quite inebriated Michael O'Laughlin awaiting him in the lobby. They went up to Booth's room, where they remained for perhaps thirty minutes. O'Laughlin would later testify that the purpose of his visit was to collect money Booth owed him for various services, money that had nothing to do with the assassination.

After getting rid of his drunken friend, Booth walked to the boardinghouse of Mary Surratt on H Street. He was aware that she, accompanied by her boarder Louis Weichmann, was planning to go to Surrattsville that afternoon. This trip, it was later alleged by the Military Commission, would present her an excellent opportunity to observe whether army pickets were still stationed on the road three miles south of Washington, along the route that Booth planned to travel that very night. The problem with this theory is that Booth was still unaware on Friday morning that he would assassinate Lincoln at ten that evening. Why would he need information concerning the location of army pickets? Poor Mrs. Surratt obviously had nothing to do with Booth's actions later that evening.

He next visited the stable he had rented several weeks earlier behind Ford's Theatre. One Mary Jane Anderson, a black woman who lived nearby, later testified that she had seen him there that morning.

About noon on Friday, Booth would drop by Ford's Theatre itself. "There comes the handsomest man in Washington," commented Harry Clay Ford, the theater's treasurer, as he watched Booth approach. Only the month before, on March 18, 1865, Booth had played Pescara in *The Apostate* at Ford's Theatre and was well known to all. He was also a long-time friend of John Ford and had free access to the theater. He even had his mail sent there when he was in Washington. Clay Ford later recalled that Booth had several letters awaiting him that morning and he had most casually sat down on the theater's steps to read them. He remembered that Booth had laughed uproariously as he read one letter.

Clay Ford then revealed to Booth that a messenger had arrived from Mrs. Mary Lincoln at about ten-thirty that morning announcing that she and her husband would attend the play at Ford's that evening. He also stated proudly that the Lincolns would be accompanied by Gen. Ulysses S.

Grant. Ford later remembered that Booth greeted this news with no special excitement, simply nodding his head. It was now approximately 1 P.M.

Booth later put in an appearance at James W. Pumphrey's stable at 224 C Street, near the National Hotel, to arrange for a saddle horse, a bay mare. Booth took the mare with him and left it in his stable at Ford's Theatre. Mr. Pumphrey never saw the horse or rider again after that morning. Booth also told Pumphrey that he was headed for Grover's Theatre to write a letter, which was probably the document he would give to fellow actor John Matthews that afternoon.

Based on the later testimony of Mrs. Ulysses S. Grant, Booth might next have strolled down Pennsylvania Avenue to the Willard Hotel at Fourteenth Street, where the Grants were staying. While Mrs. Grant and her son, Jesse, were at lunch, she later testified, she was disturbed by a "man with a wild look" who took a seat at a nearby table and stared at her throughout her meal and appeared to be listening to her conversation. Mrs. Grant felt certain that the wild-looking man was John Wilkes Booth. Despite Mrs. Grant's sincere testimony and good intentions, it appears doubtful that the man who planned to murder the president that very evening would go out of his way to arouse any suspicions. Likely, she only imagined that the rude intruder was John Wilkes Booth.

Booth planned to return to the National Hotel to change into riding clothes and get his field glasses, which Mrs. Surratt would deliver to Surrattsville that afternoon. But first he again visited the Kirkwood House and asked to see Vice President Johnson. Johnson was not in, Booth was told, but was at the White House meeting with the president.

At eight o'clock that morning, it might be pointed out, George Atzerodt had checked in at the Kirkwood House and taken a room immediately above the apartment of Vice President Johnson. A great deal would be made of this at the conspiracy trial, the commission claiming that this in itself was proof that Booth planned to assassinate the entire government of the United States.

But Booth was convinced that George Atzerodt was no

killer, and it is apparent, despite all the accusations to the contrary, that Booth never entertained the least intention of assassinating Andrew Johnson during the evening of April 14. In the first place, had he made any attempt on Johnson's life, Abraham Lincoln would never have attended the play at Ford's Theatre that evening. Moreover, he would have been spirited away under heavy military guard. In addition there was the later testimony of two Southern sympathizers who assisted Booth and Herold in their bid to escape: They stated that Booth and Herold had boasted of having assassinated Lincoln and Seward, but they had not mentioned Andrew Johnson in any way. When John Lloyd, the tavern keeper at Surrattsville, was testifying during the conspiracy trial, he stated that he had spoken with the conspirators outside his tavern on the night of the murder and one of them had stated, "I am pretty certain that we have assassinated the President and Secretary Seward." But again, not one word did the assassins mention concerning Andrew Johnson.

Booth arrived at Mrs. Surratt's boardinghouse at about 1:30 P.M. Louis Weichmann would later testify that he was just leaving to secure a horse and buggy to drive Mrs. Surratt to Surrattsville to collect money owed her by Mr. Nothey when he noticed Booth and Mrs. Surratt engaged in deep conversation. Upon Weichmann's return with the buggy, he noticed that Booth had already departed. Then, as he and Mrs. Surratt were about to leave for Surrattsville, Mrs. Surratt stopped Weichmann, saying, "Wait, Mr. Weichmann. I must get those things of Booth's," and she went back inside to retrieve the package. According to Weichmann's testimony, "those things" consisted of the field glasses that Booth allegedly planned to use during his escape. How Weichmann knew what was inside the package, we simply are not told, nor, if the package was so important, why Mary Surratt almost forgot to take it along.

But again, at this point Booth was still unaware that the president would be alone at the theater that evening, and that was the basic requirement for the execution to take place since Booth would be alone and without the assistance of any of his fellow conspirators. As Lincoln himself did not learn until approximately 5 P.M. that General Grant had snubbed his invitation to accompany him to the theater, there is certainly no way Booth could have known prior to 5 P.M. that the president would be unattended. So again the question must be asked, why would Booth send his field glasses and a message to John Lloyd at 1 P.M. that day "to have the shooting irons ready" when he himself would not know until later that afternoon that he would be engaged in his deadly work that evening.

It was Good Friday, and it seems that Booth was engaged in nothing more devious at this point than good-naturedly enjoying the warm spring weather and passing the time of day with various friends and acquaintances throughout the Washington area. Booth next sauntered to the rear exit of Ford's Theatre, where he passed some time speaking with various actresses and stagehands. Rehearsal for *Our American Cousin* had just ended and Booth entered the theater and peeped over the shoulder of William J. Ferguson, the call boy, who was making preparations for the state box where the presidential party would be seated.

Booth, accompanied by Ferguson and James Maddox, the theater's property man, then walked next door to Taltavull's Star Saloon, where they enjoyed a drink. Ferguson would later remember that Booth was in a cheerful, talkative mood, though he had remarked that he was suffering from pleurisy and not feeling well. After the drink at Taltavull's, Booth started for Pumphrey's Stable but stopped in at the National Hotel and wrote a letter, which he sealed and placed in his coat pocket.

Minutes later Booth was at the entrance to the stable, where he encountered his old friend Col. C. F. Cobb. Referring to Vice President Johnson, Booth asked Cobb if he had heard "that dirty tailor from Tennessee" speak in front of Willard's Hotel. When Cobb replied in the negative, Booth said, "If I had been there I would have shot the son of a bitch." Cobb concluded that Booth had imbibed too much brandy and simply laughed off his friend's remark.

Booth mounted his horse and trotted down Sixth Street

to Pennsylvania Avenue, then continued on towards the White House for some four blocks until he saw Charles Warwick, an actor friend, who was recovering from a recent illness. Booth stopped, reached down, and shook Warwick's hand and told him he was glad to see him looking better. Warwick would later testify that Booth seemed in unusually good spirits that afternoon. He did not appear worried or mentally preoccupied, said Warwick. He certainly did not behave like a man on a mission to execute the president of the United States. (But of course at that point he was *not* on a mission to execute the president.)

Booth then returned to Ford's Theatre and chatted briefly out front with James Maddox, explaining what a fine horse he had just rented. A few minutes later James Ferguson, owner of the restaurant that adjoined the theater, stepped out onto his porch and Booth, with boyish enthusiasm, called to him and said, "See what a nice horse I've got. Now watch, he can run like a cat!" He then wheeled, spurred the mare, and began a run back down Tenth Street towards Pennsylvania Avenue.

Minutes later, at the corners of Thirteenth and Fourteenth Streets, Booth paused in his antics to speak with John Matthews, an old friend who played an unscrupulous agent in *Our American Cousin*. Matthews would later remember that Booth appeared so pale and nervous that Matthews had asked him what was wrong. Booth assured him that there was no problem. Matthews then called his attention to a group of emaciated Confederate prisoners of war being escorted by, and Booth had shaken his head and sighed, "Great God! I have no longer a country." Booth then asked Matthews if he would do him a favor. "I might have to leave town tonight," he said, "and I have a letter here which I desire to be published in the *National Intelligencer*. Please attend to it for me, unless I see you before ten o'clock tomorrow; in that case I will see to it myself."

Some two years later, during the trial of John Surratt in 1867, John Matthews would testify that the day following the assassination, he sat down in his hotel room and read

Booth's letter to the *National Intelligencer*. The contents of that letter so frightened him, he said, that he immediately wadded it up and tossed it in the fire. Then he took a poker and stirred up the ashes. He was so terrified that the letter might somehow implicate him in the conspiracy that he kept it quiet until his testimony. But, he added as a happy afterthought, he had memorized the final paragraphs and could still recall them. Asked to repeat them, Mathews stated:

> For a long time I have devoted my energies, my time, and money to the accomplishment of a certain end. I have been disappointed. The moment has now arrived when I must change my plans. Many will blame me for what I am about to do; but posterity, I am sure, will justify me.
>
> Men who love their country better than gold or life, John W. Booth, Payne, Herold, Atzerodt.

To date, it seems that everyone—the government, historians, and the public—have accepted without question Matthews' word that Booth wrote this letter, a confession of sorts, that he, aided and abetted by Lewis Powell, David Herold, and George Atzerodt, intended to murder Lincoln. (Yet the letter only implies that Booth intends to take a drastic step. It never explicitly states the murder of Lincoln.) Still, it seems fair to ask, just how reliable was Matthews' testimony? It must be remembered that according to his own testimony, more than two years had elapsed since a trembling John Matthews had sat down the morning following the assassination and read this letter. How remarkable it is that two years later he should still retain a verbatim recollection of the final paragraphs. It also must be recalled that no one ever saw this letter except John Matthews. Therefore, we have only his dubious word that Booth was its author.

It is also troubling that Booth referred to his fellow assassin Lewis Powell simply as "Payne" since Booth knew full well that Payne was merely an alias. The truth of his name was shared by only John Surratt and the Branson sisters. To everyone else, including Federal investigators, Powell was known as Lewis Payne. It seems, if Booth were truly the author of the above missive and that missive was to be saved for posterity, he would have referred to his accomplice by his true name.

Yet, for what possible reason would Matthews want to lie, unless it was to establish at trial that John Surratt was an active collaborator of a confessed assassin? What of the rest of the letter, those paragraphs that Matthews could not recall? Did Booth implicate anyone else, high government officials, perhaps? In 1867, when Booth's diary finally appeared at trial, a passage revealed, "I am of a good mind to return to Washington and clear my name, which I feel I can do without much trouble." Could this letter that Matthews destroyed possibly shed any light on that enigmatic statement?

As Matthews pocketed the letter, the one allegedly written at the National Hotel a short time earlier, he noted a coach passing rapidly towards the Capitol. He recognized General Grant as one of the passengers and commented, "Why there goes Grant. I thought he was coming to the theater to night with the president."

"Where?" exclaimed Booth.

"There," replied Matthews, pointing towards the coach. Matthews was surprised then to see Booth spur the mare and set off at a gallop after the coach.

Moments later Mrs. Grant noticed a horseman gazing into the coach and turned to her husband. "That is the same man that sat at the luncheon table near me. I don't like his looks." As the carriage turned off on First Street, heading for the Baltimore and Ohio station at C Street and New Jersey Avenue, a frightened Julia Grant again noted a man she later identified as Booth ride by and look intently at the Grants.

Puzzled, Booth then rode to Willard's and heard from patrons there the astonishing news that General and Mrs. Grant would be departing Washington within the next three hours for Brunswick, New Jersey. This was the news that likely sealed the fate of Abe Lincoln. Had Grant been present that evening, accompanied as he would have been by his military entourage, Booth could not possibly have assassinated the president. Certainly he would have been stopped before he had gotten within ten feet of Lincoln and Grant at Ford's Theatre. Booth was very much aware of that fact, which further calls into question the assassination letter he allegedly had just given to Matthews. When that letter was written at the National Hotel an hour or so earlier, Booth was still unaware that Grant would not attend Lincoln at the theater that evening.

Booth then left Willard's and rode to the Kirkwood House and tried once again to see Vice President Johnson. But the desk clerk said that Johnson still was not in. At that point, Booth made a strange move, doubtlessly his strangest move of the day. He requested the desk clerk give him a blank card. On this card he wrote, "Don't wish to disturb you. Are you at home?" He then signed his name and asked the clerk to deliver the card to Mr. Johnson. For a century and a half now historians have argued over the significance of that card.

As he was leaving the hotel he met on the front steps John Debonay, a former Maryland infantry officer and a longtime friend. Debonay asked him if he would be playing in the Washington area again in the near future, and Booth replied, "No, I'm not going to play again. I am in the oil business."

Booth then rode to the stable behind Ford's Theatre. He left his mare with Peanuts John and went into the theater to get a halter from Edman Spangler. Minutes later Spangler walked out to the stable with the halter and was about to remove the mare's saddle when Booth stopped him. "Never mind," Booth said, "I don't want it off but let it and the bridle remain." Booth, Peanuts John, Spangler, and Maddox then jauntily made their way to the bar next door and Booth set them all up to a drink.

At six-thirty that evening, according to Henry Merrick, Booth sat at a table in the National Hotel and had a cup of tea. He then went to his room. It is assumed that it was then that he picked up the bowie knife and Derringer that he would use in the attack on Lincoln later that evening. At about seven Booth descended the stairs and walked through the lobby of the National for the last time. "Are you going to

The controversial and enigmatic note that Booth left for Andrew Johnson on the day of the assassination. It would later be used against Johnson with great effect during his impeachment trial. National Archives

the theater tonight?" he asked George Bunker, the room clerk, as he tossed his keys on the desk. Bunker smiled and shook his head. "Well, you should. There will be some fine acting there tonight."

In truth, it must be said that Booth had not given the least indication through word or deed that he planned anything extraordinary for the evening of April 14. Based on the testimony of those who observed his activities and spoke with him that day, it is most difficult to believe that it was actually John Wilkes Booth who assassinated the president. He appeared to be as calm and collected as anyone in the city. Yet there can be no doubt that it was Booth who pulled the trigger.

As for Booth's fellow conspirators, on this day, just after 3 P.M., Lewis Powell, who had a weakness for good food, called Mrs. Murray, owner of the Herndon House, and telling her he was returning to Baltimore that evening, asked if he could be served dinner at four. George Atzerodt, who had taken room 126 at the Kirkwood House at eight that morning, was seen at about 2 P.M. at Howard's Stable, where he rented a horse for five dollars. He was seen by others throughout the day. David Herold, in the company of Atzerdot, was seen at 4 P.M. at Naylor's Stable, where he also rented a horse from John Fletcher for five dollars. Herold mounted the horse and asked Fletcher how late he could keep the horse. Fletcher told him to return the animal no later than nine o'clock. Herold nodded that nine would be fine. Fletcher never saw the horse or its rider again. At this point the four conspirators had all been furnished with horses, the one used by Powell furnished by Booth himself.

Of the absent conspirators, John Surratt was in Elmira, New York, Arnold was employed in Fortress Monroe, and a drunken Michael O'Laughlin was still in Washington partying with friends. He would later deny any prior knowledge of Lincoln's execution.

About five o'clock Herold and Atzerodt returned to Atzerodt's room at the Kirkwood House and rested for a few minutes. Before they left the room, Herold drew from his waistband an army Colt revolver and a large bowie knife, which Booth had given him a short time earlier. These weapons he very casually placed under Atzerodt's pillow. Unfortunately for Atzerodt, however, investigators would find these weapons the day following the execution and use them as "evidence" to prove that Atzerodt was a murderous cutthroat bent on killing Vice Pres. Andrew Johnson, a charge which would absolve Johnson of any complicity in the conspiracy (or so it was hoped).

But again, Booth was fully aware that George Atzerodt was no killer. Then why would Booth assign him, a man reputed to be a man afraid of his own shadow, to execute the second most important man in American government? And why would Booth go to all the trouble of planting this incriminating evidence in his room? Perhaps these puzzling questions can be answered in just two words: Andrew Johnson. But this episode with Atzerodt makes sense only if Andrew Johnson had been a prime mover in the conspiracy to assassinate Lincoln.

During Johnson's impeachment trial of 1867, Sen. Ben Butler would shake his fist at Johnson and shout to the top of the Senate Chambers that it was Johnson, and only Johnson, who had stood to gain from the assassination of Abraham Lincoln. Butler (and numerous others) left no doubt that they suspected Johnson of having masterminded the execution.

The evidence strongly suggests that Stanton and Johnson collaborated in planning Lincoln's execution and that they were motivated by their anger over Lincoln's conciliatory Reconstruction plans for the South. As for William Seward, of all Lincoln's cabinet members, he alone agreed with Lincoln that the Southern states must be brought back into the Union as though they had never been away. Thus Seward too must die.

Later on the evening of April 14, William Withers, director of the band at Ford's Theatre, would remember having a leisurely drink with Booth at about 7:30. During the conversation Withers laughingly remarked that Booth would never be as great as his father. At that, recalled Withers, "a smile passed across his face and he replied, 'When I leave the stage tonight, I will be the most talked about man in America.'"

The minutes ticked by, and at eight o'clock Booth, Powell, Herold, and Atzerodt, by prior agreement, met one last time in Powell's room at the Herndon House for a final conference. Booth then told his flabbergasted colleagues that the fateful hour had finally struck and it was his intention to execute two of the heads of American government. He himself would kill Abe Lincoln, he said. He then handed Lewis Powell a .44-caliber Whitney navy revolver, a long bowie knife, and a package of medicine. Powell would pretend to be a delivery boy from a pharmacist, which would gain him entrance to the home of Secretary of State William Seward, whom he would execute. Then, astride the mare provided by Booth, he would be guided out of the city by David Herold. Booth would meet them, he said, beyond the Anacostia Bridge. Atzerodt, Booth said casually, almost in passing, would assassinate Vice Pres. Andrew Johnson. At that point the terrified Atzerodt jumped to his feet and replied that he would not, could not, harm anyone. He had agreed to assist in abducting Lincoln during their earlier meetings, but he absolutely would not kill anyone. Quietly amused, Booth smiled and told Atzerodt that he was a fool, that the authorities would hang him anyway. But Atzerodt stuck to his guns.

Once this meeting ended Atzerodt would never see Wilkes Booth again. As for Powell and Herold, Atzerodt would not see them again until they were all placed on trial before that kangaroo court known as the Military Commission, the brainchild of Edwin Stanton.

Following their meeting, a frantic Atzerodt spent most of the night wandering from barroom to barroom throughout Washington. Then, totally inebriated, he spent the rest of the night at the Kimmel House. Early the next morning he made his way to the home of his cousin Hartman Richter in Germantown, Montgomery County, Maryland, where he was arrested six days later, on April 20. Oddly enough, Atzerodt's older brother, John Atzerodt, worked as a Baltimore police detective under Provost Marshal McPhail, and it is suspected that it was a tip from John Atzerodt that led to George Atzerodt's arrest at Richter's home. And sure enough, Booth was right: they did hang Atzerodt.

The Lincolns Attend the Theater

At the very moment Booth was meeting with Powell, Herold, and Atzerodt at the National Hotel, President and Mrs. Lincoln were seated in their carriage and on their way to pick up their guests for the evening, Maj. Henry Reed Rathbone and his fiancée Clara Harris, at the home of her father, New York senator Ira Harris, at H and Fifteenth Streets, just two short blocks from the White House. With them was Charles Forbes, Lincoln's loyal footman.

As for General Grant, an intriguing question surrounds him: Was Grant himself aware of the fatal conspiracy that would unfold that evening? Was that his true reason for

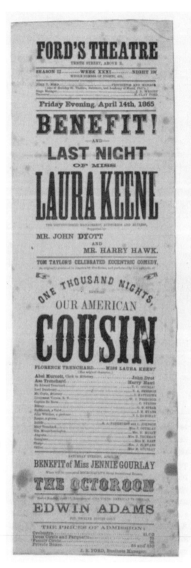

The playbill advertising Our American Cousin *and the play's primary actors, Laura Keene and Harry Hawk. It was well known that President Lincoln preferred light comedy to heavy drama and was looking forward to this particular play.*
Harvard Theater Collection, Harvard University

snubbing the president? If the secret papers of Lafayette Baker are to be believed, Grant must have been aware of it. Samuel Beckwith, Grant's cipher operator, in an article in the *New York Sun* on April 27, 1913, says, "As a matter of fact, Grant didn't want to go at all but he yielded to the President's request. When he learned at the War Department of the fears of Edwin Stanton he acquiesced at once in his suggestion that the visit to the playhouse be abandoned." As usual, when all the smoke clears away, there stands the unscrupulous Edwin Stanton.

Once the Lincolns received General Grant's refusal, Mary Lincoln immediately thought of issuing an invitation to Clara Harris, a dear young friend, and her fiancé, Rathbone. In addition to being Major Rathbone's fiancée, she was also his stepsister, his widowed mother having married Clara's father several years earlier. John Rathbone had served with distinction throughout the war and could serve as both a guest and a bodyguard for the president. (Another sad footnote to this affair: Major Rathbone and Clara Harris were married in 1867. In Hanover, Germany, on Christmas morning, 1883, Rathbone, who had gone quite mad since the assassination, murdered Clara and then spent the rest of his life in an insane asylum.)

The president and his guests were in high spirits as they drove the seven blocks from the Harris residence to Ford's Theatre. The rain of the past two days had finally given way to sunshine, now spring had burst forth in all its glory on this Good Friday, and the city was all alight in celebration of General Lee's surrender just five days before. As the carriage pulled in front of the theater, the president and his guests could see the yellowish flames of smoking tar torches stuck in barrels up and down Pennsylvania Avenue. They were part of the theater's efforts to attract patrons, with a barker standing beside each barrel shouting, "This way to Ford's Theatre."

By the time the president's party entered the theater the play had already begun and a large audience of well over a thousand persons was already becoming restless.

Many had come simply because they wanted to see President Lincoln and General Grant. And now the first scene was well underway and still no sign of the special guests. As though that were not enough, the majority had paid a dollar or more per ticket to attend a play that generally cost only a quarter.

The Lincoln party entered the theater by the southwest door and turned left towards the stairs leading to the dress circle. James O'Brien, an usher, led Lincoln and his party up the stairs. The president was escorted by Charles Forbes, his longtime attendant, and John Parker, a temporary bodyguard from the Metropolitan Police Department, whose duty it was to stand outside the president's box and make sure no one entered.

Previously Parker had been reprimanded repeatedly and suspended from duty for a series of drunken misadventures over the years. Since 1861 he had been charged with "insubordination, unbecoming conduct, loafing on beat, drunkenness while on duty, and arresting streetwalkers who had refused him their favors." In 1863, he had faced the police board to answer charges that he "had gone to bed drunk in a house of prostitution and had fired a pistol through the window of said brothel." Why Edwin Stanton would have chosen such a miscreant to guard the president on this night is anyone's guess. However, on April 2, 1865, it was Stanton who requested that Parker be excused from the military draft, taken off his beat, and detailed for duty at the executive mansion. What motivated Stanton is difficult to understand, unless he had ulterior motives.

It is also difficult to understand why Mary Todd Lincoln would agree to go along with Stanton's suggestion that Parker be assigned to the executive mansion as a bodyguard for the president. Likely she did so simply out of ignorance of Parker's ignoble behavior over the past several years, but it is a fact that she, at Stanton's suggestion, wrote a letter to Washington's provost marshal, James R. O'Beirne, requesting that Parker be transferred to the White House guard. Her note to O'Beirne reads as follows:

EXECUTIVE MANSION

Washington, April 3, 1865

This is to certify that John F. Parker, a member of the Metropolitan Police has been detailed for duty at the Executive Mansion by order of:

Mrs. Lincoln

Whatever Mrs. Lincoln's reasoning might have been in this instance, the government immediately had the matter hushed. This remains just another in a long series of enigmas that surround the assassination of Abe Lincoln.

When Booth entered the president's box during the fateful final act, Parker was nowhere to be found. It was later learned that at the moment Lincoln was attacked, Parker was at Taltavull's Star Saloon, next door to the theater, drinking whiskey and becoming quite inebriated. On May 1, A. C. Richards, superintendent of the Metropolitan Police Force, preferred charges of neglect of duty against Parker:

> In this, that Said Parker was detailed to attend and protect the President Mr. Lincoln, that while the President was at Ford's Theater on the night of the 14 of April last, Said Parker allowed a man to enter the President' private Box and Shoot the President.

Edwin Stanton, again for understandable reasons, ordered that all charges against Parker be dropped, and so a hearing into the matter was never conducted. Interestingly enough, in 1868 Parker was finally dismissed from the Washington police department for sleeping on a streetcar while on duty.

However, Lincoln suspected none of this when he entered the theater that night. The audience rose and cheered when they realized that the president and his party were now in the theater, and the band struck up "Hail to the Chief." Lincoln, who hated such demonstrations, bowed deeply, then proceeded to Box 7. The president, as usual, seated himself in the rocker in the left-hand corner of the box, and Mary sat in a chair between the president and the pillar in the center. Miss Harris sat in one of the two chairs at the opposite side of the box while Major Rathbone sat on the couch next to Miss Harris. This arrangement placed Rathbone about eight feet from the president and about the same distance from the door. Lincoln himself was only about four feet from the door. Clay Ford would later testify that Booth was thoroughly familiar with the layout of Box 7 since that was the box he always chose for himself when attending a play at the theater.

From the president's position in the box, shaded as he was by draperies, he could be seen from the theater floor only when he leaned forward. One witness testified that during intermission following the first act, Lincoln leaned forward in his rocking chair, his elbows propped on the box railing, his chin resting on his hands. He appeared to be studying the audience to see if he recognized anyone there.

Booth Moves in for the Kill

Following his meeting with Powell, Atzerodt, and Herold at the Herndon House, Booth returned to Ford's Theatre. There was now a damp chill in the air, but Booth hardly noticed. John Ford had given him the run of the theater and he was totally familiar with both the theater and the alley behind it. It was now approximately 9 P.M.

Booth stood quietly outside the theater, his eyes slowly adjusting to the darkness. At last he turned, and as he passed Clay Ford seated inside the box office, he reached his hand in the window and playfully placed a partially smoked cigar on a small shelf inside. "In a mock heroic bombastic furioso style," he gave Ford a wink and laughingly warned, "Who e'er this cigar dares displace must meet Wilkes Booth face to face." Ford recognized these lines as a parody of lines in a popular play of the day and laughed good-naturedly.

Clay Ford would later testify that if Booth planned to murder the president or anyone else that evening, he certainly gave no indication of it at that point.

This encounter with Ford marked the first of about six times Booth would be seen in Ford's Theatre on the evening of April 14. He was also seen in Taltavull's Star Saloon on a number of occasions, apparently moving back and forth between the theater and the saloon as the mood struck him. Several witnesses claimed to have seen and spoken with him at various times prior to the conclusion of the first act around nine o'clock.

It was at this time that Booth went to the stable behind the theater and retrieved the bay mare left there earlier in the evening. Leading her by the bridle, he walked her to the rear entrance of the theater. There, he met John Debonay, a scene shifter, and told him to get Edman Spangler, a carpenter and handyman at the theater. It might be pointed out that Booth and Spangler were old acquaintances, Spangler having helped build the Booth home in Bel Air years earlier. Once Spangler arrived outside, Booth handed him his horse's bridle and asked him to hold his horse for the next hour.

Booth then entered the theater and asked Debonay if he could cross the theater by the back stage. Debonay told him that the back stage was in use and he would have to walk under the stage and up on the other side. Immediately following Booth's departure, Spangler, still standing outside, called to Debonay to ask Peanuts John Burroughs, a boy of fourteen, to come out back and hold Booth's mare, claiming that he had no time. Debonay did as ordered, but Burroughs, who was sitting at a side entrance to the theater to make sure no gate crashers entered without paying, went to Spangler and stated that he could not hold Booth's horse since he could not leave his post by the side door. At that point, Spangler spoke harshly to Burroughs, ordering him to take the mare in tow. Burroughs, generally described as "a simple-minded young man," did as ordered and spent the rest of the play either sitting or lying down on a nearby bench, the mare's reins in his hands.

Following Debonay's instructions, Booth quietly lifted a trapdoor cut into the floor in the right-hand corner of the back-stage area and descended a flight of wooden steps that led to a dirt cellar directly beneath the stage. Passing under the stage to the opposite side, he came to a second set of stairs. These he ascended. Thus he was able to pass from one side of the stage to the other without bothering the actors or stagehands busy at their work.

It was approximately ten o'clock when Booth was seen for the final time in Taltavull's saloon. He came in, the owner later testified, and ordered brandy. He downed it immediately, put some money down on the bar, turned and went back to the theater. Ten minutes later Taltavull heard shouts that the president had been shot.

After leaving the saloon, Booth reentered the theater and crossed the front lobby to the staircase on the left, which led to the dress circle and boxes above. He ascended the stairs and began moving across the rear promenade that led to the box where Lincoln was seated. Because of the large crowd, Booth was forced to walk in front of dozens of people who were standing in the rear of the promenade. Two soldiers, Capt. Theodore McGowan and Lt. Alexander Crawford, were seated in chairs in the narrow passageway leading to the president's box. They would later testify that they saw a man, whom they described as Wilkes Booth, enter the passageway, and they were forced to lean their chairs forward in order to allow the man to pass behind them. Booth then did a strange thing. He apparently recognized Charles Forbes, Lincoln's personal valet and messenger, seated just outside the outer door leading to the president's box. Booth paused, spoke briefly to Forbes, then took a small card from his vest pocket. He wrote a message on the card and handed it to Forbes, who read the card then carried it to Lincoln. Moments later, he returned to his seat, leaving the door that led to the president's box open to the assassin.

Since Forbes was never called to testify at the trial of the conspirators, no one has ever learned why Booth stopped to speak with him, what Booth wrote on the card, or what

Forbes did with the card once he entered the president's box. Since Forbes could have offered testimony that would have shed much light on the events of this evening, why he was not called on to testify remains an enigma.

Powell Attacks Seward

At the very moment that Booth was approaching the president's box at Ford's Theatre, Lewis Thornton Powell and David Herold quietly reined their horses in the front yard of William Seward's home on Lafayette Square. Powell was aware that the secretary had been badly injured in a carriage wreck the week before and was now lying in bed with a heavy metal brace around his neck and chin. As a result Powell had very cleverly disguised himself as a pharmacist's delivery boy and was carrying a bottle of medicine. At that point, the fearless Powell dismounted his horse and handed the reins to Herold. He took the front steps in a single bound and gave a hearty knock at the door. To make sure that he had come prepared, he patted the big bowie knife and the heavy Whitney revolver, which he had tucked into the waistband of his trousers.

Seconds later his knock was answered by William Bell, Seward's houseboy. Powell flashed him a smile and asked him if he could come in, as he had been instructed to deliver medication to Mr. Seward personally. Totally convinced of Powell's sincerity, Bell stepped aside and motioned for Powell to enter. Bell then closed the door and told Powell that Seward was resting in an upstairs bedroom. Powell thanked him and calmly began mounting the stairs. Just as he reached the top step, he was halted by Seward's son, Frederick Seward, who told him that his father was sleeping and no one could be admitted to his room. He then held out his hand and requested that Powell give him the medication. Momentarily confused by this turn of events, Powell shook his head and stepped backwards as though to descend the stairs. But then, moving quickly as a cat, he drew his revolver from his

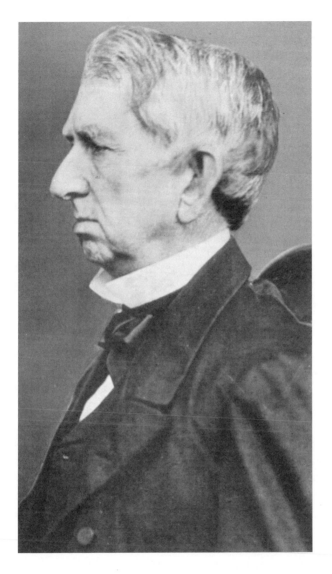

Secretary of State William Seward did everything in his power to persuade Lincoln not to go to war with the South over secession. In April 1865, because he supported Lincoln's conciliatory Reconstruction program for the South, he too was targeted for assassination. A metal neck brace saved his life. Library of Congress

waistband, whirled, and began pistol-whipping the aston-ished Frederick Seward about the head until he collapsed unconscious upon the floor, his skull shattered.

The next two minutes passed in a blur of confusion. Powell looked at his broken revolver and tossed it to the floor. He then pulled the bowie knife and crashed through the door to Seward's bedroom, leaping bodily upon the injured sec-retary. He began stabbing and slashing Seward with a force born of anger and fear until pulled away by Sgt. George Robinson, an invalid Maine soldier and acting nurse. A ter-rible fight then ensued between Powell, Robinson, and Seward's other son, Augustus, who had been awakened by the murderous brawl going on in his father's bedroom. Finally Powell broke free of his assailants and quickly fled down the stairs, stabbing and wounding a State Department messenger who made the mistake of getting in his way.

Later it would be determined that Seward, thanks to his heavy neck brace, would survive the attack. In fact, no one was actually killed, though Powell did manage to severely wound five men in less than five minutes. (At trial, Powell was asked why he attacked Seward. Very coolly, he replied, "I'm a Confederate soldier. I was merely doing my duty—as I've done for the past four years.")

Having exited the house, Powell now found to his dismay that a terrified Herold, hearing screams issuing from the house, had deserted him, leaving Powell's horse tied to a tree. He mounted his one-eyed mare and calmly trotted away from the scene of his crime. Soon, however, aware that he was totally lost and had not the least idea where he was or how to find the escape route out of Washington, he dis-mounted his horse and took to the woods. He came upon an abandoned cemetery, and there he hid for the next three days. But on Monday night, April 17, after living for three days and nights in the cold, deprived of food and fresh water, confused and frightened, Powell was finally forced to seek shelter. (It is interesting to speculate how history might have been different had Herold remained at his post that night and led Powell out of Washington as he had been assigned.

Had that been the case, it is possible that neither Powell, Mrs. Surratt, nor David Herold would ever have been hanged. In fact, there is a good chance that Powell would never have been apprehended had he managed to escape to Virginia.)

In an effort to disguise himself, he fashioned a toboggan from the sleeve of his undershirt, and this he pulled down low on his forehead. He managed to find a rusty pickax, which he threw across his shoulder. Then he began searching for the boardinghouse of Mrs. Mary Surratt. An hour later, he was being questioned by Detective John Clarvoe.

Booth Executes the President

His heart pounding, aware that neither his life nor the life of his family would ever be the same again, Wilkes Booth flashed Charles Forbes, the president's personal valet, a warm smile and quietly entered the outer door. For long moments he stood in that dark alcove, silently rehearsing his next move. He opened the door to the president's box, and there before him sat the man who had destroyed the Constitution, democracy in America, and was now on the verge of subjecting the South to a terribly vindictive Reconstruction program. There was no bodyguard, and Lincoln and his companions were totally engrossed in the play on stage. At that point Booth, who was not a violent man, must have felt a tremendous sense of anxiety over what he was about to do—as well as a sense of relief that his great plan to rid the nation of Lincoln was going as scheduled. Very quietly he reached into his coat pocket and withdrew his weapon, a tiny Derringer. He pulled back the hammer and took a silent step forward. Then, holding the pistol only inches from the back of the president's head, he pulled the trigger. There was a sudden ear-splitting explosion, and white smoke billowed forth in the darkness. The president pitched forward in his seat. Had Lincoln been sitting upright the bullet would have entered the right side of his head. But

Maj. Henry R. Rathbone and his fiancée, Clara H. Harris, were last-minute guests of the Lincolns at the theater on the evening of April 14. In 1882 Rathbone, by then an opium addict, was named consul general to Germany. A year later he went berserk and stabbed Clara, whom he had wed in 1867, to death. He spent the rest of his life in an asylum for the criminally insane in Hildesheim, Germany, dying in 1911. Library of Congress

as luck would have it, he was looking down at someone sitting in the orchestra seats. As a result, the heavy lead ball entered his head about three inches behind his left ear and ploughed seven and a half inches through his brain before coming to rest just above his right eye.

It strikes one as especially odd that Booth should have armed himself with a *single-shot* Derringer to perform this deed. In 1865 firearms were readily available, and it is known that Booth owned several six-shot .44 Colt revolvers. Considering all the unknowns faced by Booth on this most important night of his life, it seems that he would have chosen a multi-shot revolver for the assassination. One cannot help but wonder, for example, what he would have done had Major Rathbone, instead of observing the play, been standing by with a cocked .44 revolver in his hand, waiting for an intruder to open that door. Armed as he was with a single-shot Derringer, Booth conceivably could have shot Rathbone, but what would he then do about the president? What would he have done had General Grant at the last moment decided to accompany the president to the play? Or what would he have done had he encountered presidential bodyguards in the box, and he armed only with a single-shot Derringer?

It might also be pointed out that Associated Press reporter Lawrence Gobright, who was searching for his lost watch, found the Derringer on the floor of the box the afternoon following the execution and so it has always been assumed that it was the weapon Booth used to assassinate the president. In fact, it is not known for certain that Booth ever owned this weapon or if it was the murder weapon. Since this was a smoothbore weapon, it would be impossible for authorities to conduct ballistics tests to determine if it was the weapon used to kill the president. For all the authorities know, Booth might have used a six-shot .44 Colt revolver. He or one of the dozens of detectives, physicians, military men, or theater employees who crowded into the box following the assassination might very well have dropped the Derringer simply by accident.

Whatever the gun that fired the shot, the sound startled Major Rathbone, who had been sitting with his back to the door. He leapt to his feet at the noise and saw Booth through the haze of white smoke. Booth shouted something, which Rathbone remembered as "freedom," and attacked Rathbone with his bowie knife. The major grabbed Booth and began to grapple with him, but the assassin broke free and struck at the major's chest with the knife. Rathbone blocked the

Boxes 7 and 8 (far right) at Ford's Theatre were combined and gaily decorated with patriotic flags to accommodate the president and his party on April 14. Witnesses testified that Booth did not leap over the front railing of the box to the stage, some twelve feet below, but gripped the railing with his right hand and simply lowered himself to the stage, a drop of only about three feet. National Archives

blade with his left arm, receiving a wound several inches deep and an inch long. As the major bent over in agony, Booth turned to the front of the box, placed his right hand on the railing, and gently lowered himself to the stage.

Members of the audience and the cast heard the shot, but it apparently occurred to no one that the president had just been executed. Some thought the shot had come from the bar next door; others thought it had come from the theater's property room. Of course the war had just ended and still others thought the shot had come from celebrants outside, which was not uncommon. Clay Ford,

Ford's Theatre the day following the assassination, with its windows and doors draped in black crepe. Upon the orders of Edwin Stanton, the theater was not allowed to reopen for several months. Library of Congress

seated in the treasurer's office, glanced back at the stage just in time to see Booth, knife in hand, standing on the stage and thought that Booth was pursuing someone who had insulted him. During the trial of the conspirators, over a hundred witnesses would come forward and swear that they had seen Booth before, during, and after the play, then, following the shot, saw him lower himself to the stage and shout some words, though there was general disagreement as to what those words were.

When Edwin Stanton finally was forced to release Booth's diary during the trial of John Surrat in 1867, the following entry was written early in that controversial record:

> I struck boldly and not as the papers say. I walked with a firm step through a thousand of his friends, was stopped, but pushed on. A colonel was at his side. I shouted *Sic Semper* before I fired. In jumping broke my leg. I passed all his pickets, rode sixty miles that night, with the bone of my leg tearing the flesh at every jump. I shall never repent it, though we hated to kill. Our country owed all her troubles to him, and God simply made me the instrument of his punishment.

President Lincoln would finally succumb to his wounds about seven o'clock the next morning. As for Booth, thanks to incompetence—or collaboration—of Washington authorities, he would not be found for another twelve days.

VI

Booth Makes His Escape

Immediately after knocking Peanuts John to the ground, Booth mounted his horse and quickly galloped down the darkened alleyway that led to F Street. He turned east onto Pennsylvania Avenue in the direction of the Capitol as he fled toward his main goal, the Navy Yard Bridge, located at the end of Eleventh Street in southeast Washington.

Behind him the theater was in turmoil. The president lay dying and Major Rathbone badly wounded. The screams of Mary Todd Lincoln had alerted the audience that something was terribly wrong in the president's box, and confusion and fear suddenly took hold. Physicians and military personnel were beginning to pour into the president's box as hundreds of spectators seated below were wondering aloud what role Wilkes Booth had played in the great mystery swirling about them.

Within minutes Edwin Stanton, Maj. Thomas Eckert, and other Washington officials were notified that the president had been mortally wounded (Lafayette Baker was in New York on April 14). Now, one would assume, Stanton would immediately have Eckert telegraph the news of the assassination throughout the nation, and the name John Wilkes Booth, along with his physical description and probable destination, would be on everyone's lips by morning. But such was not to be. In fact, more than four hours would pass before the first dispatch announcing Lincoln's wounding left Eckert's Telegraph Office. When Eckert's dispatch finally did go out at 2:30 A.M., it still did not mention the name John Wilkes Booth. Moreover, another two hours would elapse

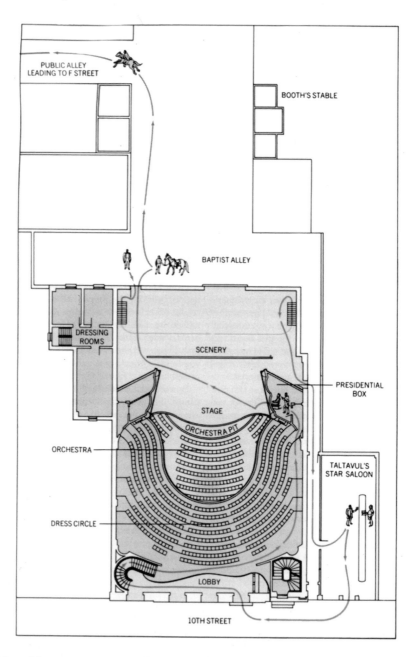

Booth's escape route from Ford's Theatre

before Eckert saw fit to wire newspapers that Booth was a suspect in the shooting. By then it was far too late for morning newspapers to announce that citizens should be on the lookout for Booth. Not until 3 A.M. did Stanton order Eckert to mention Booth by name. Since the majority of newspapers depended on the War Department for the bulk of their news out of Washington, they could not inform citizens of the assassin's identity until the afternoon of April 15.

Even more bizarre than the delay in mentioning Booth's name is the fact that all telegraph communications between Washington and the outside world were interrupted at the moment of Lincoln's wounding and remained off for over two hours. George A. Townsend, a reporter for the *New York World,* wrote on May 2:

> Within fifteen minutes after the murder, the wires were severed entirely around the city, excepting only a secret wire for government uses, which leads to Old Point. I am told that by this wire the government reached the fortifications around Washington, first telegraphing all the way to Old Point, and then back to the outlying forts. This information comes to me from so many creditable channels that I must concede it.

Obviously, if the conspirators were able to isolate Washington by disrupting its wire communications, then the conspirators must have been far more numerous than anyone has ever been aware. As the so-called break was repaired in only a few hours, the ease with which the problem was repaired suggests that there was never a break in the first place. As a result of these circumstances, rumors and suspicions concerning the failure of the telegraph immediately following Lincoln's assassination would not go away. In 1867, during the impeachment investigation of Andrew Johnson, this matter was raised, and Maj. Thomas Eckert was called to the witness stand:

> *Q.* Did you have knowledge of the telegraph lines at or about the time of the assassination of President Lincoln?
> *A.* I did.
> *Q.* Was there any interruption of the lines that night?
> *A.* Yes, sir.

*Maj. Thomas Eckert, assistant secretary of war under Edwin
Stanton and director of the Telegraph Office. Lafayette Baker
named Eckert as the man who made the arrangements for the
president's execution. He would later become a multi-million-
aire as owner of the American Telegraph Company.* Library of
Congress

Q. What was it?

A. It was my impression at the time that they were cut, but we got circuit again very early the next morning. The manager of the Commercial office reported the cause to have been crossing of wires in main batteries. Throwing a ground wire over the main wires would have caused the same trouble, and taking it off would have put it in ordinary working condition.

Q. Was there an investigation into what was the real cause of the difficulty?

A. No, sir. It did not at the time seem to be sufficiently important, as the interruption only continued about two hours. I was so full of business of almost every character that I could not give it my personal attention. The interruption was only of a portion of the lines between Washington and Baltimore. We worked our City Point lines all the time.

Q. Do you know whether the Commercial lines were interrupted at that time?

A. Yes, sir. It was only the Commercial lines that were interrupted; it was in the Commercial office and not in the War Department office. I could not ascertain with certainty what the facts were without making a personal investigation, and I had not the time to do that.

Even to the novice, that famous interruption in telegraphic services at a critical point in our history appears to have been the work of someone on Stanton or Eckert's staff. Certainly a conspirator without the support of these government offices could not have approached the main batteries without being detected. In order to avoid detection, a conspirator likely would have disrupted service by simply slipping out in the darkness and cutting the wires. But that was not done. Someone had tampered with the batteries and provided Lincoln's assassins with the time they needed to make their escape. Had Booth not been hobbled by a broken leg, he could easily have been aboard a ship bound for Mexico by the time his name was telegraphed around the nation.

It seems just as strange that once dispatches were being issued from the War Department, Stanton would first alert troops in the northern and northwestern areas of the capital, a direction the assassin would not pursue since he would find neither friends nor shelter there. The next dispatch was sent to military units in southwestern Washington, another area Booth would avoid. Indeed, by morning all western and northwestern exits out of Washington had been closed. Strangely enough, Stanton's next dispatch was to alert troops in Baltimore, northeast of the city. Such measures might have proven beneficial had Booth determined to remain in Washington. But by 4 A.M. he was thirty miles *southeast* of Washington.

Incredibly, Stanton left only one possible exit out of Washington unguarded, the road that led south from Washington to Port Tobacco. Back on February 20 Louis Weichmann and Captain Gleason had advised Edwin Stanton that this was the route the conspirators would travel if and when they should abduct the president. Had Stanton only bothered to glance at a map, he would have seen that the most reasonable escape route for Booth was the one leading to Port Tobacco. It was the one road that Booth was familiar with, the one he had planned to use from the very beginning, for it led straight to Richmond and safety. But of all the dispatches sent by the War Department Office during the morning hours of April 15, not one mentioned this particular route and no precautions were taken to guard it. There should never have existed the slightest doubt that this was the route Booth would use. This route had been known throughout the war as the underground railroad to Richmond and was constantly used by Confederate agents of every stripe. Certainly no other section of the country could boast of more rabid secessionists than the southern Maryland peninsula. The fact that Booth could remain in hiding in that area for twelve days without being detected by the swarms of Union soldiers searching for him is proof that he very wisely chose the correct route. Yet Stanton sent not a single message to guard or search that particular route.

Meanwhile, Booth's heart pounded as he neared the Navy Yard Bridge, the principle route leading from Washington into Maryland over the Potomac River. By tomorrow his name would be on everyone's lips as the executioner of Abe Lincoln, and he would be hailed as a great hero throughout the South, and in time the North as well. Indeed, his future was assured. Perhaps he would spend a few years in Mexico or Europe, at least until the truth of the execution could be made public, then he would return to Washington to accept the applause of a grateful nation.

At that point his final destination was uncertain, though he might have intended to make his way to the coast of Virginia, where he would take a British ship to Matamoros, Mexico. Booth was aware that John Surratt's older brother, Isaac Surratt, was now living in Matamoros, and certainly that city would be a perfect hiding place for him as well. Of course he would be traveling in disguise, which would be no problem for an experienced actor. Indeed, John Surratt himself would do the same when taking a ship from Canada to England months later. Regardless, Booth's future seemed assured, though his first priority at the moment was to escape the clutches of the Federal army.

Later, John Fletcher, who managed Thompson Naylor's stable, would report that by chance he had seen Booth riding furiously for the Navy Yard Bridge, followed moments later by a second rider, very possibly David Herold, who had abandoned Lewis Powell at the Seward household and was now fleeing Washington in a panic. It was approximately 11 P.M.

Unfortunately for the conspirators, Herold had rented a horse from Fletcher earlier in the afternoon and was then two hours past due in returning it, which caused Fletcher some anxiety. Simply by coincidence, Fletcher had just departed the stable and was walking up Pennsylvania Avenue when he happened to see a man who resembled David Herold trotting up Fifteenth Street. Fletcher ran after him, shouting for the man to return the horse, but the man responded by spurring the mare and taking off at a gallop in the direction of the Navy Yard Bridge. Fletcher pondered his next move.

Guarding the bridge on this evening were three Union soldiers, Sgt. Silas T. Cobb and two privates. Despite General Lee's surrender five days earlier, passage into or out of the capital still required passing a military post. Thus Cobb stepped out and challenged Booth when he galloped up to the bridge. At that point, Booth did a strange thing for a man trying to escape the authorities: he told Cobb his name was Wilkes Booth and his destination was Beantown, a small village in southern Maryland. Why Booth would reveal both his true name and his true destination remains a mystery. According to Sergeant Cobb, in testimony offered three days later, the following dialogue passed between them:

"Who are you, sir?"

"My name is Wilkes Booth."

"Where are you from?"

"The city."

"Where are you going?"

"I'm going home."

"Where would that be?"

"Charles."

"What town?"

"No town."

"Look here, you must live in some town."

"I live close to Beantown, but I don't live in the town."

"Don't you know that travelers aren't allowed to pass after nine o'clock?"

"That's new to me."

Booth then explained that he had been to Washington on an errand, and since the night was unusually dark, he had waited for the moon to rise to start home.

Cobb stated that he suspected the rider to be some rich man's son who had been "pleasuring" in the city. Such being the case and satisfied that the well-dressed gentleman posed no dire threat to the Union, Cobb waved Booth over the bridge. (If this rider had a broken leg, Cobb did not mention it.) Less than ten minutes later, a second rider came breathlessly galloping up to the bridge. Again Cobb stepped out to learn the identity and destination of this rider. This time the rider (allegedly David Herold, though Herold would later deny that he was that rider) gave an alias and said that he had been visiting a woman in Washington and had overstayed his visit and was now returning home to southern

The Navy Yard Bridge that Booth and Herold crossed from Washington into Maryland immediately following the assassination. This photograph was taken from the Maryland side looking back towards Washington. Library of Congress

Maryland. Cobb grinned at this revelation, warned the man that he had better make up a good excuse for his wife, gave him a wink, then waved him through.

Only minutes later, a third rider approached the bridge. This time it was a law-abiding citizen, John Fletcher, who patiently explained to Cobb that he managed a Washington stable and was now in pursuit of a man who had stolen his horse. Cobb eyed Fletcher warily; his story sounded a bit fishy. Not sure exactly how to handle this suspicious character, Cobb told Fletcher that he could pass over the bridge, but he could not return until morning. Frustrated and angry at Cobb's ruling, Fletcher wheeled his horse around and returned to Washington.

An hour later Fletcher was standing in the office of Gen. Christopher Augur, commander of the Twenty-second Army Corps, in downtown Washington. He asked the general if anyone had turned in a stray horse. Augur told him that no one had, but then Augur asked Fletcher if he recognized a saddle that had just been found. Fletcher looked at the saddle and immediately stated that it was the one he had rented to George Atzerodt that afternoon. Coincidentally, Fletcher told Augur, Atzerodt was a close associate of David Herold, the man who had stolen his horse and ridden it across the Navy Yard Bridge earlier that night.

Augur at that point began putting two and two together. Apparently, based on his reasoning, Atzerodt and Herold must have been the two men who had ridden across the Navy Yard Bridge and into southern Maryland. Augur reported this information to the provost marshal's office, and later that morning the provost sent a detective, John Lee, to search Atzerodt's room at the Kirkwood House. Lee was informed by the clerk at the Kirkwood that Atzerodt, a highly suspicious looking character who spoke broken English, had taken room 126, just above the room of Vice Pres. Andrew Johnson. Lee thanked the clerk, then took the steps two at a time to the second floor. When he searched Atzerodt's room he found not only a revolver and a large bowie knife hidden under Atzerodt's pillow but also a bankbook bearing the name J. Wilkes Booth. All this evidence Lee immediately returned to the provost's office. The military now had three names—Herold, Atzerodt, and Booth—and all were linked one to the other. At least two of them had passed across the Navy Yard Bridge into southern Maryland the previous night, their destination possibly the small village known as Beantown.

Only hours later, on the morning of April 15, General Augur dispatched a troop from the Thirteenth New York Cavalry, under Lt. David Dana, into southern Maryland. At noon they arrived at Bryantown, only a few miles from Beantown and the home of Dr. Samuel A. Mudd.

Booth, meanwhile, at approximately 11:30 A.M., inexplicably met with Herold at a place called Soper's Hill, some eight miles southeast of Washington. Whether this meeting was prearranged or a matter of coincidence is not known, but Herold would later swear that it was nothing more than coincidence. The two riders then headed for the tavern Mrs. Surratt had leased to John Lloyd in Surrattsville, thirteen miles southeast of Washington, their purpose to retrieve the weapons left there earlier by John Surratt.

At least this is what transpired according to the later testimony offered by John Lloyd at the trial of the conspirators. Still, several questions should be asked: first, what good would weapons do Booth and Herold at this point? They were not expecting to shoot their way out of Maryland; to the contrary, at this point their main ally was speed. As quickly as possible they must get to Virginia, where they would find friends and safety. For what reason, therefore, would they waste precious time with John Lloyd at the tavern? Lloyd, the government's star witness, testified that David Herold had awakened him from a drunken stupor on the morning of April 15 and asked for the rifles; however, Lloyd admitted that he had been so drunk at the time that he could hardly recall the event.

Another question at this point is: Was it Booth who was riding with Herold that night? Lloyd testified that the man who accompanied Herold on horseback did not enter the tavern but waited outside in the darkness, and it was impossible to make out the rider's features. Did Lloyd know Booth? No, he said, he had never seen Booth. Whoever the rider was, he yelled for Herold not to bring him a rifle since his leg hurt too badly for him to carry a weapon. That was testimony enough for the Military Commission: they concluded, based on Lloyd's recollections, that the rider must have been John Wilkes Booth.

After leaving John Lloyd to his agonizing hangover, the two men then rode to the home of Dr. Samuel A. Mudd, arriving there at about four in the morning. According to both Herold and Dr. Mudd, the man accompanying Herold did not break his leg when he jumped to the stage that night but did so hours later when the horse he was riding tripped and fell near Teebee. Herold recalled in detail how his companion had lain on the ground, clinching his fist and sobbing in agony. Herold at that point helped him to his feet and assisted him in getting back in the saddle. The man identified by the Military Commission as Booth, gasping with agony, then told Herold that they could never make it to Port Tobacco. The pain was too great. They must find a doctor. Perhaps Herold was lying, but this story makes far more sense than to say that Booth, hobbled with a broken leg when he jumped to the stage that night, could possibly have performed all the physical gymnastics he allegedly performed. It is obvious that Booth's visit to Dr. Mudd that morning (if indeed it was Booth) came about as a result of his broken leg. Had he remained healthy, doubtlessly he and Herold could easily have crossed the Potomac and struck for freedom long before pursuing Federal cavalry caught up with them.

When they reached the doctor's home, Herold pounded on the front door, awakening Mudd. The good doctor, fearing harm from the numerous guerilla bands operating in the area, opened the door cautiously. It was then that he was introduced to the man with the broken leg. It was now Saturday morning, April 15, 1865, and Dr. Mudd invited the two inside, settled the man with the broken leg on a couch, and made a splint of sorts with the pasteboard sides from a hatbox. Then the injured man, who was in terrible pain, was fed a light supper, taken upstairs and put to bed. Following his arrest, Dr. Mudd twice swore under oath that he had never seen this man before the morning of April 15, nor had he ever seen the man called Herold. According to Dr. Mudd, Herold introduced himself as "Henston" and his injured companion as "Tyson."

At breakfast that morning, Dr. Mudd informed "Tyson" that his badly injured leg would take three to four weeks to heal. Undue movement or strain would aggravate the break. The injured man buried his face in his pillow and groaned loudly at that news.

At approximately ten that morning Dr. Mudd, claiming that he had to do some shopping, traveled to Bryantown, about four miles south of the Mudd farm. Upon arriving in the village, Dr. Mudd was startled to find the troop of cavalry under Lt. David Dana milling around in a local tavern, which they were using as a headquarters of sorts. Making inquiries, Dr. Mudd was amazed to learn that President Lincoln had been shot the night before and had died at 7:22

that morning. Mudd further learned from the soldiers that the assassin had been the famous actor John Wilkes Booth. Doubtlessly, had Mudd known the man in his home was Booth, he would have immediately informed Dana of that fact, partially from a sense of patriotism but mainly from a desire to save his own neck from the noose.

Around five o'clock, says Mudd, he returned home to find his two guests departing his farm. The injured man was already about seventy-five yards down the road, with his young companion ready to follow. Herold then asked Mudd for directions to a Parson Wilmer's home, which lay southwest of Mudd's residence across the Zekiah Swamp. Following the departure of the two strangers, Mudd returned to his wife, unaware of the grief that lay ahead as a result of his having rendered medical help to the injured stranger. For the rest of his life he would maintain that never before had he seen that injured man prior to that fateful morning.

According to the trial testimony of Dr. Samuel Mudd, the man who came to his house that morning with a broken leg was decidedly not John Wilkes Booth. Dr. Mudd twice swore under oath that the man who accompanied Herold to his home on the morning of April 15 was not Booth. He knew Booth well, said Dr. Mudd, but the man with the broken leg who came to his home that morning stood about six feet tall, had sandy red hair, and wore a false beard. Obviously this was not a description of John Wilkes Booth, who stood five foot seven and had jet black hair. Was the devoutly Christian Dr. Mudd telling the truth? If so, this would lend credence to the persistent rumor that Booth did not die in Garrett's barn on the morning of April 27 but somehow managed to escape. (Dr. Mudd was the first of several witnesses who would later claim that the body they viewed at autopsy had reddish-colored hair. One witness stated that the body had red hair and freckles.)

Besides, testified Mudd, he was merely living up to his Hippocratic oath as a physician when he set the man's broken leg, regardless of who the man might have been. At four o'clock on the morning of April 15, said Mudd, he was not even aware that the president had been assassinated. No one was aware of the assassination at that early hour. The Military Commission questioned Mudd as to why he had not informed the soldiers in Bryantown the next morning that Booth could be captured at his home. The doctor again insisted that he did not know that the man was Booth. He certainly did not look like him. Of course the Military Commission believed he was lying, and thus he escaped the gallows by only one vote.

At the same time Dr. Mudd was in Bryantown shopping on Saturday morning, April 15, Mrs. Surratt's star boarders, Louis Weichmann and John T. Holohan, entered the office of Maj. A. C. Richards, superintendent of the Metropolitan Police Department, and related their story concerning Wilkes Booth and the strange goings on at their boardinghouse over the past six months. Richardson was probably the most competent officer investigating the assassination, and he knew within five minutes that he had struck gold. Considering Weichmann's personality, he doubtlessly told Richards everything he could possibly want to know about Booth, John Surratt, Lewis Powell, and the other conspirators. Richards quickly decided that he had better hold on to this talkative witness. Following the interview Holohan was allowed to return home, but Richards took Weichmann in tow as his "personal prisoner," rounded up a squad of cavalry, and immediately set out for lower Maryland. By dusk they had found nothing, but that night Richards held Weichmann incommunicado at his police headquarters. The next morning, Easter Sunday, he rushed Weichmann to Baltimore for a secret conference with Provost Marshal McPhail. Then, still hoping to cash in on Weichmann's intimate knowledge of the conspirators, Richards received special permission from the War Department to take Weichmann to Montreal in hopes of spotting the elusive John Surratt.

Despite Richards' efforts, he would never receive any credit for his splendid police work. To the contrary, Stanton and other military authorities, in a snit because Richards had failed to share Weichmann's information with them and strongly suspecting that Richards wished to claim all the reward money for himself, would later charge that Richards had "appropriated" a key witness and kept valuable information from them. During the 1867 trial of John Surratt, Richards would be questioned about this matter:

> *Q.* And why did you appropriate Mr. Weichmann?
> *A.* We wanted to use Weichmann to pursue the suspected assassins of the President.
> *Q.* You had him in charge?
> *A.* Yes, sir. But not to his knowledge. It was our intention to hold him as a witness for the reason that certain other parties were monopolizing all the information, and we wanted to hold him, as we thought we had not been treated altogether proper.

Edwin Stanton's National Detective Police chief, Lafayette Baker, had been in New York for the past week, but he arrived in Washington on Easter Sunday, April 16, to take charge of the search for Booth and his fellow conspirators. He immediately ordered additional rewards and photographs of the conspirators posted. Then he ordered his detectives to disperse throughout southern Maryland to learn whatever they could. Baker did not realize at the time that there were numerous military patrols already active throughout southern Maryland. All were breathlessly competing for the one-hundred-thousand-dollar reward being offered for the capture of Booth. Motivated by greed and jealousy, these various patrols refused to share information with anyone else. Whatever they learned, they kept it under their hat, hoping to make the arrest and claim that huge reward for themselves. Thus Lafayette Baker's detectives soon returned to Washington utterly defeated.

When Herold and his companion, Booth (or whomever), departed Mudd's home at about 5 P.M. on the fifteenth, they headed west towards the swirling gloom of the Zekiah Swamp. At about nine that evening they suddenly arrived at the cabin of a free black man named Oswell Swann, several miles southeast of Dr. Mudd's farm. Swann owned a small tract of land given him by Dr. Mudd's cousin, George Mudd, near Hughsville, Maryland, on the east side of Zekiah Swamp. Their purpose in seeking out Swann was to obtain

SURRAT.   BOOTH.   HAROLD.

War Department, Washington, April 20, 1865,

$100,000 REWARD!

THE MURDERER

Of our late beloved President, Abraham Lincoln,

IS STILL AT LARGE.

$50,000 REWARD

Will be paid by this Department for his apprehension, in addition to any reward offered by Municipal Authorities or State Executives.

$25,000 REWARD

Will be paid for the apprehension of JOHN H. SURRATT, one of Booth's Accomplices.

$25,000 REWARD

Will be paid for the apprehension of David C. Harold, another of Booth's accomplices.

LIBERAL REWARDS will be paid for any information that shall conduce to the arrest of either of the above-named criminals, or their accomplices.

All persons harboring or secreting the said persons, or either of them, or aiding or assisting their concealment or escape, will be treated as accomplices in the murder of the President and the attempted assassination of the Secretary of State, and shall be subject to trial before a Military Commission and the punishment of DEATH.

Let the stain of innocent blood be removed from the land by the arrest and punishment of the murderers.

All good citizens are exhorted to aid public justice on this occasion. Every man should consider his own conscience charged with this solemn duty, and rest neither night nor day until it be accomplished.

EDWIN M. STANTON, Secretary of War.

DESCRIPTIONS.—BOOTH is Five Feet 7 or 8 inches high, slender build, high forehead, black hair, black eyes, and wears a heavy black moustache.

JOHN H. SURRAT is about 5 feet, 9 inches. Hair rather thin and dark; eyes rather light; no beard. Would weigh 145 or 150 pounds. Complexion rather pale and clear, with color in his cheeks. Wore light clothes of fine quality. Shoulders square; cheek bones rather prominent; chin narrow; ears projecting at the top; forehead rather low and square, but broad. Parts his hair on the right side; neck rather long. His lips are firmly set. A slim man.

DAVID C. HAROLD is five feet six inches high, hair dark, eyes dark, eyebrows rather heavy, full face, nose short, hand short and fleshy, feet small, instep high, round bodied, naturally quick and active, slightly closes his eyes when looking at a person.

NOTICE.—In addition to the above, State and other authorities have offered rewards amounting to almost one hundred thousand dollars, making an aggregate of about TWO HUNDRED THOUSAND DOLLARS.

Poster advertising the rewards for Booth and his coconspirators

a guide through the swamp to the farm of Col. Samuel Cox, a farm known throughout the area as Rich Hill. How they were aware of Oswell Swann is not known, though it may be assumed that Dr. Mudd had recommended him to them.

Subsequently, at about midnight the two very weary conspirators, led by Swann, finally arrived at Samuel Cox's front door at Rich Hill. According to Swann's later testimony, Cox, a well-known Confederate agent, listened to the men's story of being pursued by Union cavalry then invited them inside his home and supplied them with food and water. However, Cox, in his later testimony, swore that the three men were never invited into his home but remained outside on horseback while he found provisions for them. Nor could he ever identify the men again, he said, since they were sitting in total darkness. His testimony was supported by a freed slave from his farm. After extending his hospitality to the two strangers, Cox made arrangements with his foreman, Franklin Robey, to hide them in a pine thicket some two miles from Rich Hill.

The next morning Cox sent his son to get Thomas Jones, another Confederate agent who lived near the Potomac River, and immediately bring him back to Rich Hill. Upon Jones' arrival, Cox informed him that he had Southern fugitives hidden in a nearby thicket and he wanted Jones to look after their welfare. His help would include ferrying them across the river into Virginia as soon as possible. Jones, who owed his allegiance to Cox, promised to do the best he could.

For the next five days, until April 20, Jones was diligent in his care of the two men, bringing them food, drink, and newspapers. Very possibly those five days were the darkest of Booth's life. Forced now to live in the woods, with no protection from the elements, cold, hungry, in terrible pain, and eager to move on to more hospitable surroundings, Booth might very well have experienced some second thoughts about his decision to rid the country of Abe Lincoln.

Jones had been unable to ferry the men across the river because of a great deal of military activity in the area. But on April 20, a Thursday, he visited them and told them what they were so eager to hear, that he would attempt a crossing later that evening. He had visited a tavern in Port Tobacco that morning, he told them, and had overheard a soldier say that Booth and Herold had been seen crossing the river at a point far to the south. Likely, he said, the cavalry would be off on a wild goose chase in that direction, and the fugitives should leave now, while the coast was clear.

True to his word, Jones came for Booth and Herold later that night. Under the cover of darkness, they made their way towards the Potomac River, Booth riding a horse Jones had brought for him while Jones and Herold traveled on foot. Less than an hour later they came to Jones' home, called Huckleberry, and while Booth and Herold waited outside, Jones went into the kitchen to get them food and water. Then, moving as silently as possible, they made their way to a high bluff overlooking the wide Potomac. From where they stood they could see the state of Virginia and safety on the far shore.

Despite his pain, Booth must have breathed a sigh of relief. After all he had been through over the past week, his goal was now within his grasp. Though his beloved Confederacy was no longer alive, and he would not be hailed as a great hero once he reached Virginia, at least he would have the satisfaction of knowing that he had rid the nation of perhaps its worst tyrant in history. As a Southern patriot he could easily fade away into that huge nation, just another face in the crowd, and live peacefully under an alias for the rest of his life, happy that he had done his best for the nation. He reasoned that he had sacrificed his own glorious life as one of America's most-celebrated (and well-paid) stage actors in order to execute the president, but he was sure it would be worth the sacrifice. Doubtlessly the death of Lincoln would sound the death knell for the Republican Party and their dastardly efforts to destroy states' rights, the Constitution, and democracy in America. More immediately, Lincoln's sudden removal from office would save the South from a devastating Reconstruction program.

Ten years from now, he reasoned, every citizen in this great nation would remember the name John Wilkes Booth, and associate it with the name Thomas Jefferson, the father of our

Constitution. Truly, they would remember forever that it was he, John Wilkes Booth, who had restored democracy to America, and there was satisfaction in that. Besides, there was his family—his mother and his brothers and sisters—to think about. Think of the honor and glory that would now come their way. How proud they would be of him—once they realized the implications of his actions. Immediately following the assassination, he had faced the audience at Ford's Theatre and shouted, "Death to Tyrants!" He had meant every word of it, especially as they pertained to Abe Lincoln. He had proven himself the worst tyrant in history, but then in a moment he had become only a bad memory.

Jones helped Herold lift Booth down from his horse. Moving now in total darkness, the three men made their way down the steep slope to the river's edge, where Jones had hidden a small skiff. He motioned for the two men to get in. Booth sat in the stern with a sculling oar while Herold pulled at the oars. With the aid of a candle and Booth's wood-boxed compass, the two began making their way towards the far Virginia shore near Mathias Point. But almost immediately things began to go badly for the two fugitives. The tide was much stronger than either had anticipated, and after two hours they were being swept back towards Blossom Point on the Maryland shore. Once arrived there, totally frustrated, they carefully made their way up Nanjemoy Creek and on to the farm of Peregrin Davis, another Confederate agent well known to David Herold.

Davis was not at home, but his son-in-law, John J. Hughes, provided them with food and water and then directed them to a nearby pine forest where they could find refuge. Totally exhausted from their efforts to cross the river, they spent all day Friday and part of Saturday sleeping and resting.

Late Saturday night, April 22, they again attempted a crossing. This time, after battling tides, fatigue, and pain, they were finally successful, landing near Mathias Point on the Virginia shore. They then made their way southward, stumbling blindly in the darkness, their feet bogging down in the muddy shoreline, Booth staggering along on the homemade crutch

Dr. Mudd had given him, until they reached Machodoc Creek.

Near the mouth of this creek lived another Confederate agent, Mrs. Elizabeth Quesenberry. Thomas Jones had advised Booth and Herold that they should contact Mrs. Quesenberry as quickly as possible, and she would direct them to another agent who lived in the area, Thomas Harbin. Booth had earlier met Harbin through Dr. Mudd, back in November 1864, at the Bryantown Tavern. At that meeting, Booth had informed Harbin of the conspiracy to abduct Lincoln and engaged his promise of help in transporting Lincoln from the Potomac on to Richmond. Mrs. Quesenberry immediately sent for Harbin, who arrived early that afternoon, a Sunday, with another of his Confederate agents in tow, one Joseph Baden.

Not wishing to keep Mrs. Quesenberry in such a dangerous situation, Harbin and Baden led the two fugitives a short distance away to the home of another operative, William Bryant, and left them in his care. It was Bryant who supplied them with horses and agreed to pass them along to yet another operative, Dr. Richard Stewart, who owned a large summer home known as Cleydael, eight miles south of the Potomac in an isolated area of King George County. Dr. Stewart, it might be pointed out, had earlier been arrested by Federal authorities for running medical supplies to the Confederacy and had only recently been released from the Old Capitol Prison. Thus when Bryant and the fugitives arrived at Dr. Stewart's home on Sunday evening, they found him less than welcoming. He doubtlessly knew fugitives' identities, was aware of the charges against them, and was frightened to have anything to do with them. He refused them shelter or medical attention, though he did allow them to enter his kitchen and eat, but only after a lengthy argument. Dr. Stewart then quickly sent them on their way, this time to the log cabin home of William Lucas, a freed slave, who lived only a short distance away.

Booth at this point was highly insulted at Dr. Stewart's lack of hospitality. After all, Dr. Stewart was another Southern partisan, and Booth had expected at least some show of courtesy. Instead, he and Herold had been treated like common criminals. He tore a page from his diary and sent Stewart a note thanking him in kind for his lack of hospitality, and, as a final insult, enclosed $2.50 to pay for the small amount of food he and Herold had eaten, a definite affront to any Virginia gentleman. Taking several lines from *Macbeth,* Booth wrote:

> Dear Sir:
> Forgive me, but I have some little pride. I hate to blame you for your want of hospitality; you know your own affairs. I was sick and tired, with a broken leg, in need of medical advice. I would not have turned a dog from my door in such a condition. However, you were kind enough to give me something to eat, for which I not only thank you, but on account of the reluctant manner in which it was bestowed, I feel bound to pay for it. It is not the substance, but the manner in which kindness is extended that makes one happy in the acceptance thereof. The sauce in meat is ceremony; meeting were bare without it. Be kind enough to accept the enclosed two dollars and a half (though hard to spare) for what we have received.
> yours, respectfully,
> Strangers

Booth took the lines "The sauce in meat is ceremony; meeting were bare without it" from *Macbeth.* His point being, of course, that even though Stewart had offered food to Booth and Herold, the manner in which the offer was made was as important as the offer itself. And "the manner in which the offer was made," unfortunately, was an insult. Later, during the trial of the conspirators, Stewart produced Booth's note to prove he had not befriended the fugitives. That note very possibly saved his neck from the noose. (This note was last seen during the impeachment trial of Andrew Johnson in 1867. What might have happened to it after that remains a mystery.)

During the early morning hours of Monday, April 24, Bryant led Booth and Herold to the rustic cabin of William Lucas. Now totally exhausted and still angry from their rude treatment at the hands of Dr. Stewart, they ordered the elderly Lucas and his wife out of their cabin. They thanked Bryant for his help and bid him farewell then they fell into an exhausted sleep until dawn.

Upon awaking, Booth attempted to persuade Lucas to lead

them to the next point on their escape route, Port Conway on the Rappahannock River. According to Lucas's later testimony, he declined to help the fugitives in any way until Booth pulled a large revolver from his waistband and threatened to shoot him unless he did as ordered. (Where Booth got this revolver remains a mystery. Possibly it was the same one he used to shoot the president.) At that point, Lucas appointed his son, Charlie Lucas, to transport Booth and Herold in his wagon to Port Conway, located some ten miles away on the banks of the Rappahannock. For this service, Booth very graciously paid Lucas twenty dollars.

Two hours later Charlie drew up at the home of William Rollins and his wife, Betsy, situated along the northern banks of the Rappahannock River in Port Conway. Betsy Rollins, as fate would have it, apparently collected all the local gossip, including that from nearby Bowling Green, and she would later reveal information to the Federal cavalry that would prove fatal to both Booth and Herold.

Booth tried to persuade Rollins to take them across the river to Port Royal, but they were unable to reach an agreement. He and Herold had no choice but to drive down to the ferryboat landing and wait there. The boat, they were told, was owned by Champe Thornton, who lived on the far side of the river in Port Royal, so they would have to await his arrival. It was at that point, while waiting impatiently for the return of Champe Thornton, that three Confederate cavalrymen arrived. They were Lt. Mortimer B. Ruggles, Pvt. Absalom Bainbridge, and Pvt. William Jett. They had ridden with Col. John Mosby's famous Partisan Ranger regiment until that unit had been disbanded the week before, and now they were trying to make their way back home. While Booth lay stretched out on the bank, sleeping deeply under the warm sun, Herold told the soldiers that he and Booth were the Boyd brothers. Booth now called himself James W. Boyd because of the initials J. W. B. tattooed on his right arm. After a great deal of easy talk and laughter had passed between the five men, Herold finally took them into his confidence, admitting their true identities and that they were the assassins of Abe Lincoln. Rather than being appalled or frightened, these war-hardened Rangers said that they were all soldiers of the Confederacy and vowed to assist in their escape in any way possible. They would take them with them across the river, they said, and help them find a hiding place.

At noon that day James Thornton, a free black who operated the ferry for Champe Thornton, finally arrived with the ferryboat and took the five men and their three horses across the Rappahannock to the Port Royal side. Once arrived there, the five men, riding two to a horse, rode up a small incline that led to the home of Randolph Peyton. Young Willie Jett, who was an old friend of the Peytons, knocked on the front door. Lucy Peyton answered and Jett asked to see her brother, Randolph. Lucy replied that Randolph was away on business and would not return until the next day. Only she and her sister, Sarah Jane, were at home. Jett pointed to the men waiting in the yard and asked if a wounded Confederate soldier and his friend could spend the night there. Lucy thought carefully for a moment then shook her head and replied that she was sorry, but it would not be proper for two strangers to spend the night while the man of the house was out. Young Jett graciously thanked the lady for her time and returned to his friends.

The five men continued down the road to Bowling Green, ten miles to the south. They had traveled about four miles when they decided to follow a road leading to the home of Richard Garrett, a highly respected farmer and Southern sympathizer in the area. Jett was again elected to approach the house and ask if the wounded Booth, whom he introduced as James W. Boyd, could rest there before continuing. Old Mr. Garrett eagerly agreed to receive a wounded Confederate lad and gave Booth a welcoming wave. Booth managed a pained grin, then climbed down from his horse and limped up the steps to Garrett's front porch. With that good news, Jett and the three others tipped their hats to Garrett, mounted their steeds, and rode toward Bowling Green.

A few miles from Garrett's farm, about midway to Bowling Green, a woman named Mrs. Martha Carter and her four

Pvt. William Jett in 1873, then a tobacco salesman in Baltimore. A former member of Mosby's Rangers, Jett arrived home in April 1865 just in time to help hide Booth and Herold as they made their race for freedom. Federal soldiers captured Jett on the morning of April 26 at the Star Hotel, from where he led them to the Garrett farm and the fugitives. He later died in an insane asylum, still berating himself for the grief he had brought upon the Garrett family. National Archives

beautiful daughters lived in a small frame house. It was well known in the area that these five women provided "entertainment" for men who sought such pleasure. It was there that Herold and his three adventuresome Confederate friends decided to stop for a while. They had no money, so their visit to Mrs. Carter's establishment was more of a lark than anything else. They sat on the front porch with the girls, laughed, joked, flirted, and enjoyed a free glass of brandy. But that apparently was all.

Just after dark, Herold and his three friends bid the ladies goodbye and mounting their horses, continued on to Bowling Green. There they stopped at the Star Hotel operated by a Mr. Gouldman. He had a beautiful young daughter named Izora, whom Willie Jett had been courting for some time. After stopping outside the hotel, the four men decided that Jett and Mortimer Ruggles would spend the night at the Star Hotel while Herold and Absalom Bainbridge would ride just a few miles down the road to the home of Joseph Clarke, an old friend who had served with Jett, Bainbridge, and Ruggles as a member of Mosby's Rangers.

Booth, meanwhile, living now as James W. Boyd, had been shown every courtesy by the Garrett family. He immediately became the petted patient of young Annie Garrett and Lucinda Holloway, a young school teacher and Mrs. Garrett's sister, who was boarding with the Garretts. Booth was, Lucinda and Annie whispered to Mrs. Garrett, one of the most handsome men they had ever seen, despite his terrible wound and his dirty and disheveled appearance. They had tended his broken leg as well as possible, considering their limited knowledge and materials, then provided him a tub of hot bathing water and clean clothing. An hour later they cooked him a dinner of fried chicken. Booth and his handsome benefactors exchanged pleasant conversation until he had completed his meal. Later, they tucked him into the guest bedroom, where he fell into an exhausted slumber on a big feather bed.

At this point, on the evening of Monday, April 24, things were looking up for Booth and Herold. They had experienced some rough times following their flight from Washington ten days earlier, but now, among friends in northern Virginia, escape and freedom seemed within their grasp. Booth spent that night sleeping the sleep of the just, knowing that he had rid the country of the greatest tyrant of all time.

The following morning dawned bright and sunny, an unusually warm day for northern Virginia, as Herold and Bainbridge returned to Bowling Green to meet Jett and Ruggles. After exchanging some small talk, two of the men, Bainbridge and Ruggles, decided to continue on to their homes. Willie Jett, however, wished to remain with Izora Gouldman at the Star Hotel.

Soon thereafter, Herold, Ruggles, and Bainbridge departed Bowling Green for Richard Garrett's farm to reunite with Booth. A few miles later, however, as they approached Mrs. Carter's establishment, they suddenly decided that there was no big rush to rejoin Booth. Perhaps they should stop and socialize a bit with the Carter sisters. They spent several hours in polite conversation with those ladies, proving that boys will be boys, regardless of the circumstances. It was late afternoon when Ruggles and Bainbridge delivered Herold to Richard Garrett's farm before riding back to Thornton's Ferry.

Two hours later, having arrived at Thornton's Ferry, Ruggles and Bainbridge were startled to find a large number of Federal cavalrymen gathered there. They were mounted and apparently about to ride in the direction of Garrett's farm. The two Rangers looked at one another and silently agreed that they should return immediately to Garrett's to warn Booth and Herold that they might be in imminent danger of capture. It was about dusk when the two former Rangers rode up in a cloud of dust and related to Booth and Herold what they had witnessed. They then tipped their hats, wished their fugitive friends the very best, and galloped away. Booth and Herold, deciding that discretion was advisable at that point, made straightway for a pine thicket that stood nearby. The Garretts, meanwhile, looked askance at one another. What were these men afraid of?

Back at Thornton's Ferry, Federal lieutenant Edward P. Doherty and his troop of twenty-five veterans of the Sixteenth New York Cavalry rode out of Port Royal and headed due south. How they found themselves so near their quarry is interesting to review.

On April 24, while Booth was resting at the Garrett farm, Col. Lafayette Baker visited the War Department's Telegraph Office, commanded by Maj. Thomas Eckert. Eckert had just received a telegraphed message from Port Tobacco erroneously claiming that Booth and Herold had crossed the Potomac into Virginia on Sunday evening, April 16, just two days following the assassination. In fact, they did not cross over until Sunday evening, April 23, some nine days later. The two men seen crossing the river on April 16 were later identified as Thomas Harbin and Joseph Baden, whom the fugitives had met through Mrs. Elizabeth Quesenberry. But from Booth's standpoint, it made little difference that the two men had been misidentified for Baker went to Stanton and immediately received an order to start a cavalry troop for the Port Royal area. They were going to Port Royal for the wrong reason, but for Booth and Herold the arrival of the Federals at that point could not have been more untimely.

By late evening of April 24, Lafayette Baker had rounded up a troop of twenty-five men from the Sixteenth New York Cavalry under Lt. Edward Doherty. At the urging of Edwin Stanton, Lieutenant Doherty and his troop were placed under the command of Lt. Luther Baker, Lafayette Baker's first cousin. They were accompanied by Col. Everton Conger, who was on sick leave in Washington. Why Stanton urged Baker to place his cousin in command of the team is unclear, though it must be remembered that there was a one-hundred-thousand-dollar reward on the heads of the fugitives. Translated into today's money, that sum would be the equivalent of over three million dollars. As a matter of speculation, might Stanton have urged Baker to make sure that his cousin brought in two captives—any two—whom they could claim were Booth and Herold so that a large part of that magnificent reward would find its way into their hands? During the impeachment trial of 1867, Luther Baker testified that his cousin said to him, "You are going after Booth. Lieutenant, we have got a sure thing." Those who know Stanton and Baker, two of the most unscrupulous men ever to hold public office, would not be in the least surprised. Such motivation might also explain why Boston Corbett inexplicably murdered Booth before he could be taken captive—dead men tell no tales.

It was at this point that Maj. James R. O'Beirne, who had been on Booth's trail now for several days, reported to Stanton from Port Tobacco that witnesses had informed him that the two fugitives were in the immediate vicinity, and he expected to have them in custody within the next twenty-four hours. To O'Beirne's lasting dismay, he received a message from Stanton informing him that he was to abandon his pursuit of Booth and return to Washington immediately. O'Beirne claimed for the rest of his life that he would have captured Booth had Stanton not stepped in when he did.

If Lafayette Baker had calculated correctly, it was he and his conspirators who soon would be sharing the reward money. Inexplicably, Baker had calculated correctly. In his memoirs entitled *Recollections*, Baker's attorney, Albert G. Riddle, would give the following account of how Baker pinpointed Booth's whereabouts:

> Before the starting of the party, the Chief spread out a map of Virginia and designated the crossing-place of the fugitives and the place where they had probably landed; then, taking a compass, he placed one point at Port Conway, where a road crossed the Rappahannock, and drew a circle, which he said included a space of ten miles around that point, and within that territory they would find the fugitives. The fugitives were captured within Baker's circle.

Doherty, Baker, and their men boarded a steamer, the *John S. Ide,* at the Old Washington Arsenal, then headed down the Potomac to Belle Plaine, northeast of Port Conway on the Rappahannock. They docked at ten o'clock that

evening and rode southeast, stopping and questioning people along the way about the possible whereabouts of the two
fugitives, one known to be a cripple.

By noon of Tuesday, April 25, Doherty and his cavalry had
worked their way down to Port Conway. There, Doherty visited the home of William Rollins and learned from Rollins that
two men fitting the description of Booth and Herold had been
ferried across the Rappahannock just the day before. There
were three Confederate soldiers with them, said Rollins, one
a local boy by the name of William Jett. It was then that Betsy
Rollins eagerly spoke up and informed Lieutenant Doherty
that it was well known that Jett and Mr. Gouldman's daughter, Izora, were deeply in love, and that in all probability Willie
Jett could be found wherever Izora was, which was without
doubt the Star Hotel in Bowling Green. Doherty tipped his hat
and backed out the front door. As an afterthought, he paused
and suggested that William Rollins accompany him and his
troop to Bowling Green. Rollins reluctantly agreed. After a
short discussion with the other two officers, Doherty
mounted up and led his men straightway to Bowling Green. If
they found Jett, he reasoned, they might very well find Herold
and Booth. If not, then it was a sure bet that Jett could tell
them where to find them. It's amazing how a noose around
the neck can loosen a reluctant tongue.

Lt. Luther Baker could already smell that big reward
money being offered for Booth's capture. He was not sure how
much of the reward money would be his, but he was sure that
Stanton and his cousin would be forced to treat him fairly
when he plunked down the body and said, "Here's John
Wilkes Booth." He already had been told that the biggest
mansion in Washington could be built for less than five thousand dollars, so even if he received only one-tenth of that one-
hundred-thousand-dollar reward, he would be set for life.

As darkness approached, Doherty and his men rode past
the Garrett home where Booth and Herold were now fear-
fully hiding in the woods. A few miles farther and they
halted at the home of Mrs. Carter and her four daughters.
Quite possibly these very active young ladies might have

seen the fugitives over the past few days. Doherty, Conger, and Baker went inside the house while the troop waited outside. Exactly what transpired with the girls remains unknown, though they did assure Doherty that they had never seen any characters such as he had described. Luther Baker spoke up at that point and told Mrs. Carter and her girls that the two fugitives had raped a young girl and were attempting to escape justice by getting out of the state. At that, an angry Mrs. Carter suddenly remembered that a local boy, Willie Jett, had visited her home just the day before, and there were two other men with him, but neither was injured. Doherty found the absence of Booth puzzling, but it mattered little. Find Jett, he decided, and Booth had to be nearby.

It was just past midnight when Doherty and his troop of totally exhausted cavalrymen rode into Bowling Green and quietly surrounded the Star Hotel. They had been riding hard for the past twenty-four hours in Rebel territory, with little to eat or drink, and now some of his dusty troopers were asleep in the saddle. But now, suspecting that the kill was at hand, most of them perked up. Doherty burst into the hotel, found Private Jett, and dragged him from his bed (which he shared with Izora's brother) and out into the front yard. Doherty, in no mood at this point to negotiate, rammed a .44 Colt revolver in Jett's right ear and cocked the hammer. "Where are they?" he asked. Over the next thirty seconds Jett told Doherty everything he could concerning the whereabouts of Booth and Herold. Jett was then placed under arrest and tied to his saddle in order that he might lead the Federals to Garrett's farm.

Booth and Herold, meanwhile, had anxiously observed the Federal cavalry ride by earlier in the evening and had hurried out to hide in a nearby pine forest. Since they had heard nothing further from the Federals, they returned to Richard Garrett's home. It was just past midnight, and they were bedded down in a tobacco barn located to the rear of the house. The Garretts had observed their guests' suspicious behavior earlier in the evening, and apprehensive that their guests

Wilkes Booth at the age of twenty-seven, when he assumed the terrible responsibility of assassinating Lincoln. McClellan Lincoln College, Brown University

might be thieves or crooks of some sort, Mr. Garrett's two sons, William and Jack, had gone out and quietly placed a padlock on the barn door. Now the two men could not possibly steal any horses and ride off during the night. As a further safeguard, William and Jack hid themselves in a nearby corn-crib where they could take turns watching the barn.

At about 4 A.M. the sleeping Garrett boys were suddenly awakened by the sight and sounds of Doherty's Federal cavalrymen encircling their home. When everyone was in position, the three officers strode to the porch and began roughly banging on the front door and yelling for Mr. Garrett to come out. Garrett, awakened from a deep slumber, was startled by the noise, and fearful that it might be outlaws, he slowly opened the door. At that point he was roughly grabbed by the collar and pulled out onto the porch. Doherty stuck his Colt revolver in Garrett's face and demanded to know where Booth and Herold were hiding. Mr. Garrett stuttered when excited, and under such stress his affliction became even more pronounced.

Tired and frustrated, Doherty ordered two soldiers to drag Mr. Garrett to a big tree in the front yard. There a rope was tossed over a limb and a noose was placed around the old man's neck. He had a choice, he was told: he could talk or hang. At that point, a furious Jack Garrett jerked the rope from a soldier's hands, and he told Doherty what he wanted to hear. The two fugitives were locked in an outbuilding. Doherty gave an order and soldiers immediately surrounded the barn. Jack Garrett was told to unlock the door and bring out the two fugitives.

Jack did as instructed, but Booth refused to come out. Booth patted him on the back and thanked him for his family's hospitality. As for himself, he said, he could never surrender to those miserable curs in blue. Jack came back outside at that point, shaking his head that it was no use. Luther Baker then tried to persuade Booth to come out, but again to no avail. Indeed, Booth at that point yelled for the soldiers to back off and give him a chance to shoot his way out. Doherty refused.

After further negotiation, Booth informed Doherty that David Herold wanted to surrender. Doherty agreed and Herold stumbled from the barn. Then he made a statement that has puzzled and troubled historians ever since. He looked Doherty straight in the face and said, "That man in the barn is *not* John Wilkes Booth." How Baker's heart must have sunk when he heard those words. There went his share of the reward money. Union soldiers grabbed Herold and dragged him to a nearby tree, where he was tightly bound. One of the Union soldiers asked him if would like a drink of water, but Herold merely smiled and shook his head.

By now it was becoming obvious to Doherty that the man in the barn, regardless of who he was, would not come out of his own free will. He therefore decided to set fire to the barn to flush the man out. He gave a quick order and soldiers began piling pine brush against one corner of the barn. Someone struck a match, and soon the fire was blazing bright enough to illuminate the man inside. Doherty could see him plainly. He was leaning on a crutch and carrying a carbine in one hand and an army Colt in the other. The man noted the flames leaping up all around him and frantically twisted to both his right and left as though confused by this turn of events. He made a move towards the door and dropped his crutch. At that point a single shot suddenly shattered the stillness and the man crumpled to the floor. Sgt. Boston Corbett, in defiance of orders, had just shot John Wilkes Booth through a crack in the barn wall.

Or did he? For a hundred and forty years now historians have been bedeviled by the question: Just who shot John Wilkes Booth? According to Colonel Conger's testimony at the trial of the conspirators, he and Baker heard a shot. Baker rushed into the barn, Conger at his heels. Before them, sprawled on the floor like a broken doll, lay the body of Wilkes Booth. The two officers immediately began to argue over who had shot him. "I supposed he had shot himself," said Conger.

I stooped over, looked down at him, and said that he had shot him-self. Baker said, "No, he did not!" He had the appearance of a man who had put a pistol to his head and shot himself, shooting a little too low; and I said again, "He shot himself." Baker said, "No, he did not." He spoke very positively about it. I thought it a little strange rather, as if he doubted my word when he said so.

Baker did indeed doubt Conger's word. In 1867, during the impeachment trial of President Johnson, Baker would testify: "I supposed at the time that Conger shot him, and I said, 'What on earth did you shoot him for?' Said he, 'I did not shoot him.' Then the idea flashed on my mind that if he did, it had better not be known."

Startled and chagrined at this turn of events, Baker hur-riedly dragged the mortally wounded Booth from the barn. He did not want to see his one hundred thousand dollars cremated. With the help of several soldiers they carried the fatally wounded man from the barn and laid him down on the grass beneath a big locust tree growing next to Garrett's front porch.

Jack and Robert Garrett were now desperately cranking the well and carrying buckets of water across the yard in hopes of saving the burning barn. They could see that their efforts were hopeless. (Edwin Booth later reimbursed the Garretts for the loss of their tobacco barn.)

"Water!" Lieutenant Baker shouted, kneeling by Booth's side. At that, Jack Garrett brought a bucket of water to the dying man. "I took Booth's head upon my knee and threw some water in his face," Baker reported. "His mouth being open, I poured some in his mouth." Booth strangled on the water and gave Baker an agonized look. "He made his lips go as though he would say something," Baker stated. "'Tell mother—' he started, and then he swooned again." Baker revived him with more water splashed on his face. "I was washing his face all the time. He said in a whisper, 'Tell Mother I died for my country.' Then I saw his wound. That was the first time I saw it. I saw that he was shot in the back of the neck."

At that point, Baker ordered that Booth be lifted and carried

Thomas "Boston" Corbett was the killer of John Wilkes Booth and certainly one of the most bizarre personalities ever to wear the uniform of the U.S. Army. Born in England in 1832, he later migrated to Boston and became an evangelical Christian. He wore his hair long in imitation of Jesus, and in 1855 castrated himself so as not to be tempted by evil thoughts concerning females. Following the war he moved to Kansas and in 1887 was named doorkeeper of the Kansas State Legislature. He entered their chamber one morning and opened fire with his .44 revolver. He was sent to the Topeka Asylum for the Insane but escaped shortly thereafter. It was rumored that he finally died in Enid, Oklahoma. National Archives, The National Park Service

to Garrett's front porch. There they laid him on a mattress that had been brought from the house. Lucinda Holloway came out and placed a pillow under his head, a damp cloth upon his forehead, and knelt by his side, speaking soothingly to him until his death three hours later. She could see that he was dying as he lay bleeding and paralyzed from the bullet that had entered his neck from the rear, severing his spinal cord.

It was then that Baker, Conger, and Doherty put their heads together in hopes of making up a plausible story to give to Lafayette Baker. Colonel Conger began to roughly question his cavalrymen, demanding to know if any of them had witnessed a fellow trooper shoot the man in the barn. At that point, Boston Corbett came forward and proudly admitted that it was he who had shot the assassin. Conger swore at him and asked him why he had done such a thing, but Corbett shrugged and replied that God had demanded he do it. Speechless, Conger turned away in frustration and returned to Luther Baker. Together they searched Booth's pockets. There was a map upon which Booth had traced the route he planned to take from Richmond to Mexico, which was apparently his ultimate destination. Among the items found there was also small red diary. In the months and years to come, that diary would prove a matter of great controversy and a curse to Edwin Stanton.

Conger began thumbing through the diary. For April 14 Booth had written:

Ti Amo
April 13-14 Friday the Ides
Until today nothing was ever thought of sacrificing to our country's wrongs. For six months we had worked to capture. But our cause, being almost lost, something decisive & great must be done. But its failure was owing to others, who did not strike for their country with a heart. I struck boldly and not as the papers say. I walked with a firm step through a thousand of his friends, was stopped, but pushed on. A colonel was at his side. I shouted *Sic Semper* before I fired. In jumping broke my leg. I passed all his pickets, rode sixty miles that night, with the bone of my leg tearing the flesh at every jump. I can never repent it, though we hated to kill. Our country owed

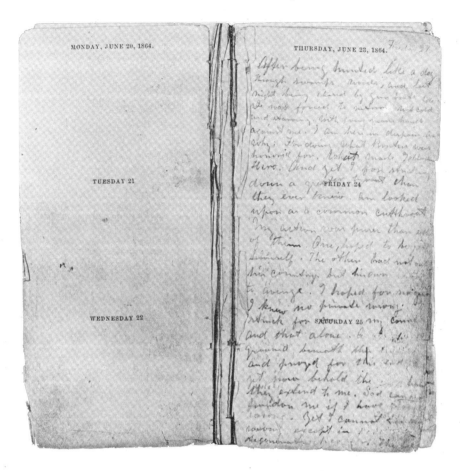

Booth's diary entry for April 13-14, 1865. National Park Service

all her trouble to him, and God simply made me the instrument of his punishment. The country is not what it was. This forced union is not what I have loved. I care not what becomes of me. I have no desire to out-live my country. That night (before the deed), I wrote a long article and left it for one of the editors of the *National Intelligencer,* in which I fully set forth our reasons for our proceedings.

Here Booth states in plain language that prior to April 14 he had never considered murder as a solution to the

Booth's diary entry for April 21, 1865. National Park Service

Lincoln problem. But then something extraordinary occurred on that date to convince him that Lincoln must be executed immediately.

Then came the entry for April 21:

Friday 21
After being hunted like a dog through swamps, woods, and last night being chased by gun boats till I was forced to return wet cold and starving, with every man's hand against me, I am

here in despair. And why? For doing what Brutus was honored for. What made Tell a Hero. And yet I for striking down a greater tyrant than they ever knew am looked upon as a common cutthroat. My action was purer than either of theirs. One hoped to be great himself. The other had not only his country's but his own wrongs to avenge. I hoped for no gain. I knew no private wrong. I struck for my country and that alone. A country groaned beneath this tyranny and prayed for this end, and yet now behold the cold hand they extend to me. God cannot pardon me if I have done wrong. Yet I cannot see any wrong except in serving a degenerate people. *The little, the very little I left behind to clear my name, the Govmt will not allow to be printed* [emphasis added]. So ends all. For my country I have given up all that makes life sweet and Holy, brought misery upon my family, and am sure there is no pardon in Heaven for me since man condemns me so. I have only heard of what has been done (except what I did myself) and it fills me with horror. God try and forgive me, and bless my mother. To night I will once more try the river with the intent to cross; though *I have a greater desire and almost a mind to return to Washington and in a measure clear my name, which I feel I can do* [emphasis added]. I do not repent the blow I struck. I may before my God but not to man. I think I have done well, though I am abandoned, with the curse of Cain upon me, when if the world knew my heart, that one blow would have made me great, though I desire no greatness.

Tonight I try to escape these blood hounds once more. Who, who can read his fate? God's will be done.

I have too great a soul to die like a criminal. O may he, may he spare me that and let me die bravely.

I bless the entire world. Have never hated or wronged anyone. This last was not a wrong, unless God deems it so. And it's with him to damn or bless me. And for this brave boy with me who often prays (yes, before and since) with a true and sincere heart. Was it crime in him, if so, why can he pray the same. I do not wish to shed a drop of blood, but "I must fight the course." 'Tis all that's left me.

This entry contains the sentence that has proven an enigma to historians: "I have almost a mind to return to

Washington and clear my name, which I feel I can do." Certainly, if Conger were thinking at all, he must have seen the implications in that statement. It would seem that when he read those puzzling lines he would have started asking Booth some fast questions. How could Booth possibly return to Washington and clear his name when he was obviously guilty of murder? Was he saying that it was not he who had shot the president after all, or was he hinting that when he pulled the trigger, he was merely carrying out an order from some government official? Today, it is highly unlikely that we will ever know just what Booth intended.

Booth would remain conscious until his death at dawn, though whatever comments he might have made were not recorded. In addition to his alleged request to Doherty, "Tell Mother I died for my country," he made one last statement. As the light of dawn finally began to break on this terribly tragic scene, Booth asked that his arms be raised so that he could see his hands. Looking at them, he gasped, "Useless, useless." As far as is known, those were his last words.

The old saying "Dead men tell no tales" holds special meaning in the case of John Wilkes Booth since the answers to so many nagging questions died with him on Garrett's front porch on the morning of April 26, 1865. For well over a century the nation has puzzled over whether the body pulled from Garrett's barn was that of John Wilkes Booth or the body of an unlucky Confederate agent who was mistaken for the assassin. Was it Booth's body that was buried beneath the flooring of the Old Penitentiary, or did he somehow manage to escape his pursuers and make his way to freedom? And was the execution of President Lincoln strictly Booth's idea, acting on a moment's impulse? Was he truly the mastermind of this terrible deed, working alone and independently of others, or was he simply the tool of certain high-ranking government officials?

Upon Booth's death at 7 A.M., Lieutenant Doherty ordered that his body be sewn into a saddle blanket with needle and thread obtained from the Garrett house. His body was taken aboard a wagon to Belle Plain, where the steamer

John S. Ide was waiting. Trotting along behind the wagon, a long rope around his neck, came the loyal but very subdued David Herold.

Also under arrest was Sgt. Boston Corbett, who was charged with disobeying orders. Later, when awaiting trial for murder, Corbett began to behave in a most bizarre manner, claiming that Booth was the devil while he, Corbett, was the Lord's avenging angel. It was God who had commanded him to shoot that devil, he shouted, waving his arms about wildly. Insane or not, the army would later drop all charges against Corbett—by order of Edwin Stanton.

Over an hour before Booth finally died, Colonel Conger, smelling that big reward money, had lit out like a comet for Washington to make a report to Lafayette Baker. The detective chief was ecstatic when told that Booth was dead. Indeed, his death marked the end of the matter—there could be no questions. Baker grabbed his cap, motioned to Conger, and the two men dashed to the home of Edwin Stanton on K Street. Stanton was resting on a couch in his parlor when Baker burst in. Without preamble, Baker exclaimed, "Mr. Stanton, we have got Booth!" Baker would later write that Stanton did not move or show any sign that he had even heard. Instead, he put his hands over his eyes and sighed deeply, as though he expected a deadly blow. Then Baker added, "He is dead, but we got him." For fully two minutes, says Baker, Stanton lay without moving or saying a word. At last, with his hands still covering his eyes, he sat up and very quietly asked, "Are you sure he's dead?" When Baker assured Stanton that Booth was quite dead, the secretary arose, flashed Baker and Conger a quick smile, put on his coat, and began to examine the articles that Colonel Conger had taken from Booth's pockets. They included a holster, a pipe, a compass, a Canadian bill of exchange, a knife, two pistols, and a small diary.

Stanton flipped through the pages of the diary then casually slipped it into his jacket pocket. It would not be seen again until the trial of John Surratt in 1867. Initially, Stanton denied that he had ever seen such a diary, but Surratt's attorney entered a subpoena and Stanton was forced to turn it over to the court. Even at that there were eighteen pages torn from it. Stanton testified that those eighteen pages were missing when he received the diary, but Lafayette Baker contradicted that testimony, swearing under oath that no pages had been torn from the diary when he turned it over to Stanton.

Oddly enough, Baker would later say that Stanton did not react angrily when informed that Booth had been killed. To the contrary, said Baker, Stanton seemed to be greatly relieved at the news. Since Lincoln's assassination thirteen days before, Stanton had seemed to grow increasingly depressed as his Federal cavalry drew closer and closer to capturing Booth. Baker would later recall that "Stanton had become very despondent regarding the capture, and had often spoken of the disgrace it would be if the base assassin should escape." In other words, Stanton never explicitly ordered Booth's murder, but he strongly hinted to Lieutenant Baker and Colonel Conger that it would be of great benefit to the government (that is, Edwin Stanton) if Booth should somehow die before being questioned in a court of law. One suspects that it was Booth's testimony that might prove a "disgrace" to the government and Edwin Stanton. What that testimony might have been remains a matter of speculation.

But there remains Booth's enigmatic statement in his diary that he was tempted to return to Washington "and clear my name, which I believe I can do without too much trouble." How he planned to clear his name also remains a matter of speculation. Did he think to reveal that he was an operative of high-ranking authorities and merely following their orders when he executed the president? During the impeachment trial of 1867, former Union general Ben Butler (then a U.S. congressman) voiced the attitude of many when he shouted in the House:

> How clear himself? By disclosing his accomplices? Who were they? If we had only the advantage of all the testimony, Mr. Speaker, we might have been able to find out who, indeed, were these accomplices of Booth; to find out who it was that changed Booth's purpose from capture to assassination; who it was that could profit by assassination who could not profit by capture and abduction, who it was expected by Booth would succeed to Lincoln if the knife made a vacancy.

Butler did everything but name Vice Pres. Andrew Johnson as the moving force behind Lincoln's execution. It was an opinion held by many.

Had Stanton seen fit to turn over Booth's diary to the Military Commission back in June 1865, it might very well have saved lives for it proved conclusively that it was not until the fatal day itself, April 14, 1865, that it first occurred to Booth to assassinate the president instead of abducting him. But the diary remained the secret possession of Edwin Stanton for over two years. By that time Lafayette Baker had been dismissed from the War Department for spying on the president and had published his book, *The History of the Secret Service*. It was in that book that Baker made repeated references to Booth's diary, and it created a sensation throughout the nation. At that point, the Judiciary Committee of the House, then in session, ordered Baker to take the stand and repeat his statements under oath. It was then that Baker flabbergasted his listeners when he revealed that the diary had been mutilated since it had been taken from Booth's body the morning of his death. Again, Ben Butler thundered forth: "That diary, as now produced, has eighteen pages cut out, the pages prior to the time when Abraham Lincoln was massacred, although the edges as yet show they had been written over. Now, what I want to know, was that diary whole? Who spoliated that book?"

On February 7, 1867, Baker took the stand and testified under oath that he had read portions of Booth's diary on the afternoon of the day Booth had been shot, and he thought there had been a great deal more to the original volume at that time. "In my opinion," he said, "there have been leaves torn out of that book since I saw it."

On April 1, 1867, Stanton himself was put on the stand and gave his own version of events. The leaves of the diary, he swore, were missing when the diary was given to him.

Q. When you first saw the diary in the room of the Committee on the Judiciary, was your attention called to the circumstance that certain leaves had been cut or torn from it?

A. My attention was called to it at that time. I had observed the fact at the time on which I first saw the diary. I examined it then with great care; read over all the entries in it, and noticed that leaves had been cut or torn from it at the time.

Q. According to your recollection, was the diary, when you saw it in the committee-room, in the same condition it was when you first saw it?

A. It was precisely in the same condition.

Three days later Baker again would be called to the stand. This time he testified that some of his detectives had made copies of Booth's diary but had been forced to give them up on orders from Edwin Stanton. He was still certain that no leaves were missing when he turned the diary over to the secretary of war.

Q. Do you mean to say that at the time you gave the book to the Secretary of War there were no leaves gone?

A. I do.

Q. That is still your opinion?

A. That is still my opinion.

Q. Did you examine it pretty carefully?

A. I examined the book, and I am very sure that if any leaves had been gone I should have noticed it.

Q. Did you examine it carefully?

A. It did not require careful examination to discover the absence of so many leaves.

But Baker saved his best shot at Stanton for last, when he stated that Stanton had not questioned the absence of eighteen pages when the diary had first been given to him. "I think Mr. Stanton would have asked me what had become of the missing leaves, if any had been missing." Knowing Stanton's personality, said Baker, it was highly unlikely that he would have accepted a mutilated piece of evidence without question.

On May 13, Colonel Conger, who had actually taken the diary from Booth's body and returned it to Washington, was called to the stand, but he said he could recall very little concerning the condition of the diary at the time he turned it over to Lafayette Baker. It had been two years since he had last seen the diary, and he could not recall whether pages had been torn out at that time or not. (It is interesting to note that when Stanton distributed the final reward money, Conger received by far the largest amount, some fifteen thousand dollars, while Lt. Luther Baker received only three thousand dollars.)

Following Lafayette Baker's report to Stanton concerning the death of Booth, Stanton ordered him to meet the *John S. Ide* at Alexandria and see to it that David Herold and Booth's body were taken by tugboat to the Navy Yard. With Baker in command, the tugboat arrived at the Navy Yard at about two in the morning of April 27. There both David Herold and Booth's body were transferred to the monitor *Montauk*. Herold was chained to the wall down in the hold while Booth's body was stretched out on a carpenter's bench up on deck. Baker, possibly concerned about the reward money, determined that his first order of business was to identify the corpse as that of John Wilkes Booth. Both Booth's physician, Dr. John Frederick May, and a Washington dentist were called to the monitor. A canvas awning was stretched over the deck to shield the corpse and the witnesses from a merciless sun. Under that airless tent a hurried inquest was conducted at 10 A.M. Dr. May was led on deck and Surgeon General Joseph K. Barnes and an assistant stood by. According to Dr. May's written statement:

> By Dr. Barnes' order the cover was removed, and to my great astonishment revealed a body in whose lineaments there was to me no resemblance to the man I had known in life! My surprise was so great that I at once said to General Barnes, "There is no resemblance in that corpse to Booth, nor can I believe it to be that of him."

Lafayette Baker's chagrin was total when he read those words. His jaw dropped and he rushed forward to confront the doctor. Not Booth? It had to be Booth. Otherwise, not only would he lose his share of the reward money but probably his government job as well. In a panic, Baker urged Dr. May to examine the back of Booth's neck for an old surgery scar. He motioned to Dr. Barnes, and together they turned the corpse on its stomach. Dr. May stared at

Booth's neck. The big lead bullet from Corbett's Colt .44 had blasted away most of the skin and muscle from that area, but after some deliberation Dr. May said he believed he recognized what appeared to be a scar on the back of Booth's neck, though this particular scar had "the appearance of the cicatrix of a burn." The dentist stated that he recognized Booth's two dental fillings as his own work.

As for Dr. May, he saved his most astonishing bombshell for his written report to Secretary Stanton. One can imagine Stanton's reaction when he read, "The right lower limb was greatly contused, and perfectly black from a fracture to the fibula." The right lower limb? According to official testimony, as well as eyewitness testimony, the fugitive for whom the government had been searching since April 14 had suffered a break to his lower *left* limb. Dr. May dropped a lesser bombshell when he noted that the corpse had a freckled face, which made it difficult to identify as that of John Wilkes Booth.

How Stanton must have leapt to his feet and began pacing his office in circles, trying to decide how he could keep this amazing revelation from reaching the press. He failed. Once this inquest report somehow escaped the secretary's control, a frantic Edwin Stanton excused Dr. May's statement by informing the press that Dr. May had been standing at the feet of the corpse when he made his examination. From that position, he said, it was a simple matter to confuse left and right. Obviously Dr. May had meant to say Booth's left leg instead of his right. Still, there were critics who maintained that Dr. May, regardless of his position while conducting the examination, should have surrendered his medical license if he could not distinguish Booth's right leg from his left.

A mortified Dr. May forever after refused to comment on the matter, but the press was beginning to enjoy a field day. The *Washington Daily Constitution's* headline screamed, "HOAX!" In the accompanying article the *Constitution* claimed Booth's capture, death, and burial amounted to a fraud and contended that Booth had managed to escape. The *Richmond Examiner* copied this same headline and article. The *Louisville Journal* stated that the body aboard the *Montauk* was not that of John Wilkes Booth: "Baker and his associates have willfully conspired to swindle the United States Treasury."

Surgeon General Joseph K. Barnes presided over the autopsy. According to Barnes' subsequent report, Booth had been "struck on the back of the neck by a conoidal pistol ball, fired at the distance of a few yards, from a cavalry revolver." The bullet had severed Booth's spinal cord and thus had brought on "general paralysis." Booth, the report concluded, had died from asphyxiation. Since according to Dr. May, the body aboard the *Montauk* did not resemble John Wilkes Booth, officials had to rely on "special marks," especially the initials J. W. B. supposedly tattooed on his right hand. One witness stated that he failed to see any such mark, but a second stated that he did see the tattoo on Booth's right hand.

Certainly everyone knew by then that Booth had J. W. B. tattooed on the back of his right hand; yet, a secret letter, recently found in the files of the War Department from Gen. J. L. McPhail, provost marshal for the state of Maryland, to Edwin Stanton contradicts that testimony:

> Hon. E. M. Stanton
> Secretary of War, Washington, D.C.
>
> Sir: The following marks are upon the person of Booth by which he may be recognized: On his right arm are the initials of his name, and on his left hand, between the forefinger and thumb, a small cross, and across the same hand several spots, all in India ink.
>
> J. L. McPhail
> Provost-Marshall, State of Maryland

Following this so-called identification of the body, Edwin Stanton ordered that it be turned over without delay to Lafayette Baker. At 2:45 that afternoon, immediately following the "examination" of the body and while outraged naval officials stood quietly by with the metal casket they had made especially for this occasion, wondering what this frantic rush was all about, Baker and his cousin, Luther Baker, snatched the body away and lowered it to a small boat manned by two sailors.. In order to fool the large gathering of curious onlookers lining the shore into believing that the body would be buried at sea, Baker also had a large metal ball and chain lowered to the boat. Then the boat, the Baker cousins, the two sailors, and the body headed down the Potomac several miles to Geeseborough Point, a dark, dismal, and desolate marsh. In addition to other debris, it was littered with the decaying corpses of horses and mules cast off by the army. It was also the site of the Old Penitentiary, now used as a storage building for the Washington Arsenal.

In order to avoid any witnesses, the two Bakers and the sailors sat in their boat until almost two in the morning, when the four men carried the body to a large room in the penitentiary, a room selected by Edwin Stanton himself. By the ghostly light of a single lantern, the sailors performed their grim task. They pried bricks from the room's flooring and dug a shallow grave then lowered the body, now resting in a wooden rifle box, into the hole. They covered it with dirt and replaced the bricks. All present were then sworn to secrecy concerning the whereabouts of the body. For reasons known only to himself, Edwin Stanton wanted to make sure that no one knew the location of this body. It definitely would not be made available to anyone for purposes of identification. This body would remain hidden away until Pres. Andrew Johnson had it released to Booth family members in 1867. It was interred in the Booth family plot at Green Mount Cemetery in Baltimore. Till this day a great many question the identity of the body buried in Booth's grave. Perhaps it is that of John Wilkes Booth. Perhaps it is not. No one will know for certain until that body is exhumed and DNA tests conducted.

VII

The Trial of the Conspirators

The Conspirators Are Hauled In .

The first of the conspirators to be arrested following the execution of the president was Michael O'Laughlin, perhaps the most reluctant of all Booth's recruits, who did not wait to be arrested but surrendered himself to the Metropolitan Police on Sunday afternoon, April 16. According to O'Laughlin's reasoning, he had nothing to fear from the police because he was certainly not guilty of anything. True, he had spoken with Booth on several occasions concerning the possible abduction of the president, but those conversations had come to nothing. They were just talk, nothing more than what numerous other citizens were speaking of during the final year of the war. He also had an ironclad alibi for his whereabouts on the night of April 14. True, he had been in Washington, but he had been in the company of perhaps a dozen of his friends, sporty young men who were totally loyal to the Union. They had spent that night, as well as Saturday night, staggering from one barroom to the next and from one bawdy house to another, having a wonderful time. It had been a most delightful weekend, and, he laughed, he had not executed a single president. The police failed to see the humor in his remarks, and he was thrown into a cell and kept there until his trial began, a most sobering experience.

Then came Edman Spangler, whose worst crime was briefly holding the reins of Booth's horse on the night of April 14 before he turned the job over to Peanuts Burroughs. Still, there was one witness who testified that Spangler had also held open the door at Ford's Theatre as Booth rushed out the rear exit. There were others who testified that they had seen Spangler and Booth speaking together and enjoying drinks together over the years. Spangler too was thrown into a cell to await trial.

Samuel Arnold was arrested on Monday, April 17, and charged with conspiring to assassinate the president. Despite his protests that he was at work in Point Comfort, Virginia, on that past Friday, and his fellow workers could verify his presence, Federal authorities insisted that he be jailed until trial. Apparently, if he was not guilty of murder, then he was probably guilty of something else.

Concerning Mary Surratt and Lewis Powell, it seems that the hand of fate was most definitely at work in their arrests. Only hours following Lincoln's being shot, at two o'clock in the morning, Metropolitan Police detective John A. Clarvoe led a squad of four detectives to Mrs. Surratt's boarding-house in search of either Wilkes Booth or John Surratt. Louis Weichmann, dressed in his pajamas, answered the loud knock at the door. While the detectives searched the house, Weichmann woke Mary Surratt then returned to the living room to demand the reason for the intrusion. When told, quite mistakenly, that Booth had shot the president and John Surratt the secretary of state, Weichmann threw his hands in the air and cried, "My God! Now I see it all." At that point Mrs. Surratt entered the living room and Weichmann told her the startling news. Her hands flew to her mouth in horror. "Good Lord, Mr. Weichmann, do not tell me so!" Clarvoe would later testify that Mrs. Surratt's reaction seemed genuine and unforced. She freely admitted that she had seen Booth only the day before, but, she insisted vehemently, her son had been out of town for the past two weeks and she did not know where he was. He certainly was not in Washington murdering anyone. At that point the police departed, leaving an excited Louis Weichmann and a distraught Mary Surratt to dissect what they had just heard.

But on Monday evening, just before midnight, some

seventy-two hours following the shooting of the president, the Metropolitan Police returned to Mrs. Surratt's boarding-house to arrest her. She was charged with conspiracy and assisting the assassins as well as aiding their escape. Arrested along with her were her daughter, Anna, and her niece. Mrs. Surratt was astounded at this turn of events and swore that she knew nothing of any conspiracy against Lincoln. Her protestations of innocence were so convincing that the detectives now began to look at one another doubt-fully. Perhaps this lady might be telling the truth after all.

It was just at that point that an astonishing bit of fate intruded in the proceedings in the form of a knock at the front door. Surprised, John Clarvoe threw open the door, and there stood the infamous Lewis Powell. A big, muscular man, standing six foot two in his bare feet, he filled the doorway. His clothing and boots were covered in mud, a woolen tobog-gan pulled down low over his forehead, and a pickax thrown over his shoulder. He had been hiding in an abandoned graveyard since his flight from the Seward home the previous Friday night, but cold and hunger had driven him to seek refuge with the Surratts. Startled, his jaws agape, Powell stood looking speechlessly at Clarvoe. Clarvoe, suspiciously rubbing his chin, looked back at Powell.

"Yes?" Clarvoe asked with mock pleasantness. "May I help you?"

Powell, thinking quickly, stuttered that he had been hired by Mrs. Surratt to dig a gutter around her house, and he had just dropped by to discuss the job with her.

"At midnight?"

Powell nodded a tentative yes.

Clarvoe looked at Mrs. Surratt for confirmation of Powell's story. But in the dark front parlor and with Powell in dis-guise, the very nearsighted Mrs. Surratt shook her head emphatically and said, "I swear before God, I do not know this man, and have never seen him before, and I did not hire him to dig a gutter for me."

Upon further questioning, Powell pulled a document from his pocket indicating that Lewis Payne (his alias) had taken

an oath of allegiance to the Union. The police were not familiar with the name Lewis Payne, but the episode struck them
as sufficiently suspicious to haul Powell in along with the
rest. Mary Surratt was locked in a cell in the Carroll Annex
of the Old Capitol Prison to await trial. From then until her
hanging some ten weeks later, an utterly distraught Mary
Surratt daily dressed in a black dress, black bonnet, and
black veil. She could not stop weeping.

As for Lewis Powell, the police were stymied. No matter
what they asked, no matter what they threatened, Powell
stuck to his story—he was just a poor laborer looking for
work. However, police were convinced that this strange crea-
ture must be guilty of something. Then, just after daybreak
the following morning, it suddenly occurred to police that
perhaps this mud-spattered young man might have been
involved in the attempt on William Seward's life. They immediately sent for William Bell, Secretary Seward's houseboy.
Upon his arrival, Bell took one look at Powell and then asked
him to smile. Surprised at the request, Powell gave Bell a
quick, cold look, but then he sighed, shrugged his shoulders and flashed Bell a big smile. Bell began jumping up
and down excitedly. He told police that Powell was indeed the
man; he would recognize those big dimples in his cheeks
anywhere. Powell was thus charged with conspiring to murder not only William Seward but also Abraham Lincoln.

George Atzerodt, meanwhile, had eluded police for some six
days without much effort. Police had found the incriminating evidence that David Herold had left in Atzerodt's room at
the Kirkwood House only hours following the shooting of the
president, but they had no idea where to look for him. Then
came a mysterious tip, and police immediately picked up
Atzerodt at his cousin's home in Germantown. There is evidence that the tip came from none other than George
Atzerodt's older brother, John Atzerodt, a Baltimore detective.

As of April 20, police now had in custody Michael
O'Laughlin, Samuel Arnold, Edman Spangler, Mary Surratt,
Lewis Powell, and George Atzerodt. Booth, Herold, and Surratt
were still at large, their whereabouts supposedly unknown.

Photos of Lewis Powell taken following his arrest. In the photo at right he, like the other conspirators, is wearing metal manacles that proved most painful to the wrists. He was also required to don a western hat for identification purposes.
Library of Congress

Subsequently, on April 26, Wilkes Booth would be killed (allegedly at least) in Garrett's barn, and his accomplice, David Herold, taken into custody. Upon his arrest on April 27, Herold swore that he was not even in Washington on the evening of April 14 but was in southern Maryland trying to sell a horse. He agreed that he did meet with Wilkes Booth during the early morning hours of April 15 at a place known as Soper's Hill, but that meeting, he said, came about strictly by chance. He swore that he did not even become aware that Lincoln had been assassinated until the afternoon of April 15. (At the trial of the conspirators not a single witness could positively identify Herold as one of the conspirators seen on the evening of April 14.) Little good it did him.

As for John Surratt, once the government could no longer ignore his existence, he was finally arrested some nineteen months later, on November 27, 1866, in Alexandria, Egypt, and returned to Washington for trial.

Following their arrests, all the conspirators, with the exception of Mary Surratt, were thrown into the dark bowels of the monitor *Saugus* on the Potomac River, a truly terrifying experience for the conspirators, for in that deep, silent hold there penetrated not a spot of light.

Upon Lewis Powell's arrest, his clothes were taken from him, and he was given a dark blue navy uniform which he would wear twenty-four hours a day for the next eighty-one days. In fact, on July 7, 1865, following his execution, he would be buried in that same uniform.

Trial by Military Court-Martial

Secretary of War Edwin Stanton, aided and abetted by Pres. Andrew Johnson, immediately made the decision to prosecute the Lincoln conspirators by military court-martial rather than in a civil court of law. Thus Stanton himself could control not only the investigation but the trial as well since it was he who would appoint the military officers who supposedly would conduct the trial and act as the jury.

Those officers would report to Stanton on a daily basis and receive orders from him. As a result, the trial immediately became a farce and the military tribunal nothing more than a kangaroo court.

Certain influential government officials strongly objected to trying these civilians before a military court. In his personal diary, Secretary of the Navy Gideon Welles wrote, "I regret they are not tried by the civil court, and so expressed myself, but Stanton, who says the proof is clear and positive, was emphatic, and Speed advised a military commission, though at first, I thought, otherwise inclined." Welles was not alone in his objections. Indeed, Edward Bates, former attorney general under President Lincoln, opposed the military commission, believing it to be unconstitutional. In his diary he wrote,

> Trial of the Assassins at Washington, by a secret Military Court. Some one sends me the Philadelphia 'Ledger' of May 12, containing copious extracts from the N. Y. Post, the Tribune and the Times—all denouncing bitterly the proceeding as, at once, a dangerous breach of law, and a gross blunder in policy. I wrote the other day, to tell how the government fell into the blunder of insisting upon trying the conspirators by a military court.

Despite such objections, on May 1, 1865, Pres. Andrew Johnson issued a special executive order removing jurisdiction of the conspirators from the civil courts and placing them under the jurisdiction of the military. It is interesting to note that the original draft of this order, dated April 20, 1865, some ten days prior to Johnson's order, was handwritten by Edwin Stanton on stationary with a War Department letterhead. There can be no doubt that it was Stanton's decision to try the conspirators in a military court, where he could control the proceedings, the findings, and the judgments. His order of April 20 reads, in part: "All persons harboring or secreting the said persons [Booth and Herold] or aiding their concealment or escape, will be treated as accomplices in the murder of the President, and shall be subject to trial before a military commission, and the punishment of death."

Stanton's decision to try the conspirators before a military commission has infuriated historians across the nation. In the first place, General Lee had surrendered his army weeks earlier and thus the war was at an end. The city of Washington was no longer under martial law, and the civil courts were operating just as they had prior to the war. Indeed, days earlier Stanton had issued an order stating that since the capital no longer faced a threat from Confederate forces, passes no longer would be necessary for citizens entering or exiting the city of Washington. In other words, Washington had returned to a state of prewar normalcy—except in the courtroom where the accused conspirators would face murder charges.

Before the Military Commission, as both Johnson and Stanton were well aware, the accused would have none of the constitutional rights they would enjoy in a civil court. They would be treated (or mistreated) not as American citizens but as U.S. soldiers charged with terrible crimes. At Johnson's behest, James Speed, the attorney general of the United States, issued a written justification for the establishment of a military commission. He pointed out, rather unconvincingly, that though Lee had surrendered his Army of Northern Virginia, there were still several Confederate units fighting in the field, especially in the area west of the Mississippi, and since Lincoln had been commander in chief of the armed forces, it seemed reasonable that the accused should be tried before a military commission.

Johnson was delighted when James Speed came trotting into his office one morning with his written justification for denying the accused their right to be tried in a civil court of law. Johnson immediately called Stanton into his office. Together they beamed when Speed finished reading his justification. With the creation of this Military Commission, they would become both judge and jury, or at least they would have total control of the judge and jury. The conspirators would quickly be found guilty, as everyone knew they were, and subsequently hanged by the neck until dead, thereby taking to the grave with them any secrets that might prove embarrassing to the government. Johnson and Stanton shook hands with Speed, then with each other. How very clever they were.

Reacting against such a flimsy justification for a court-martial, former attorney general Edward Bates' sense of outrage grew even stronger. In his diary, he wrote,

> I am pained to believe that my successor, Atty Genl Speed, has been wheedled out of an opinion, to the effect that such a trial is lawful. If he be, in the lowest degree, qualified for his office, he must know better. Such a trial is not only unlawful, but it is a gross blunder in policy: It denied the great, fundamental principle, that ours is a government of Law, and that the law is strong enough to rule the people wisely and well; and if the offenders be done to death by that tribunal, however truly guilty, they will pass for martyrs with the world.[1]

It was determined that the trial should be conducted in the jail itself, the Arsenal building, located on the banks of the Potomac River. It was decided that "the following persons should be tried as principals and accessories for the murder of the President and the attempted assassination of the Honorable William H. Seward and others: David E. Herold, George A. Atzerodt, Lewis Payne [Powell], Michael O'Laughlin, Edman Spangler, Samuel Arnold, Mary E. Surratt, and Samuel A. Mudd." According to the orders of Edwin Stanton, the Military Commission should be composed of the following officers: Gen. James A. Ekin, Gen. Robert S. Foster, Gen. T. M. Harris, Gen. Albion P. Howe, Gen. David Hunter, Gen. August V. Kautz, Gen. Lewis Wallace, and Col. C. H. Tompkins. Col. Joseph Holt would serve as judge advocate and recorder. Judge Holt would have as his assistants (special judge advocates) the Honorable John A. Bingham and Gen. Henry L. Burnett. Holt, it might be pointed out, had been appointed by President Lincoln to serve as judge advocate general of the U.S. Army in 1862. The marshal of the court would be Gen. John F. Hartranft. Despite all the official hullabaloo out of Washington, the Military Commission quickly proved itself little more than a gang of Edwin Stanton sycophants.

The Military Commission (left to right): Col. David Clendenin, Col. C. H. Tompkins, Gen. T. M. Harris, Gen. Albion Howe, Gen. James Ekin, Gen. Lew Wallis, Gen. David Hunter, Gen. August Kautz, Gen. Robert Foster, Special Judge Advocate John Bingham, Judge Advocate Henry Burnett. Library of Congress

The makeshift courtroom itself was some thirty feet long and twenty-five feet wide, its entrance located in the wall opposite the penitentiary. Lengthwise it was divided into two sections, that on the right being occupied by the court, which sat around a long table. Judge Holt and his assistants were located on the left side. Another portion of the room was set aside for spectators, citizens who would be admitted only if they had a pass signed by General Hunter, president of the court. Newspaper reporters were seated in a special section near the witness box in the center of the room.

The prisoners had been transferred from the monitors to the Arsenal Prison on the night of April 29, and each was placed in a pitch-dark solitary cell. Stanton had ordered that the prisoners would be forced to wear tight fitting, heavily padded hoods that would essentially render them blind, deaf, and mute. Each prisoner wore heavy steel cuffs on his hands and feet. Certainly in May and June the heat inside those cells, a guard would later write, was unbearable. The psychological effects of living under such conditions—in total darkness, extreme heat, and unable to communicate—can be imagined. It is generally conceded that such psychological tortures are employed to exact confessions from the accused. In this case, Stanton's sadistic measures served to prevent any confessions.

The prisoners were fed four times a day a steady diet of "a soft piece of bread, two slabs of salt pork, and a cup of water." Six days later, after the move to the Arsenal Prison, on May 5, each prisoner was brought a pail of water and allowed to bathe for the first time since their incarceration eighteen days earlier. They were also given a fresh change of underclothes.

The Trial Gets under Way

On May 12, the trial finally got under way with the taking of first testimony. Unfortunately for the defense attorneys, they were given no time for pretrial preparation or consultation with their clients. They had almost no time to locate, prepare, and call all the witnesses they wished and little time to investigate the government's witnesses. They had no influence over the agenda or timetable of the trial, no right to put their clients on the stand, and no citation to particular statutes that the defendants were alleged to have violated. They faced a court of nine judges, all of them army generals and not one a lawyer, men who had no professional knowledge of criminal law or rules of evidence. A simple majority vote would result in conviction; a majority of two-thirds could impose the death sentence. There was no right of appeal, except to the president of the United States. The verdicts and sentences of the commission would, in other words, be final. At trial's end, it was found that every objection entered by the commission was sustained while every objection entered by the defense was overruled. (Not a bad average for the commission!)

The defendants were seated at one end of the courtroom, behind a wooden railing, all in a row on a raised platform. From the left sat Mrs. Surratt, then David Herold, Lewis Powell, George Atzerodt, Michael O'Laughlin, Edman Spangler, Dr. Samuel Mudd, and Samuel Arnold. Between every two prisoners sat an armed guard. With the exception of Mrs. Surratt, all the prisoners wore heavy handcuffs, and each wore a thirty-two-pound iron ball chained to his ankle. The heavily padded hoods that the prisoners were ordered to wear were removed once they entered the courtroom, one of the few rules of legal decorum observed by the Military Commission. Just to the right of Mrs. Surratt stood a stout iron door that led into a corridor where the cells of the accused were located.

On Tuesday morning, the ninth of May, 1865, the accused were brought into court for the first time. They were asked if they had any objections to any member of the Military Commission. Silently, they shook their heads. They had none. Judge Holt then read a long, rambling charge against the accused. In addition to those now on trial, the commission also indicted the following individuals: Jefferson Davis, George N. Sanders, Beverly Tucker, Jacob Thompson, William C. Cleary, Clement C. Clay, George Harper, and George Young. With the exception of Jefferson Davis, of course, these individuals were all agents of the Confederate Secret Service, operating largely out of Canada and deeply incriminated in the conspiracy to murder Lincoln.

Stanton hoped that by indicting the heads of the Confederate government for the assassination, he would divert suspicion from where it rightly belonged: with the heads of the U.S. Federal government, in particular Edwin Stanton and Andrew Johnson. Jefferson Davis, now in prison at Fortress Monroe, eagerly looked forward to his day in court for he had not the least doubt that he could prove the Southern states were never in a state of rebellion but merely exercising their constitutional rights when they seceded from the Union. After carefully considering the matter for some two years, in 1867 Pres. Andrew Johnson and Edwin Stanton quietly ordered

Davis's release. They were afraid that should Davis ever be allowed a hearing in a court of law he might prove his points.

The accused now on trial, according to the indictment, had been

incited and encouraged thereunto by Jefferson Davis, George N. Sanders, Beverly Tucker, Jacob Thompson, William C. Cleary, Clement C. Clay, George Harper, George Young, and others unknown, . . . did in aid of said armed rebellion, on the 6th day of March 1865, and on divers other days and times between that day, and the 15th day of April A.D. 1865, combine, confederate and conspire together at Washington City with the Military Department of Washington, and within the entrenched fortifications and military line of the United States, there being, unlawfully, maliciously, and traitorously to kill and murder Abraham Lincoln, the President of the United States aforesaid; and unlawfully, maliciously and traitorously to kill and murder Andrew Johnson, now Vice-President of the United States aforesaid . . . ; and to kill and murder Ulysses S. Grant, Lieutenant-General of the Army of the United States . . . ; and to kill and murder the said William H. Seward, then Secretary of State of the United States aforesaid.

In addition to the main ring of conspirators, there were many others charged with "aiding the escape" of Booth and Herold, and if found guilty, warned Stanton, their punishment would be "death." This pronouncement had ominous implications for those Southern patriots who had assisted Booth and Herold in their bid for freedom: John M. Lloyd, Col. Samuel Cox, Peregrin Davis, Oswell Swann, John J. Hughes, Franklin Robey, Dr. Richard Stuart, William Lucas, Charlie Lucas, Elizabeth Quesenberry, Thomas Harbin, Thomas Jones, William Bryant, Joseph Baden, Pvt. William Jett, Pvt. Mortimer Ruggles, and Lt. Absalom Bainbridge. However, none of these persons were ever brought to trial, to their great relief. Why the government chose not to prosecute the above conspirators remains one of the great mysteries of the Lincoln assassination.

Continuing with their indictments, the Military Commission charged Edman Spangler with very few crimes.

He was accused of aiding John Wilkes Booth in gaining entrance to the president's box at Ford's Theatre and with aiding and abetting him in his escape from the theater. Though his crimes had been few, if convicted, he could be hanged as an accessory to murder.

Poor George Atzerodt, a hapless victim of circumstances if ever there was one, was accused of lying in wait at his hotel, the Kirkwood House, for the vice president, whom he supposedly planned to murder. The commission apparently failed to realize that this charge was patently ridiculous. Had Atzerodt made any move against Johnson on April 14, President Lincoln would never have appeared at Ford's Theatre that evening, spoiling Booth's plan.

Michael O'Laughlin did not even meet with his fellow conspirators on April 14. In fact, he and Samuel Arnold had both withdrawn from the plot following the failed attempt to abduct the president on March 17. But for lack of a better charge, he was accused of lying in wait for Gen. Ulysses S. Grant for the purpose of murdering him. The commission failed to explain just how O'Laughlin was expected to find and murder Grant at a time when the general and his wife were on a train bound for New Jersey.

Samuel Arnold, who, along with Michael O'Laughlin, had withdrawn from the conspiracy on March 17, was charged with a variety of offenses, including conspiring with, aiding, counseling, abetting, comforting, and supporting Booth and his band in their murderous conspiracy. Surely, if he were charged with enough offenses, at least one would stick.

David Herold was accused of assisting Booth in the assassination of the president, as well as with assisting him in both his escape from Washington and in his later flight from justice as he hid from Federal authorities in the woods of Maryland and Virginia. As though the noose were not already tight enough around Herold's neck, he was also accused of aiding Lewis Powell in his murderous attack upon Secretary of State William Seward. It was obvious to Herold's mother and sisters, as optimistic as they tried to be, that there was little hope that Davy would escape the hangman.

Upon his return to Washington on April 27, Herold had been questioned by Judge John Bingham and sworn that he was not in Washington on April 14 after 8 P.M. Herold swore that he had nothing whatsoever to do with the assassination of Lincoln or the attempted assassination of William Seward. He had had an opportunity to sell a horse in southern Maryland, he said, and was on the south side of the Potomac when Lincoln was assassinated. Riding back to town, he met Booth, strictly a matter of coincidence, at about 11:30 P.M. at the bottom of Soper's Hill, about eight miles southeast of the capital. He wanted to return home, but Booth persuaded him to accompany him to Bryantown, where they would start out on a hunting party, Herold's favorite pastime. He was suspicious of the circumstances, he said, because Booth was heavily armed and apparently had a badly injured leg.

Q. What time did you start from Washington on that journey?

A. I don't know. I was tight. I had been tight nearly all day.

Q. Who asked you to go?

A. No one; I asked myself. Atzerodt wanted to sell a horse, and loaned him to me at Shreve's stable. He had two horses he wanted to sell. Mr. Greenswalt, the proprietor of the Pennsylvania House, bought one of them for $140. It was when the circus was here.

Q. What I want to know is, who asked you on Friday evening to take that horse and sell him? How did you come to go that Friday afternoon?

A. I don't know how, any more upon that afternoon than any other.

Q. Did nobody tell you anything about going that day?

A. No, sir; it is nothing unusual for me to leave home seven or eight o'clock at night to go to the country. As I have said, I took one, if not two drinks. I owed Mr. Lloyd two dollars. I gave him a bill—I think it was either one or two dollars—and told him it was all the money I had in change. I said, "Mr. Lloyd, here is a bill; you need not give me any change, let it stand." On my way home, at the foot of Soper's Hill, between seven and eight miles from Washington, I met Booth. He spoke to me.

Q. What time was that?

A. I think it must have been about half-past eleven o'clock at night.

Q. The same Friday night you went down?

A. Yes, sir; the same Friday. Says Booth, "Come go back down the country; we will have a gay old time." I told him I was obliged to go back home. He said it was impossible to cross the bridge, for the gates were shut, and he had had difficulty in getting over himself. I think Booth must have been drinking; I am quite confident that he had been. He insisted upon my going down to Bryantown with him.

Q. How was he traveling?

A. He was riding a bay mare, which I saw in the morning.

Q. Did you not drink that evening in town with Booth?

A. I did not. I did not see Booth that evening.

Q. Is there any other statement in regard to your conduct or your connection with this matter, or in regard to the conduct or connection of anybody else with the murder of the President or the attempted murder of Mr. Seward, that you wish to make?

A. I do not know of any. I had no idea that there was any such thing in view, by any party at all. I knew nothing of it. I never knew any party in existence that had the slightest idea of injuring the President or any of the Cabinet.

Herold also stated that he turned away from Washington and accompanied Booth to Bryantown. There they separated for the night. The next morning the two met again, and Herold could see that Booth's injured leg had been set. Over the next week, Herold and Booth spent their time hiding out in various pine thickets. Booth kept him in line, he said, with the promise of a big reward if he cooperated and threats of death should he not cooperate.

There is a possibility that Herold was telling the truth. At trial, he was only partially identified by only two witnesses. John Fletcher, manager of the stable, said that he had seen a horse and rider on the evening of April 14, but the night had been quite dark, and the horse and rider were some two blocks away. Still, he "thought" the rider was David Herold. Then there was Sergeant Cobb, who had stopped a horse and rider at the Navy Yard Bridge on the evening of the assassination. His testimony was very similar to that of Fletcher. The night had been quite dark and he had spoken with the rider for only a minute. "He is very near the size of the second horseman, but I should think taller, although I can not be sure. He had a lighter complexion than this man," explained Cobb. In other words, neither could Cobb identify

David Herold, the youngest child in a highly respected Washington family, was sometimes described as "slow of mind," though he in fact held a certificate in pharmacy from Georgetown College. He was third in line to be hanged on July 7, 1865. Library of Congress

Herold. These were the only witnesses against Herold. Had his attorney, Frederick Stone, examined them more aggressively, his client might have escaped the hangman.

Lewis Payne (Powell) was charged with the attempted murder of William Seward. Armed with a revolver and a large knife, he inflicted grievous wounds upon William Seward, Frederick Seward, Augustus Seward, Emrick Hansell, and George Robinson. Neither the commission nor anyone else knew the true identity of the stoic young man who gave his name as Lewis Payne, and Powell refused to tell. In fact, he would say nothing at all. Despite the press's intense efforts to learn his true identity, Powell would go through his entire trial and execution on July 7 as Lewis Payne. Powell's attorney, Col. William Doster, would later write that Powell would reveal nothing even to him. Doster reported that fully a week had elapsed before Powell would speak to him at all, except to brazenly admit that he was guilty of all charges.

Edwin Stanton assigned Maj. Thomas Eckert to visit and interrogate Powell on a daily basis. Indeed, it is recorded that Eckert became an almost constant companion to Powell during his incarceration. Was Eckert assigned to question Powell to see just what, if anything, Booth had told him concerning the government's role in the execution? It is said that Eckert was most kind to Powell when in his company. On one occasion Powell refused a direct order from Col. H. H. Wells, a provost marshal from Washington. Angry, Wells drew his sword and struck Powell a sharp blow on his arm. At that, the muscular Eckert stepped forward and grabbed Wells by the hand. "We don't permit that sort of treatment, Colonel," he said. Furious, Wells walked away.

The prisoner did not only have the government's attention, he also aroused great public interest at trial. George Townsend, a reporter from the *New York World*, was obviously intrigued by this unusual young man. On May 10 he would write:

> Taller by a whole head than either his companions or the sentries, Payne the Assassin, sits erect and flings his barbarian eye to and fro, radiating the tremendous energy of his colossal physique. He is the only man worthy to have murdered Mr. Seward. The mystery attending Payne's home and parentage still exists to make him more incomprehensible. With this man's face before me as I write, I am reminded of some Maori Chief waging war from the lust of blood or the pride of local dominion. His complexion is bloodless yet so healthy that a passing observer would afterward speak of it as ruddy. His face is broad, with a character nose, sensual lips, and very high cheekbones, while the head runs back to an abnormal apex at the tip of his cerebellum. He is entirely beardless, yet in his boyish chin, more of a man physically than all the rest combined.

Powell's jailers would later remember that Powell always

maintained a sense of dignity unusual in a boy of his age and that he remained stoic and silent during his weeks of imprisonment, never attempting to communicate with anyone in any way, unless spoken to first. On one occasion in particular, while being questioned by an officer of the court, he broke his silence not to plead for his own life but to swear in the name of God that Mrs. Mary Surratt had nothing whatsoever to do with the conspiracy. Certainly Powell's sangfroid won the grudging admiration of everyone who came into contact with him during his long weeks of imprisonment. Even the night prior to his execution, while the other condemned prisoners spent their final hours weeping and praying with their family members and spiritual leaders, Powell, say his guards, spent part of the night in earnest conversation with his minister, the Reverend Abram Gillette, then later slept like a baby.

Aside from Lewis Powell, the prisoner who generated the most interest was the very handsome Mary Surratt. How could such a fine, gentle, Christian woman conspire with thugs to commit such dastardly deeds, wondered the press. She would remain for the press a puzzle throughout the trial and a daily topic for discussion. One reporter summed up the situation with Mary Surratt very succinctly when he wrote that she "just proves the old saying that you cannot tell a book by its cover."

Very much like Samuel Arnold, Mary Surratt was charged with a multitude of serious crimes. According to the commission, over the past few months she did "receive, entertain, harbor, and conceal, aid, and assist" the conspirators in their "murderous and traiterous [sic] conspiracy." And she did, without doubt, "aid, abet, and assist them in the execution thereof." As a happy afterthought, the commission added that she also assisted the conspirators in "escaping justice" following the assassination of Lincoln. She was, in other words, an accessory to murder.

Mrs. Surratt, who wore a veil throughout the trial, sat weeping bitterly and shaking her bowed head as the charges against her were read. Even Lewis Powell's composure was disturbed for a moment. He sat straight up in his seat, teeth clenched, and glared at the commission. He could recall one incident when he, a visitor to her boardinghouse, had inadvertently mentioned in her presence a minor detail related to the abduction of the president. John Surratt had immediately collared him and pulled him out into the hallway. "Never mention anything about our plot in front of my mother," Surratt warned. "She knows nothing about this, and I want it to remain that way. She must be protected." "Of course," Powell agreed. "I would not want my mother involved, either."

As for Dr. Samuel Mudd, Judge Holt read out the indictment against him, charging that between March 6 and April 20 he did "receive, entertain, harbor, and conceal, aid, and assist" the conspirators "with the knowledge of the murderous and traitorous conspiracy aforesaid, and with intent to aid, abet, and assist them in the execution thereof, and in escaping from justice after the murder of the said Abraham Lincoln."

To both the charges and specifications, the accused all voted not guilty. The court then adjourned for the day.

The court again convened the following morning, Thursday, May 11, 1865. At this time the commission granted Dr. Samuel Mudd's request that he be represented by Frederick Stone and Gen. Thomas Ewing, who would also represent Edman Spangler. The commission granted Mary Surratt's request that she be represented by Frederick Aiken and John W. Clampitt as well as George Atzerodt's request that he be represented by Col. William E. Doster and Walter S. Cox. On the following day, Friday, May 12, 1865, David Herold's request that he be represented by Frederick Stone was granted. The commission then granted requests from Dr. Mudd, Samuel Arnold, and Michael O'Laughlin that they be represented by Walter Cox.

The commission granted Mrs. Surratt's request that Reverdy Johnson serve as additional counsel for her. It might be pointed out that her attorneys, Aiken and Clampitt, enjoyed excellent reputations in the Washington area. As for Johnson, he was a senator from Maryland and a man of distinguished reputation. Unfortunately, he devoted far less time to defending Mrs. Surratt than to repeatedly denying the commission's jurisdiction to try the case. It was a ploy that aroused the ire of the commission and led repeatedly to heated exchanges between Johnson and Judge Bingham.

As for Gen. Thomas Ewing, he was considered perhaps the best of the defense attorneys and worked incessantly for his clients. A native of Ohio, his sister was married to Gen. William T. Sherman, and he was a cousin of the Honorable James G. Blaine. He himself was a highly decorated war veteran. His appearance in court to represent Spangler and Dr. Mudd caused some consternation among the judges. Perhaps they should exercise some discretion when responding to General Ewing, especially if they valued their military careers.

Lewis Powell at this time still had not secured counsel, though Atzerodt's attorney, Col. William E. Doster, would soon agree to represent him. Doster was an excellent attorney, a Harvard graduate who had fought valiantly throughout the war. Initially, he was not eager to represent Powell, but after speaking with him privately, he became as fascinated with him as everyone else. His efforts on Powell's behalf were most admirable.

Following the commission's approval of attorneys, the accused withdrew their not guilty pleas and filed a petition to the commission denying its jurisdiction to try their cases. After some deliberation, Judge Holt announced, to no one's surprise, that the defendants' pleas to be tried in a civil court had been overruled. Such being the case, the accused again entered not guilty pleas.

Once the preliminaries ended, the trial itself finally began. Court convened at ten o'clock each morning, six days a week, and lasted until late in the afternoon. In all, the government presented 180 witnesses, the defense 160.

It was now mid-May, and by early afternoon the temperature in Washington reached into the high eighties, and inside the packed courtroom the heat was stifling. The members of the Military Commission, dressed in their heavy dress blue uniforms, as well as the cuffed and chained defendants and their attorneys, appeared to have lapsed into comas as they sat listening to the droning testimony of an endless list of witnesses. One reporter wrote that members of the Military Commission seemed to periodically rouse themselves from their stupors just long enough to wipe away the rivulets of perspiration that streamed down their faces. Then again they would lapse back into their comas.

The commission first presented its case against David Herold. They maintained that Herold had known John Surratt as far back as April 1863. In March 1865 he had visited Mrs. Surratt's boardinghouse, where he met with Booth and Lewis Payne. He, they maintained, had been a party to the group of conspirators who had attempted to abduct the president on March 17. Most damaging of all, however, was the commission's contention that on April 14, the day of the assassination, he had met with Booth, Payne, and Atzerodt in Atzerodt's room at the Kirkwood House, where he had inadvertently left his overcoat. He also had been observed by witnesses leaving the Seward home at the time of the attack. A military guard identified him as the horseman he observed crossing the Eastern Branch Bridge just moments following the assassination. Too, he had accompanied Booth to the home of Dr. Mudd and had later been captured in Garrett's barn the night that Booth was killed. Things did not look good for David Herold. Still, his attorney, Frederick Stone, mounted a stout defense. Stone did everything possible to save Herold's life, but in the end, there was no denying the facts.

Since the testimony against his client was incontrovertible, Stone attempted to create sympathy for Herold by pointing out that he had always enjoyed an excellent reputation in the community, and he had worked since childhood to help support a widowed mother and seven older sisters. More importantly, said Stone, Herold had always been considered by those who knew him as weak and simple minded, a man with the mind of a child. Obviously Booth had taken advantage of his mental problems and used him for his own selfish purposes. Herold could be held responsible for his actions no more than could a child. Admittedly, it was not much, but it was the best Stone could offer. The commission, unfortunately for Herold, were not impressed. They could hang childlike men as well as worldly men.

Judge Bingham then presented the government's case against Lewis Payne. Beginning with Payne's arrival at the Branson house in January 1865, Bingham traced in great detail his movements until the attack upon Secretary Seward on the evening of April 14 and his subsequent arrest at Mrs. Surratt's boardinghouse on April 17. William H. Bell, the Seward's houseboy, took the stand and positively identified Payne as the young man who had forced his way into the Seward home under pretext of delivering medication to the injured secretary of state. Then came the detectives who arrested Payne at Mrs. Surratt's boardinghouse on the evening of April 17. They described how he was dressed and related the lies he told. The big bowie knife he used to assault Seward was entered into evidence, and the prosecution brought out a pair of boots that Payne had allegedly been wearing the night of his arrest. Stamped inside the top of one boot were the initials J. W. B., proving, said the prosecutor, that these boots once belonged to John Wilkes Booth, who had obviously given them to Payne.

Powell avidly followed this testimony with unblinking eyes. But when the prosecutor stated that the boots had belonged to John Wilkes Booth and that Booth had given them to Payne, who was wearing them the night of his arrest, Powell showed emotion for one of the few times in the entire trial. He threw back his head and laughed out loud. When Doster later asked him why he had shown such an outburst, Powell explained that Booth stood about five feet, seven inches tall and probably wore a size eight boot. He, on the other hand, stood six-two and wore a size eleven boot. There was no way, he laughed, that he and Booth could possibly wear the same size boots. He wondered why the prosecution would fabricate such dubious evidence to connect him with Booth when he freely admitted the connection. Doster agreed. He knew, but did not tell Powell, that the prosecution was convinced that Powell was guilty and would go to any lengths to hang him, even if they were forced to create a pair of boots.

The press would later report that Doster's defense of Powell was absolutely magnificent. It "was like an epic poem," one reporter wrote, "and one of the finest productions in the English language. During its delivery, the audience sat as if entranced with the orator's thrilling utterances." First, Doster stated that there were three things in the case against his client that were admitted beyond dispute:

1. That he is the person who attempted to take the life of the secretary of state.

2. That he is not within the medical definition of insanity.

3. That he believed what he did was right and justifiable.

Doster then presented a detailed portrait of Powell's life, relating his childhood on his father's farm in Florida, his joining the Confederate army, his wounding and capture at Gettysburg, his days with Mosby's Rangers, his taking a room with the Bransons in Baltimore, his meetings with Booth and his recruitment in the scheme to abduct the president, and finally his attack on Secretary Seward. "I have asked him why he did it," said Doster. "He responded only, 'Because I believed it my duty.'"

Doster denied nothing; Powell had done everything of which the government had accused him. However, Doster did attempt to present justification for his deeds. Powell was a Confederate soldier. He had attacked and killed Federal soldiers on the battlefield and won applause from his comrades for doing so. On the evening of April 14 he attacked and attempted to kill another Federal officer. What was the difference, really, between a Federal soldier and a Federal secretary of state? They were both enemies of the Confederate States of America. Besides, continued Doster, consider the opposite. Was there a single soldier in the Union army who would not have been delighted to take a shot at Jefferson Davis or Judah Benjamin should the opportunity have presented itself? Probably not. The people of the North would have wildly applauded that soldier's efforts should he have been successful in incapacitating one of those Confederate gentlemen.

During Doster's address to the Military Commission, wrote one reporter, "Payne sat stolid and indifferent; not a muscle in his face moved, and his stout frame exhibited no signs of emotion or fear. He was apparently the most unconcerned and the bravest man in the court room." It is well that he was, for the Federal hangman was already preparing a noose to fit Powell's neck.

Poor Atzerodt's defense was next presented. His case was hopeless and he knew it. Indeed, one reporter wrote that "he was the most wretched and woebegone-looking prisoner among them all." He now realized the enormity of the charges against him, and he appeared wracked with despair. Despite the sentiment against his client, Colonel Doster did the best he could for Atzerodt. He admitted that Booth and Surratt needed a boatman who could row them across the Potomac once they had abducted the president, and their boatman turned out to be George Atzerodt. Booth had told him of the conspiracy and promised him riches beyond his wildest dreams if he would simply ferry them and their party across the river. This the naive Atzerodt had agreed to do even though Booth had revealed to him that the victim of the abduction would be the president of the United States.

There was one great redeeming factor in favor of Doster's client. On the evening of April 14 at 8 P.M., during a meeting with Payne and Atzerodt at the Herndon House, Wilkes Booth had unveiled his latest plan. Abduction was no longer an option. According to Doster's explanation, if the conspirators were to have any hope of saving the South, they must throw the Federal government into a state of disorganized confusion by assassinating the heads of the U.S. government. Powell would assassinate the secretary of state. Atzerodt would assassinate the vice president, Andrew Johnson, who was currently living in the Kirkwood House, in the apartment just below his. Booth would assassinate the president. It took the German-born boatman a few moments to fully interpret Booth's words, but finally comprehending, a terrified Atzerodt leapt to his feet, upsetting his table and chair, and told Booth in no uncertain terms that he would

George Atzerodt, an immigrant from Germany. His primary role in the conspiracy was to ferry Booth, the conspirators, and Lincoln across the Potomac. On the night of the assassination he loudly refused to kill Vice President Johnson. Library of Congress

have absolutely nothing to do with the murder of another human being. And he wanted nothing further to do with any conspiracy against anyone, especially the president of the United States. He just wanted to return to Port Tobacco, forget the conspiracy, and get on with his life. Atzerodt had started for the door when Booth stopped him with the words, "You might as well do it. They're going to hang you anyway."

After fleeing the Herndon House, continued Doster to the Military Commission, Atzerodt had gone to the Oyster Bay and took drinks for the next hour, or until ten o'clock. From there he went to the Union, where he had drinks with a young man who worked at his stable. About 10:30 P.M. he visited the bar at the Kirkwood House. Then it was on to the Kimmel House, where he had several more drinks. Totally inebriated, he took to his horse and began aimlessly riding about the city. After returning his horse to the stable, he caught a streetcar to the Navy Yard. There, he met and spoke with Robert Briscoe, an acquaintance who operated a store at the Navy Yard. Around 2 A.M., he visited the Pennsylvania House and requested a room for the night. Feeling somewhat ill from all the drinking he had done the previous evening, he awakened about five that morning, took breakfast, then departed the Pennsylvania House. Several blocks away he threw his knife into a gutter on F Street near the Herndon House. Somehow, Atzerodt was not quite sure how, he made his way to Georgetown, where he pawned his two revolvers. Then he fled northward to Montgomery County, to the home of Hezekiah Metz, where he spent a day and a night. Washington detectives finally discovered him on April 20 at four o'clock in the morning at the home of his cousin, Hartman Richter. He was immediately taken into custody and placed aboard the monitor, the *Saugus*, and interrogated at great length.

It was true, argued Doster, that Atzerodt did have prior knowledge that Booth and Payne were talking of assassinating the president and the secretary of state, but the naive and poorly educated Atzerodt had no idea that they would actually attempt such an insane idea. He was as surprised and appalled as everyone else when he heard that they had carried through with Booth's plan. Therefore, Atzerodt should certainly not be viewed as an accessory to the murder of Lincoln and the attack on Seward. He was just a simple man whose generosity had been exploited by John Wilkes Booth.

Members of the Military Commission roused themselves long enough to wipe away their perspiration, then lapsed back into their comas. Here was another assassin whose presence the world would hardly miss.

Dr. Mudd's attorney, Gen. Thomas Ewing, fought strenuously and bitterly to have charges dismissed against his client. The Military Commission's charges against Dr. Mudd stemmed not so much from what he might have done prior to the assassination but from what he did afterward, allegedly shielding and harboring Booth and Herold in their flight from justice. If the government could prove that Dr. Mudd had known Booth and Herold prior to the assassination, a fact which they easily established, then he was rendered an accomplice and coconspirator after the fact of murder.

The most damning evidence against Dr. Mudd was provided by the ubiquitous Louis Weichmann, who related how he and John Surratt had been out for a stroll on December 23, 1864, when they accidentally met Mudd and Wilkes Booth on Seventh Street outside the National Hotel. They had gone up to Booth's room, where Booth, Mudd, and Surratt had engaged in whispered conversation while he was left to entertain himself. Obviously they were conspiring with one another, Weichmann offered to the commission. In return, commission members nodded knowingly and smiled approvingly at Weichmann. Encouraged, Weichmann went on to relate every incident he could possibly recall where Dr. Mudd might have somehow been involved with Booth or Surratt.

It must be remembered that Weichmann was initially arrested along with Mrs. Surratt and charged with conspiracy to murder the president, a charge he strongly denied. How could a man like Weichmann, wondered the detectives, a man who impressed everyone as something of a busybody, an inquisitive pest, have lived at the boardinghouse with a grand conspiracy swirling about him on a daily basis for months and not be aware of it? It was later written that upon his arrest he was thrown into a cell at the Arsenal, a rope tossed over a rafter and a noose looped around his neck while detectives threatened that he must tell them what they wanted to know or else he would be hanged on the spot. His death, they told him, would be reported as a suicide. The incident truly frightened Weichmann, and on May 5, in a letter written from his solitary cell at Carroll Prison to judge advocate Col. H. L. Burnette, he made the following comments: "I have the honor to call your attention to the following additional facts in my recollection. You confused and terrified me so much yesterday that I was most unable to say anything." At that point, Weichmann told them everything he knew, as well as a few things he merely surmised. Too, Weichmann was the sort of fellow who desired the approval of superiors more than anything, and his testimony would certainly win him not only his life but big smiles from the Military Commission.

During John Surratt's trial in 1867, Lewis Carland, who had been imprisoned with Weichmann in 1865, testified that Weichmann had confided in him during Mrs. Surratt's trial that "it would have been very different with Mrs. Surratt if I had been let alone." Weichmann also told Carland that prosecutors had written a statement for him and he was threatened with prosecution as one of the conspirators if he did not swear to it. James J. Gifford, who had also been in prison with Weichmann, corroborated Carland's testimony:

> Q. Did Weichmann say in your presence that an officer of the government had told him that unless he testified to more than he had already stated they would hang him too?
> A. I myself heard the officer tell him so.

In his testimony at trial in 1867, John Surratt vociferously denied Weichmann's account of Dr. Mudd introducing him to Wilkes Booth in December 1864. Surratt stated that Dr. Mudd did not introduce him to Wilkes Booth, as he had known Booth for months prior to that time. Surratt also testified that Weichmann had indeed been a party to the conspiracy, using his position as a clerk in the Prisoner of War Commissary to funnel information concerning Confederate prisoners of war, their numbers and whereabouts, to Surratt, who would carry the information to Richmond. Of course it must be remembered that Surratt blamed Weichmann's testimony for sending Mrs. Surratt to the gallows. Perhaps this testimony was his revenge.

General Ewing attacked Weichmann's testimony with everything he had, presenting witness after witness who swore that Dr. Mudd was not in Washington on December 23. He, too, accused Weichmann of having been a party to the conspiracy, but General Ewing could tell from the bored expressions of the Military Commission that his efforts were having little affect.

But there was one occasion when Weichmann knowingly lied under oath to the Military Commission. He testified that on April 2 Mrs. Surratt had sent him to deliver a message to Wilkes Booth in his room at the National Hotel. "It was on the 2nd of April," said Weichmann, "when Mrs. Surratt sent me to the hotel; and I at that time found in Booth's room Mr. John McCullough, the actor; and I communicated my message to Booth. I told him that Mrs. Surratt would like to see him." McCullough later offered incontrovertible proof that he had departed Washington on March 12 for an engagement in New York City and had been nowhere near Washington on April 2. After some deliberation, the Military Commission concluded that since McCullough could offer thousands of witnesses who would swear that they saw him on stage in New York on April 2, perhaps Weichmann was mistaken as to his date. Perhaps it would not be wise to indict McCullough after all.

In the end, it was a beaming Louis Weichmann who stepped down from the witness stand. Several weeks following his testimony he received a very nice note from none other than Edwin Stanton himself thanking him for his unimpeachable courage.

As for Dr. Mudd, said the Military Commission, by setting Booth's broken leg he had aided and abetted Booth and Herold, fugitives from justice, in their escape from Washington. But it must be remembered that Booth and Herold had called at Mudd's home at about 4 A.M. on the morning of the assassination, at a time when neither Dr. Mudd nor anyone else in Maryland had even become aware that Lincoln had been assassinated. Since the news had not been circulated, how could he have known that he was aiding and abetted the escape of desperate criminals by simply following his oath as a physician?

In addition, Dr. Mudd twice testified under oath that the man who came to his home on that morning was not Wilkes Booth. He certainly knew Booth, he said, and the man who came to his home that morning was decidedly not the man he knew. The two men went by the names Tyson and

Henston and were totally unknown to him. The injured fellow, recalled Mudd, wore a false beard and stood about six feet tall (Booth stood five-seven). Who he was and where he came from, Mudd swore that he did not know, but he was sure that the man with the broken leg was not Wilkes Booth and the smaller man was not David Herold. Members of the Military Commission looked at one another and smirked. Mudd could not fool them.

Among a bevy of other witnesses against Dr. Mudd, there was one Elzee Eglent, a former slave, who was called to the stand simply to swear that the doctor had once taken a shot at him with his pistol. At that testimony, members of the Military Commission roused themselves from their lethargy long enough to jot down Eglent's testimony then nod knowingly at one another. That just proved what a murderous thug Mudd really was.

In the end, the Military Commission missed hanging Dr. Mudd by only one vote. Instead, he was sentenced to life imprisonment in the Dry Tortugas.

As for Samuel Arnold and Michael O'Laughlin, the evidence against them proving their collaboration in the plot to murder the president was not nearly as strong as against some of the others. In his confession of April 17, Arnold freely had admitted that he and O'Laughlin were members of the conspiracy to abduct Lincoln, but he swore that they knew nothing of any conspiracy to assassinate him. Following their failed attempt to abduct Lincoln on March 17, said Arnold, he and O'Laughlin had thrown up their hands and returned home to Baltimore. From their standpoint, he said, they would have nothing else to do with Booth or his conspiracies. Thus on April 1 he went to Fortress Monroe and took a job in a store owned by John W. Wharton and was there the night Booth shot Lincoln.

Throughout the trial the Military Commission had dismissed any testimony that suggested the conspirators were ever committed to abducting the president. It was assassination they had in mind from the beginning, not abduction. General Bingham related to the commission Booth's plan to abduct

Michael O'Laughlin was a schoolmate and friend of John Wilkes Booth. A former Confederate soldier, he was unemployed and living at home with his parents when recruited for the conspiracy. O'Laughlin died in prison during the yellow fever epidemic in 1867. Library of Congress

the president at Ford's Theatre by grabbing him in his box and lowering him to a waiting accomplice on stage then riding with him down through Maryland and into Virginia. "Can you imagine," cried Bingham, "a pigmy catching a giant!" Both Bingham and his cohorts on the Military Commission enjoyed a long and hearty laugh at the absurdity of such an idea. Arnold and O'Laughlin, therefore, were wasting their time if they thought the Military Commission could be fooled into believing that they were innocent of plotting the murder of the

Samuel Arnold, another schoolmate and friend of Booth, like Arnold, was unemployed and living with his parents when approached to help abduct the president. He and O'Laughlin joined the conspiracy primarily for the easy money that Booth promised. Arnold was pardoned in 1869. Library of Congress

president. "Besides," added Bingham, "if Arnold were truly through with the conspiracy, why did he not make known the fact to Abraham Lincoln and his constitutional advisors that these men, armed with the weapons of assassination, were daily lying in wait for their lives?" It was a difficult question to answer, except that Arnold was truly convinced that Booth and the others would never take further steps against the president and that the conspiracy was essentially at an end. Doubtlessly he was lying, reasoned the Military Commission, though they would not hang him but send him to the Dry Tortugas for the rest of his life.

For O'Laughlin's trial, the government paraded a dozen witnesses to the stand to swear that they had seen O'Laughlin in Washington on the day of the assassination. O'Laughlin did not contradict them; indeed, he freely admitted their claim, but he said he was not involved with Booth or any of the others on that day. In fact, he spent that afternoon and evening getting wildly drunk in a succession of Washington barrooms. His attorney brought six witnesses to the stand who sheepishly testified that they had been with O'Laughlin during his weekend of revelry. They had visited numerous barrooms, they swore, seeking drink and female companionship and had not even gone near Ford's Theatre. In fact, no one had even mentioned Ford's Theatre or President Lincoln. The Military Commission, in their infinite wisdom, would also sentence O'Laughlin to life in prison in the Dry Tortugas.

Despite the Military Commission's vindictive attitude and the fear with which they were regarded by almost everyone, there emerged a few citizens who were not afraid to speak out in opposition to what was obviously a mock court. On June 24, John T. Ford, the owner of Ford's Theatre, outraged that his employee Edman Spangler was now on trial for his life, demonstrated a great deal of courage when he published in Washington newspapers a transcript of Spangler's testimony along with a condemnation of the commission for their treatment of Spangler:

> The part of the GREAT CONSPIRACY TRIAL contains all the evidence which in any and every way relates to my Theater, and to the acts of EDMAN SPANGLER, the only person connected with it upon trial,—it is published from the OFFICIAL COURT RECORD for the use of my friends and for the sake of truth. Much exaggeration incidental to the charges upon which this trial was founded was indulged in at a time of great public excitement. The offer of rewards for information brought many ambitious detectives to the surface, who were manifestly more ambitious to convict than to learn truth—willing and florid newspaper correspondents caught up their tales and attractively

placed them before the public, and through such means PUBLIC OPINION was created, condemning the accused before trial. How much wrong has been done in this way, the patience and fairness of the reader must now judge.

Unfortunately, there were just too few citizens with the courage to speak out in defense of justice, and the trials by military court-martial continued.

Then came the evidence against Mary Surratt. Of all those on trial, it was she who aroused the most attention and excitement. The courtroom was packed to the rafters with curious onlookers and members of the press the morning that Judge Bingham called her case to the attention of the court. Not only was this defendant a female, which was most unusual, but she was also, at the age of forty-two, the oldest member of the conspirators. If convicted, she would become the first woman ever to be executed in America.

The evidence against her, said Judge Bingham, was strong, far stronger than against Atzerodt, Arnold, O'Laughlin, Mudd, or Spangler. Her involvement in the conspiracy began on December 23, 1864, the day on which her son had met with Booth and Dr. Mudd, and did not end until the date of her arrest on April 17, 1865. Bingham charged that her boardinghouse had become a headquarters of sorts for the conspirators, a place where they frequently met and conspired to murder the president. Her own daughter, in fact, had testified that Lewis Payne had visited her boardinghouse on at least two occasions, and obviously he was not visiting simply to pass the time.

The major evidence against Mary Surratt concerned her activities on April 14, the day of the assassination. According to the testimony of Louis Weichmann, Booth had visited with her at two o'clock that afternoon and left in her possession a pair of binoculars. Later, Weichmann had driven her to Surrattsville, ostensibly to see a Mr. Nothy concerning a debt of five hundred dollars which he owed her, but in reality her purpose was to warn John Lloyd to have the guns ready when Booth came by that night. She also gave to Lloyd the binoculars that Booth had left with her. Mrs. Surratt's supposed knowledge of the carbines hidden away at Lloyd's Tavern and her awareness that they would be needed that very night was enough to convince the Military Commission that Mary Surratt was a confidante of Wilkes Booth and that she was involved in the conspiracy to murder the president. Little matter that this testimony was provided by Louis Weichmann, who was hoping to save his own neck from the noose, and John Lloyd, who was so drunk during Mrs. Surratt's visit, testified his own wife, that he could not sit upon a horse or even lie down without vomiting.

Also bringing into question the truth of the men's testimonies, there was strong disagreement concerning the time of Booth's visit to Mrs. Surratt. Weichmann testified that the visit occurred about two in the afternoon, but Reverdy Johnson contradicted that statement, maintaining that Booth had arrived earlier, at approximately noon. At noon, argued Johnson, Booth had not even been aware that Lincoln and Grant would be in attendance at Ford's Theatre that night. Indeed, Booth had not learned that they would be in attendance until he read the news in the afternoon newspaper, which did not hit the streets until about 2 P.M. Furthermore, Booth did not learn until after 5 P.M. that Grant would not be in attendance. Since he himself was not aware that he would be assassinating the president that night, he would have had had no reason to tell Mrs. Surratt at noon that day to instruct Lloyd to have the carbines ready for that evening. The government's timeline simply did not fit. Besides, if Booth and Herold were being pursued by Federal cavalry, what good would two carbines do them? To the contrary, their greatest concern would be time, and they would want to ride out of Maryland and into the South as quickly as possible, not pausing for carbines or anything else. These arguments aroused no reaction from members of the Military Commission.

Then Judge Bingham called to the stand the police officers who arrested Mrs. Surratt on the night of April 17. They related how Lewis Payne had come to her house that night disguised as a workman and that he had stated that Mrs. Surratt had hired him to dig a ditch for her. When taken inside the house, Payne was introduced to Mrs. Surratt, and she was asked to verify his story. Instead, she became visibly upset and swore that she had never seen Payne before. Why Mrs. Surratt would deny knowing Payne is unclear, especially when her own daughter and every boarder at her house would testify that Payne had visited with them on at least two previous occasions. But it must be remembered that it was after midnight when the detectives burst into her house, awakening her from a deep sleep and frightening her badly. They informed her that she and her daughter were to be taken to prison and charged with conspiracy to commit murder. At that point, weeping, her body trembling in fear, probably already in shock at this turn of events, Mary Surratt was suddenly confronted with a giant of a man wearing a toboggan low over his forehead, carrying a pickax over his shoulder, his clothes spattered with blood, and asked to identify him. In the dim light of her parlor, under the most negative circumstances, it is entirely possible that the myopic Mrs. Surratt truly did not recognize Powell, a man she had met only briefly on two previous occasions.

But of all the evidence presented against her, it was Lloyd's testimony concerning her request that the carbines to be ready the night of the assassination and the detectives' testimony concerning Payne's visit to her home the night of April 17 that proved most damning. The testimony of Louis Weichmann was incriminating, yes, but it was the testimony of John Lloyd and the arresting detectives that would hang her.

In a statement Mary Surratt gave to Col. H. S. Olcott on April 28 concerning her visit to Lloyd on April 14, she would state under oath:

> Q. How long a conversation did you have with Mr. Lloyd?
> A. Only a few minutes conversation. I did not sit down. I only met him as I was leaving for home.
> Q. Where was Mr. Weichmann?
> A. He was there.

Q. He heard the conversation?

A. I presume he did. I don't remember.

Q. What did the conversation relate to?

A. He spoke of having fish and oysters. He asked me whether I had been to dinner, and said that he could give me fish and oysters. Mr. Weichmann said that he would return home as he was in need of his bread and butter.

Q. What did you say about any shooting irons or carbines?

A. I said nothing about them.

Q. Any conversation of that kind? Did you not tell him to have the shooting irons ready, that there would be some people there that night?

A. To my knowledge no conversation of that kind passed.

Q. Did you know any shooting irons were there?

A. No, sir, I did not.

Mary Surratt's attorney, Reverdy Johnson, made a valiant effort to impeach the testimony of John Lloyd on the grounds that on the afternoon of April 14 Lloyd was so drunk that he could not even stand up. Johnson then introduced six witnesses who swore that Lloyd was practically comatose with alcohol on the day in question. Johnson recalled Lloyd to the stand and established that Lloyd was unsure whether Mrs. Surratt had spoken about carbines on the two occasions when they had previously met. "It was a very quick and hasty conversation," Lloyd said. "I am confident that she named the shooting-irons on both occasions; not so positive about the first as I am about the last. I know she did on the last occasion." When Johnson asked if he was absolutely positive she had mentioned "shooting-irons" on the April 14 meeting, Lloyd replied, "I am quite positive about that, but not altogether positive. I am quite positive but cannot determine that she said 'shooting-irons.'" Lloyd then admitted that he had been drunk on April 14: "I was right smart in liquer that afternoon," he said, "and after night I got more so."

Two years later, during John Surratt's trial of 1867, Lloyd again would be called to the stand and admit that he had been "hopelessly drunk" during the meeting of April 14, 1865. He would volunteer, "I knew what effect liquer had on me. It makes me forget a great many things." And how much liquor had he consumed by the time of Mrs. Surratt's arrival? "I drank enough to make me drunk. I was so drunk that when I lay down I felt sick. I could not lie down."

In the course of his testimony at Mrs. Surratt's trial, Lloyd was asked by Johnson if the Military Commission had threatened him in any way prior to his testimony. Lloyd testified:

> While I was there in Carroll Prison, this military officer came there and told me he wanted me to make a statement, as near as I remember. I told him I had made a fuller statement to Colonel Wells than I could possibly do to him under the circumstances, while things were fresh in my memory. His reply was that it was not full enough.
>
> *Q.* What else did he say?
>
> *A.* He said that it was not full enough.
>
> *Q.* Did he say anything to you in the way of offering a reward, or use any threat towards you, for the purpose of getting you to make it fuller?
>
> *A.* When I told him what I had repeated before, he jumps up very quick off his seat, as if very mad, and asked me if I knew what I was guilty of. I told him, under the circumstances I did not. He said you are guilty as an accessory to a crime the punishment of which is death.

"Seeing his case against Mary Surratt about to evaporate before his eyes," wrote one reporter, "Judge Bingham sprang to his feet, and with his whole frame quivering with emotion, seized one of the carbines lying on the table before him, and raising it aloft, eloquently and forcibly exclaimed, 'Gentlemen, they say that Lloyd lies and that he was drunk, but these carbines, these mute witnesses, were not drunk and they do not lie. Where did Booth get them? One was found at Lloyd's tavern, and the other, its mate, was taken from the body of the dying assassin in Garrett's barn.'" Perhaps Lloyd was lying, perhaps Mary Surratt was lying, but carbines do not lie. Members of the Military Commission looked at one another and nodded agreement. Judge Bingham had just scored an excellent point.

Despite Bingham's "truthful carbines," a fighting Reverdy Johnson was not finished presenting a defense for Mary

Surratt. He next called to the stand Louis Weichmann, a witness for the prosecution, in hopes of establishing that Mary Surratt was a woman of unimpeachable character.

Q. During the whole of that period, you never heard Booth intimate that it was his purpose, or that there was a purpose to assassinate the President?

A. Never, sir.

Q. You never heard him say anything on the subject, or anybody else during the whole period from November until the assassination?

A. No, sir.

Q. During the whole of that period what was Mrs. Surratt's character?

A. It was excellent; I have known her since 1863.

Q. You have been living in her house since November?

A. Since November.

Q. During the whole of that time as far as you could judge, was her character good and amiable?

A. Her character was exemplary and lady like in every particular.

Q. Was she a member of the church?

A. Yes, sir.

Q. A regular attendant?

A. Yes, sir.

Q. Of the Catholic Church?

A. Yes, sir.

Q. Are you a Catholic?

A. Yes, sir; I am a Catholic.

Q. Have you been to church with her?

A. I generally accompanied her to church every Sunday.

Q. As far then, as you can judge, her conduct in a religious and in a moral sense was altogether exemplary?

A. Yes, sir. She went to her religious duties, at least every two weeks.

Q. Then, if I understand you, from November up to the 14th of April, whenever she was here, she was regular in her attendance at her own church, and apparently, as far as you can judge, doing all her duties to God and to man?

A. Yes, sir.

Reverdy Johnson had one more point to make. He had tried to establish through the testimony of several witnesses that Mrs. Surratt and Louis Weichmann departed Washington for Surrattsville at about noon on April 14, hours before Booth had decided to execute the president. This timeline, as Johnson pointed out, negated Mary Surratt's involvement in Booth's potential need for weapons that night. The members of the Military Commission simply sighed and shook their heads. After all, what difference did a few hours make? This woman was the mother of John Surratt, a confidante of John Wilkes Booth, and she obviously deserved to be hanged.

Immediately following this effort from Reverdy Johnson, it was announced that the trial of the conspirators was adjourned. Members of the Military Commission would meet again on June 29 and 30 to discuss the guilt or innocence of the accused.

At that point John Clampitt began the closing argument for Mrs. Surratt and all the defendants by reading a brief that had been prepared by Reverdy Johnson. This brief was, by all accounts, a brilliant move on the part of Johnson, and it struck the Military Commission where they were most vulnerable: the question of War Department jurisdiction and the legality of the Military Commission. Johnson contended that trying civilians before a Military Commission was unconstitutional. "Military tribunals can try none but military offenses," he argued, "and even those only when the persons committing them are members of the military forces." Johnson then reminded the commission that "traitorous conspiracy" is defined as treason, and according to the Constitution, treason trials could be held only in civil courts. Gen. Thomas Ewing reinforced Johnson's argument when he stated, "Under the Constitution none but courts ordained and established by Congress can exercise judicial power over civilians. Congress has not ordained nor established you as a court. You are, therefore, no court, and you have no jurisdiction in this case."

Ben Poore would write that Judge Holt and his assistants paid little notice to the readings of Johnson and Ewing. General Hunter dozed while Lew Wallace drew idle sketches. The other officers expressed their boredom in various ways. The commission, it was obvious, was not interested in being told that they were an illegal body.

After recessing to consider the guilt or innocence of the accused, the Military Commission announced the following verdicts and sentences:

David E. Herald [*sic*]: Guilty as charged. And the Commission do, therefore, sentence him, the said David E. Herald, to be hanged by the neck until he be dead, at such time and place as the President of the United States shall direct; two thirds of the Commission concurring therein.

George A. Atzerodt: Guilty. And the Commission do, therefore, sentence him, the said George A. Atzerodt, to be hanged by the neck until he is dead, at such time and place as the President of the United States shall direct; two thirds of the Commission concurring therein.

Lewis Payne: Guilty. And the Commission do, therefore, sentence him, the said Lewis Payne, to be hanged by the neck until he be dead, at such time and place as the President of the United States shall direct; two thirds of the Commission concurring therein.

Mary E. Surratt: After mature consideration of the evidence adduced in the case of the accused, Mary E. Surratt, the Commission find the said accused guilty. And the Commission do, therefore, sentence her, the said Mary E. Surratt, to be hanged by the neck until she be dead, at such time and place as the President of the United States shall direct; two thirds of the members of the Commission concurring therein.

Michael O'Laughlin: . . . On the nights of the 13th and 14th of April 1865, at Washington City, and within the Military Department and military lines aforesaid, the said Michael O'Laughlin did there and then lie in wait for Ulysses S. Grant, the Lieutenant-General and Commander of the Armies of the United States, with intent there and then to kill and murder the said Ulysses S. Grant.
Of the charge: Guilty. The Commission do, therefore, sentence the said Michael O'Laughlin to be imprisoned at hard labor for life, at such place as the President shall direct.

Edman Spangler: Guilty. And the Commission do, therefore, sentence the said Edman Spangler to be imprisoned at hard labor for six years, at such place as the President shall direct.

Samuel Arnold: Guilty. The Commission do, therefore, sentence the said Samuel Arnold to imprisonment at hard labor for life, as the President shall direct.

Samuel A. Mudd: Guilty. The Commission do, therefore, sentence the said Samuel A. Mudd to be imprisoned at hard labor for life, at such place as the President shall direct.

It has struck some historians as strange that the four conspirators who were sentenced to be taken out immediately and hanged—Mrs. Surratt, Lewis Powell, David Herold, and George Atzerodt—were the four who were known to have associated with Wilkes Booth on April 14, the day of the assassination. Did Edwin Stanton fear that Booth had imparted some great secrets to these four that would prove incriminating to the government should they ever be made public? Such an idea makes for interesting speculation.

Another oddity is inherent in President Johnson's order of July 5 that those who received prison sentences would serve their sentences at a state prison in Albany, New York, but just days later, on July 15, Johnson suddenly changed his order to read that the prisoners would serve their time at a military prison in the Dry Tortugas. No reason for this change was given, though according to Gideon Wells, secretary of the navy, it was Stanton who persuaded Johnson that it would be better if the prisoners should be exiled to a place inaccessible to the public or press. In other words, they would again be placed in solitary confinement, where they could be kept silent. (In the spring of 1869, upon orders from Pres. Andrew Johnson, Dr. Samuel Mudd, Edman Spangler, and Samuel Arnold received presidential pardons for their roles in the conspiracy and were immediately released from prison. Spangler had nowhere to go, so kindly Dr. Mudd took him into his own home, where he would remain until his death several years later. Michael O'Laughlin had died in prison during the yellow fever epidemic of 1867.)

Years later the news leaked out that the commission initially had voted five to four against a death sentence for Mrs.

Surratt, with only Generals Wallace, Harris, and Howe and Colonel Clendenin voting to hang her. A dismayed Judge Holt, who knew that he soon would be forced to answer to Edwin Stanton, was totally outraged when he read the decision of the commission. Without bothering to don his blue dress coat, he dashed over to the War Department for an emergency session with Edwin Stanton. Thirty minutes later a smiling Holt returned to the commission with a workable compromise. If the commission would unanimously vote a death sentence for Mrs. Surratt, they could draw up a petition of mercy and forward it to Pres. Andrew Johnson, and Stanton would see that Andrew Johnson acted on that petition of mercy. With this compromise, the commission could save face and spare the life of a not-very-guilty Mary Surratt at the same time. Little did the commission suspect that Stanton would later convince President Johnson to ignore their petition of mercy.

Truly, Edwin Stanton was a study. In just a few moments he had convinced the commission, against their better judgment, to vote unanimously to execute Mrs. Surratt and then draft a petition of mercy to President Johnson. Stanton then, in a secret move, would literally forbid the president from honoring that petition. Mrs. Surratt would be executed after all, and President Johnson would suffer the blame for it from an outraged citizenry. This cold-hearted move could very well remove Johnson from consideration when the Republicans and Democrats were selecting a candidate for president in 1868. If so, Stanton would be quietly standing by, the most likely replacement, having cleverly parlayed Mary Surratt's execution into the nation's top office for himself.

Thus the commission prepared a petition and it was signed by five members of the court, a majority, addressed to the president of the United States, recommending that on account of the age and sex of Mrs. Surratt, the sentence that the commission was constrained to render in her case from the testimony presented be commuted from death to imprisonment for life if the chief executive, in considering the case, could, in his judgment, so determine. President

Johnson did not respond to the commission's petition.

On July 5, 1865, following President Johnson's approval of the findings of the Military Commission, an outraged Orville Browning, secretary of the interior, wrote in his diary: "This commission was without authority, and its proceedings void. The execution of these persons will be murder." But Browning and many others who shared his opinion were simply crying in the wilderness.

On the morning of July 6, in hopes that a direct appeal from herself might save her mother from the hangman, a distraught Anna Surratt paid a visit to General Hancock at his hotel and asked him what she could do to save her mother. The general replied that there was but one way left, and that was "to go to the President, throw herself upon her knees before him, and beg for the life of her mother." Anna then hurried to the executive mansion, to President Johnson's office. She was met at his door by two Radical Republicans, the senators Preston King and James H. Lane. They very coldly told her that the president absolutely would not see her, that he would see no one on behalf of the condemned prisoners. Crudely, they pushed Anna away from the door. (On November 13, 1865, Preston King committed suicide by tying a bag of bullets around his neck and diving into the Hudson River. Some eight months later, on July 11, 1866, James H. Lane committed suicide by shooting himself through the head in Ft. Leavenworth, Kansas.)

Father Jacob Walter, Mrs. Surratt's confessor, also made several unsuccessful attempts to see Johnson. In 1891 he would write a scathing article for the *Catholic News of New York City* in which he proclaimed Mrs. Surratt's innocence and charged that the government had knowingly executed her wrongfully.

Having exhausted all attempts to save her mother, Anna Surratt spent the night of July 6 with Mary in her cell. The following afternoon at the fatal hour, guards were forced to tear Anna away from her mother so that they could carry her to the gallows.

The scaffold had been constructed on the grounds of the

Anna Surratt in 1865. Born in 1839, Anna was educated at a Catholic seminary in Bryantown and was considered an accomplished pianist and a young lady of culture. When her attempt to win President Johnson's pardon for her mother failed, she spent the rest of the day before the execution and that night holding her mother's hand and trying to comfort her. Courtesy the Surratt House Museum

old Arsenal. Execution day, July 7, 1865, was excessively hot, and there was no shade to protect the visitors who crowded in to witness the hangings. They had begun gathering about ten o'clock that morning, and some three hours later they still waited patiently, knowing they would soon see Mrs. Mary Surratt, the first woman in America to be executed.

Just after 9 A.M. that morning Mrs. Surratt's attorneys had won a writ of habeas corpus from a Washington civil court, ordering that she be immediately released from military custody. Her attorneys were jubilant and could hardly wait to break the good news to her that she had just received a reprieve. But their joy was short lived. Immediately upon receiving this startling news, General Hancock and Atty. Gen. James Speed rushed to court with an executive order

The gruesome sight that greeted the condemned as they walked to their death: their graves dug just to the right of the gallows. Following the executions their bodies were placed in simple pine boxes and buried here in holes four feet deep.
Library of Congress

from the president suspending the writ. It had been a close call, but Edwin Stanton and his Military Commission would shortly see Mrs. Surratt hang.

Just after 1 P.M. the front door of the Arsenal slowly opened and the condemned prisoners and their guards began their mournful procession towards the gallows. Accompanied by their spiritual advisors, the condemned climbed the thirteen steps and took their places as ordered: Mrs. Surratt, Lewis Powell, David Herold, and George Atzerodt. Atzerodt was attended by the Reverend George

Butler, pastor of St. Paul's Lutheran Church of Washington, and Herold by the Reverend Mr. Olds of the Episcopal Church. Lewis Powell was attended by Dr. Abram Gillette, pastor of the First Baptist Church in Washington, who had spent many hours with Powell in his cell over the past few weeks. It was Gillette who would assist Powell's father in claiming his son's body in 1869. Following his own death, he would leave behind some very revealing comments about Powell. Mrs. Surratt was attended by Father Walter and Father Wigget of the Catholic Church, who stood on either side of her. Father Walter held a crucifix, which Mrs. Surratt kissed. Weak and unsteady, she mounted the thirteen steps, was led to her place at the end of the gallows, then sat down in the chair that had been provided for her. Father Walter shielded her from a cruel sun with his umbrella.

George Atzerodt very admirably rallied enough courage at that point to say, "Gentlemen, may we meet in a better place some day." A faint Mary Surratt was brought to her feet and straps placed around her chest and ankles. She murmured to the two soldiers supporting her, "Please, don't let me fall." Powell, wearing a straw hat to protect his head from the sun, looked bold and defiant and held his head high. His tight-fitting sailor suit, it was written, the same one he had been forced to wear since his arrest ten weeks earlier, accentuated his robust physique. As he sat in a chair upon the scaffold a gust of wind blew his hat off. The Reverend Abram Gillette picked it up and replaced it on Powell's head. Powell looked at Gillette and said, "Thank you, Doctor. I'm afraid I shall not need it much longer." As for Herold, he seemed totally dazed by the situation. If he had any last words, they were not recorded.

Even then, since Andrew Johnson had never rejected the commission's petition for mercy for Mrs. Surratt, there was still hope among the assembled that a messenger would arrive at any moment with a stay of execution from the president. General Hancock had stationed couriers with swift horses at various locations between the White House and the Arsenal so that should the president decide at the last moment to commute Mrs. Surratt's sentence, the message would reach him as quickly as possible. But the U. S. marshal who would deliver the writ never came, and no rider from the White House bearing news of presidential clemency ever appeared.

The executions were under the direction of General Hancock, who ordered General Hartranft to carry them out. When the fatal moment arrived, both officers stood in front of the scaffold. After the president's order for the executions had been read by General Hartranft the clergymen left the condemned and Mrs. Surratt's chair was taken away. White hoods were placed over their heads and nooses placed around their necks. The order to proceed startled the hangman, Capt. Christian Rath. As he was ordered to place a noose around Mrs. Surratt's neck, he looked beseechingly at General Hancock.

"Her, too?"

"She can not be saved," replied Hancock.

When Captain Rath came to Powell, who stood next to Mrs. Surratt, he whispered into Powell's ear, "I have grown to admire you a great deal over the past few weeks, Lewis. I want you to know that I'll place this noose good and tight around your neck, so that you won't suffer. You'll die quick."

"You know best, Cap'n," Powell said simply, with typical sangfroid.

In fact, Powell's neck did not break and it took him fully eight minutes to strangle to death, a terrible way to die.

Some forty-eight years following this tragic event, Cpl. William Coxwell, one of the four soldiers responsible for knocking the posts from under the drops, still had vivid recollections of the hanging. "The soldiers were promised a canteen of whiskey for doing a good job, but we never got that drink." As he waited for the order to drop the prisoners, he became extremely nauseous, leaned against the post for support, and vomited violently. While the spectators remained totally silent, General Hartranft gave a signal with his hand. Four Union soldiers—Cpl. William Coxwell, Pvts. Daniel Sharpe, George F. Taylor, and Joseph Hazlett—then delivered sharp blows to the pins supporting the traps. At exactly 1:26 P.M. the traps collapsed and four bodies dropped into eternity.

It was a terribly hot day, with the sun beating down upon the heads of the guilty and innocent alike. Mrs. Surratt, seated in a chair, is covered by an umbrella while being comforted by her two priests. The others are forced to stand as Gen. John F. Hartranft reads their death warrants. Cpl. William Coxwell can be seen leaning against the far left post in this photo. Library of Congress

Their guilt or innocence no longer mattered. They were dead.

Their bodies were left hanging for thirty minutes. Then they were cut down and their bodies inspected by three military doctors—Otis, Woodward, and Porter—who pronounced them dead. Despite having dropped some five feet from the scaffold,

Hoods are being placed over the heads of the condemned, and Capt. Christian Rath fits a noose around David Herold's neck. (Left to right): Mrs. Surratt, Lewis Powell, David Herold, and George Atzerodt. Library of Congress

not a neck was broken. The nooses had all slipped to the back of the necks, and all the conspirators had obviously strangled to death. The bodies were then placed in simple pine boxes and dropped into holes four feet deep on the penitentiary grounds, just to the right of the scaffold. There they would remain until February 1869, when by order of the president their bodies were released to their families. Mrs. Surratt's body was laid to rest in Mount Olive Cemetery in Washington,

A close-up of the preceding photograph. Apparently Captain Rath fitted the nooses very poorly, for a postmortem examination indicated that all the condemned died of strangulation rather than broken necks. Library of Congress

The noose that Capt. Christopher Rath placed around the neck of Lewis Powell on the afternoon of July 7, 1865. National Archives

The bodies of the conspirators dangle from the gallows before being cut down, placed in U.S. Navy equipment boxes, and buried in shallow graves just to the right of the gallows. It was said that Powell's neck did not break, and it took him eight minutes to strangle to death. (The gallows and ropes were cut into pieces and distributed as souvenirs.) Library of Congress

the burying ground for the Catholics of that city. David Herold's body was buried in the Congressional Cemetery at 1801 East Street SE in Washington. Lewis Powell's body, still dressed in the navy uniform he had been issued the day following his arrest, was claimed by his father and older brother, George, and returned to Geneva, Florida, where he was buried beside his mother.[2]

Following the executions the other accused, Dr. Mudd, Arnold, Spangler, and O'Laughlin were placed on board a gunboat and taken to the Dry Tortugas to begin serving their sentences.

One might assume that with the death of Mary Surratt her case came to a close. However, the ghost of Mrs. Surratt lived on long after her death. Almost immediately citizens and newspapers throughout the country began to voice their outrage that the government would actually go through with their plan to execute her, a woman whose greatest sin apparently was to operate a boardinghouse where her son and his friends would meet from time to time. Three years later, in November 1868, just in time for the presidential election of that year, a disturbing rumor was beginning to make its way across the nation: the Military Commission had petitioned President Johnson to commute the sentence of Mary Surratt, but Johnson had failed to approve that petition. By December a virtual firestorm of anger erupted, much of it ignited by the Catholic Church, which firmly believed Mrs. Surratt innocent of all charges, and directed at President Johnson and his callous disregard for justice and mercy.

In his defense, President Johnson heatedly denied that Judge Joseph Holt had ever presented such a petition to him, and he was totally ignorant of any petition for mercy for Mary Surratt from the Military Commission. If Johnson's denials were true, then Judge Holt was guilty of a most cruel betrayal of the public trust. Indeed, his withholding the petition from the president was a murderous action since a woman had died as a result of his treachery.

On December 5, 1868, the Reverend George Butler, pastor of St. Paul's Lutheran Church in Washington, presented a most persuasive argument against Johnson in the following letter to Judge Holt:

> The interview occurred during a social call upon the family of the President in the evening, a few hours after the execution.
>
> I had been summoned by the Government, I then being a hospital chaplain, to attend upon Atzerodt, and was present at the execution.
>
> Concerning Mrs. Surratt the remarks of the President, by reason of their point and force, impressed themselves upon my memory. He said, in substance, that very strong appeals had been made for the exercise of executive clemency; that he had been importuned; that telegrams and threats had been used; but he could not be moved, for, in his own significant language, Mrs. Surratt "kept the nest that hatched the eggs."
>
> The President further stated that no plea had been urged in her behalf, save the fact that she was a woman, and his interposition upon that ground would license female crime.

As for ignoring the commission's recommendation for mercy, it is interesting to note that Johnson used the same words to Butler that Edwin Stanton had used with him just prior to Mrs. Surratt's execution.

Five years would elapse before Johnson and Holt went public with their debate. In 1873 Holt would write to John A. Bingham, the judge advocate during the trial,

> In the discharge of my duty when presenting that record to President Johnson, I drew his attention to that recommendation, and he read it in my presence, and before approving the proceedings and sentence. He and I were together alone when this duty on his part and on mine was performed. The President and myself having, as already stated, been alone at the time, I have not been able to collect circumstantial evidence enough to satisfy any unbiased mind that the recommendation was seen and considered by the President, when he reviewed and approved the proceedings and sentence of the Court. Still, in a matter so deeply affecting my reputation and official honor, I am naturally desirous of having the testimony in my possession strengthened as far as practicable, and hence it is that I trouble you with this note. While I know that the question of extending to Mrs. Surratt the clemency sought by the petition was considered

by the President at the time mentioned, I have, in view of its gravity, been always satisfied that it must have been considered by the Cabinet also; but from the confidential character of Cabinet deliberations I have thus far been denied access to this source of information.

Judge Holt then went on to ask whether Judge Bingham had ever discussed with Secretary Seward or Edwin Stanton the commission's petition for mercy for Mrs. Surratt. If so, would he please relate to Judge Holt, as closely as he could, Seward and Stanton's response to the petition.

On February 17, 1873, Bingham sent the surprising response to Judge Holt's query:

Before the President had acted upon the case, I deemed it my duty to call the attention of Secretary Stanton to the petition for the commutation of sentence upon Mrs. Surratt, and did call his attention to it, before the final decision of the President. After the execution, the statement that you refer to was made that President Johnson had not seen the petition for the commutation of the death sentence upon Mrs. Surratt. I afterward called at your office, and, without notice to you of my purpose, asked for the record of the case of the assassins; it was opened and shown me, and there was then attached to it the petition, copied and signed as hereinbefore stated. Soon thereafter I called upon Secretaries Stanton and Seward and asked if this petition had been presented to the President before the death sentence was by him approved, and was answered by each of these gentlemen that the petition was presented to the President, and was duly considered by him and his advisers before the death sentence upon Mrs. Surratt was approved, and that the President and Cabinet, upon such consideration, were a unit denying the prayer of the petition; Mr. Stanton and Mr. Seward stating that they were present.

Having ascertained the fact as stated, I then desired to make the same public, and so expressed myself to Mr. Stanton, who advised me not to do so, but to rely upon the final judgment of the people.

To this startling bit of information, a chagrined Judge Holt, who had been assailed and slandered from every quarter of the public for the past eight years for his withholding the petition from the president, responded:

It would have been very fortunate for me indeed could I have had this testimony in my possession years ago. Mr. Stanton's advice to you was, under all the circumstances of the case, most extraordinary.

This asking you "to rely upon the final judgment of the people," and at the same time withholding from them the proof on which the judgment—to be just—must be formed, was a sad, sad mockery.

As further proof that Johnson did in fact ignore the recommendation of the commission, there is this letter to Judge Holt from Gen. R. D. Mussey, dated August 19, 1873:

In a few days after the assassination I was detailed for duty with Mr. Johnson and acted as one of his secretaries, and was an inmate of his household until sometime in the fall of 1865.

On the Wednesday prior to the execution (which was on Friday, July 7, 1865), as I was sitting at my desk in the morning, Mr. Johnson told me that he was going to look over the findings of the Court with Judge Holt, and should be busy and could see no one. . . . I am very confident, though not absolutely assured, that it was at this interview Mr. Johnson told me that the Court had recommended Mrs. Surratt to mercy on the ground of her sex. But I am certain he did so inform me about that time; and that he said he thought the grounds insufficient, and that he had refused to interfere; that if she was guilty at all, her sex did not make her any the less guilty; that about the time of her execution, justified it; that he told me there had not been women enough hanged in the war.

On March 30, 1875, Judge Holt also received verification of his version of events from James Speed, the former attorney general who had approved the trial by Military Commission in the first place, who stated that prior to the executions he had seen the findings of the Military Commission lying on the president's desk. Attached to those findings, said Speed, was a document signed by five members of the commission recommending that the sentence against Mrs. Surratt be commuted to imprisonment for life. Whether President Johnson had read and considered that document or not Speed did not feel at liberty to say.

From Johnson's standpoint, perhaps the most damning

testimony on this issue is contained in a letter dated May 23, 1875, that Holt received from James Harlan, senator from Iowa and secretary of the interior in 1865.

> After the sentence and before the execution of Mrs. Surratt, I remember distinctly the discussion of the question of the commutation of the sentence of death pronounced on her by the Court to imprisonment for life and by members of the Cabinet in presence of President Johnson. Present at that meeting, in addition to myself, were President Johnson and Secretary Edwin Stanton.

Harlan recorded Stanton's words to Andrew Johnson:

> Surely not, Mr. President, for if the death penalty should be commuted in so grave a case as the assassination of the head of a great nation, on account of the sex of the criminal, it would amount to an invitation to assassins hereafter to employ women as their instruments, under the belief that if arrested and condemned, they would be punished less severely than men. An act of executive clemency on such a plea would be disapproved by the Government of every civilized nation on earth.

It is hardly surprising to learn that it was none other than Edwin Stanton who persuaded Johnson to reject the commission's petition for mercy for Mrs. Surratt. Surely the ambitious Stanton was aware that for Johnson to disregard the commission's recommendation would be to drive a stake through his heart with the voting public, thereby opening the way for Stanton to receive the Republican nomination for the presidency in 1868. Such correspondence with Judge Holt should prove conclusively that it was Andrew Johnson and not Judge Holt who was lying concerning Mrs. Surratt and her fate on the gallows.

Johnson compounded his sins, first when he ignored the recommendation of the commission, costing Mrs. Surratt her life, and later by telling a cruel lie when he accused Judge Holt of withholding the petition from him. Why would President Johnson refuse to honor the Military Commission's recommendation for mercy for Mary Surratt?

Perhaps that question was best answered by Col. William P. Wood, keeper of the Old Capitol Prison and one of Stanton's closet associates, in an undated article that appeared in the *Washington Gazette* soon after the death of Edwin Stanton.

> Some time after the execution of Mrs. Surratt, President Johnson sent for me and requested me to give my version of Mrs. Surratt's connection with the assassination of President Lincoln. I did so, and I believe he was thoroughly convinced of the innocence of Mrs. Surratt. He assured me he sincerely regretted that he had not given Mrs. Surratt the benefit of Executive clemency, and strongly expressed his detestation of what he termed "the infamous conduct of Stanton" in keeping these facts from him. I asserted my unchangeable friendship for Mr. Stanton under all circumstances, and while I regretted the course adopted by the Secretary of War towards Mrs. Surratt, I would never hesitate to perform any act of kindness for him. President Johnson commended me for my devotion to friends, and the subject of the assassination was never afterwards discussed between him and myself. The great War Secretary of the Union was no longer in power. He was a plain citizen of our Republic, broken in health and tottering between life and death.

Wood continued:

> The Republican leaders had, after much pleading, induced President Grant to name Mr. Stanton for a judge of the Supreme Court. The Senate promptly confirmed the nomination, but Grant, for some reason best known to himself, did not put his signature to the commission, or if he did sign the commission he did not forward it to Mr. Stanton. It was at this time the latter sent for me, and I called at his residence on K Street. When ushered into his presence I was startled at his woe-begone and wretched appearance. He inquired if I knew the reason why that man (meaning President Grant) withheld his commission. I told him. Then we drifted in our talk to the executions herein referred to, and he rebuked me for not making greater effort to save the woman that was hanged. He said he would have trusted his life in my keeping; that *I would have saved him the torment of hell had I been more persistent in my efforts. I reminded him of my call on President Johnson to plead for mercy for Mrs. Surratt, and that I was met by Lafayette Baker at the entrance of the President's house, and Baker produced an order over his (Stanton's) signature which set forth that I should*

not be permitted to enter the building or communicate with the President.

"Too true," Stanton responded, "and the Surratt woman haunts me so that my nights are sleepless and my days miserable, and Grant aids my enemies by refusing to sign my commission, which would afford me temporary relief and perhaps prolong my life. He will not do it, and, Wood, this is at last the end." Placing his hands to his head he continued: "I cannot endure the pressure; I am dying, dying, surely, dying now!"

A few parting words were exchanged between us, and the following day the death of Edwin M. Stanton was publicly announced.

In fact, it was widely rumored throughout Washington that Stanton committed suicide by cutting his throat with a razor. Regardless, his passing marked the end of one of the most dismal chapters in American history.

VIII

The Escape, Capture, and Trial of John Surratt

On the evening of Monday, April 3, 1865, following his return from Richmond to Washington, John Surratt and Louis Weichmann went out and Surratt treated his old chum to an exciting stage drama. Afterwards they sat in a fine restaurant, where they enjoyed the usual dinner of beer and roasted oysters. Then Surratt told Weichmann that he was being watched by Federal detectives and therefore did not wish to return home. He bid Weichmann goodbye and walked to the Metropolitan Hotel. There he spent the night, leaving by train the next morning for New York City. The following day, April 5, he called at the beautiful home of the Booth family but was told that Wilkes had already departed for Boston to fulfill an acting engagement. Disappointed that he had not been able to speak with Booth, he took the late-evening train for Montreal, where he arrived at 10:30 A.M. on April 6. He registered at the St. Lawrence Hall, the leading hotel in that city (and a headquarters of sorts for the Confederate Secret Service), and he signed in as John Harrison, the alias he generally used when on business for the Confederacy. He remained in Montreal until late that afternoon, then on orders from Jacob Thompson, director of the Confederate Secret Service in Canada, he returned to the United States. His destination was Elmira, New York, and his assignment was to make sketches of the Confederate prison camp in that city and ascertain if a raid on that camp would be feasible. Over the past year various other agents had been given this same assignment, but the others had

John Harrison Surratt in a photo taken immediately following his trial in 1867. His whereabouts on the night of April 14, 1865, remain in question, and the jury at his trial, like everyone else, could not decide whether or not he was involved with the president's assassination. Charges against him were later dismissed, and he walked away a free but very bitter man.
National Archives

failed for one reason or another, usually out of fear of being captured. Surratt, a man of only twenty when these stirring historical events transpired, handled himself well for a lad of such an early age.

He was still in Elmira on April 14, the day Booth executed Lincoln. On April 18, having gotten the information he needed, he returned once again to Montreal. As before, he registered at the St. Lawrence Hall under the alias John Harrison. By the following day, aware that he was now suspected in the assassination and being pursued by Federal agents, he left the hotel and for a brief period was hidden in the home of a "Mr. Porterfield," a Confederate agent.

On April 22, Joseph Du Tilly, a devout Catholic, ferried a disguised Surratt by horse and wagon to the home of Fr. Charles Boucher, a priest who resided at St. Liboire, some ten miles distance from Montreal. For the next three months Surratt lived in comfort, spending most of his time secreted from view. He would occasionally go hunting with Father Boucher and other Catholic parties who drove up from Montreal to speak to him, including one prominent priest by the name of Father LaPierre.

Surratt remained with Father Boucher until the latter part of July, when the priest found it necessary that he leave because of widespread rumors suggesting Father Boucher was keeping a woman in his home. At that point Father Boucher and Father LaPierre brought him, again in disguise, to the home of LaPierre's father, an elderly gentleman living on Old Cemetery Street. Here Surratt lived in the greatest secrecy, venturing out of the house only at night, but it soon became obvious to his priestly benefactors that Surratt must be accorded safer quarters. After much deliberation they decided that he should be sent to Rome, or should that not prove feasible, to the papal army. They began making preparations to that end, and on September 13, 1865, passage was secured for Surratt aboard the Canadian steamer *Peruvian*, which was set to sail out of Quebec.

Prior to the ship's sailing, Father LaPierre happened to meet on the street a parishioner named Dr. Lewis McMillan, the ship's doctor. LaPierre told McMillan that he had a friend by the name of McCarty who was going over on the same vessel as he and that he would like to introduce him to his friend. The doctor agreed, and it was arranged that they should meet aboard the steamer *Montreal,* which would leave for Quebec on September 15. On that date Father LaPierre met McMillan and led him to a locked stateroom on the steamer. He unlocked the door and introduced the young man hidden there. His name was given as McCarty and he was dressed as an English gentleman. The two young men greeted one another warmly and spent most of the evening together. Dr. McMillan noticed upon closer inspection that his new friend wore green spectacles, and his hair was dyed dark brown and cut quite short. He thought that odd but passed it off as probably the latest fashion among English gentlemen.

Surratt and Dr. McMillan reached Quebec the following Saturday morning. Surratt bid his benefactors, Father LaPierre and Father Boucher, goodbye and promised to write as soon as he reached England. They had essentially saved his life, he told them, for had he been captured and returned to Washington, he surely would have been hanged along with his mother, Powell, Atzerodt, and Herold. A tugboat transported Surratt and Dr. McMillan out to the waiting *Peruvian.*

An Odyssey Stranger than Fiction

During the course of their passage across the wide Atlantic, Surratt and McMillan spent almost every waking hour together. As is normal in such situations, in time Surratt began to reveal intimate details of his life to the young surgeon. In 1867, during the trial of John Surratt, much of what he told the doctor would prove of great value to the government.

Only one day out from port, Surratt pointed to another passenger and commented to McMillan that he could tell by the man's manner of dress that he was doubtlessly an

American detective sent there to arrest him. "Tell me, McCarty, what have you done that you should so fear a detective?" asked the doctor in great surprise. Surratt very boyishly replied that he had done more things than the doctor could imagine, and if he knew even half those things, he would be astounded. McMillan passed over Surratt's remarks as simply the idle boasts of a very immature young man and told him that they were aboard a British ship in British waters and he had nothing to fear from an American detective.

At that, Surratt smiled and pulled a small four-barreled revolver from his pocket. He knew how to handle American detectives, he told McMillan, should it ever come to that. Once the problem of the "American detective" had been resolved, Surratt revealed to McMillan that he had been an operative of the Confederate Secret Service. On one occasion, he said, he had accompanied a female agent from Montreal to Richmond. Just outside Fredericksburg, walking through the countryside to the train station, they saw running towards them four escaped Union prisoners of war. The woman said, "Let's shoot them." When he remembered the cruelties his own people had suffered at the hands of Yankees, he pulled his four-barreled revolver from his belt and shot them down without a second thought, leaving their bodies for Southern officials to find.

On another occasion, said Surratt, he and four other agents were attempting to cross the Potomac in a boat when they were hailed by a Union gunboat and ordered to surrender. They immediately replied that they would do so. The gunboat sent a small boat out to take them, but when it drew alongside, Surratt and his friends drew their revolvers and fired into the surprised Yankees, then escaped to the Virginia shore. "I can still hear their screams," he laughed.

Surratt also revealed that he was with a regiment of Southern soldiers one night when they came to an apple orchard. Hungry, they began picking apples and happily devouring them. There was a large house adjacent to the orchard, and when they approached the house, they heard what they surmised to be the ticking of a telegraph machine. A quick search of the house revealed that indeed there was a Union soldier secreted there and he was telegraphing messages to the commander of a Union army camped a few miles away. Surratt and his Confederate comrades took the Union telegrapher outside and happily hanged him from an apple tree.

Surratt also told the flabbergasted McMillan that he had visited Richmond just prior to that city's fall and met twice with Judah Benjamin, from whom he had received two large sums of money: thirty thousand dollars on one occasion and seventy thousand dollars on another. This money he left with Jacob Thompson in Montreal.

Concerning his escape from the United States following the assassination, Surratt revealed that he had arrived at St. Albans on April 16. While waiting for his train to Montreal, he had entered a hotel restaurant for breakfast. He noticed a great deal of excited talk among the other patrons, and when he had seated himself at a table, he asked an elderly gentleman what all the hullabaloo was about.

"Why, don't you know? The president has been assassinated."

Surratt laughed quietly. "Oh, that story is too good to be true."

The elderly gentleman handed him the morning newspaper, and sure enough there it was—John Wilkes Booth had assassinated President Lincoln. Among the names of the other assassins, Surratt saw his own. He was so unnerved by this news that he dropped the newspaper and quietly fled the room. As he was walking towards the door, three men excitedly burst in and told everyone that John Surratt, one of Lincoln's assassins, must be in town, for someone had just found a handkerchief in the street with his name on it. At that he reached in his jacket pocket, where he normally carried his handkerchief, and sure enough it was gone.

He wasted no more time, but immediately boarded the train for Montreal. Once arrived there he at once made for the home of Mr. Porterfield, a Confederate agent, who was delighted to see his old comrade, especially now that he was a fugitive from

American justice. Several nights later, aware that Surratt was being actively pursued by Federal agents in Montreal (Louis Weichmann and Mr. Richards), Porterfield expressed the opinion that it would be suicide for him to remain in the city. The following night Porterfield arranged for two carriages to draw up at his house just before midnight. Surratt, now calling himself Mr. McCarty, entered one carriage, and another agent similar in physical appearance to Surratt entered the other. The two carriages were driven in opposite directions. Surratt's carriage drove about ten miles outside Montreal, where another agent was waiting to paddle him in a canoe to the southern shore of the St. Lawrence River. From there he was led to a small village on the Grand Trunk Railroad called St. Liboire. Once arrived in that village he was greeted by the parish priest, Fr. Charles Boucher, and taken into his home. Father Boucher assured Surratt that he could at last rest easy, that the Catholic Church would not give him up to American authorities without a fight, which was just the news that young Surratt wanted to hear. At last, for the first time in many days he could breathe again.

For months things went well for Surratt, hidden away in that small Canadian village many miles from the nearest telegraph or law enforcement office. Isolated as he was from civilization, he would pass his time in reading books or talking with Father Boucher and other new friends, blissfully unaware that his poor mother had been hanged on July 7. When news of his mother finally reached him in September, he was totally devastated. He would spend much of his life thereafter defending himself against claims that he had very selfishly abandoned his mother to her fate, a cowardly thing at best.

But Surratt's luck could not hold forever, and about the first of September it finally ran out when a young female servant, curious as to the identity of Father Boucher's secret guest, slowly pushed his bedroom door open just a crack. Surratt, lying on his couch, watched in astonishment as the door slowly began to open. When the girl stuck her head inside, he jumped off his couch and shouted, "Boo!" The girl fled in terror and immediately circulated the rumor that

Father Boucher was keeping a woman in his room. At that point, Father Boucher, fearing the gossip that was making the rounds, informed Surratt that he would be forced to take him to Father LaPierre in Montreal. It was from there that he was forced to book passage to Europe.

On Sunday, September 24, 1865, Surratt's last day aboard the *Peruvian,* he sought out Dr. McMillan and asked to talk with him. They sat down in deck chairs, and Surratt pointed towards the coast of Ireland, now in sight. "Here is a foreign land at last. I hope I shall be able to return to my country in two years. I hope to God!" Then, doubtlessly thinking of his mother whom Andrew Johnson had refused to reprieve, he again showed the doctor his revolver and spat, "Mark my words, I shall live to see the time when I can serve Andrew Johnson as Abraham Lincoln has been served."

Surratt then asked McMillan whether he should land in Ireland or go on to Liverpool as the doctor himself planned. The doctor shook his head and said that he would not want to offer him advice on that matter. McMillan was surprised, therefore, several hours later when he met Surratt on the vessel preparing to go ashore. Surratt explained, "I have thought over the matter, and I believe it is better for me to get off here. It is now dark, and there is less chance of being seen."

McMillan, very curious as to the true identity of his friend, said, "You have been telling me a great many things about what you have done and seen, and I believe the name under which you are traveling is not your true name. Will you please give me your true name?"

Surratt glanced around to make sure that no one was within hearing, then he leaned forward and whispered in the doctor's ear, "My name is John Surratt."

Perhaps fearing that he had divulged too much to the doctor, Surratt suddenly became visibly excited and asked McMillan if would give him a drink of brandy. The doctor produced a full flask, and Surratt turned it up and drained it in several gulps. By the time the ship docked, McMillan could see that Surratt was quite inebriated and somewhat unsteady on his feet. He called for a ship's officer to lead

Surratt by the arm down the gangway onto Irish soil.

The next day, Monday, September 25, Dr. McMillan made it a point to visit the American consul in Liverpool and made a full report to officials there concerning his strange encounter with John Surratt, a fugitive from American justice. Several weeks later McMillan returned to Canada and would next see Surratt at his trial in 1867.

This raises an interesting point: for the past century and a half historians have known that Secretary of War Edwin Stanton and his National Detectives were aware of Surratt's every move from April 1865 until he was finally taken into custody in May 1867. Yet Stanton never made the least move to have Surratt arrested and brought back to America to stand trial. He had been informed by Col. John Richards and Louis Weichmann that Surratt was in Canada. However, he did not send a single Federal agent in pursuit. Instead, merely as a screen, that summer he ordered Lafayette Baker to send agents on a wild goose chase to the mountains of Pennsylvania. For a period of nineteen months Stanton allowed Surratt to roam the Western world and would not have arrested him when he finally did had not circumstances demanded that he do so. Some historians have speculated that Stanton might very well have been afraid of what Surratt might have known and could have revealed while under oath in a court of law concerning Lincoln's assassination.

On September 27, 1865, the vice consul in Liverpool would write to Secretary of State William Seward:

> No. 538
> Sir:
> Yesterday, information was given me that John Surratt, one of the persons implicated in the conspiracy to murder Mr. Lincoln, was in Liverpool, or expected there within a day or two. I took the affidavit of the person who gave me the information.
> A. Wilding

Three days later, on September 30, Wilding would again write to Seward:

No. 539

Sir:

Since my dispatch No. 538, the supposed Surratt has arrived in Liverpool and is now staying at the oratory of the Roman Catholic church of the Holy Cross.

I can, of course, do nothing further in the matter without Mr. Adam's [U.S. minister to England] instructions and a warrant. If it be Surratt, such a wretch ought not to escape.

A. Wilding

Mr. Wilding probably received the shock of his life when he received the following reply from Secretary of State Seward:

Sir:

Your dispatches have been received. In reply to your No. 538 I have to inform you that, upon a consultation with the Secretary of War and the Judge Advocate General, it is thought advisable that no action be taken in regard to the arrest of the supposed John Surratt at present.

W. Hunter

Acting Secretary

On the same day as Wilding's first message to Seward, September 27, Surratt paid a surprise visit to McMillan at his rented room in Birkenhead and asked to be given directions to a certain house in Liverpool. To that end, McMillan called for a cab and gave the driver directions to the house that Surratt had asked about. Surratt, of course, had letters of introduction from Fathers Boucher and LaPierre which he was to deliver to certain Catholic priests upon his arrival in England.

Surratt Goes to Rome

After remaining in hiding in Liverpool for several weeks, Surratt made his way to France. As soon as he could, he caught a train for Rome, arriving there in November 1865. Father Boucher, Surratt's great benefactor to this point, had also given him a letter of introduction to Father Neane, rector of the English College in Rome. As luck would have it,

Surratt was detained for several days in Civitavecchia. Without funds to pay his expenses, he wrote to Father Neane. The priest sent him fifty francs.

By this time Dr. McMillan had returned to Canada. Eager to get his hands on the twenty-five-thousand-dollar reward being offered for Surratt's capture, he quickly visited the United States consul in Montreal and informed authorities there that it was Surratt's intention to seek refuge in Rome. On October 25, 1865, the consul wrote to the State Department:

> No. 236
> It is Surratt's intention to go to Rome.
> I requested instructions in my telegram, but hearing nothing yet, I scarcely know what course to take. If an officer could proceed to England, I have no doubt that Surratt's arrest might be effected, and thus the last of the conspirators against the lives of the President and Secretary of State be brought to justice. . . .

Finally, two weeks later, on November 11, the consul received the follow rather cool reply:

> Your dispatches have been received. The information communicated has been properly availed to.
> F. W. Seward
> Assistant Secretary

Dr. McMillan must have felt that his last communiqué would finally bring action against Surratt and he would soon become a wealthy man. How his jaw must have dropped when he was notified on November 24 that according to Edwin Stanton's decree, "The reward offered for the arrest of John H. Surratt is now revoked."

Thanks to the apathy of the American government, Surratt was free to travel unmolested throughout Europe. In April 1865 he finally arrived in Rome and went immediately to the English College, where Father Neane made him welcome. They decided that he was not safe, not even in Rome, so Surratt assumed the alias John Watson. Still, he did not feel safe. Day after day he would walk the campus of the English College feeling vaguely uneasy, sure that American detectives were in close pursuit. He conferred with Father Neane, and together they decided that Surratt should enlist in the Papal Zouaves.

And thus in January 1866 Surratt enlisted as John Watson in the Third Company of Volunteers, Papal Zouaves, and was stationed at Sezze, about forty miles from Rome. Even here, among foreign soldiers, two thousand miles from Washington, Surratt did not feel entirely at ease. His intuition told him that something was amiss, that there were eyes out there watching him from the shadows. Indeed, several months later, while walking guard duty one morning, he was approached by a fellow Zouave, a deeply tanned young man with black curly hair and dark eyes. The young man almost had passed Surratt when he appeared to pause in mid-stride. He turned back and looked Surratt straight in the face.

"What is your name?" he asked in a strong Canadian accent.

Surprised and somewhat taken aback, Surratt managed to mumble, "John Watson. Why do you ask?"

"No, your name is not Watson," the young man cried. "I know you. Your name is John Surratt, and you were introduced to me by Louis J. Weichmann at Little Texas, Maryland in 1863. Surely you remember."

Surratt was incredulous. Here, in the hinterlands of Italy and after all this time, stood a man, a member of his own company of Zouaves, with whom he had spoken for less that five minutes over three years ago. Yet that man still remembered his face and his identity. It was an unbelievably unfortunate coincidence. Or was it merely coincidence?

The scene came back to Surratt. He and Louis Weichmann had visited St. Charles College, and a priest there, a native of Montreal, had given Weichmann a letter, which he asked be delivered to Henri Sainte Marie, a French Canadian from Montreal, who had been marooned in Little Texas, Maryland, some months before. They did as the priest requested and

John Surratt as a member of the Papal Zouaves. In 1867 he was discovered and imprisoned to await extradition, but he escaped and took refuge in Egypt, where he finally surrendered to American authorities. He was brought back to Washington and tried in a civil court for his role in the assassination of the president. (When this story and photograph were made public, it led to widespread rumors that the Vatican was involved in the assassination.) Library of Congress

spoke with Sainte Marie for only minutes. After all this time, here he was—a relentless nemesis.

Surratt admitted that Sainte Marie was quite correct in his identification of him but said that he was now a wanted man. "Please, for God's sake, don't give me up to the authorities," he pleaded.

Despite Surratt's pleas, Sainte Marie lost no time in visiting the American minister in Rome, Gen. Rufus King. Seated in King's office, Saint Marie told a story too incredible to be believed. He had been living in Canada when Lincoln was assassinated. Somehow, he became aware that Surratt, after hiding out with priests in Montreal, had fled by ship to England and Italy. At that point, said Sainte Marie, from an intense desire to see justice done, he had resolved to pursue the slayer of the president. This he did and finally found his murderous prey hiding out in the Papal Zouaves. To finally close the trap, he himself became a volunteer. Sainte Marie, this notorious Southern sympathizer, said he was only performing his patriotic duty to the Union. Then he asked if he qualified to receive the big reward being offered for Surratt's capture. King's response was not recorded.

As soon as General King heard Sainte Marie's report, he wrote the following letter to William Seward, secretary of state, in Washington:

April 23, 1866

Sir:

On Saturday last, 21st instant, a private in the Papal Zouaves, given his name as H. B. St. Marie, and claiming to be Canadian by birth, called upon me for the purpose, as he said, of communicating the information that John H. Surratt, who was charged with complicity in the murder of President Lincoln, but made his escape at the time from the United States, had recently enlisted in the Papal Zouaves, under the name of John Watson, and was now stationed with his company, the 3rd, at Sezze. My informant said that he had known Surratt in America; that he recognized him as soon as he saw him at Sezze; that he called him by his proper name, and that Surratt, taking him aside, admitted that he was right in the guess. He added that Surratt acknowledged his participation in the plot against Mr. Lincoln's life, and declared that Jefferson Davis had incited or was privy to it. St. Marie further said that Surratt seemed to be well provided with money, and appealed to him as a comrade not to betray his secret; and he expressed an earnest desire that if any steps were taken towards reclaiming Surratt as a criminal, he, St. Marie, should not be known in the matter. He spoke so positively in answer to my questions as to his acquaintance with Surratt, and the certainty that he was the man, and there seemed such entire absence of motive for any false statement on the subject, that I could not very well doubt the truth of what he told me. I deemed it my duty, therefore, to report the circumstance to the Department and ask for instructions.

Upon receipt of this letter, much correspondence then passed between Seward, Edwin Stanton, Rufus King, and the judge advocate general, Joseph Holt. The wheels were beginning to turn, but very slowly. Another eight months would pass before any steps were taken to actually arrest Surratt. He, meanwhile, went about his duties as before, blissfully unaware that he had been betrayed by Sainte Marie.

A perplexing question confronting authorities in Washington concerned the fact that no extradition treaty existed between the United States and the Vatican. In hopes of resolving this sticky question, on November 2, 1866, General King paid a visit to Cardinal Antonelli, secretary of state for the Vatican. The cardinal, after hearing the American government's charges against Surratt, stated that the Vatican was opposed to extraditing any prisoner to a country where capital punishment was in affect. However, because of the severity of the charges against Surratt, he could assure King that Surratt would be extradited to the United States following his arrest.

Or maybe not.

Soon thereafter, on November 7, 1866, King received a letter from a Colonel Allet of the Papal Zouaves, who had been ordered to arrest Surratt, in which he announced that the fugitive had been captured and locked safely away in a mountain prison where escape was virtually impossible. King, who served at the pleasure of Secretary Seward, felt tremendous relief at this news. Now it would be simply a matter of placing a heavily manacled Surratt aboard an American ship bound for this country, and King's responsibilities for the assassin would be at an end. The next day, unfortunately, King was again plunged to the depths of despair when Colonel Allet wrote that despite all his precautions Surratt had somehow managed to escape.

King was incredulous. Had not Allet assured him that Surratt was surrounded by armed guards and that the prison was escape proof? How could Surratt possibly have escaped?

Allet simply shrugged and reminded King that God works in strange ways. He offered the following questionable explanation. According to Allet, he had sent a Sergeant Halyerid and six armed guards to Tresulte, where Surratt was on duty, to arrest him. But they found that he was on leave that day in Veroli. He was finally arrested in that village and taken to the escape-proof prison where armed guards were posted at the door. All went well, according to Allet, until four o'clock the next morning.

> Then the prisoner was awakened, arose, put on his gaiters, and took his coffee with a calmness and phlegm quite English. The gate of the prison opens on a platform which overlooks the country; a balustrade prevents the promenaders from tumbling on the rocks, situated at least thirty-five feet below the windows of the prison.
>
> Beside the gate of the prison are situated the outhouses of the barracks; Watson [Surratt] asked permission to halt there. Corporal Warrin, who had six men with him as guards, allowed him to stop, very naturally nothing doubting, either he or the zouaves present, that their prisoner was going to escape at a place which it seemed quite impossible to us to clear. The perilous leap was, however, to be taken, to be crowned with success. In fact, Watson, who seemed quiet, seized the balustrade, made a leap, and cast himself into the void, falling on the uneven rocks, where he might have broken his bones a thousand times, and gained the depths of the valley. Patrols were immediately organized, but in vain. We saw a peasant, who told us that he had seen an unarmed zouave who was going towards Casa Mari, which is the way to Piedmont.
>
> I am assured that the escape of Watson [Surratt] savors of a prodigy.

A fine understatement if ever there was one!

In the Hanson Hiss interview published in the April 3, 1898, issue of the *Washington Post,* Surratt himself would verify the above account of his escape in all its particulars and add the following details. He looked over the balustrade and noted a vertical drop of some one hundred feet to the roadway below, but he had scouted this site in advance, just in case an escape should ever become necessary. He closed his eyes and made a vertical leap into the inky darkness, fully expecting to fall to his death. But as luck would have it, he somehow managed to land on his feet on a rocky outcropping some thirty feet below, the one he had noted earlier and had aimed for when he made his leap. Miraculously, he was not injured, he says, but for a moment he did lose consciousness. His Zouave guards, meanwhile, finally recovered from their great astonishment, began firing their rifles down at him. The loud reports of their rifles and the sounds of the bullets splattering themselves against the rock near his head revived Surratt. Dizzy and shaken, he pulled himself together and somehow managed to crawl down the rocky precipice to the roadway far below. Soon, his legs throbbing, he made his way to the small nearby village. Once arrived there, he found to his chagrin that he still was not out of danger. Indeed, while jogging down the main street he immediately ran into a squad of pursuing Zouaves. They were as surprised as he, but he had the advantage of being on the alert and quickly turned about and began running in the opposite direction, the Zouaves running after him, firing their rifles as they ran. But Surratt was running for his very life and he quickly outdistanced his pursuers. Still, the alarm had been sounded, and now all the gates to the wall that enclosed the village had been closed and locked. Young Surratt, however, was not beaten. He silently selected a dark place along the wall obscured from view by the foliage of a large tree. Surratt was nothing if not resourceful, and in a moment he had scampered up the tree and over the wall. He then took to the road that led to the coast. After jogging for about a mile, just as he was congratulating himself on making his escape, an alarmed voice called out of the darkness.

"Who goes there?" the voice challenged.

"Friend," Surratt responded in Italian. He realized now that he had blundered into a Garibaldian camp. The guard eyed his Zouave uniform and raised his rifle to his shoulder. Surratt quickly put up his hands. The guard cocked his rifle.

"Lower your rifle," Surratt cried. "Can't you see that my hands are raised?"

At that, the guard called out over his shoulder for the sergeant of the guard. That officer quickly arrived on the scene, took a look at Surratt's uniform and called for the officer of the guard. Within moments Surratt was totally surrounded by the entire company of excited Garibaldians. He told them as best he could in Italian that he was an American, a deserter from the Papal Zouaves, and he wanted to get to the coast, where he could make his getaway. Immediately, they began to treat him as a welcome guest, taking turns speaking to him, shaking his hand, and slapping him on the back.

The following morning, after a nourishing breakfast, Surratt, who had lost his British passport, made his way to Naples, where he visited the local police station. He told the officer who interviewed him that he was a Canadian citizen who had arrived as a visitor to Rome some two months earlier, but a pickpocket had stolen all his money. At that point, totally without funds, desperation had forced him to enlist in the Papal Zouaves. The week before, he said, Zouave authorities had arrested him and put him in prison for insubordination, but he had escaped by jumping from a high wall. In doing so, he had injured his back and arm. He then asked the police, since he was still without funds, for shelter. He had committed no crime, said the police, so they furnished him with meals and a cell where he could sleep for the next three days. At that point, bearing a Canadian passport, he requested to be taken to the British consul, and the police complied with his request.

Once arrived at the British consulate, he told the consul that he was John Watson, a Canadian citizen, and he wished to return to England. The consul looked at his red fez, baggy trousers, and leggings of the Papal Zouaves and expressed surprise that he had not been killed by the Garibaldians who then occupied Naples. But Surratt told him that the Garibaldians were the best friends he had—his only friends, in fact—and what little money he had in his pocket came from them.

Surratt remained in Naples for nine days. Surprisingly, he did not return to England, but traveled to Alexandria, Egypt, aboard the steamer *Tripoli*. Some English gentlemen, it seems, noting his pleasant appearance and speech, had felt sorry that such an outstanding young Britisher should be suffering dire financial difficulties and volunteered to pay his passage to Alexandria and give him spending money in the bargain.

As for American authorities, Gen. Rufus King had contacted Frank Swann, American consul in Naples, and urged him to spare no efforts in tracking down the elusive Surratt. Then he wrote to Secretary William Seward concerning Surratt's escape from Papal authorities and American efforts to recapture him:

> I was apprised yesterday that Surratt had left Naples the preceding day, November 17, for Alexandria, by a steamer which stopped at Malta to coal. I also immediately telegraphed to Mr. Winthrop at Malta, urging the arrest of Surratt, but up to the moment of closing the dispatch I have received no reply from Mr. Winthrop. The probabilities I fear, are, that Surratt will make good his escape.

A flurry of communications then ensued between King and other consuls in the Mediterranean area. The noose was being drawn tighter around Surratt's neck. Finally, on November 27, 1866, Consul General Charles Hale wired Secretary William Seward that John Surratt had indeed been taken into custody. Fortunately for the government, said Hale, Surratt was quartered among the third-class passengers aboard the *Tripoli*, and though there were seventy-eight of these, it was easy to spot Surratt, for he was still wearing his bright red Zouaves uniform, hardly proper attire for a fugitive on the run.

Hale approached Surratt, and said, "You are the man I want; you are an American."

Surratt, apparently resigned to his fate, replied, "Yes, sir, I am."

"You doubtless know why I want you. What is your name?"

Without batting an eye, Surratt replied, "John Watson."

Hale smiled. "I believe your true name is Surratt."

Later, when taken to Hale's office, Surratt was asked if he would like to make a statement, to which he replied, "I have nothing to say. I want nothing but what is right."

Twenty-four days later, on December 21, 1866, Surratt, in heavy chains, was placed aboard the corvette *Swatara.* He reached Washington on February 15, 1867, and was immediately placed in the Old Capitol Prison to await trial.

The war had ended almost two years earlier, and Surratt could hardly be treated with the same cruel disregard as his fellow conspirators back in the spring of 1865. A heavily padded hood was not strapped around his head, for example. But he was placed in solitary confinement, and all communication with the outside world was forbidden. What secrets he might know could not be told to anyone else.

Nor could the government's Military Commission try Surratt, thanks to a Supreme Court ruling, but still the government did the best it could. In his published diary, Gideon Welles states that William Seward, for reasons known only to himself, employed attorney Albert G. Riddle to find or, if necessary, manufacture evidence against Surratt. On June 10, 1867, Surratt was brought before the Criminal Court of the District of Columbia. The prosecutors named were Edwards Pierrepont and Albert G. Riddle. Pierrepont was a known Stanton favorite while Riddle served as Lafayette Baker's attorney. The case was put in charge of Judge Fisher, whom Secretary of the Navy Welles described as "a coarse, vulgar Radical in the hands of Stanton." Nor did Fisher disappoint his Radical friends. Under his control, the trial became a mockery of justice. Welles wrote, "The judge was disgracefully partial and unjust, and his charge highly improper."

Surratt proved of great interest to the Radicals, and before he went on trial he was frequently visited by Stanton's close friend, Congressman J. M. Ashley of Ohio, perhaps the prime mover in the efforts to impeach Pres. Andrew Johnson for treason. Obviously Ashley hoped to learn assassination secrets from Surratt that would aid in that impeachment.

The Trial of John Surratt

The trial of John Surratt was scheduled to begin on June 10, 1867, nearly two years since the executions of his mother, Lewis Powell, David Herold, and George Atzerodt. He himself had been in prison since February 15. He was charged with collaborating with Booth and the others in the assassination of Abraham Lincoln. He, on the other hand, swore that he had been in Elmira, New York, on April 14.

Despite efforts on the part of Edwin Stanton to have Surratt tried before a military court for the murder of Lincoln, as the other conspirators had been, where he would have very few rights and even fewer opportunities to defend himself, the Supreme Court ruled that since the war had ended and Washington was therefore not under martial law, Surratt must be tried in a civil court. Richard Merrick, a most well-respected Washington attorney and a noted Southern partisan, would defend him.

The trial opened with the prosecution explaining the charges against Surratt to the jury. They were told that the government would produce eighty-five witnesses to prove those charges. Merrick stated that he would delay his opening statements until the government had completed its testimony.

The first witness for the prosecution was Surgeon General Joseph K. Barnes, who testified that on the night of the assassination he had been called to attend the president both before and after his death. He had performed a post-mortem and removed the bullet from his skull. To the surprise of no one, Barnes further testified that the president died as a result of this gunshot wound.

Then came testimony that a Derringer pistol, the weapon that caused the fatal wound, had been found lying on the floor of the president's box. Prosecutor Wilson then produced both the Derringer and the flattened ball removed from Lincoln's skull for the jury to examine. Since this Derringer was a smoothbore weapon, with no lands or grooves in the barrel, it would have been impossible to conduct a ballistics test. How could the prosecution be so certain that this Derringer caused the president's fatal wound? Since no other weapon was found, reasoned the authorities, this must have been the murder weapon. (How long such reasoning would stand up in a modern court of law can be imagined.) It apparently occurred to no one that this Derringer could have been accidentally dropped, not by Booth, but by one of the numerous individuals who crowded into the president's box during the hours following the assassination.

At this point witness after witness was called to the stand. Most of those witnesses had testified before the Military Court in 1865. There were many new ones, including both Dr. Lewis McMillan and Henri Sainte Marie, who gave damning evidence concerning Surratt's connection to the conspiracy to abduct the president. Sainte Marie swore that Surratt had confessed to him that he was not in Elmira on April 14, but in Washington, escaping on the morning of April 15 disguised as an Englishman. He gave the following testimony:

Q. Did the prisoner tell you at this time anything about his disguises? If so, what?

A. Yes, sir; I asked the prisoner how he got out of Washington; if he had a hard time in escaping. He told me he had a very hard time.

Q. How did he say he got out of Washington?

A. He told me he left that night.

Q. What night?

A. The night of the assassination, or the next morning. I am not positive.

Q. What was the disguise, if any, he told you he had?

A. He told me he was so disguised that nobody could take him for an American; that he looked like an Englishman; that he had a scarf over his shoulders. He did not mention any other disguise that I remember.

Then came more witnesses who swore that they knew Surratt at least by sight and were positive they had seen him in Washington on April 14, the day of the assassination. A Washington barber, William Wood, testified that he shaved Surratt on the afternoon of April 14. He came into the shop with Booth, said Wood, and was travel worn and dusty. Mr. D. C. Reed, who had known Surratt since early childhood, testified that he had passed him on the street on the afternoon of April 14 and stopped and spoke with him. Mr. Ben Rhodes testified that he saw Surratt in the president's box at Ford's Theatre on the afternoon of April 14, adjusting the piece of wood that would prevent anyone from opening the door to the box. Then came a Mr. Benjamin Vanderpoel, a New York lawyer, who swore that he had seen Surratt in the company of John Wilkes Booth in a saloon on the afternoon of April 14. Despite Merrick's efforts to shake his testimony, Vanderpoel remained confident that Surratt was the man he had seen. Dr. William E. Cleaver, a veterinary surgeon, testified that he had seen Surratt on horseback on the afternoon of April 14 and that Surratt had paused and spoken with him. Sgt. William M. Dye swore that he had seen Surratt at Ford's Theatre on the evening of April 14, just prior to the president's assassination, in the company of John Wilkes Booth. But one of the most convincing witnesses for the prosecution was Susan Ann Jackson, the servant girl in Mrs. Surratt's boardinghouse, who testified that Surratt had returned home that evening, eaten supper, changed clothes, and then left again.

Merrick, upon cross-examinations, ripped into these prosecution witnesses with a vengeance, something to which they were not accustomed since they had been pampered, catered to, and encouraged during their testimony before the Military Commission two years earlier.

Then Surratt's old friend, the ubiquitous Louis Weichmann, was called to the stand. He would testify for the next three days. He told everything he had stated in 1865, with "many additional facts which had come to my mind since that time." Merrick showed no mercy when he later cross-examined him. Weichmann, however, stuck to his story.

Weichmann was followed to the stand by Dr. McMillan, who had made the crossing to England with Surratt. He related to the jury all the various conspiracy stories Surratt had told to him, but he could not confirm that Surratt had participated in the assassination of the president.

The next witness was Ezra B. Westfield, a conductor for the Northern Central Railway, who testified that a man he identified as Surratt came to him at 10:30 A.M. on the morning of April 13, 1865, in Elmira, New York, and asked what time the train would arrive in Washington. Westfield stated that the train arrived in Washington at 10:30 A.M. on the morning of April 14. He then pointed to Surratt as the man who had approached him in Elmira.

When it became Merrick's turn to present witnesses for the defense, he set about to refute the testimony of the prosecution's witnesses who placed Surratt in Washington at the time of Lincoln's murder. He first called Joseph Carroll, F. C. Atkinson, and Charles Stewart, employees of Stewart and Ufford Clothing in Elmira, New York. All three were highly respected citizens of that city, and all recalled without hesitation Surratt's visit to their clothing store on April 14, 1865.

Then came Dr. Augustus Bissell, an Elmira physician, who swore that on the afternoon of April 14 he met Surratt at the Brainard House in Elmira, where they enjoyed a lengthy conversation. Bissell's testimony was thrown into doubt, however, when the prosecution produced witnesses who swore that Dr. Bissell could not be believed, even under oath, and that he was a man totally devoid of character.

Another witness, John Cass, swore that Surratt, whom Cass took to be a Canadian, came into his clothing store in Elmira on the morning of April 15. During their conversation, Cass mentioned that he had read some bad news in the morning newspaper. Surratt asked what that news was, and Cass replied that the president had been assassinated.

Surratt had shrugged and made a noncommittal response. Despite Surratt's lack of sympathy for President Lincoln's death, Cass's testimony further indicated that Surratt had been in Elmira on the evening of the assassination.

Then the defense attempted to have admitted into evidence the register of the Webster Hotel in Canandaigua, New York, showing that Surratt had registered for a room under his alias John Harrison on the evening of April 15. The register was produced and in the middle of the page, with six names preceding his and six names following, was written the name John Harrison. David Bates, an expert hired by the government, swore that the handwriting was without doubt that of John Surratt. Judge Fisher stated that he would consider this evidence overnight and render an opinion the next morning, July 15, 1867.

Richard Merrick slept well that night, knowing that this hotel register should prove conclusively that Surratt could not possibly have been in Washington on the evening of April 14. Merrick would soon learn, however, not to underestimate the long arm of the government.

The following morning a packed courtroom was hushed as Judge Fisher rendered his decision. He gruffly informed the court that the register would *not* be entered as evidence. Why? Well, because it would have been too easy for Surratt to have manufactured that evidence. He simply could have signed the register at a later date and left it at the hotel in hopes that he could use it as an alibi should he ever be forced to stand trial for the assassination.

Merrick was astonished. How could Surratt possibly have manufactured this evidence, especially when his name appeared in the middle of the page, with six names above his and six below, unless he could have arranged for twelve collaborators to meet him at the hotel on a given day and have them all sign the register? Merrick looked at Surratt and shook his head: Don't expect any favors from Judge Fisher. Fisher was a federal judge whose career depended on the goodwill of Edwin Stanton, and his decisions throughout the trial proved to all that Fisher would force Surratt to *prove his innocence* at every step of the proceedings.

The prosecution then produced a witness, Charles Blinn, a night watchman at the depot of the Vermont Central Railway Company in Burlington, Vermont, who swore that on the night of April 17 he was approached by two men, one tall, one short. The taller of the two men asked if he and his companion could sleep on benches at the depot until their train to St. Albans and Montreal arrived. Blinn gave them his permission, and they both stretched out on benches. Their train arrived, said Blinn, at 4:30 A.M. on Tuesday morning, April 18. About two hours following their departure, Blinn found a pocket handkerchief under the bench occupied by the taller of the two men. On it was written "J. H. Surratt, 2." Two days later Blinn handed the handkerchief over to a detective, George Chapin, who was then in pursuit of Surratt.

This was damning evidence and would have disproved Surratt's story that he had arrived in Montreal on April 16. But Merrick immediately brought forth a rebuttal witness, John T. Holohan, who had been a longtime resident at Mrs. Surratt's boardinghouse. Holohan swore that the wash lady at the boardinghouse apparently had placed that particular handkerchief in his drawer by mistake, and it was he and not John Surratt who had lost it in Burlington on or about April 17.

The prosecution countered with testimony that Holohan, in the company of Federal detectives and Louis Weichmann, had been in Philadelphia on April 17 and 18, the time when Blinn said that he had found the handkerchief. Therefore, said the prosecution, Mr. Holohan was obviously mistaken in his testimony.

The prosecution then produced another witness, Carroll Hobart, a conductor for the Vermont Central Railway, who essentially verified Blinn's testimony when he testified that he too had encountered a tall man and a short man on the road to Essex Junction about five o'clock in the morning of April 18. They were standing on the platform at the rear entrance to the passenger car, said Hobart, and told him that they had no money for a ticket. They must get to St. Albans, said the taller man, and they could walk to Montreal from there. Hobart allowed them to go through to St. Albans, he said, but what happened to them after that he did not know. At that, the prosecutor asked Surratt to stand, and Hobart said, "The man that stood up before me resembles the man I saw, very much. I should not recognize his face since he had at that time a moustache with no whiskers on the chin and wore a cap."

Eventually, in both his "Rockville Lecture" and an interview with Surratt published in the *Philadelphia Times*, October 4, 1885, Surratt admitted that the testimony of Hobart at trial was essentially correct. He wrote that he and his companion, who was not identified, were without funds at that point, and hence they walked from St. Albans to Franklin, Canada, about fifteen miles distant, where they immediately met a Confederate agent who supplied them with money. They reached Montreal, said Surratt, the same day, April 18.

Louis Weichmann would later write that at this point in the trial, with so much conflicting testimony, some proving that Surratt was in Washington on April 14 and some proving that he was in Elmira on April 14, he truly became confused and did not know what to believe:

> Knowing this young man as intimately as I did, and he always presented to me only the honorable side of his character, I cannot reconcile myself to the belief that he was the man who stood in front of Ford's Theater, as narrated by Sergeant Dye, nor can I believe that it was he who at midday, as told by Mr. Rhodes, was in the President's box preparing the wooden bar which Booth would use that night. Still less can I entertain the story as told by Susan Mahoney that he entered his mother's house that night, partook of supper, changed his clothing and then left. I was in the house during the whole of that time after eight o'clock, and there was not the slightest indication to satisfy my mind that Surratt was there at that time.

Despite Weichmann's doubts concerning Surratt's guilt, the government wanted to take no chances with the jury. By this time Pres. Andrew Johnson had returned to the

Democratic fold, and Southern sympathizers in Washington, as throughout the nation, were beginning to take heart. The talk in Washington at this time, fueled by these Southern sympathizers who were no longer intimidated by the Black Republicans, concerned the national government's "murder" of Mrs. Mary Surratt in 1865. Indeed, these people, complemented by Surratt's old friends from southern Maryland, daily filled the courtroom, leaving little doubt in the jury's mind where public sympathy lay.

The government's fears became so great that Weichmann was visited one morning by two ladies, a Mrs. Griffen and a Mrs. Tullock, who informed him that they came with a message from Edwin Stanton, who feared that the jury might be swayed by public support for Surratt. Rest assured, they told Weichmann, that he should not feel intimidated by those in the audience, as Stanton had assigned some twenty "colored soldiers" to occupy three rows of benches in the courtroom, their duty to insure that no one in the audience engaged in unseemly demonstrations of support for Surratt.

Religion also came into play during the trial. Surratt and his family were devout Catholics, and he thus received unrestrained support from the Catholic community. In particular, Fr. Jacob Walter, who had served as Mary Surratt's confessor prior to her execution, and Fr. Lewis Roccofort attended every day of the trial and never missed an opportunity to smile and speak with Surratt and his attorney, Mr. Merrick.

On one occasion Merrick called Father Roccofort to the stand and asked him whether Louis Weichmann, a clerk in the War Department Office, had ever stated to him outside the confessional that he was involved in the conspiracy against the president or that he was used to send secret information to the Confederacy in Richmond. Before Roccofort could answer, however, there burst forth a storm of objections from the prosecution, which was sustained by Judge Fisher, and at that point Roccofort was excused from the stand. What his answer might have been, is not known. But it does not matter. From the jury's standpoint the veracity of Weichmann's testimony against Surratt had been badly damaged.

On another occasion some twenty students, led by their professor, Fr. John Menu, all from St. Charles College in Maryland, where Surratt and Weichmann had studied some years before, came into court and were permitted by the court marshal to greet and shake hands with Surratt. At one point, while an awed jury and a furious prosecutor looked on in disbelief, Father Menu himself gave Surratt a warm embrace. What effect this had on Catholic members of the jury can only be imagined. As for Weichmann, Father Menu and his students pointedly ignored him. Sitting alone and rejected, the self-righteous Weichmann, a man who could truly wax eloquent when discussing his own piety, seethed with silent resentment.

When testimony had been completed, closing arguments began on July 27. Edward Carrington, an attorney for the prosecution, spoke at great length, and he did everything to convict Surratt, even suggesting to the jurors that they could demonstrate their love of America if they voted to convict him. Then came Richard Merrick for the defense. He too spoke strongly and eloquently for an entire day. Observers would state that if Surratt were not acquitted it was certainly not the fault of Richard Merrick. Edwards Pierrepont then closed for the prosecution. He seemed to be genuinely convinced of Surratt's guilt, and he did a masterful job of presenting the evidence against Surratt in such a way that the jury could surely follow the chronology of the crime and gain a complete picture of Surratt's role in that crime. Judge Fisher, who apparently was also convinced of Surratt's guilt, then made a lengthy charge to the jury.

At 11:30 A.M. on Thursday, August 7, 1867, the jury retired to their chamber. Judge Fisher, who was convinced that the prosecution had an open-and-shut case, waited in his courtroom until five o'clock that afternoon, confident that the jury would quickly reach a guilty verdict. He also sat and waited all day on Thursday and Friday. By this time he was becoming frantic. On Friday afternoon, his worst fears were realized when he received a note from the jury foreman informing him that the jury was hopelessly deadlocked.

John Surratt as an elderly gentleman in 1914. Following his acquittal on murder charges in 1867, he taught school for several years then became an official with the Old Bay Line of Chesapeake, a freight company in Baltimore. He married and fathered seven children (his wife was the great-granddaughter of Francis Scott Key). He died in 1916, taking whatever secrets he might have known to the grave. Courtesy the Surratt House Museum

Fisher commanded the jurors to appear in the courtroom the following morning. Once Fisher arrived on that brutally hot August morning, the bailiffs handed him a stack of notes written by the twelve jurors stating that they currently stood just as they had on first balloting, and they were convinced that they could not reach a verdict. They stood at eight for acquittal, four for conviction. Judge Fisher threw his hands in the air at that point, dismissed the jury, and remanded Surratt to the custody of the marshal.

In the fall of 1867 Surratt was released from jail on twenty-five thousand dollars' bail—the amount initially offered by the War Department for his capture and subsequently canceled by Edwin Stanton.

Eventually, he was again brought to court, but this time the prosecution brought no murder charges. Instead, Surratt was tried for treason and conspiracy. Surratt's attorney, Mr. Merrick, made a mockery of the indictment. With a big grin on his face, he stood and pointed out to both the judge and the prosecution that the statute of limitations had expired on such charges. Merrick was quite correct, the statute of limitations had indeed expired. The judge looked at the prosecutors, shook his head, banged his gavel, and said quietly, "Case dismissed." Surratt walked out of court a free man. That marked the end of the affair; he was never again brought to trial.

And this too is puzzling. For doubtlessly Stanton and Judge Holt were both aware that the charges brought against Surratt would never fly, that the statute of limitations had expired. Did Stanton fear that Surratt might reveal evidence that would prove his mother innocent of all charges? Did he fear a revival of interest in the body that now lay beneath the flooring in the Arsenal Penitentiary? The case against Mary Surratt would never be reopened. However the body of Booth refused to remain at rest, and today, a century and a half later, the debate continues: Just who is buried beneath that stone in Baltimore labeled John Wilkes Booth?

As for Surratt's true guilt or innocence, that question has

bedeviled historians since the trial. John Surratt himself forever after refused to make any comments concerning his trial. On one occasion, by way of explanation, he stated, "I traded my life for a vow of silence." Perhaps that is the answer.

IX

Who Is Buried
in Booth's Grave?

Since April 1865 it has been persistently rumored that Booth, aided and abetted by high government officials, somehow managed to elude capture and make his way to freedom. Over the years these rumors have been fueled by testimony from numerous witnesses, reliable citizens for the most part, who viewed the body pulled from Garrett's barn on the morning of April 26, 1865, and swore that the body they examined was definitely not that of John Wilkes Booth.

The *Beloit (Wis.) Daily News* of April 20,1898, for example, carried an interview with John Kenzie, a former member of Lt. Edward Doherty's Sixteenth New York Cavalry, the unit that captured Booth at Garrett's farm. Kenzie stated that only moments after Booth was declared dead on the front porch of Garrett's farmhouse, he lifted the blanket that covered the corpse's face and found that the "body had reddish hair and ruddy features," hardly a description of John Wilkes Booth. In fact, it seems that "red hair" would become a common denominator for many of the witnesses who viewed the body.

On June 24, 1931, the *Des Moines Register* carried an article on H. L. Frost, a former cavalry colonel who had been present at Booth's capture in 1865:

> H. L. Frost, who led the New Hampshire Cavalry in the search for John Wilkes Booth after the assassination of President Lincoln, was buried here yesterday. He always maintained Booth was not burned to death in a barn while trying to elude his pursuers, but escaped and died later in Enid, Oklahoma.

In 1937 a fairly well-known author named Izola Forrester published a biography entitled *This One Mad Act,* in which she announced that she was the daughter of actress Rita Wilkes Booth, daughter of John Wilkes Booth and Izola Mills D'Arcy. According to old records, says Miss Forrester, Booth and Izola Mills D'Arcy had been married by the Reverend Peleg Weaver at North Cos Cob, Connecticut, on January 9, 1859.

Booth and Izola met while both were appearing on stage in Richmond. Following a whirlwind courtship, they were secretly married in Connecticut, and Izola later bore him a daughter. Booth purchased a home for his wife and daughter near Hampton Roads, Virginia. But with the outbreak of war, he essentially abandoned his new bride and began to spend his time performing clandestine operations for the Confederate Secret Service. He and Izola would meet from time to time and made plans for a reunion once the war ended, but his wartime activities prevented him from playing the family man. In time, says Forrester, Booth and Izola had two children, a son, Harry Jerome Booth, and a daughter, Rita Wilkes Booth (Miss Forrester's mother).

Following Lincoln's assassination, Izola Booth began life under an assumed name, living as a widow in fear that she and her children, Harry and Rita, would be ostracized if word of her secret marriage to Wilkes Booth ever leaked out. Izola, however, did, maintain constant contact with the Booth family throughout this period. Indeed, Booth's sister Rosalie Booth furnished financial support for Rita and her children. Edwin Booth, on the other hand, remained aloof from his brother's secret family.

Miss Forrester furnishes a vivid description of her unsettled childhood, living backstage with her mother and grandmother in theaters across America. Through it all, she says, there were mysterious letters from Aunt Rosalie Booth. A special friend of the family was actor John Matthews, who had earlier, at least allegedly, destroyed Booth's letter to the *National Intelligencer.*

She maintains that Booth survived long after the war, and that her grandmother, Izola Mills D'Arcy Booth, met with

Booth and his mother in San Francisco in 1869 and remained there for quite some time. As for "proof" that Booth survived the war, Miss Forrester points to her uncle, Harry Jerome Booth, as living proof that Booth did not die at Garrett's farm. Jerome was not born until 1870, some nine months following Izola's reunion with Booth in San Francisco in 1869.

Miss Forrester goes on to relate a meeting she arranged in 1908 with Gen. James R. O'Beirne, by then a judge on the New York bench. They discussed O'Beirne's role in the pursuit of Booth following the assassination and the killing at Garrett's farm. "In concluding his recollection of the chase," she writes, "the old soldier smiled grimly. 'I am telling you something that you will never find on any record. We were all pledged to secrecy in those days. You can't use it now, but follow it up. There were three men in that barn that night, and one got away.'" He left it up to Miss Forrester to guess which one. Miss Forrester says she did not have to guess. The man who got away was her grandfather, John Wilkes Booth.

Aside from the "proof" of Izola Forrester's family tree, there are numerous eyewitness accounts of citizens who encountered Booth long after the episode at Garrett's farm. There is much conflicting testimony arising from the various autopsies, inquests, and examinations of Booth's body. Perhaps the most obvious example of this would be Dr. John May's sensational report that the body he viewed aboard the *Montauk* on the morning of April 28 had a broken right leg. The government, of course, had advertised for the past two weeks that the fugitive suffered a broken *left* leg.

On February 17, 1869, following Edwin Stanton's removal from office, Pres. Andrew Johnson ordered that Booth's body be disinterred and delivered to Mrs. Mary Ann Booth and her family in Baltimore. It was then, for the first time, that the Booths and a few family friends were permitted to view the remains.

According to Francis Wilson, in his *John Wilkes Booth*, the body was disinterred by Harvey and Marr Funeral Home in Washington and turned over to Edwin Booth and John

Weaver, owner of Weaver's Undertaking Parlor in Baltimore. In a back room at Weaver's Undertaking, the body was viewed by old theater friends: John T. Ford, comedian Charles Bishop, actress Blanche Chapman and her sister Ella, Henry Clay Ford, Col. W. M. Pegram, and Henry C. Wagner.

Later, Blanche Chapman would recall that John Ford had called her out of rehearsal late one afternoon and told her he wanted her to view the body. "Very pointedly, he told me to keep my eyes and ears open and my mouth shut." Accompanied by Ella Chapman and Charles Bishop, she hurried to Weaver's Undertaking Parlor. They entered a back room and were greeted by Joseph "Doc" Booth, elderly Mrs. Booth, and Rosalie Booth. Edmund Booth, it was said, waited in the front parlor.

Ella then saw what appeared to be "a mummy wrapped in a brown colored blanket" lying on a table on the far side of the room. In a letter written to Francis Wilson in 1927 (see *John Wilkes Booth*, 1929), Ella Chapman recalled that the corpse's "nose and eyes, though shrunken a little, had not receded as is usual. The skin was brown and shriveled, the lips gone, and wonderful teeth were exposed." Miss Chapman goes on to say that Charles Bishop unwrapped the blanket from the corpse and stood for long moments gazing at the remains. Says Miss Chapman:

> Mr. Charles Bishop then carefully drew off one of the long riding boots, which were still on the feet and limbs of the body, which had evidently lain in the earth for years, and as he did so the foot and lower portion of the limb remained in the boot. An examination was then made, and it was plainly seen that the ankle had been fractured.

The fact that the corpse was apparently wearing two boots is a most remarkable revelation, for according to the official records of the assassination, Dr. Samuel Mudd cut away the boot encasing Booth's fractured leg on the morning of April 15, 1865. Dr. Mudd inadvertently kept that boot at his home, where it was later discovered by Federal officers. It was then turned over to the War Department and later used as evidence against Dr. Mudd by the Military Commission to prove that Mudd had collaborated with John Wilkes Booth in his flight from justice.

At the risk of being thought picky, the question begs to be asked: If the Military Commission had this boot in their possession long before "Booth" secretly had been buried beneath the flooring at the Military Arsenal, just how could that boot possibly have gotten back on the corpse being investigated at Weaver's Undertaking Parlor in Baltimore, Maryland, in February 1869? There is no way that such a transition possibly could have been made. Was the Military Commission lying when they stated that they had in their possession the boot of John Wilkes Booth, or was the government lying when it said that the body aboard the *Montauk,* the body wearing *two boots,* was that of John Wilkes Booth? Obviously there is a huge discrepancy here. Either the Military Commission was lying, or the government was lying. Or did Ella Chapman simply imagine that she saw two boots, one of which still held the foot of Booth? If the Military Commission was telling the truth when they displayed the boot of John Wilkes Booth, then it stands to reason that the corpse examined at Weaver's Undertaking Parlor, the corpse wearing two boots, was not that of John Wilkes Booth.

If in fact Booth had somehow made his escape and been in frequent contact with his family, then it stands to reason that Charles Bishop could have uncovered any corpse, and the Booth family still would have sworn that the body was that of John Wilkes. To have done otherwise would have been to sic the dogs on Booth once again. And of course the same is true of Booth's dearest friends who were present that day. Certainly they would not inform the government of Booth's escape by denying that the body under scrutiny was that of Booth. Indeed, we recall John Ford's admonition to Blanche Chapman to "keep my eyes and ears open and my mouth shut."

Whatever its identity, the body would remain at Weaver's while Edwin Booth acquired a family plot in Green Mount Cemetery in Baltimore. There on June 26, a quiet funeral was conducted with only family and intimate friends present.

One of those present that afternoon was Basil Moxley, the doorman at Ford's Theatre, who had been a close friend of Booth for many years and who served as a pallbearer at the funeral. Thirty-four years later, in an article that appeared in the *Baltimore American,* on June 6, 1903, Moxley described the ceremony as a "mock funeral." Headlines in the *Baltimore American* for that day shouted the news:

NOT BURIED HERE!
REMARKABLE DISCOVERY BY MR. BASIL MOXLEY!
He says another body was interred in
Green Mount for that of the assassin!
   Family and friends at the funeral, said Moxley, were all "party to a well-intended deception," that the body buried that afternoon was not Booth's. Moxley went on to say that prior to the funeral, he himself had visited Weaver's Funeral Home and examined the body closely. To his consternation, he found that "the body at that funeral home had red hair."

Yet another eyewitness account stating that the body brought back from Garrett's farm had "red hair" emerges in the March 31, 1922, *Beloit Daily News,* which carried a story concerning two elderly war veterans who had the previous day sworn out an affidavit stating that the body brought from Garrett's farm was definitely not that of John Wilkes Booth. The two veterans, Joseph Ziegen and Wilson D. Kenzie, were members of Lt. Edward Doherty's cavalry troop, which cornered Booth at Garrett's back in April 1865. They stated that the man dragged from the barn that night wore the uniform of a Confederate soldier, and on his feet he wore yellow brogans, the footgear of the Confederate soldier at that time. Ziegen and Kenzie also stated in their affidavit that the soldier had "red hair." "There was no chance of a mistake," said Kenzie. "One of our three officers seized the blanket and shouted to me: 'Don't you repeat that.' My company commander, Lieutenant Morris, husband to the niece of Edwin Stanton, also warned me to keep quiet." Lieutenants Doherty and Baker and Colonel Conger then forced all present to swear that they would never reveal what they had seen. Of course keeping the men quiet did not require much effort since they were as eager to share in that big reward money as were their officers.

Another witness present at Weaver's Undertaking Parlor was a quiet, middle-aged woman clad in black. She was Eliza B. Rogers, a close friend and neighbor of Booth's mother, Mary Ann Booth. She was present as a favor to Mrs. Booth, who was too distraught to view her son's body, and had asked Eliza if she would do so in her place. According to Terry Shulman in his article "What Really Happened to the Assassin?" (*The Civil War Times Illustrated*, July 1992), a recently discovered letter from Eliza Rogers to a Dr. William S. Forward, now on file at the Maryland Historical Society, further adds to the confusion surrounding the body viewed at Weaver's on February 17, 1869. Eliza Rogers wrote, "John Wilkes was there at Mr. Weaver's. When John's coffin was opened, he was lased [*sic*] up in 2 Government blankets. His leg was broken square off below the knee and the bones had passed each other, and was protruding out of the flesh." Eliza Rogers' statement just adds another puzzling aspect to the case. Thank goodness she did not bother to mention *which leg* was broken.

Heretofore, all official testimony concerning Booth's broken leg had been to the effect that it was the small bone in his leg, the fibula, that was broken, and that just above the ankle. Booth could not possibly have made such a daring escape from the theater with a broken tibia, the large bone in the leg. It would have been difficult enough to get about with a broken fibula, but it would have been virtually impossible with a broken tibia. Yet Eliza Rogers, an eyewitness to the examination of Booth's body, stated with the utmost equanimity that the body clearly had a broken tibia. Not only that, but the bone was broken off just below the knee, and not just inches above the ankle. It should be recalled that Dr. Samuel Mudd, in his testimony before the Military Commission, swore that the injured man who visited his home on the morning of April 15 had suffered a break to his tibia. Eliza Rogers' statement would seem to verify Dr. Mudd's testimony.

Only Surgeon General Joseph K. Barnes, who examined the body aboard the *Montauk,* ever stated that Booth had suffered a break to his fibula, but that statement became accepted as fact. Barnes' statement about the fracture in the small bone of the left leg accounts for Booth's ability to get about as he did for another twelve days. It is a simple fact that Booth could not have functioned for twelve minutes with a broken tibia. Indeed, had he broken his tibia he still would have been writhing in pain on the stage at Ford's Theatre when the police came to take him away minutes following the shooting.

The discrepancies surrounding the official examination of the body are also obvious in light of the statement of Dr. John Frederick May. Dr. May, Booth's personal physician and one of the first to view the body, stated, "By Dr. Barnes' order the cover was removed, and to my great astonishment revealed a body in whose lineaments there was to me no resemblance to the man I had known in life! My surprise was so great that I at once said to General Barnes, 'There is no resemblance in that corpse to Booth, nor can I believe it to be that of him.'" At that point the body was quickly turned over and Dr. May was asked to identify a surgical scar on the back of Booth's neck. After some breathtaking hesitation, Dr. May finally agreed that there did appear to be a scar there, but it looked like a scar from a burn. That quasi-identification was good enough for Lafayette Baker, and he immediately had the body removed before other embarrassing questions could be raised.

And again there was Dr. John May's blockbuster testimony following his examination of the body aboard the *Montauk.* The good doctor, it will be recalled, wrote in his official report that the body had suffered a broken right leg. His testimony created consternation in Stanton's War Department and led to a barrage of questions from curious journalists. We can only imagine Stanton mumbling a response: "Well, there is a simple explanation for that small oversight. You see, gentlemen, Dr. May was standing at the feet of the cadaver when he made his examination. From that vantage point it is easy to confuse your right from your left. Now, if you gentlemen will excuse me, I'm late for a very important appointment."

Were all these witnesses telling the truth? At this point we will never know. But it is a fact that in April 1865 Washington was filled with powerful and unscrupulous politicians who could plot, without a twinge of conscience, to assassinate the president who had betrayed their party by allowing the South to escape unscathed following the war. Doubtlessly, they could have connived to arrange for that assassin to make a clean getaway. In fact, they would much prefer that the assassin did make a clean getaway. That way he would not be available at a later date to answer embarrassing questions or name names in a court of law.

According to perhaps the most popular and widespread rumor concerning Booth's escape, on April 21, 1865, a week following the assassination, just after he had finally crossed the Rappahannock River into Virginia, Booth met a Confederate soldier by the name of Ruddy, who gave Booth and Herold the alarming news that there were Union cavalrymen in the area. Thus Booth quickly hired a dilapidated wagon driven by a former slave to drive him out of the area. Booth himself hid on the wagon's flooring while Herold and Ruddy covered him with baskets of vegetables, old blankets, and various other farm items. Later, now miles away from that danger area, Herold and Ruddy removed the farm items from atop Booth and dragged him from the wagon.

Several days later, on April 25, now a guest of the Garrett family, Booth noted that the items he had kept in his coat pocket, including photos of female friends and his personal diary, were missing and surmised that he had somehow dropped them while riding in the wagon. He asked Herold and Ruddy if they would return to find the former slave and his wagon and retrieve those lost items. They did so.

Late that night, forewarned that Union cavalry was in the area, Booth fled the Garrett household and hid in a nearby pine thicket. Herold and Ruddy returned later and took refuge in Garrett's barn. And that is where they were when the barn was fired and Ruddy was shot. Ruddy still had Booth's items in his pocket when he was pulled from the barn mortally wounded.

According to this story, it was Ruddy who was killed and not Booth. But finding Booth's articles in Ruddy's pocket, Lt. Luther Baker assumed that the victim was his prey, Wilkes Booth. And so upon Colonel Conger's return to Washington that morning, he reported to Lafayette Baker that Booth had been killed and his body was on its way to Washington. Soon thereafter Edwin Stanton ordered Baker immediately to remove Booth's body from the monitor where it lay, as soon as an examination of sorts could be conducted, and bury it under the cover of darkness in a secret location.

It might be noted that of the fourteen people who viewed the body aboard the monitor that afternoon, ten of them were employees of the War Department. Still, a number of people examined Booth's body at one time or another, and there were indeed great discrepancies in their testimony and some disagreement as to whether it was truly the body of Wilkes Booth.

The Appearance of Booth in Sewanee, Tennessee

In 1872, some seven years following the terrifying episode at Garrett's farm, an individual suddenly appeared in Sewanee, Tennessee, and began living life there very comfortably as though he were native to the region. His name was Booth, he said, and he was a cousin to John Wilkes Booth, the famous actor. He appeared to be a most respectable individual, well spoken and obviously well educated, and thus the local justice of the peace, Cleburn C. Rose, suffered not the least reservation about renting him an upstairs room in his own home.

In Franklin County, Tennessee, it is still common knowledge that John Wilkes Booth once spent almost a year as a resident of that area, where he established relationships with quite a few of the local citizens, most of them well-educated and highly respectable individuals, many associated with Sewanee: The University of the South. Numerous stories concerning Booth's residency in Franklin County have been passed down from generation to generation, and it seems that today citizens of Franklin County still have stories to relate concerning Booth's stay in Sewanee. These may be considered either folktales or oral histories, depending on one's attitude.

This Mr. Booth, an unmarried man of thirty-four, was quite lonely, and in time he began courting a woman in Sewanee, a handsome young widow born and raised in the area. Her name was Louisa Price Payne, and she and Booth were married on February 24, 1872. Local legend has it that the day prior to their wedding, Louisa's fiancé confessed to her that his real name was John Wilkes Booth, and he was indeed the famous actor. At that point Louisa, who apparently was not intimately familiar with the Lincoln assassination, became very upset and said that she would never marry a man under a false name, and so Booth was forced to marry Louisa under his real name or not at all.

Louisa Payne Booth had a son, McCager Payne (1863-1932), a boy of nine at the time of his mother's marriage to Booth. In later years, while working as a security guard at the Elk Cotton Mill in nearby Fayetteville, McCager Payne still had vivid (and quite fond) memories of his stepfather. He recalled sitting in the living room at night and Booth pulling up his pant leg and showing McCager his terribly scarred leg. McCager also remembered on one occasion, when there was little food in the house, hearing his mother and Booth discussing the possibility of Booth's selling his very valuable gold watch to raise badly needed money. After some discussion, Booth and Louisa agreed that the family needed food more than a gold watch, and so Booth left the house with a long face to find a buyer. McCager recalled the feeling of gladness that filled the family hours later when his stepfather returned with bags of groceries.

Booth told Louisa and McCager that he had walked to the village and pawned his watch to a local merchant, Preston S.

Booth's marriage licenses. Courtesy Franklin County (Tenn.) Archives

Brooks, Jr., who was the son of South Carolina's illustrious congressman by that same name, the man who had badly beaten Sen. Charles Sumner with his cane on the floor of the Senate prior to the war. Booth told Brooks that he felt so much sentimental attachment to his watch that he would prefer to pawn it rather than sell it. Brooks assured him that such an arrangement was satisfactory, and Booth could retrieve the watch once he had repaid the loan.

Many years later Brooks' two daughters, Amy Brooks Eggleston and Polly Brooks Kirby-Smith, would recall that their father had shown them a beautiful gold watch when they were mere girls and told them that he had taken it from John Wilkes Booth as security on a loan. Both Amy Brooks Eggleston and Polly Brooks Kirby-Smith were related to illustrious Southern families. Mrs. Eggleston's husband was the grandson of Capt. Jack Eggleston, commander of the *Merrimac.* Mrs. Kirby-Smith married the son of Gen. Kirby Smith, who himself served as president of Nashville College following the war. These ladies would recall that Booth's invaluable watch later was stolen from their father's trunk on the Brooks' back porch and never seen again.

McCager Payne says that his mother and Booth lived in Sewanee until July 1872. At that time the family packed their few belongings and moved to Memphis, where Booth claimed he expected to collect a large sum of money. Louisa was three months pregnant at the time and was delighted to hear that their financial situation would soon be improving. But after only a short while in Memphis, Booth and Louisa were sitting at the kitchen table when he quietly broke the news to her that he was sure he was being followed by federal agents. He had no choice, he said, but to flee to Texas, where he had old friends who would offer him shelter until he could become self-supporting. He promised that within the coming three months, he would send for her, McCager, and the child that would be born. Louisa began weeping at that point, but Booth quieted her fears by again vowing that he would send for her within three months.

Louisa never heard from him again. An Episcopal church

gave her the money to return home with McCager. Three months later, in Pelham, Tennessee, she gave birth to a daughter, Laura Ida Elizabeth Booth. Five years later Louisa Booth died from burns received after her clothes caught fire while she was burning leaves in her front yard. Laura would swear that as her mother lay on her deathbed she called young Laura to her side. There was something Laura should always remember, Louisa whispered, her father was the famous actor John Wilkes Booth.

Laura grew up in the Sewanee area, finished school, became an actress, and married actor Charles LaVine. She had a son whom she named after his father. Later she married actor L. A. Howard, whose name she was using on the stage in 1903.

Coincidentally, at about that same time, on January 13, 1903, a man by the name of David George committed suicide in Enid, Oklahoma Territory. Immediately upon his death, a woman in the community swore that David George several years earlier had confided to her that he was in fact John Wilkes Booth. When Laura Booth Howard, now an actress in New York City, heard the news, she contacted officials in Enid in hopes of establishing whether this man was in fact her father. But nothing definitive could be determined, at least not at that time.

It was also at that time that an attorney in Memphis, one Finis Langdon Bates, heard the news of George's death. Without a second thought, he dropped everything, packed his bags, and caught the next train to Enid, Oklahoma Territory. He had to see this David George for himself. It seems that some twenty-five years earlier, in 1878, while practicing law in Granbury, Texas, Bates had enjoyed the friendship of a local gentleman well known throughout the region as a most talented actor and sophisticated man about town named John St. Helen. During the course of their friendship, St. Helen confessed to Bates that he was in reality none other than John Wilkes Booth, the assassin of Pres. Abraham Lincoln. Bates, a skeptic by both nature and profession, was initially incredulous. But as time progressed, he slowly became convinced that John St. Helen was telling the truth, that he was in fact John Wilkes Booth.

In 1903, having investigated the life and death of David George in some detail, he became convinced that George was the same John St. Helen. Bates wrote a book, *The Escape and Suicide of John Wilkes Booth, Assassin of President Lincoln,* which he published in 1907. The publication of this sensational work aroused tremendous interest throughout the nation and Bates sold seventy thousand copies the first year.[1] According to Bates, he was a young attorney of nineteen practicing law in Granbury, Hood County, Texas, in 1872, the year he first met in his law office a gentleman of thirty-four named John St. Helen.

St. Helen said to him, "I desire to retain you as my attorney; that you may represent me in all matters of legal business concerning my affairs, and ask that you fix your reasonable retainer fee." Bates immediately did as requested and St. Helen continued his statement, saying, "Now that I have employed you and paid your retainer fee, you, as my lawyer, will and must keep secret such matters as I shall confide in you touching my legal interest and personal safety."

Bates replied that he quite understood the conditions of his being retained as St. Helen's attorney. To which St. Helen responded: "I say to you, as my attorney, that my true name is not John St. Helen."

Bates was puzzled, but he agreed to whatever St. Helen had to say. Too, said Bates, "He was a man whose physical beauty and mental attainments no man could fail to appreciate and no woman fail to admire."

The weeks, months, and years went by. Then, in 1877, St. Helen came down with an unnamed illness and was confined to bed in a back room of his store. Bates and other friends, assisted by a local physician, cared for him as well as possible. But St. Helen's condition worsened, and the doctor gave no hope for his recovery.

Bates recalled that it was about ten o'clock one night a week later when he, exhausted from hours of attending St. Helen, had fallen asleep in a chair on the store's front porch.

Finis Langdon Bates, a Memphis attorney, whose friendship with John Wilkes Booth, alias John St. Helen, in Granbury, Texas, 1872-78, led him in 1907 to publish a book describing Booth and his experiences following the assassination. His book swept the nation and he sold seventy thousand copies the first year. The Swaim Collection, Georgetown University Library, Washington, D.C.

He was awakened by a friend who told him that St. Helen was now in the final death throes and wanted to see him before he died. When Bates arrived at St. Helen's side the physician was holding his wrist and counting his faint pulse. The doctor said, "St. Helen is dying and wishes to speak to you alone." The doctor then withdrew from the room.

At that point, St. Helen, who could only whisper his words, said, "I am dying. My name is John Wilkes Booth, and I am the assassin of President Lincoln. Get the picture of myself from under the pillow. I leave it with you for my future identification. Notify my brother Edwin Booth, of New York City."

Bates withdrew the picture from beneath St. Helen's pillow and placed it in his pocket. Then he and an employee rubbed down St. Helen's body with brandy in hopes of rejuvenating him. St. Helen slept through the night, and the next day, to his doctor's amazement, he seemed to be on the road to recovery.

Several weeks later, now fully recovered from his illness, St. Helen joined Bates for a leisurely stroll in the country. Without prompting, St. Helen continued his confession. As for his motive in assassinating the president, he said, "I was persuaded at the time that the death of President Lincoln and the succession of Vice President Johnson, a Southern man, to the presidency, was the only protection of the South from misrule and the confiscation of the landed estates of the individual citizens of the Southern Confederate States."

After swearing that Mary Surratt was totally innocent of any knowledge of the conspiracy, St. Helen stated that John Surratt had no knowledge of his plan to assassinate the president.

He described his actions of April 14, the day of the assassination: At about 3 P.M. he and David Herold went to the Kirkwood House, where Vice Pres. Andrew Johnson was in residence. Then, in a most startling confession, St. Helen stated that over the past several months he and the other conspirators were in the habit of meeting at the Kirkwood House with Vice President Johnson to discuss the progress of their plans to abduct the president. On the day of the assassination, he went straight to Johnson's room, and there he and Johnson discussed the surrender of General Lee and how that great event would change, or even obviate, his plans for the capture of the president.

Vice President Johnson turned to me and said, in an excited voice and apparent anger:

"Will you falter at this supreme moment?"

I could not understand his meaning, and stood silent, when with pale face, fixed eyes and quivering lips, Mr. Johnson asked of me:

"Are you too faint-hearted to kill him?"

As God is my judge, this was the first suggestion of the dastardly deed of the taking of the life of President Lincoln, and came as a shock to me. While for the moment I waited and then said:

"To kill the President is certain death for me," and I explained to Vice President Johnson that it would be absolutely impossible for me to escape through the military line, should I do as he suggested, as this line of protection completely surrounded the city. Replying to this, Mr. Johnson said:

"General and Mrs. U. S. Grant are in the city, the guests of President Lincoln and family, and from the evening papers I have learned that President Lincoln and wife will entertain Gen. Grant at a box party to be given in his honor by the President and Mrs. Lincoln at Ford's Theater this evening."

At my suggestion Vice President Johnson assured me that he would so arrange and see to it himself, that Gen. Grant would not attend the theater that evening with the President and his family, and would also arrange for my certain escape. I replied:

"Under these conditions and assurances I will dare strike the blow for the helpless, vanquished Southland, whose people I love."

Mr. Johnson left his room and after a little more than an hour returned, saying that it had been arranged as he had promised, and that Gen. Grant had been, or would be suddenly called from the city, and that, therefore, he and his wife could not attend the theater that evening with the President and Mrs. Lincoln, as had been pre-arranged, and that such persons as would attend and occupy the box at the theater with the President and his wife would not interfere with me in my purpose and effort to kill the President.

I would be permitted to escape by the route over which I had entered the city during the forenoon of that day. That is, I was to go out over the East Potomoc river bridge, that the guards would be called in from this point by order of Gen. C. C. Augur that afternoon or evening, but if there should be guard present, I was to use the password "T. B." or "T. B. Road," by explanation, if need be, which would be understood by the guards. I would be permitted to pass and protected by himself (Mr. Johnson) absolutely in my escape. On the death of President Lincoln, he (Vice President Johnson) would become president of the United States, and *in this official capacity I could depend on him for protection and absolute pardon, if need be, for the crime of killing President Lincoln, which he had suggested to me and I had agreed to perform.*

I had no grudge against President Lincoln but wished to kill so that Andrew Johnson, a Southern man, a resident of Tennessee, should be made President of the United States, to serve the interests of the South.

Mr. Johnson promised me that as President of the United States he would protect the people of the South from personal oppression and the confiscation of their remaining landed estates. Relying upon these promises, and believing that by the killing of President Lincoln, I could practically bring victory to the Southern people out of defeat for the South.

Moved by this purpose and actuated by no other motives, assured by Mr. Johnson of my personal safety, I began the preparation for the bloody deed.

Several hours later, he again met with Johnson at the Kirkwood House and informed him that everything was in readiness.

About 8:30 that evening we left his room, walked to the bar in the hotel and drank strong brandy in a silent toast to the success of the bloody deed. We walked from the bar-room to the street together, when I offered my hand as the last token of good-bye and loyalty to our purpose, and I shall not forget to my dying day the clasp of his cold, clammy hand when he said:

"Make as sure of your aim as I have done in arranging for your escape. For in your complete success lies our only hope."

I replied, "I shall shoot him in the brain."

"Then practically, from this time I am President of the United States."

St. Helen then recounts how he visited the theater and brazenly entered the president's box and shot Lincoln behind his left ear. He makes an interesting statement: He says that

in leaping down to the stage his spur caught in a flag and he
landed off balance, "and threw my shin bone against the edge
of the stage, which fractured my *right* [emphasis added] shin
bone about six inches above the ankle." So St. Helen claims
that it was the fibula in his right leg that was broken!

Bates comments: "At this point St. Helen, exposing his
shin, called attention to what seemed to be a notched or
uneven surface on the shin bone. This I did not notice
closely, but casually it appeared to have been a wound or
fracture."

Of his successful escape, St. Helen says,

> When I came to the gate across the east end of the bridge there
> stood a Federal guard, who asked me a question easy to answer:
> "Where are you going?"
> I replied, using the simple letters "T. B." as I had been instructed,
> and the guard then asked:
> "Where?"
> I then replied, "T. B. Road," as I had been instructed by Mr.
> Johnson, and without further question the guard called for assistance
> to help raise the gate quickly.

He and Herold spent that night and much of the following
day at the home of Dr. Samuel Mudd, then it was on to the
farm of Samuel Cox, a Southern sympathizer. Cox called for a
local man "by the name of Ruddy," who agreed to guide Booth
and Herold to friendly forces located near Bowling Green,
Virginia, some thirty-five miles to the south. (Bates says that
there was an entire family of Ruddys in a nearby village.)

Several days later, on April 21, Booth and Herold, guided
by Ruddy, began the long journey to Bowling Green. They
were now in open country heavily scouted by Union cavalry
and so were fearful of discovery. It was then that they came
upon "an old negro near the summer home of Dr. Stewart,
who possessed two impoverished horses and a dilapidated
wagon." Booth immediately determined that this wagon
would make an excellent hiding place, so they hired the freed
slave and his wagon to transport them. To improve Booth's
hiding place, "straw was placed in the bottom of the wagon

bed. I got in on this straw and stretched out full length; then slats were placed over the first compartment of the bed, giving me a space of about eighteen inches deep, which required me to remain lying on the straw during the entire trip." Various farm goods were placed on top of the slats to further hide Booth's secret compartment. Herold and Ruddy, meanwhile, rode their horses far to the rear of the wagon.

About an hour after leaving the wagon, he noticed that his coat pocket was now empty. He says, "In my side coat pocket I had a number of letters, together with my diary, and I think there was a picture of my sister, Mrs. Clark, all of which must have worked out of my pocket en route or came out as I was hurriedly taken from the wagon." There was also in his pocket, says St. Helen, a check drawn on a Canadian bank for sixty dollars, which he planned to use to pay Ruddy for his services. That too was missing. He was forced to ask Ruddy and Herold to retrace their route and find the wagon and retrieve the missing items. Once they had found these items, instructed Booth, Ruddy and Herold should bring them to the Garrett farm, where he would be waiting. It was then "about 2 o'clock in the afternoon of April 23."

Booth, now in the care of the three Confederate soldiers, William Jett, A. R. Bainbridge, and Mortimer Ruggles, was led to Mr. Garrett's farm to wait for Ruddy.

Two days later, says St. Helen, on April 25, Bainbridge and Ruggles rode up to the Garrett farm in a state of great excitement. They had spotted a squad of Federal soldiers and said that Booth had best flee to the woods north of the Garrett farm. They would return to that place in about an hour with a horse for his escape. Under the circumstances, with Union cavalry practically at his doorstep, Booth immediately fled to the woods north of the Garrett farm. He did not even take time to inform the Garretts that he was leaving. Bainbridge and Ruggles soon arrived with a horse "which I mounted, and we rode away in a westerly direction, riding the remainder of the afternoon and the following night until about twelve o'clock, when we camped together in the woods. We talked over the situation, they giving me directions by which I should travel."

John St. Helen, c. 1876 The Swaim Collection, Georgetown University Library, Washington, D.C.

John Wilkes Booth, c. 1864 National Archives

Following Booth's departure, Ruddy and Herold returned to the Garrett farm with the items belonging to Booth that they had retrieved from the wagon. While Herold and Ruddy waited for Booth, Ruddy would go to sleep in the barn. Thus it was the unfortunate Ruddy and not Booth who was shot and killed a few hours later. It was Booth's items in his pocket that led Conger, Baker, and Doherty to conclude that they had indeed killed the assassin of President Lincoln and could now claim that huge reward being offered for his capture. As for the broken leg, the man pulled from the barn did not have one, but after his death, it required only a single swing of a rifle butt, and Ruddy's corpse featured a broken leg. Whether it was the left or right one, no one noticed. Now there could be no doubt: The body was that of John Wilkes Booth. Indeed, Colonel Conger left Lieutenants Baker and Doherty to watch "Booth" expire while he rocketed off to Washington to lay claim to that incredible fortune awaiting them.

St. Helen says that he continued to ride southwesterly for days on end, passing himself off as a wounded Confederate soldier to numerous country folks who were kind enough to take him in for a day or two. "Continuing on down through West Virginia, I crossed the Big Sandy River at Warfield, in Eastern Kentucky, and after traveling from Warfield for about two days, and covering a distance of fifty or sixty miles in a southwesterly direction from Warfield, I was forced to rest for about a week."

After recuperating some of his strength, he continued in his bid for freedom:

> I traveled south until I could reach the Mississippi River at a safe point for crossing, and find my way into the Indian Territory as the best possible hiding place. I finally reached the Mississippi and crossed at what was called Catfish Point in the state of Mississippi. Then I followed the south and west bank of the Arkansas River until I reached the Indian Territory, where I remained at different places, hiding among the Indians for about eighteen months.

At that point, aware that he was no longer being pursued—that according to official statements out of

Washington he had been killed on April 26, 1865—he felt confident enough to migrate to Nebraska City, Nebraska. Using the alias Jesse Smith, he took a job with a Mr. Treadkel, who had a government contract to deliver supplies to the U.S. Army in Salt Lake City, Utah.

Interviewed in later years, Treadkil told Bates:

> There was always a strange thing about Jesse Smith, or Booth. While he was a good driver of mules four in hand, he did not have the slightest knowledge in how to harness his team nor even how to hitch them to the wagon. But he was the life of the camp at night and rendered himself so agreeable that I never once thought of discharging him. He would recite Shakespeare's plays, poems, etcetera, and tell of his travels, which seemed to have been extensive. His recitations were grandly eloquent.

A few years later, says Bates, Treadkel purchased a book concerning the assassination of President Lincoln and was amazed to find therein a photograph of John Wilkes Booth, whom Treadkel identified as his old teamster Jesse Smith.

Just before reaching Salt Lake City, Booth abandoned the wagon train and traveled by rail to San Francisco, where he experienced a prearranged and joyous reunion with his mother and brother Junius Brutus Booth. After several weeks of resting comfortably with his mother and brother, his pockets now filled with cash, he traveled to Matamoros, Mexico, where he lived as an itinerant Catholic priest. Two years later he migrated northward to Glenrose Mills, Texas.

Bates remained highly skeptical of St. Helen's story, supposing him to be just a bit off when it came to believing that he was John Wilkes Booth. Yet they remained the best of friends and frequently enjoyed the company of one another. But in the spring of 1878, a restless Bates decided to move his law practice to the more fertile fields of Memphis, Tennessee. John St. Helen, at the same time, determined to sell his store in Granbury and try his hand at silver mining, and thus he moved to Leadville, Colorado.

For the next twenty years, says Bates, until 1898, he

heard nothing from St. Helen. However, Bates remembered his strange friend from Granbury, and as time passed his curiosity grew increasingly stronger. He recalled that in 1897 he had read a newspaper article written by Gen. David Dana, who had gone in pursuit of Booth following the assassination in April 1865. Assuming that Dana would have intimate knowledge of both Booth and David Herold, Bates wrote him a letter explaining his relationship with St. Helen. He included a copy of the tintype that St. Helen had given him and asked Dana if that might be the image of either John Wilkes Booth or David Herold. On January 17, 1898, Bates received the following response from General Dana:

> Dear Sir: Your favor of January 8th at hand and read. I must say I was somewhat surprised at the turn things took, for I expected the likeness of Herold, or that it would have some of the features in it of the man Herold you wrote me about, but it seems it was Booth instead.
>
> Can this be J. B. Booth [Junius Brutus], brother of John Wilkes Booth? Will it be asking too much of you to send me a copy of the confession which you have? I would like to have it for my own satisfaction. If I can be of any help to you, will gladly aid all I can. Regarding J. B. Booth, I shall write to some one of the Booth family and learn all I can of his death, and where. When received will send to you.
>
> Respectfully yours, David D. Dana

This letter, says Bates, revived his interest in St. Helen and motivated him to again begin his investigation into the life of John Wilkes Booth. Had Booth truly been killed in 1865, or did he have in his possession a photograph of Booth taken in 1876? Finis Bates was a man of great intellect and deep curiosity, and he could not rest until he found the answers.

He wrote to Gen. Lew Wallace, among others, requesting information concerning the death of John Wilkes Booth but received only contradictory responses. Then, he wrote to Secretary of War John P. Simonton. On May 13, 1898, he received the following response:

Dear Sir:

I am collecting matter for a detailed account of the assassination of President Lincoln by J. Wilkes Booth, and seeing your letter to this department concerning the evidence you therein state you possess, that Booth was not captured and killed by the Federal troops, I have been prompted to write to you in my private capacity as a citizen, and not as an employee of the War Department, and inquire if you will kindly give me for publication, if found available, such information on the subject as you may possess.

While I have not what may be styled direct or positive evidence that the man killed was Booth, I have such circumstantial evidence as would seem to prove the fact beyond doubt. Still, I would be glad to examine any evidence to the contrary.

Hoping to hear from you soon, I am, very respectfully, your obedient servant,

JOHN P. SIMONTON

As Bates points out, this letter from the secretary of war himself strongly indicates that the government was not totally convinced that the man killed at Garrett's farm in 1865 was the assassin of the president, John Wilkes Booth. The government had "circumstantial evidence," yes. But as Simonton says, they had always lacked "direct or positive" evidence that they had the right man.

On May 18, 1929, historian Lloyd Lewis wrote an article for the *Washington Star* concerning John P. Simonton and his conviction that Booth had somehow escaped justice:

In hunting new material about John Wilkes Booth and the assassination of Abraham Lincoln, I was referred to John P. Simonton by Major Willis Crittenberger of the War Department. Simonton had shortly before retired after 40 years of service. His researches into the mystery surrounding the death of John Wilkes Booth, assassin of Lincoln, exceed those of any other man of his time. During his service in the Judge Advocate's Office he was regarded as an expert on evidence, and his search into the papers and facts concerning Booth was microscopic. At the end of 40 years study of the question from all angles he still believes that Booth avoided justice and that the War Department in 1865 killed an innocent man for the assassin.

Even Edwin Stanton and Lafayette Baker seemed to entertain grave doubts as to the true identity of the body brought aboard the *Montauk* on April 27, 1865. Such doubt certainly explains their rush to "identify" the body and then have it immediately hauled away for a secret burial under the cover of darkness, much to the consternation of family and friends of Booth who were never given a chance to view the body.

Once he had located St. Helen in Leadville, Colorado, Bates wondered if the U.S. War Department might be interested in hearing that he had conclusive evidence that Booth still lived. In early January 1897 he wrote to the judge advocate general, Norman Lieber, outlining St. Helen's story. When a secretary showed Bates' letter to Lieber, that gentleman simply responded, "It is recommended that he be informed that the matter is of no importance to the War Department." Essentially, John Wilkes Booth was now a free man.

Bates persisted with his investigation, now to satisfy his own curiosity if nothing else. To that end, he contacted a retired soldier, Col. Edward Levan, then living in Monterey, Mexico. Bates had heard from a anonymous source that Levan had once been acquainted with a man who might have been John Wilkes Booth. Levan's response was most gratifying. He wrote that he had once roomed with a man during the winter of 1868 in Lexington, Kentucky, one J. J. Marr, who represented himself as an attorney. Levan, who had once been stationed in Washington and had seen Booth on stage on many occasions, one day voiced his suspicions to Marr that he was either John Wilkes Booth or his identical twin. "Mr. Marr did not deny the allegation," says Levan, "but shortly thereafter he left Lexington." Levan says he later learned that Marr had settled at Village Mills, Texas, and from there he moved to Glenrose Mills, where Bates had first made his acquaintance.

Bates contacted Col. M. W. Connolly, distinguished editor in chief of some of Texas's leading newspapers. Connolly responded to Bates' inquiry:

While in the little town of Village Mills, Texas, I met St. Helen, although I never knew his name, and cannot say whether he went under that name or not. . . . Later I went to Fort Worth as editor of the *Gazette.*

One night I was in the Pickwick Hotel barroom talking to General Albert Pike, who had come down from Washington on legal business. Captain Day was behind the bar.

Tom Powell, mayor of Fort Worth joined us, and Temple Houston, son of the ex-Governor of Tennessee, was there. . . . Just then the fellow known as St. Helen from Village Mills came in. I was watching General Pike closely, when suddenly he threw up his hands, his face went as white as his hair and beard, and he exclaimed:

"My God! John Wilkes Booth!" He was much excited, trembled like an aspen, and at my suggestion went to his room. He seemed weakened by the shock.

There were other witnesses who swore that they had met St. Helen prior to his settling down in Glenrose Mills. There was a Dr. H. W. Gay, who told Bates:

I knew John Wilkes Booth in 1857. As for the assassination, I was horrified to think of such a thing, for Booth, though a boy when I knew him, in appearance was the most accomplished gentleman with whom I had ever come in contact. All who knew him were captivated by him. He was the most hospitable, genial fellow to be met.

I read of his capture and death and never doubted it until the year 1869. I was then living in what is now Tate County, Mississippi. One evening about dusk a man came to my house claiming that he was one of the Ku-Klux Klan run out of Arkansas by Clayton's militia.

During his stay at my house he told me that John Wilkes Booth was not killed but made his escape and spent a short while in Mexico. The man also told me that during Booth's short stay in Mexico he had lived in disguise an itinerant Catholic priest. He also told me the story of how Booth had escaped after the assassination was done, and it corresponded exactly with Mr. Bates' story as told by John St. Helen, even to the crossing of the Mississippi River at Catfish Point.

Bates says that after tracing St. Helen's progress across the country for a number of years, he next found evidence of him in Hennessy, Oklahoma Territory, in 1896. Using the alias George D. Ryan, he was thought to be a gentleman of leisure. He remained there for about three years, then moved to El Reno, some sixty-five miles to the south.

The Appearance of David George

It was in El Reno, Oklahoma Territory, in 1899 that John St. Helen suddenly became David E. George. If he was indeed John Wilkes Booth, he would have been sixty-one years of age at that time. His first step was to take a room at the Anstein Hotel. The following day he opened a bank account at the State Bank of El Reno under the name David E. George.

After staying at the Anstein Hotel for quite some time, George paid thirty-five hundred dollars cash for a nice home in El Reno. His next move was to allow a Mrs. Simmons and her family to live in several rooms of his home absolutely free if she would agree to take care of his domestic needs. She would cook, clean, and wash his clothes; otherwise, he would stay out of her way. Mrs. Simmons readily agreed to this arrangement. He also rented rooms to the Methodist minister in El Reno, the Reverend and Mrs. E. C. Harper. Mr. Harper, it was said, was a man of means and did not depend on the ministry for a livelihood, while Mrs. Harper was a lady of great refinement and culture and occupied a high position in El Reno society.

In time, associating with each other on such close terms, the Simmons family and the Harpers all became quite friendly with David George, a man of unusual education, talents, and charm. But after several months George became ill with an asthmatic condition, and on April 15, 1902, he requested that he be moved to the Kerfoot Hotel. There, he was attended to by Mrs. Simmons and Mrs. Harper and other kind-hearted ladies of the city.

Several days later, everyone, including David George, thought that he was dying. A year later, following his suicide in 1903, Mrs. Harper would write an excellent account of George's earlier confession to her during his illness:

Mr. George (Booth) had been a resident of the Territory for several years. He had always been well supplied with money, the origin or source of which no one knew, for from some mysterious source he received a regular remittance. He was a familiar figure in Guthrie, El Reno and Enid. My acquaintance with Mr. George led me to believe him to be a very different person from what he represented himself to be. He was eccentric, and was possessed of the highest degree of intelligence, had always the bearing of a gentleman of cultivation and refinement, and in conversation was fluent and captivating, while he discussed subjects of the greatest moment with learning, familiarity and ease. There were very few people with whom he cared to associate. Generally he was gloomy, though at times he would brighten up, sing snatches of stage songs and repeat Shakespeare's plays in an admirable manner. He was so well versed in these plays and other writings that he would often answer questions with a quotation.

At one time the young people of El Reno had a play of some kind. One of the actors became ill and Mr. George (Booth) filled his place to the great admiration and entertainment of those who saw him. When surprise was expressed at his ability as an actor he replied that he had acted some when he was a young man.

He seemed very lonely at times, and said that he had not a relative in the world. He was subject to fits of melancholia, was extremely sensitive, quick tempered and rather excitable. He said he had never married. There seemed to be something constantly on his mind about which he thought, and which made him miserable. He seemed to love to have one understand that he was in trouble and appreciated sympathy.

He remained with the Simmons family three months and treated everyone with the greatest kindness and consideration. Never do I remember his mentioning the history of his past life or that he was other than David E. George until the time he thought he was going to die—that was about the middle of April, 1902.

He had gone up town, but returned shortly and, entering the room where Mrs. Simmons, Mrs. Bears and myself were seated, he made some remarks regarding the weather, which was unusually fine for that time of year. He then went to his room and in about fifteen minutes called for us, and said:

"I feel as if I am going to be very sick." He was lying on his bed and asked me to get him a mirror. For some time he gazed at himself in the mirror.

Mrs. Bears said she could see the pupils of his eyes dilate and believed that he had taken morphine. Being uneasy, she went out of the room and got him a cup of coffee and insisted until he drank it, but when she suggested sending for a physician he roused himself and in a peculiar and dramatic manner and voice said, while holding the mirror in front of his face:

"Stay, woman, stay. This messenger of death is my guest, and I desire to see the curtain of death fall upon the last tragic act of mine," which passionate utterance brought tears to our eyes. And when I turned to wipe the tears from my eyes he called me to his side and said:

"I have something to tell you. I am going to die in a few minutes, and I don't believe you would do anything to injure me. I killed the best man that ever lived." I asked him who it was and he answered:

"Abraham Lincoln."

I could not believe it. I thought him out of his head and asked: "Who was Abraham Lincoln?"

"Is it possible you are so ignorant as not to know?" he asked. He then took a pencil and paper and wrote down in a peculiar but legible hand the name "Abraham Lincoln," and said:

"Don't doubt it, it is true. I am John Wilkes Booth."

"Am I dying now?" he asked. "I feel cold, as if death's icy hand was closing my life as the forfeit for my crime."

He then told me that he was well off. He seemed to be perfectly rational while talking to me. He knew me and knew where he was, and I believe he really thought in fact that he was dying, and asked me to keep his secret until he was dead, adding that if any one should find out now that he was J. Wilkes Booth they would take him out and hang him, and the people who loved him so well now would despise him. He told me that people high in official life hated Lincoln and were implicated in his assassination. He said that the suspense of possibly being detected preyed on his mind all the time and was something awful, and that his life was miserable. He said that Mrs. Surratt was innocent and he was responsible for her death as well as that of several others. He said that he was devoted to acting, but had to give it up because of his crime, and the fact that he must remain away from the stage, when he loved the life and profession of acting so well, made him restless and ill tempered. He said he had plenty of money, but was compelled to play the character of a working man to keep his mind occupied.

In the meantime Dr. Arnold arrived and as a result of his efforts, Mr. George was restored. After this he was very anxious for weeks regarding what he had told me and questioned me concerning it. I answered him that he had told me nothing of importance, but he seemed to know better. One day he saw me looking a picture of Abraham Lincoln and asked me why I was looking at it. I told him that I had always admired Lincoln.

"Is that the only reason you have for looking at it?" he asked, regarding me with a fierce look. A peculiar expression came over his face, his eyes flashed and he turned pale and walked off.

One peculiar feature of Mr. George, or Booth's, face was that one eyebrow was somewhat higher than the other. I have noticed him limp slightly, but he said it was rheumatism. That Mr. George had a past we all knew, but what his secret was remains unknown except in so far as he may have communicated the truth to me.

Never one to remain long in one place, on December 3, 1902, David E. George, now completely recovered from his illness in the spring, moved to Enid, Oklahoma Territory, and registered at the Grand Avenue Hotel as David E. George. At this point he had less than two months to live.

Coincidentally, the Reverend and Mrs. E. C. Harper also moved to Enid around the same time. They soon were startled to read that David George had committed suicide. Ten days after George's suicide, on January 23, 1903, Mrs. Harper would write and sign a notarized statement:

> On the evening of January 13th, I was startled and surprised by reading in the *Enid Daily News* of the suicide of David E. George, of El Reno, with whom I first became acquainted in March, 1900, in El Reno, at the home of Mrs. Simmons.
>
> Mr. Harper went down on Wednesday morning, the 14tht instant, and recognized him, and told the embalmers of a confession that David E. George had made to me, and that they had best investigate.
>
> I went to the morgue with Mr. Harper on the 15th and identified the corpse of David E. George as the man who had confessed to me at El Reno that he was John Wilkes Booth, and as brevity has been enjoined on me, will reaffirm my former statement made in detail of David E. George's confession to me at El Reno, about the middle of April, 1900, as fully as if same were set forth herein.
>
> Mrs. E. C. Harper

On January 17, a sensational article appeared in the *Enid*

Wave, which was soon picked up by newspapers across the country.

> David E. George, a wealthy resident of the Territory, who committed suicide here, announced himself on his deathbed to be John Wilkes Booth, the assassin of President Lincoln. He stated that he had successfully eluded the officers after shooting Lincoln and since had remained incognito. Surgeons examined the body and stated the man to be of the same age Booth would be at this time, and announced that his leg was broken in the same place and in the same manner as that of Booth. All the time George has received money regularly from unknown sources, and telegrams arriving yesterday and today ask that the body be held for identification. It is claimed that one telegram came from the address, George E. Smith, Colfax, Iowa, the same as the mysterious money remittances. Smith is unknown to any one in Oklahoma. Upon his arrival in Enid today he commanded that no other person be allowed to view the remains, and promised to return for the body later.
>
> Mr. Smith was asked if George had ever confessed any of his life's history to him, to which he answered: "Well, yes, to some extent. He has had a past of which I do not care to speak at the present. I think he killed a man in Texas. He may be Booth."

Four days later, on January 21, 1903, the *Enid Wave* published a subsequent report on David George and the possibility that he could be John Wilkes Booth.

> The Wave is still of the opinion that the possibility of the dead man being all that is mortal of John Wilkes Booth remains in doubt, but it must be admitted that the evidence goes to show that if George was not Booth he was his double, which, in connection with his voluntary confession to Mrs. Harper, makes the case interesting and worthy of the attention of the Attorney General's department of the United States.
>
> Doctors Baker and Way unearthed the December, 1901, number of the Medical Monthly Journal. In this pamphlet we found a portrait of J. Wilkes Booth, with quite a writeup as to his character, a physical and anatomical description among other descriptions.
>
> Yesterday, the editor of the paper, in company with Dr. McElreth, visited the corpse and compared it with the description of Booth in the Journal, and we must acknowledge that the dead man shows all the marks credited to Booth in every particular. . . . The eyebrows of

the dead man are not mates in appearance, which fits the description of Booth. The Booth chin, mouth, upper lip and general description is absolutely perfect in the corpse.

Five months later, on June 5, 1903, the *Perry (Okla.) Republican* published another sensational story:

It is now fully developed that the man at Enid, who committed suicide on January 13th last, was none other than John Wilkes Booth, the slayer of President Lincoln. Junius Brutus Booth, the nephew of John Wilkes Booth, has fully identified the picture of David E. George as that of his uncle, John Wilkes Booth.

It has always been known by the Booth family that John Wilkes Booth was alive, and they have been in constant communication with him ever since April 14, 1865, the day of President Lincoln's assassination and the escape of John Wilkes Booth. This knowledge on the part of Junius Brutus Booth, the actor, was what prompted him, or his brother Edwin, to make remarks about the supposed grave of J. Wilkes Booth. He or they well knew that the body in the grave was not that of J. Wilkes Booth.

. . . From the time of Booth's supposed capture in April, 1865, until January of this year, J. Wilkes Booth has been in almost constant touch with his friends. . . . Through the anxious efforts of friends and relatives to preserve his life, it has been an easy matter for Booth to conceal his identity.

Among George's effects was a letter addressed to his attorney, Finis Bates of Memphis, Tennessee. Authorities in Enid cabled Bates on January 17 to come to Enid as quickly as possible and identify the body. Bates dropped everything and caught the next train for Enid. Once arrived in that city, and moving about under an alias, Bates visited Pennaman's Undertaking Parlor, which was located at the rear of Pennaman's Furniture Store. Pennaman did not take him immediately to view the body, but simply showed him photographs of the corpse. Bates says, "The recognition of St. Helen, or Booth, in the pictures provided was instantaneous."

At that point, Pennaman led Bates to the rear morgue, where David George's body was waiting. "In the presence of

Signatures of D. E. George
and John Wilkes Booth.

*On the night of January 12, lying on his deathbed, David
George attempted to prove his identity by signing his name (top),
John Wilkes Booth. The bottom signature is a known Booth signature. Though the two are not identical, it is interesting that
they are so similar. Too, it must be remembered that George was
in agony at the time he furnished this sample, suffering the
affects of arsenic poisoning.* Finis Bates

Mr. Pennaman," says Bates, "cold, stiff and dead, I beheld
the body of my friend, John St. Helen. After a separation of
more than twenty-six years I knew him as instantly as men
discern night from day." Bates and Pennaman then examined the body:

> We then compared the high thumb joint on the right hand, the
> small scar in the right brow—the uneven brow—the scar received in
> the accident mentioned by Miss Clara Morris, raises this brow to an
> uneven line with the left; the right leg was examined and we found a
> slight indentation on the surface of the shin bone. And there were
> small scars plainly discernable, where particles of bone seemed to
> have worked out through the skin, leaving small round scars. His
> weight was about one hundred and sixty pounds, height about five
> feet, seven inches.

Before leaving the morgue, Bates was delighted to learn that Mr. Pennaman was not exactly a naive country bumpkin, having once served as a reporter for the *New York Sun.* He was a man accustomed by nature and training to looking beneath the surface, and he was convinced that the body lying before them was that of John Wilkes Booth.

Bates suggested, first, that efforts be made to perfectly preserve the body, and, secondly, that Pennaman take out letters of administration on the estate of George, which should include his body. Thus Finis Bates essentially became the owner of the body of David E. George. Two days later Bates returned to Pennaman's and found the body in a state of "perfect preservation." He thereby took legal possession of it and had the body shipped to his home in Memphis.

So ends Finis Langdon Bates' book on the strange history of the man who would be Booth. But that is by no means the end of the story. Nor is it the end of Finis Bates and David George.

In 1907, greatly encouraged by the sale of his book, he offered the mummified body of George to Henry Ford for one hundred thousand dollars to display in his Americana Museum. When that deal failed to materialize, Bates found himself with a mummy on his hands, which he proceeded to exhibit at carnivals and county fairs. Soon, because of its popularity, the mummy became a featured sideshow attraction. Following Bates' death in November 1923, his widow quickly sold the mummy to the promoter of a carnival sideshow. It was last seen about 1940.

The Research of Nathaniel Orlowek and Ben Chitty

Enter Nathaniel Orlowek, an historian from Silver Springs, Maryland, who became fascinated with Bates' story about a quarter of a century ago. Since that time, his research has led him to the conclusion that Booth did indeed escape Federal clutches in 1865, and he did, as Bates maintained,

David E. George, who claimed on his deathbed to be John Wilkes Booth. George had been dead for eleven days when Finis Bates made this posed photo at the morgue on January 25, 1903. George was sixty-four years of age at this time, and his face was swollen from the effects of the arsenic he had ingested. The Swaim Collection, Georgetown University Library, Washington, D.C.

live out his life in Texas and Oklahoma as John St. Helen/David E. George.

In 1991 Orlowek, in collaboration with Dr. Arthur Ben Chitty of Sewanee, Tennessee, convinced the producers of the popular television show *America's Most Wanted* to film the Booth story. They did so, and the show aired to wide acclaim in September 1991. Thus Bates' narrative, augmented by Orlowek and Chitty's latest research, reached its largest audience ever. Those who witnessed that show agreed that it was a most convincing presentation, one that Orlowek and Chitty felt very good about.

In the January 1992 issue of the *Surratt Courier*, Orlowek published his rationale for believing that Booth did escape from Garrett's barn to live out his life as outlined by Finis Bates. He says that there is overwhelming physical evidence that proves Booth died on January 13, 1903, in Enid, Oklahoma Territory, under the alias David E. George. For example, Booth had a scarred right eyebrow (suffered in a stage fight) that arched upwards, a broken right thumb (sustained when Booth caught it in the cogs of a curtain crank), and a broken left leg.

In an affidavit, still unpublished, that was sworn out by the Chicago Press Club on December 19, 1931, six Chicago physicians thoroughly examined the body of David E. George in an attempt to prove or disprove his identity as John Wilkes Booth. In 1992 Orlowek obtained a copy of their findings from Dick Mudd, the grandson of Dr. Samuel Mudd. (In 1977 Orlowek had helped Dick Mudd with his congressional petition to clear the name of his grandfather.) Those six physicians wrote as follows:

Gentlemen:

At your request, we were asked by Dr. Orlando F. Scott to examine in his office at 330 South Wells Street, Chicago, Ill., the body and x-rays of same, properly identified by us as being the body of an individual who died under the name of D. E. George, on the 13th day of January, 1903, in the Grand Hotel, City of Enid, Territory of

Oklahoma, United States of America, and we did examine said body and x-ray plates.

On examining this body physically, we found and noted the following peculiarities:

1. There was a peculiar elevation or upward riding of the right eyebrow, it appearing on the body at a higher level on the forehead than the left eyebrow. There was an area about the eyebrow that looked like an old healed scar.

2. The right thumb was seen to be considerably thickened at its knuckle joint, and sort of bowed up, or arched, producing a deformity of the right thumb; the left thumb was seen to be long and slender, and lying snugly along and in contact with the hand, there being no evidence of any deformity in this left thumb, and the left thumb appearing to be slender in size, as compared to the right thumb.

3. On examination of the legs, there was seen to be an apparent slight thickening over the outside of the left ankle: that is, over what is commonly called the ankle joint and what is technically called the lower end of the fibula, or external malleolus.

4. Examination of the back of the neck revealed that a piece of skin and underlying tissue had been removed. This we were informed, was removed by Dr. Charles E. N. Fischer, of the Fischer Laboratories, for the purpose of making a microscopic examination in order to determine whether or not there was any scar tissue in the skin at this point.

The next examination conducted was an examination of the x-ray films taken in the laboratory of and under the supervision of Dr. Orlando F. Scott of this body, these pictures being of the head, hands, and legs. These pictures were identified by a photograph imprint upon them, and were further identified to us by Dr. Scott as having been made by him and having been continuously in his possession since they were made. He further stated that the x-ray machine was a Victor x-ray machine in good working order the time the pictures were made; that he was present when they were made, and that they are in the same condition now as when they were made; and further that it is his opinion that they are true and correct representations of that portion of the body of this man that they purport to show.

1. Examination of the right lateral (side) view of the skull of this body shows a thickening of the tissues over the right eyebrow line. This may have been produced by the scar from an injury causing a thickening of the soft tissues over the eyebrow and forehead at this

level, or may be due to an actual thickening of the bony covering from an injury, or may be due to both a thickening of the soft tissue and the bony coverings.

2. Comparative examination of the x-ray pictures of the right and left leg, antero-posterior view: That is, taking the picture from front to back: this examination revealed that both the right and left legs as determined by the shadows in the x-ray films were taken in a correct and true antero-posterior position. On comparing the ankle joints, we find that the left fibula is markedly thickened at its lower end at the level of that portion which is called the external malleolus, it being the lateral (side) part of the ankle joint. This fibula is approximately 25 percent thicker at this point than the right fibula. This thickening indicates that at some time there has been a fracture of this left fibula just above the ankle joint, which has resulted in the thickening of this bone and bulbous appearance of it. This thickening is not due to any deform or defect that the body was born with; that is, it is not a congenital defect, but is an actual change in the bone due to a previous fracture of this fibula.

3. Comparative x-ray examination of the right and left hands: the left thumb is long and tapering, with slender bones, as seen in the x-ray, and the thumb is seen to be lying close to the hand and parallel with the index finger, and is perfectly straight: whereas the x-ray of the right hand shows that there is a thickening of the entire thumb and thickening of the joints of the thumb, with a deformity, or bowing out of the thumb, which is very marked in comparison with the straightness and lack of this deformity in the left thumb. It is my opinion that this thickening of this right thumb and the bones of the right thumb and joints is due not to any congenital defect, but due to changes in the bones with thickening of the bones and joints, and that such a condition is commonly caused by only one thing, and that is, an injury of a crushing nature.

In summing up our findings, it is my opinion that:

1. The elevation or upward riding, of the right eyebrow has been produced by injury and could have been produced by the thrust of a sharp instrument, the scar forming when healing ensued.

2. Examination of the right thumb shows that the condition present has been produced by the injury and is not a congenital deformity of this right thumb.

3. The condition of the left ankle is not congenital. The bony thickening found around the deformity was produced, in my opinion, by a fracture of the fibula at some remote date.

Signed:
Dr. Louis K. Eastman
Dr. Charles K. Barnes
Dr. Bernard Conway
Dr. Charles E. M. Fischer
Dr. Edward L. Miloslavich
Orlando F. Scott, MD

In 1976, says James Orlowek, he traveled to Chicago, where he interviewed Dr. Charles K. Barnes, the only surviving physician who examined the mummy of David George in 1931, and Dr. Barnes verified every detail of the report. Two other citizens who witnessed the examination in 1931, Fred F. Bloodgood of Madison, Wisconsin, and Viola Gould of Glencoe, Minnesota, were interviewed by *America's Most Wanted,* and they also verified, without the least hesitation, that the mummy of David George bore all the physical deformities described above. Says Orlowek:

> Contrary to what has been asserted by some, *Unsolved Mysteries* did not air the story to promote my conclusions. In fact, they were most reluctant to do the story, and it took me well over a year to convince them that they ought to do it at all. Moreover, they offered to interview on camera a Government historian, who is, of course, along with Mr. James O. Hall, a proponent of the 1865 theory, to balance out Dr. Chitty and myself, but that individual and the Government refused to participate. The director, Mike Mathis, also cut out a great many of my answers that I felt were particularly important to our side, and they were very scrupulous to portray only incidents that were well documented.
>
> I believe that an examination of that body [David George], that the Government refused to allow in 1865, will prove conclusively that it is that of Booth, and that if we can ever find the mummy (I've received some recent leads), we can prove what documentary and contemporary eyewitness accounts have already shown—that John Wilkes Booth really died in 1903.

In the spring of 1994, in an effort to resolve once and for all the rumors and controversy surrounding the identity of the body now lying in Booth's grave in Green Mount Cemetery, Nathaniel Orlowek and Dr. Arthur Ben Chitty, joined by Booth's great-grandnieces, Virginia Humbrecht Kline and Lois Rathbun, filed a petition to exhume Booth's body in Green Mount Cemetery.

They had hoped to use most modern DNA testing to determine the identity of the body. If the body turned out to be that of Booth, then Edwin Stanton would be exonerated and all his critics could turn their attention elsewhere. If the body turned out not to be that of Booth, then skeptics across the nation could say, "Ha, told you so!" and begin rewriting our history books. But for reasons known only to themselves, authorities at Green Mount Cemetery resisted all efforts to have the body exhumed. Thus Orlowek, Chitty, Virginia Kline, and Lois Rathbun took the matter to court in the fall of 1994, filing a petition in the Baltimore Circuit Court. In May 1995, Judge Joseph H. Kaplan ruled that only Virginia Kline and Lois Rathbun, as Booth's next of kin, had a right to petition the court, which meant that Orlowek and Chitty had to remove themselves from the petition. They did so, and Virginia Kline and Lois Rathbun filed their petition with the Court of Special Appeals in Annapolis.

The intellectually curious across the nation were jubilant. At last, after a wait of over 140 years, the truth would soon be known. Thanks to the most modern DNA testing, doctors could immediately determine whether the body buried in Green Mount Cemetery was or was not that of John Wilkes Booth.

Unfortunately, and to the consternation of Virginia Kline and Lois Rathburn, as well as Nathaniel Orlowek and Dr. Chitty, in the fall of 1996, Judge Kaplan ruled in favor of Green Mount Cemetery. The body lying in Booth's grave could not be exhumed, and no DNA tests could be conducted to resolve the question of its identity.

At that point, Orlowek's efforts came to a halt. Still, in a recent telephone conversation with the author, Orlowek said that he was on the verge of finding David George's long-lost mummy, and he hopes that DNA from that mummy should provide the evidence he needs to prove or disprove his thesis. Those who are truly curious about the identity of the body buried in Booth's grave wish Orlowek the very best of luck!

Notes

II

1. This material originally appeared in the August 1961 issue of the *Civil War Times*, written by Robert H. Fowler, former publisher of the *Civil War Times*, and is published here courtesy of Mrs. Robert H. Fowler, widow of the former publisher. The author is most grateful to Mrs. Fowler. I would also like to thank Jim Kushland, current publisher of the *Civil War Times Illustrated*, for his assistance in securing permission from Mrs. Fowler to republish this article.

IV

1. Much of the data in this section is based on Louis Weichmann's *The True History of the Assassination of Abraham Lincoln*, Alfred A. Knopf, 1975. Weichmann was a friend and classmate of John Surratt and later a boarder at Mrs. Surratt's boardinghouse, where he personally observed many of the comings and goings of the various conspirators. It was his testimony that was partially responsible for Mrs. Surratt's being executed. His purpose in writing his book, he says, was to vindicate himself for his testimony at trial.

VII

1. In April 1993, a moot court was convened at the University

of Richmond Law School to determine the guilt or innocence of Dr. Samuel Mudd and the other conspirators. Celebrated attorney F. Lee Bailey served as defense attorney, while John Jay Douglas, dean of the National College of District Attorneys, served as the chief prosecutor. After hours of testimony and debate, the three-judge panel ruled two to one that the Military Commission of 1865 had had no right to preside over the case, that the trial of 1865, as well as the guilty verdicts against the defendants, were therefore unconstitutional. Simply stated, said the judges, because the defendants were not members of the military, they should have been tried in a civil court. They cited as justification of their ruling Supreme Court decision *Ex Parte Milligan*, which states that "a person not in the armed forces should be tried by a civil court if those courts are functioning." The judges pointed out that civil courts were indeed functioning in Washington, D.C., at the time of the trial in the spring of 1865. Robinson O. Everett, a retired senior judge of the U.S. Court of Military Appeals, stated, "There was really no necessity to use a military tribunal in this case. Thus all of the proceedings of the military commission were in nullity."

2. In 1992 a Caucasian skull was found among a collection of Native American skulls in the anthropology department of the Smithsonian Institute. It was skull number 2244. A quick investigation revealed that this was "the cranium of Lewis Thornton Powell, hung at Washington City for Complicity in the Assassination of Abraham Lincoln." In 1994 the skull was returned to the Powell family in Geneva, Florida, and interred with the rest of his remains. How it came to be in the Smithsonian Institute is unkown.

IX

1. See: Finis Bates, *The Escape and Suicide of John Wilkes Booth, Assassin of President Lincoln*, Pilcher Printing Co., Memphis, 1907.

Bibliography

Adams, Charles. *When in the Course of Human Events: Arguing the Case for Southern Secession.* New York: Roman and Littlefield, 2000.

Arnold, Samuel Bland. *Defence and Prison Experiences of a Lincoln Conspirator.* Hattiesburg, Miss.: The Book Farm, 1943.

Baker, Lafayette C. *History of the United States Secret Service.* Philadelphia: L. C. Baker, 1867.

Basler, Roy P. *Abraham Lincoln: His Speeches and Writings.* New York: Da Capo Press, 1946.

Bates, David Homer. *Lincoln in the Telegraph Office.* New York: Century, 1907.

Bates, Finis Langdon. *The Escape and Suicide of John Wilkes Booth.* Memphis: Pilcher Printing Co., 1907.

Baxter, Maurice. *Henry Clay and the American System.* Lexington: University of Kentucky Press, 1995.

Beale, Howard K., ed. *The Diary of Edward Bates.* Washington, D.C.: Government Printing Office, 1933.

Bishop, Jim. *The Day Lincoln Was Shot.* New York: Harper & Bros., 1955.

Bowers, Claude. *The Tragic Era: The Revolution After Lincoln.* New York: Houghton and Mifflin, 1929.

Bryan, George S. *The Great American Myth.* Carrick & Evans, 1940.

Campbell, Helen Jones. *The Case for Mrs. Surratt.* New York: G. P. Putnam and Sons, 1943.

Chittenden, L. E. *Personal Reminiscences, 1840-1890.* New York: Richmond, Groscup, 1893.

Clark, Champ. *The Assassination: Death of the President.* Alexandria, Va.: Time-Life Books, 1987.

Clarke, Asia Booth. *The Unlocked Book.* New York: G. P. Putnam's Sons, 1938.

Cottrell, John. *Anatomy of an Assassination.* New York: Funk & Wagnalls, 1966.

Coulter, Merton L. *The South During Reconstruction.* Baton Rouge: Louisiana State University Press, 1947.

Crook, William H. *Memories of the White House.* Compiled and edited by Henry Rood. Boston: Little, Brown & Co., 1911.

Dana, Charles A. *Recollections of the Civil War.* New York: D. Appleton & Co., 1898.

DiLorenzo, Thomas J. *The Real Lincoln.* New York: Random House, 2002.

Donald, David. *Inside Lincoln's Cabinet.* New York: Longmans, Green & Co., 1954.

——. *Lincoln Reconsidered.* New York: Vintage Books, 1961.

Eisenschiml, Otto. *Why Was Lincoln Murdered?* New York: Grosset & Dunlap, 1937.

Ferguson, William J. *I Saw Booth Shoot Lincoln.* New York: Houghton Mifflin, 1930.

Fletcher, George P. *Our Secret Constitution: How Lincoln Remade America.* New York: Oxford University Press, 2001.

Flower, Frank A. *Edwin McMasters Stanton, the Autocrat of the Rebellion, Emancipation and Reconstruction.* New York: W. W. Wilson, 1905.

Forrester, Izola. *This One Mad Act: The Unknown Story of John Wilkes Booth and His Family.* Boston: Hale, Cushman & Flint, 1937.

Garrison, Webb. *The Lincoln No One Knows.* Nashville: Rutledge Hill Press, 1993.

Grant, Ulysses S. *Personal Memoirs of U. S. Grant.* Vol. 2. New York: Charles L. Webster & Co., 1886.

Grimsley, Mark. *The Hard Hand of War: Union Military Policy towards Southern Civilians, 1861-65.* Cambridge: Cambridge University Press, 1995.

Gutman, Richard and Kellie. *John Wilkes Booth Himself.* Dover, Mass.: Hired Hand Press, 1979.

Guttridge, Leonard F., and Ray A. Neff, *Dark Union: The Secret Web of Profiteers, Politicians, and Booth Conspirators that Led to Lincoln's Death.* Hoboken, N.J.: John Wiley & Sons, 2003.

Hertz, Emanuel. *The Hidden Lincoln.* New York: Viking Press, 1938.

Kimmel, Stanley F. *The Mad Booths of Maryland.* Indianapolis: Bobbs-Merrill, 1940.

Litwak, Leon. *North of Slavery: The Negro in the Free States, 1790-1860.* Chicago: University of Chicago Press, 1961.

Lomask, Milton. *Andrew Johnson, President on Trial.* New York: Farrar, Straus & Cudahy, 1960.

Luthin, Richard H. *The Real Abraham Lincoln.* Englewood Cliffs, N.J.: Prentice Hall, 1960.

Miers, Earl S., ed. *When the World Ended: The Diary of Emma LeConte.* Lincoln: University of Nebraska Press, 1987.

Milton, George Fort. *The Age of Hate.* New York: Coward-McCann, 1930.

Moore, Guy W. *The Case of Mrs. Surratt.* Norman: University of Oklahoma Press, 1954.

Mudd, Nettie. *Life of Samuel A. Mudd.* New York: Neale Publishing Co., 1906.

Oldroyd, Osborn H. *The Assassination of Abraham Lincoln.* Washington, D.C.: O. H. Oldroyd, 1901.

Ownsby, Betty. *Lewis Thornton Powell, Alias Paine, the Mystery Man of the Lincoln Conspiracy.* McFarland & Co., 1987.

Perkins, Howard. *Northern Editorials on Secession.* Gloucester, Mass.: Peter Smith, 1964.

Peterson, T. B. *The Trial of the Alleged Assassins and Conspirators at Washington City, D.C., in May and June, 1865.* Philadelphia: T. B. Peterson & Bros., 1865.

Pittman, Benn, comp. *The Assassination of President Lincoln and the Trial of the Conspirators.* Cincinnati: Moore, & Wilstach, 1865. Facsimile edition. New York: Funk & Wagnalls, 1954.

Pratt, Fletcher. *Stanton, Lincoln's Secretary of War.* New York: W. W. Norton & Co., 1953.

Reck, W. Emerson. *A. Lincoln: His Last 24 Hours.* Jefferson, N.C.: McFarland & Co., 1987.

Roscoe, Theodore. *The Web of Conspiracy.* Englewood Cliffs, N.J.: Prentice Hall, 1959.

Rossiter, Clinton. *Constitutional Dictatorship.* New York: Harcourt and Brace, 1948.

Shelton, Vaughn. *Mask for Treason.* Harrisburg, Pa.: Stackpole Press, 1965.

Stampp, Kenneth, and Leon Litwack, eds. *Reconstruction: An Anthology of Revisionist Writings.* Baton Rouge: Louisiana State University Press, 1969.

Steers, Edward. *The Escape and Capture of John Wilkes Booth.* Gettysburg, Pa.: Thomas Publications, 1983.

Swanson, James, and Dan Weinberg. *Lincoln's Assassins: Their Trial and Execution.* New York: Arena Editions, 1991.

Tarbell, Ida M. *The Life of Abraham Lincoln.* 2 vols. New York: McClure, Phillips & Co., 1904.

Trial of John Surratt in the Criminal Court for the District of Columbia. 2 Vols. Washington, D.C.: French and Richardson; Philadelphia: J. B. Lippencott & Co., 1867.

U. S. Congress. *The House Impeachment Investigation.* House Report no. 7. 40th Cong., 1st Session. Washington, 1867.

Welles, Gideon. *Diary.* 3 vols., ed. by Howard K. Beale. New York: W. W. Norton & Co., 1960.

Weichmann, Louis. *The True History of the Assassination of Abraham Lincoln and the Conspiracy of 1865.* New York: Alfred A. Knopf, 1976.

Index